The Chester
Book Club, 1824

The Chester
Book Club,1824

People, places and events of the late Georgian era

Chris Fozzard

Portcullis Press

First published by Portcullis Press in 2024

ISBN: 978-1-0685991-0-1

A good book is the precious lifeblood of a master spirit

John Milton, *Areopagitica* (1644)

Chester pleases my fancy more than any town I ever saw

James Boswell in a letter to Samuel Johnson (1779)

Contents

Introduction	1
1. Mrs Coupland	9
2. *January*	59
3. Mrs Glynne	67
4. *February*	87
5. Mrs Humberston	95
6. *March*	117
7. George Johnson, Esq.	125
8. *April*	149
9. Mrs Mainwaring	157
10. *May*	175
11. Mrs Massie	183
12. *June*	205
13. Mrs Nicholls	215
14. *July*	229
15. Mrs Panton	237
16. *August*	251
17. Rev Geo Pearson	259
18. *September*	271
19. Mrs Potts	277
20. *October*	303
21. The Misses Townshend	313
22. *November*	325
23. Miss Venables	331
24. *December*	339
25. Dr Norris	351

Epilogue	359
Notes	367
Family Trees	385
Acknowlegements	393
Index	395

Introduction

During the course of historical research, it is not uncommon to come across a fragment of data which has little bearing on the primary focus of the research but is of singular interest, nonetheless. There are three ways of dealing with this: ignore it; find a way, however tenuous, to incorporate it into the scope of the work; or treat it as a research project in itself. Ignoring it demonstrates a steely discipline and sense of purpose but may consign a worthy topic to oblivion; compromising on scope may be a distraction from, or at odds with, the objectives of the research; initiating a separate project requires commitment and a conviction that it represents a justifiable investment of time.

Such was my dilemma when, whilst researching my book *A Short History of Newton Hall, Chester,* I came across a passage in a jaded volume of *The Cheshire Sheaf* about a book club that existed in the city in the early 19th century. Having extracted a couple of facts that I regarded as relevant at the time, I was left with an abiding feeling that further research into the passage would not go unrewarded. Once my book was published, I decided to put that instinct to the test.

The Cheshire Sheaf appeared intermittently in numerous volumes between 1878 and 1990. It presents, in its own words, 'Local Gleanings, Historical and Antiquarian Relating to Cheshire, Chester and North Wales, From Many Scattered Fields'.[1] This is a wide remit, entailing somewhat arbitrary and esoteric content posted by enthusiasts keen to share or enquire about points of historical detail. It is comparable with the correspondence section of newspapers, and, indeed, the editorial and publication functions of the *Sheaf* for a time came under the auspices of a local newspaper, the *Chester Courant*, which had previously published such notes and queries within its own column inches.

The emphasis was less on expressing opinion than establishing or amplifying historical fact. For the most part, entries received responses – printed later and cross-referenced – written in a spirit of collaboration rather than contention. The modern-day equivalent, albeit without the same degree of editorial control, would be the social media post, attended by an array of comments based on the level of knowledge or strength of feeling of the readership. Contributions were, by and large, completely anonymous or accompanied by an initial or pseudonym, befitting the conventions of the time. Any risk that the content would be mere ephemera, lost to posterity, was mitigated by the hard work and application of generations of editors and publishers, wedded to the cause. The word 'sheaf' is a nod to the flag of Cheshire, which has borne three yellow wheatsheaves against a blue background since the time of the Norman Earls of Chester in the 12th century, as well as reflecting its fertile agrarian landscape. It is also emblematic of a publication which harvests its material from disparate sources into a digestible whole.

The entry that particularly caught my eye appears in the second volume of the first series of the *Sheaf* in 1880:

THE CHESTER BOOK CLUB, 1824

THE CHESTER BOOK CLUB consisted of 12 members, who, after circulating the books, sold them by auction, at an evening party, at one of their houses in turn, DR NORRIS usually being the auctioneer: it was he also that drew up the following playful catalogue, descriptive of the members of the Club. He had apparently just issued a list of the Books then in circulation, and the one now printed he calls a 'SUPPLEMENTARY CATALOGUE, 1824'.

Lot 1

A brief sketch of Mr. Owen's New Settlement, with notes, and an abridged extract of the late Marriage Act, neatly bound together in superior law binding ....(Mrs. Coupland.)

Lot 2

Tales of the Castle, the best edition, embellished with a fine view of Hawarden Castle, a single volume, neatly bound ....(Mrs. Glynne.)

Lot 3

Contributions to Natural History, containing some very fine specimens of the Cotton plant, and an interesting sketch illustrative of the mineralogy of the banks of the Humber; 2 vols., bound in Russia ....(Mrs. Humberston.)

Lot 4

Johnson's *Rasselas*. – A valuable edition, by mistake in common law binding. Letter'd ....(Mr. George Johnson, Esq.)

Lot 5

The Art of Social Life, imperial quarto, splendidly bound in Russia, gilt extra, a fine copy in the highest preservation, and worthy of a place in the best collection ....(Mrs. Mainwaring.)

Lot 6

The Guide to Domestic Happiness, 2 vols., beautifully bound in purple Morocco. Scarce; only 18 copies extant, exclusive of this ....(Mrs. Massie.)

Lot 7

Flora Britannica, 2 vols., 8vo, richly bound in green Morocco, gilt extra; the second vol. embellished with a highly finished drawing of the beautiful plant Magnolia-Hybernica, faithfully copied from nature ....(Mrs. Nicholls.)

Lot 8

The Sisters, a popular tale of Lepanto, but translated from the Welsh, 2 vols., crown 8vo, handsomely bound in red, gilt, and letter'd ....(Mrs. Panton.)

Lot 9

Coelebs in Search of a Wife, a new edition, corrected after the manner of Bowdler's Shakespeare, the objectionable passages omitted, the good only retained. 1 vol., curiously printed in black leather ....(Rev. Geo Pearson)

Lot 10

The Comforts of Human Life, a fine folio edition, particularly well bound, and in excellent preservation ....(Mrs. Potts.)

Lot 11

Illustrations of Country History, 2 vols., embellished with two fine portraits; hand-somely bound in blue Morocco. Very choice copies.............(The Misses Townshend.)

Lot 12

The Balance of Comfort, a new edition, interspersed with original poetry, a handsome copy in high preservation, embellished with an expressive title page...(Miss Venables.)

The names given within the brackets are supplied from a list left in MS. by Dr. Norris on the copy from which I transcribe this for THE SHEAF.

Newton,   H.,[2]

There is much information here, but it lacks elucidation by the subscriber. 'H' presents it, 56 years after the event, in all its pristine clarity without saying where it came from or why it is then being submitted for publication. Knowledge of the size of the membership, the modus operandi and the particulars of this meeting suggest an intimacy with proceedings which is left undisclosed. The reference to a 'playful catalogue' implies that there are 'in-jokes', which, on the surface at least, are beyond our understanding and must have been equally impenetrable to H's readers in 1880. The final sentence appears to inform us that Dr Norris had handwritten the names on the printed sheet, perhaps for him to read aloud at an appropriate point. They are listed in alphabetical order, avoiding potentially sensitive alternative rankings, for example by age, gender or social status.

For whatever reason, there was no reaction or follow-up to H's contribution within the pages of the *Sheaf*. There it hangs, in suspended animation, cocooned by time, unregarded and forgotten. Until now, that is.

This book, and the research that sits behind it, raises and seeks to address some funda-mental questions: is it possible to establish who these people were, where they lived and what the relationships were between them? Can we, two centuries later, even pretend to grasp the humour? Can we use the entry as a basis for assembling facts that enhance our understanding of Chester and life in general in the late Georgian period?[3]

In part, the book takes a cross-section through the year 1824, including an examination of significant local, national and global issues of the time. To identify and understand the people, a broader view is required, including of their forbears and successors. Attention is directed towards matters of relevance, importance and – occasionally and unashamedly – curiosity.

Book clubs were by no means new. People had met to discuss literature and ideas since the time of Socrates in Ancient Greece. The modern-day concept of a social gathering with books at its heart dates from 18th century England, when reading matter was relatively scarce and expensive. Literacy levels were increasing, printing was evolving and the novel was becoming popular as an art form. Meeting and exchanging books provided access to a wider range of material as well as the opportunity for social intercourse. It was common for these occasions to also involve food and drink.[4]

Libraries were beginning to appear in most towns and cities, and Chester was no exception. Indeed, there are references to a library in the abbey dating back to Ranulph de Meschines, Earl of Chester in the early 12th century.[5] The City Library was established by Alderman Broster in 1770. After a strong and sustained period of expansion, it moved from White Friars to the Commercial Buildings on Northgate Street in 1815. There were over a hundred proprietors, a subset of whom formed a committee. There was a separate newsroom beneath, run on similar lines. The General Public Library opened in 1817, initially in Bolland's Entry, before also finding a more generous space, in its case in Fletcher's Buildings, on the east side of Bridge Street Row. John Fletcher, who ran the *Chester Chronicle*, was the main patron. There was a need to subscribe, but this carried an entitlement to introduce a friend.[6] *Pigot's Commercial Directory* of 1820 lists six booksellers, mostly on the Rows.[7] Literate Cestrians of adequate means could therefore decide how best to obtain their chosen publication.

The year 1824 saw the country in transition. Napoleon's forces, and the very real and protracted threat they represented to British security and sovereignty, had been defeated nine years earlier at the Battle of Waterloo. A significant peace dividend resulted and continued to accrue in our period. With unprecedented growth in manufacturing and British domination of global markets, economic prosperity seemed assured. The Act of Union had formally created the United Kingdom of Great Britain and Ireland in 1801 and the British Slave Trade had been abolished in 1807. Revolutions were taking place in industry and transport, opening new avenues of wealth and opportunity for a greater proportion of society. Enclosure of the common land was well-advanced and innovations in agriculture were helping to feed a growing and increasingly urbanised population. There was a confidence, perhaps even a swagger, amongst the upper and middle classes that Englishmen – and it was, for the most part, English men – were at the head and front of the civilised world and that they had a divinely-ordained duty to guide other nations in their ways and means.

Not everyone enjoyed the fruits of military and economic success, however. As is so often the case, it was amongst the lower orders that the greatest adverse impact and uncertainty was felt. Demobilisation led to unemployment for many men unaccustomed to peacetime who must have thought themselves career-soldiers by dint of circumstance. The Corn Laws, introduced in 1815 to protect British agriculture from foreign imports in recently re-opened markets, made staple foodstuffs expensive and unaffordable for some. There was disquiet in the countryside where many an honest labourer felt dispossessed by enclosure. Mechanisation in farms and factories threatened jobs and gave rise to social unrest. Parliamentary representation – or rather the lack of it in the case of many growing industrial towns and cities – was a further source of discontent. Friction between Great Britain and Ireland was by no means diminished by the Act of Union: if anything, it aggravated a long-weeping sore. Religious differences were at the heart of the issue, with Catholic rights rigidly circumscribed by law. Whilst enslaved people were no longer transported on British ships or forced to labour in British households, the use and abuse of them in the colonies continued unabated. Society grappled with these challenges and struggled to keep pace with events in a rapidly changing world.

It is against this backdrop that the Chester Book Club met. Genteel as they were, our protagonists would have been aware of the instability and pressures around them. Not only did they read books, but they read newspapers and corresponded, home and abroad. They would have shared what news and gossip they had, human nature being what it is. This book puts these people centre-stage, examining their lives and charting what they would have been exposed to in the calendar year. Let's step into their world.

Chapter One

Mrs Coupland

Lot 1

A brief sketch of Mr. Owen's New Settlement, with notes, and an abridged extract of the late Marriage Act, neatly bound together in superior law binding

It would appear from the detail given that the key to identifying Mrs Coupland lies in establishing her connection with Mr Owen and his 'New Settlement' and understanding the relevance of the reference to 'the late Marriage Act'. There could also be a clue implicit in the words 'superior law' binding, otherwise why state it?

The Mr Owen who would have enjoyed the highest profile in this period was Robert Owen, the renowned industrialist, social reformer and philanthropist. A successful Manchester-based textile manufacturer, Owen relocated to New Lanark in Scotland following his marriage to the daughter of the mill owner, David Dale. Owen was soon involved in a partnership which bought out Dale's interest in the business, resulting in him becoming part-owner and manager of New Lanark Mills. To some extent his continued commercial success was at odds with his moral principles as it was fuelled by the exploitative working practices of the day. Owen was progressive and socially aware, his philosophy informed by the Enlightenment ideas of the 17th and 18th centuries and the humanist principles they embodied.

He paid attention to the living and working conditions of his employees – many of whom were children – introducing innovative educational and social enterprise schemes which, in turn, added significant impetus to the nascent co-operative movement. Despite the expense this entailed, the business prospered and began to attract attention from far and wide. Statesmen, industrialists, dignitaries and reformers visited from across Europe.

They were astonished to see how Owen succeeded whilst challenging existing norms by promoting and harnessing the welfare and contentment of his workforce.

In the early 1820s Owen began to seek opportunities to implement his utopian ideas in the Americas. In 1824 he sailed to the USA, visiting Harmony, a small community in Indiana which had been founded ten years earlier by German settlers on socio-religious principles. He soon struck a deal to purchase the land and property.

Is this the new settlement and the Mr Owen that Dr Norris refers to? A problem here is that Robert Owen's acquisition of what would become 'New Harmony' was not completed until January 1825. Preparations would have been well-advanced before that, however, and, as a prominent figure, his transatlantic ventures would have been firmly in the public domain.

Then we have the reference to 'the late Marriage Act', suggesting that matrimony was significant in Mrs Coupland's life at that time. Care needs to be taken not to read too much into the title 'Mrs' as an indicator of marital status. As in the present day, it was used for married women and widows, but also, in some cases, for spinsters. The practice in the latter case was a mark of veneration for more mature women and perhaps occasionally a cover, as there were societal expectations on women not to remain single.

The Marriage Act of 1823 is pertinent here. It qualified and extended the provisions of Lord Hardwicke's Marriage Act of 1753, which was mainly directed towards the prevention of clandestine marriages. It dealt with the process for reading the banns, the period of residency required to marry in a particular place, and the means by which a marriage licence may be obtained.[1] The jurisdiction extended across England and Wales. The fact that Mrs Coupland was afforded an 'abridged extract' of the Act may suggest that certain parts were more relevant to her, or simply that presenting her with the full text – extensive and loquacious as it was – may have been regarded as an affront. There is tact and obeisance too in the words 'neatly bound' and 'superior'; a technique which Dr Norris uses repeatedly to butter up his audience.

Bishops' transcripts of Cheshire parish registers show a marriage between Thomas Coupland and Ann Sloughter at St John the Baptist Church, Chester on 20th February 1806. An entry in the 'Married' section of the *Lancaster Gazette* of 1st March 1806 states: 'On Tuesday se'ennight [of last week], the Rev. Thos. Coupland, of the Priory, Chester, to Miss A. W. Sloughter, of that city.' One or other report is awry in a minor detail as 20th February was a Thursday, but the core facts are established. Ann W. Coupland, née Sloughter, is now in our sights.

The references to the surname Sloughter and the locations – The Priory and St John's Church – are informative too. Edmund Burke's Landed *Gentry of Great Britain and Ireland* (1855) contains an entry for an Anne Warburton who was directly descended from George Warburton of Arley, created a baronet immediately after the Restoration in 1660.[2] She, we are told, married Thomas Sloughter, who was High Sheriff of Cheshire in 1755. Their only son, another Thomas Sloughter, Captain in the 16th Light Dragoons, left, by his wife, Sarah, an only child, Anne Warburton Sloughter. This Anne – commonly spelt with an 'e' – married Reverend Thomas Coupland of the Priory, Chester.

The Warburton family trace their origins through the Duttons, who arrived in Cheshire in the wake of the Norman Conquest. Around 1260, Sir Piers de Dutton adopted the name 'de Werburton' due to his ownership of ancestral lands at Werburton, near Warrington in Cheshire.[3] This village – which later became known as 'Warburton' – was most likely named after St Werburgh, the patron saint of Chester. In other words, it was Werburgh's 'ton', this suffix denoting a settlement or farmstead in Anglo Saxon.

St Werburgh was a 7th century Abbess of Ely and a leading figure in convent reform across England. She died and was buried in Staffordshire but her remains were removed to the walled city of Chester, supposedly for safekeeping against Viking raids, in the 9th century. Her name became synonymous with the Abbey church up to the time of its dissolution in the late 1530s, which led to the creation of Chester Cathedral and its rededication to Christ and the Blessed Virgin Mary. There is a shrine to St Werburgh in the cathedral to this day. Places of worship that still bear her name include St Werburgh's

Catholic Church in Chester and two churches in Warburton itself. There is also a St Werburgh's Chapel at Mount Barker in Western Australia, established in 1872 by family member and noted explorer, George Egerton-Warburton.[4] The Warburtons have lived at the
magnificent Arley Hall in east Cheshire since the 15th century.

This provides an insight into Mrs Coupland's pedigree through her paternal line and
explains the derivation of her middle name. What of her maiden name, however?
'Sloughter' is often corrupted to 'Slaughter', presumably by analogy with the everyday
word. We know that her father and grandfather were both called Thomas Sloughter and
that her grandfather in particular must have had some social standing to become High
Sheriff. Despite this, there are few references to his lineage. One exception is in a Warburton family tree which identifies none other than Sir George Warburton, 3rd Baronet
and three times Member of Parliament (MP) for Cheshire in the early 18th century, as his
father.

Sir George's first and only widely disclosed marriage was to Diana Alington, daughter
of Lord Alington and granddaughter of the Duke of Bedford. She died in 1706, followed
by their only son a year later. They had a daughter too, another Diana, who would later
marry Sir Richard Grosvenor of Eaton Hall. Sir George had just turned 30 when he lost
his wife, and he would live on for almost four decades more. The family tree includes a
cursory mention of a second marriage, to 'Slaughter', with whom he had one child, the
elder Thomas Sloughter. This means that Thomas married his cousin, as Anne was the
daughter of Thomas Warburton, younger brother of Sir George. Questions arise, such as
why Thomas's mother's identity is so mysterious, why he bore the surname 'Slaughter' or
'Sloughter' rather than 'Warburton', and why, as Sir George's only son, he didn't succeed
to the title.

One possible explanation is that there was something deemed disreputable about this
second marriage. Perhaps the bride was from a lower social stratum, which was not the
convention and would not have been encouraged in elite circles at the time. Perhaps it
was a 'shotgun' wedding: whilst we know Thomas Sloughter was born in 1711, there is
no obvious record of his parents' wedding date. Indeed, the detail is so sparse that the

marriage may not have occurred at all. Burke, whose *Landed Gentry* captures the Warburton dynasty meticulously, only mentions the two Thomas Slaughters, and that only in the context of the elder Thomas's marriage to Anne. If the birth took place out of wedlock, the cloak of secrecy may be better understood.

One factor that supports the theory that the lady Sir George was involved with was socially inferior is that, from a relatively early age, their son was engaged in the day-to-day running of the estate. In the 1730s – when he would have been in his 20s – Thomas was Steward at the Manor Court at Arley.[5] However humble his maternal origins – it is possible that his mother was in domestic service – he gradually acquired social status. This is borne out by his marriage to Anne Warburton, which took place at St Paul's Cathedral in London in October 1739, and therefore must have been a grand affair. Such elevation could only have come about with the support and patronage of the most senior members of the Warburton family.

There may also have been influence on his wife's mother's side. She was Anne Dockwra, who came from an ancient baronial family and whose father, William, had founded the London Penny Post in 1680. There is a plaque commemorating this achievement in Lime Street in the City. William was also the uncle of Mary Davies, whose marriage into Grosvenor family endowed them with land in west London – most notably Mayfair – which would enhance their wealth immensely in later centuries. It may also explain why we see such close connections between the Warburtons and the Grosvenors, including several marriages, down the generations.

In the ensuing years, Thomas Sloughter's centre of gravity would shift towards Chester. His father died in 1743, at which point the baronetcy and Arley estate passed – controversially perhaps – to his cousin and brother-in-law, Sir Peter Warburton. Thomas was granted the township of Newton-by-Daresbury, south of Warrington and, although this land was sold soon after his death, there remains a part of it known as 'Slaughter's Rough'; 'rough' denoting an area of uncultivated land. By now, Thomas's stewardship at Arley had run its course, not least because Sir Peter had plans to renovate the property.[6] The Warburtons also had at their disposal a substantial estate in Hertfordshire through marriage with the Dockwras, which would become their temporary place of abode.

The most significant indication of Thomas's move to Chester was his purchase of property in 1750. It is no co-incidence that he chose to live near the church of St John the Baptist – Chester's original cathedral, dating back to the 7th century, and later a collegiate church – of which we will hear more in these pages. The Warburton family had long owned property in the area and been patrons of the church. An area dedicated to the family is a major feature of the Lady Chapel to the south of the nave. It includes conspicuous memorials to Sir George Warburton, 1st Baronet (1633-1676) and, separately, his wife Diana (1630-1693). One curiosity is a large stone set in the floor of the chapel, commemorating their daughter, Lady Christiana Warburton of Arley, who died in 1689; her name was misspelt as 'Christian' by the engraver and never corrected.

The property that Mrs Coupland's grandfather, Thomas, bought in 1750 was St John's House, which occupied the north-east section of the site of Chester's Roman amphitheatre.[7] The Warburton family already had a stake in this fine Georgian mansion. Thomas paid £275 to Sir William Yonge of Escot House in Devon and £275 to 'Warburton and other good causes … that they did grant, release and confirm to the said Thomas Slaughter and his heirs all that messuage or dwelling house, stable and garden with appurtenances in the said city of Chester called St John's Lane, nr St John's Church, late in the possession of Ann Warburton, widow, deceased mother of Walter Warburton and then in possession of the grantors'.[8] The Yonges and the Warburtons were connected through the Williams family of Penrhyn Castle, Caernarvonshire, of which the Ann just mentioned was a member. The total purchase price equates to approximately £64,000 today; not excessive for such a substantial residence and perhaps sold at undervalue because of the relationships involved.[9] The transaction appears not to have been concluded satisfactorily, however, and those relationships may have been fractured by it. A legal document of July 1751 shows a fine levied in the Portmote – an old legal term denoting a court stationed in a port area – of the City of Chester, in which Thomas Sloughter was the plaintiff and Sir

14

William Yonge and Walter Warburton the deforciants, accused of forcibly withholding property. The court found in Thomas's favour.

It is worth reflecting for a moment on the location of St John's House and the fact that it stood above the amphitheatre. We know this today, but they didn't know it then. It was as recently as 1929 that the discovery was made, more than 1,500 years after the Romans abandoned it. It would be another three decades before the building was demolished and excavation could begin on the portion of the site beneath. Despite ignorance of this price-less heritage, the road network in the area retained traces of the Roman footprint. John Wood's *Plan of the City of Chester* of 1833 shows Little St John Street arching round the north of the site of the amphitheatre, as if it were known about and visible at the time. St John's House also features in the plan, as does Dee House on the remaining part of the site behind it.

Once established in Chester, Thomas became more prominent in gentlemanly circles. From the early 1750s we see him as a racehorse owner, competing in classic races against the bloodstock of landed families such as the Stanleys, the Egertons and the Grosvenors. Two of his bay mares – 'Creeping Kate' and 'Smiling Dolly' – were particularly successful at Chester in this period.[10] Civic office came his way too. As well as becoming High Sheriff of Cheshire, he held the office of joint Treasurer of the City of Chester in 1758, alongside wealthy wine-merchant Henry Hesketh. He was Sheriff of Chester the following year, during Sir Richard Grosvenor's mayoralty. The ancient city was undergoing some urban renewal and development at this time, under the patronage of the local nobility and gentry. A significant transaction took place in October 1758 involving the provision of security by Thomas Sloughter and Henry Hesketh for a loan of £1,500 to the Corporation to purchase rooms in the Exchange, recently built shops immediately to the west of it and a building by the racecourse to serve as a workhouse.[11]

It is reasonable to ask how a man who litigated over comparatively small amounts and with no apparent trade to his name, could achieve this degree of aggrandisement and financial standing. The fact is that he had inherited handsomely from Sir George Warburton, reinforcing the notion that Sir George was his natural father. On top of that, there is a crisp entry in the *Chester Courant* of Tuesday, 4th October 1757 which reads: 'The Lottery Ticket, No. 25,990 which has drawn a prize of £5,000 was the property of Thomas Slaughter, Esq.'

State lotteries had been popular since the time of Queen Anne. They appealed to a nation with a taste for gambling – often fraught with skulduggery and ruinous financial loss, but, in the case of the lottery, attended by a contained outlay and the prospect of a stupendous return, however remote that may have been. Thomas's win, independently of his other assets, would have made him not quite a millionaire in present day terms but very comfortably off all the same. There is no question of mistaken identity here because the fact is corroborated within his family, as we will soon see – with a twist.

The appeal of a large house on what was then the fringe of the city would have would have been heightened by the fact that Thomas and Anne Sloughter had started a family. Another Thomas – let's call him Thomas junior – had been born in 1747, followed by a sister, Elizabeth, two years later. Elizabeth will feature the more prominently in our story due to her greater longevity and her closer attachment with the city of Chester and her niece, our Mrs Coupland. Thomas junior, by comparison, is an elusive figure. We know that he was baptised at St Mary's-on-the-Hill in Chester in the year of his birth but he is likely to have been on the move relatively early in adult life, as he joined the military. He was a captain, having bought a commission in the 16th Light Dragoons. This regiment was raised by Colonel Burgoyne to fight against the French and Spanish in the Seven Years' War that began in 1756. The conflict in which Thomas junior would have seen most action, however, was the American War of Independence from 1776 to 1779. As a mobile and flexible unit, the 16th Light Dragoons were initially effective against the Americans' guerrilla tactics but, ultimately, were so depleted in battle that the few remaining men were redeployed into other regiments. The officers were sent back to England to recruit.[12]

Perhaps this peripatetic military existence explains why Thomas junior's life is so little documented at home. What we do know is that he married relatively late, aged 33, and died relatively young, aged 41. His wife was a Cotswold lady: Sarah Hands of Chipping Camden, where the marriage took place in 1780. He settled and was still living there at the time of his death in 1788. His burial record of 22nd October that year describes him simply as 'Mr Thomas Sloughter of Chester'. It was in Chipping Camden that Anne Warburton Sloughter – later Mrs Coupland – was born, on 21st January 1782. There appear to have been no siblings.

In November 1789 Thomas senior died. A notice in the recently established *Chester Chronicle* on Friday 27th November states: 'Monday night died, after a short illness, Thomas Sloughter, Esq., one of the alderman of this body corporate.' Whilst obituaries were less common in those days, this is still a rather perfunctory parting reference to a well-connected citizen who had held high office and played an important role in the architectural renaissance of Chester. Soon afterwards, notices began to appear asking all creditors and debtors to account to Elizabeth Sloughter of St John Street.

Judging by his will, he died well in credit. He devised to Elizabeth a dwelling place and burial place in the grounds of St John's; land at Broughton and Saltney, to the west of Chester; and mines that he owned. The mining interests were extensive, comprising lead, calamine (a form of zinc), copper, ore and coal. There was also a stipulation that £500 be placed in trust for his granddaughter, the interest to be applied to her education and the capital to be paid to her at the age of 21 or upon marriage, provided she was given up by her mother to the care and direction of her Aunt Elizabeth for her education and improvement. The will was proved by Elizabeth in the Consistory Court in Chester on 30th November 1790.

The conditional bequest to Anne is financially generous but morally suspect. Indeed, one reading of the facts is that she is being bought, and bought with money due to her rather than her mother. It is impossible to know the full circumstances, but it is unlikely Anne would have had much say in the matter at the tender age of seven or eight. Sarah slips from view at this point, suggesting that the arrangement was accepted or enforced. For the next three decades Anne's life would revolve around Chester and her aunt.

The Chester Directory of 1792, listing tradespeople and residents in the city, has two distinct entries of relevance to us. One is to the 'Miss Slaughters, Little St John Street' and the other to 'Mrs Sloughter, St John Street'. Despite the inconsistencies, neither is plain wrong. The first reference is to Elizabeth and Anne, aunt and niece, and the second simply to Elizabeth. We are reminded of the accepted and unchallenged variability in the spelling of the surname and the interchangeability of the 'Miss' and 'Mrs' epithets for mature un-married ladies (Elizabeth, a lifelong spinster, would have been in her early forties at this time). The fact that we have two marginally different street names is inconsequential too, as St John's House was where those two thoroughfares meet. It seems they were settled here, for now at least, keeping each other company and with Elizabeth overseeing Anne's 'education and improvement'. There would have been household staff and a governess, of course, but their stations in life would have been too humble to merit mention in the commercial directories of the day.

This state of affairs persisted into the new century, with the next significant milestone in Anne's life occurring in early 1806. This, as we have seen, was her marriage to the Reverend Thomas Coupland. We could ask, as you may have done already, why Dr Norris at the book club in 1824 talked about the 'late Marriage Act' in addressing Mrs Coupland when the event had taken place and she had acquired that married name some 18 years earlier. It is a valid question, and we must wait for the chronology to unfold before provid-ing an answer.

It is to be hoped and expected, given the propitious circumstances leading up to it, that Anne developed into a cultivated and discerning young lady upon whom the eye of many a prospective suitor might fall. As a man of the cloth from outside Anne's immediate social circle, Thomas may be regarded as a surprising choice of husband. If it were true love that they felt for each other, its course was scarcely to run smooth.

Thomas Coupland, born in Ormskirk, north of Liverpool, in 1773 – making him nine years older than Anne – arrived in Chester at the turn of 1804. A letter to him from a 'W.A.L.' of the Navy Pay Office dated 3rd January 1804 congratulates him on finding a permanent residence in the city in an 'exceedingly good and respectable neighbourhood … being a short distance to your friends'.[13] The tone of the letter is intimate, suggesting it is of a personal rather than professional nature. We don't know who 'W.A.L.' was or whether Thomas was previously involved with the navy. There is an oblique reference to the loss of a child and how well-placed Thomas would have been to empathise in this regard. Once more, the underlying detail eludes us. The 'friends' to whom the writer refers are likely to have been based in Liverpool, which, being 'a short distance' away, implies that Thomas had moved to Chester from far afield.

Thomas's father, Richard, was a leather dealer, who, with his wife Elizabeth, had several children. Such was the extent of infant mortality amongst them that two were called Elizabeth and two Sarah because the first namesake died before the second was born.[14] It was not uncommon to create a bond with deceased children in this way. Thomas was one of two surviving brothers – Peter being the other – who went into the clergy. There was an elder sister too – Mary – who married Samuel Bardsley, a Manchester-based doctor. Richard died in May 1791 and appointed his brother, Valentine, as trustee to his teenage sons. There was adequate income to send Thomas to Cambridge University, where he studied at Trinity Hall.

Correspondence from this time between Valentine and his agent shows the extent of the money circulating in the family. In August 1791 the agent reported receiving a request from 'your younger nephew [Thomas] asking for £60', which would be sent that day. He adds the rider, 'I fancy matriculation is attended with considerable expense.' In February 1793, Dr Bardsley requested that £2,000 from his wife's fortune be released to him, including an immediate advance of £1,000 and the balance shortly thereafter. A statement from the Executors of Richard's will in November 1794 shows Thomas inherited £3,100 from his father and drew £744 of this between May 1791 and January 1794. There is a comment that he 'has had a greater share than the interest on his fortune', implying that this was in breach of the terms of the will.[15] It seems, at this stage of his life at least, that Thomas was more interested in mammon than in God.

The word 'fortune' in this context is not overblown when we consider that Thomas's inheritance at an early age would be worth in the region of £230,000 today. If we aggregate this with legacies to his siblings and keep in mind that his uncle was a gentleman of leisure, we start to build a picture of substantial family wealth. Leather dealing had been the primary family trade for at least two generations but now there seemed no need to sustain it. Though an honourable and skilled profession, it is unlikely to have to have generated the level of the financial resources that we now see in play.

There are indications that Thomas's early life may have been beset by ill health. He was in his twenties when he entered Cambridge, which is later than most by the standards of any period. A letter from Joseph Jowett, a tutor at his college, dated January 1797 expresses regret at his illness and suggests that he spends some weeks with him, during which he 'could perform his exercise and proceed to his degree as soon as he had kept another term'.[16] Soon afterwards Thomas received a testimonial from the college, possibly in lieu of a degree, recommending him to the Church.

So it was that Thomas arrived and settled in Chester a few years later, possibly attracted by the fact that it was a bishopric, with all the ecclesiastical apparatus that entailed, as well as its proximity to Liverpool. His choice of precisely where to live could not have put him closer to an Anglican church. The Priory, which he appears to have bought, was appended to the south-east corner of St John's, a stone's throw from where Anne Sloughter was then living. A visitor information plaque sited in that area today states:

The ruins have had a curious history. In the 18th century a large brick and stucco house called Priory House was built over part of the site. It was owned by Mrs de Quincey, mother of the author Thomas de Quincey. Robert, Earl Grosvenor lived in this house when he was Mayor of Chester in 1808. Priory House was demolished in 1871.

This is a brief but informative piece. The image of the house on the plaque and the fact that two such notable figures occupied it creates an impression of some grandeur. Victorian restoration – necessary and transformative – did not completely erase the remains of the ancient collegiate church. A small section of what would have been part of the Priory – walls, a few windows and a door – are still there to be seen.

Thomas Hughes, the first editor of *The Cheshire Sheaf*, commented on the property and its situation in that publication in 1882:

Mrs de Quincey for several years resided in a house known as 'The Priory' in St John's churchyard, Chester, the kitchens and cellaring of which formed portions of the chapter house and crypt of the Norman and early English cathedral. When St John's ceased to be collegiate, and the massive nave became transformed into a parish church, the chapter house and offices along with the eastern chapels all passed rapidly into decay, and were in utter ruin when the Priory was erected ...

A more picturesque home for the mother of the 'Opium Eater' could scarcely be found, within her means, in this part of England: there she and her household lived in retirement and at ease, within the walls occupied two or three centuries previously by the collegiate authorities. There she was visited frequently from his Manchester home, by her distinguished son: there she saw one of her children taken away by death and laid his solitary grave just outside the Priory door, as the inscription on his gravestone still remains to tell.

Mrs de Quincey's kitchen was the chapter house itself; the door of her entrance hall was a beautiful Norman window, still existing in the most perfect state, through so long having been covered over by the modern dwelling; and it used to be said by those who knew him well at that period that, during those filial and frequent visits, the son would seclude himself for hours together in the ruins, and under the noble trees that flourished there; nor is it unreasonable to believe that he drew some of his brilliant inspiration from those sacred shades.

It seems that Mrs de Quincey bought the house around 1798, perhaps a couple of decades or so after it was erected. She paid £500 and spent another £1,000 restoring and expanding it to include a drawing room and seven or eight bedrooms. She moved in with her brother, a retired East Indian officer, and her younger children.

Thomas de Quincey himself mentions the property in his *Confessions* of 1821, in which he enlarges upon 'the beautiful ruins which adorned the lawn', 'the exquisite beauty of the shrubs, wildflowers and ferns that surmounted the arches with natural coronets of the richest composition' and 'a very pretty residence, with the grace of monastic antiquity hanging over the whole little retreat'. [17] It is not difficult to see why this spot was a favourite haunt for artists and sketch-makers and how other writers also took their inspiration from it. Indeed, Priory House is a central location in the 1854 romantic novel *Kate Vernon* by the popular Victorian novelist, Mrs Alexander, with a vivid description of the approach and interior featuring in the third chapter of the first volume.

It is not entirely clear when or why Mrs de Quincey left her Chester home, but her investment in it suggested she intended to plant her roots there and stay for some time. It is therefore conceivable that Thomas Coupland acquired it directly from her. We know he had the means to buy it and there is evidence in later family records that he did just that. What better location could there be for he and Anne – aged 31 and 22 respectively – to become romantically involved with each other than in that venerable, green and secluded place? They would have had time at their disposal too, not least because there is scant record of Thomas having held a church commission, in Chester or elsewhere. Perhaps one reason for this, alongside the lack of a financial imperative, was his state of health.

We saw how infirmity had impaired his studies and now, it seems, he fell prey to it again. One of his first acts of 1804 was to subscribe two pounds and two shillings to Chester Infirmary, which would have assured him of treatment and entitled him to put forward two non-subscribers per annum for admission.[18] Two years later, Thomas and Anne crowned their courtship with marriage, the event taking place at St John's on 20th

February 1806. The extent of his health issues through this period, and Anne's awareness of them, is uncertain, but they appear not to have been trivial or fleeting.

A letter from his sister, Mary, dated 2nd February 1806 states: 'I fear our complaints are so similar that nothing but milder weather will restore us,' adding, 'I cannot understand your reason for going to Lisbon in spring as Dr Bardsley [her husband] says the climate in winter is excellent for tender lungs, but too hot in summer. Besides, Spain and France threaten to invade Portugal and you may be forced to fly at some risk to your person and property.'[19] Curiously, there is no mention of the impending wedding. The feared invasion did take place, and it precipitated the Peninsular War, which began in July 1807, albeit that would be of no consequence to Thomas.

Two weeks after marrying, Thomas drafted his will at Falmouth, Cornwall, the witnesses being an innkeeper, a waiter and the Surveyor of Customs at the port. All his household goods were left to Anne and his land and estate placed in trust for her use during her natural life, to devolve thereafter to Thomas's brother, Peter, and sister, Mary.

What is to be made of this swift and alarming concatenation of events? It appears almost certain that Thomas was gravely ill when he married and that he proceeded with his plan to seek respite in a warmer climate, as many wealthy people did at that time. Whether Anne went with him is unclear. Later correspondence from friends in Lisbon show that she had contacts there at the very least. The circumstances in which Thomas wrote his will – presumably at the coastal hostelry he stayed at immediately before the crossing – look peremptory. Perhaps he was advised to do this to ensure its legitimacy under English law or perhaps his condition had deteriorated as he travelled to such an extent that he was persuaded it was a necessary step.

We know he arrived in Lisbon but, tragically, he did not survive much longer. An entry in the 'Deaths' section of the *Manchester Mercury* dated 21st October 1806, reads: 'On 30th September, at Lisbon, of a putrid fever the Rev. Thomas Coupland of the Priory, Chester.' This is echoed in the Chester newspapers, though without mention of the fatal ailment, which may have been too graphic for friends and acquaintances in the local area. The 'putrid fever' was typhus, an infectious disease of often epidemic proportions before modern medical advances. Thomas's underlying lung condition may have made him more susceptible to it.

Recently married, Mrs Coupland now found herself newly widowed. Upon his death, Thomas's will came into effect and Anne was contractually engaged with his trustees, whom the document names as 'my friends William Earle of Everton near Liverpool and Thomas Earle of Spekelands near Liverpool'. William and Thomas proved the will at Chester, in front of Registar, Will Nicholls, and later on oath in London. This latter step was common where there was value in the estate because it was the highest court in the land and therefore made the document less amenable to challenge. The reference to the Earles in the will and the extent of the trust it places in them is illuminating. Knowledge of them sheds new light on Thomas Coupland and his family background, and it is less than edifying.

On 1st December 1699, a ship departed from Liverpool bound for West Africa. It was owned by Thomas Clayton, after whom Clayton Square in Liverpool is named, and John Earle, grandfather of the Earles mentioned in Thomas Coupland's will. This was the first slave ship to leave Liverpool. It collected its human cargo and set off for Barbados, arriving in September 1700. Records show that 220 slaves were disembarked, net of a twenty per cent mortality rate resulting from the brutal middle passage.[20] In the next hundred years or so, the Earle family would be involved in at least 270 slave voyages, transporting approximately 40,000 kidnapped Africans to the Americas.[21] This grim legacy places them at the forefront of the many Liverpool-based families of this period that were involved in the transatlantic slave trade.

The International Slavery Museum in Liverpool, which does a magnificent job of presenting this repugnant aspect of our history as it was, holds in its archives a collection of papers relating the Earle family spanning their entire maritime operation.[22] They are richly informative and unparalleled in the level of detail they provide about how this abject trade was undertaken. They also help us to understand the composition of the business and the

Earle family over time and, usefully for our purposes, make occasional references to the Couplands.

Thomas Earle of Spekelands and younger brother, William Earle of Everton, were referred to by their place of residence to distinguish them from their predecessors. John Earle, who proved that slave trading was no bar to social climbing by becoming Mayor of Liverpool in 1709, was succeeded as head of the family by his son Thomas in 1719. He became known as Thomas of Leghorn – a British moniker for the Italian port city of Livorno – because of his diversification of the business into that part of the world. It became his base for trade with Liverpool in products such as coffee, oil, pimento, hides and marble. He was the first importer into Britain of fine white marble for sculpture and ornamental purposes.[23] This move reflected a new level of affluence for the family and perhaps also where he preferred to spend his time. Far from representing a departure from the slaving business, it augmented it. For shipowners, slave voyages were long and precarious, and returns, though bountiful, were slow to come through and not always guaranteed. Vessels could founder and were targets for an enemy in times of war. Income from other sources maintained cashflow and provided the opportunity to acquire products which could then be bartered for humans amongst tribal chieftains in West Africa.

Thomas Earle of Leghorn's younger brother, and eventual successor as head of the business upon his death in 1781, was William Earle of West Derby, the area of Liverpool with which he was most closely associated. Together, they were registered owners of 110 slave ships that left Liverpool in the third quarter of the 18th century. William Earle of West Derby's two sons were the trustees and legatees in Thomas Coupland's will. The brothers combined to form T & W Earle & Company, operating from premises in Hanover Street, Liverpool. They continued the family's established lines of business there and in Livorno and further expanded into the iron, wine, silk and sugar trades. As well as transporting enslaved people, the firm acquired sugar plantations in Berbice in modern day Guyana through the forfeiture of a bad debt. When compensation claims were settled in the 1830s, William Earle of Everton received more than £10,000 for 197 enslaved people in Berbice, equating to approximately £600,000 today.

To understand the connection between the Earles and the Couplands, we need to look at the generation before. The variability in the spelling of some surnames, even well into the 19th century, is an obstacle to research. With literacy levels relatively low, official orthographers were most concerned with capturing the phonetic essence of a name. 'Coupland' is a case in point. Hence, we see an entry in a marriage register in Liverpool in 1815 where a Thomas Coupland – no apparent relation to ours – is spelt as such and yet he signs an inch below as 'Thos Copeland'. 'Copland' and 'Cowpland' are other common variants. Articles of Partnership for 1766 show the elder Thomas and William Earle involved with a number of partners – this being another way to spread the risk – including 'John Copeland'. The spelling and a dearth of Coupland family records for this period complicate the genealogy, but all the indications are that he was a member of the family. Amongst the uncles of Thomas Coupland of the Priory, Chester was a John Copeland, but it appears he remained in the immediate Ormskirk area, marrying and raising a family there.[24]

The John Copeland who partnered the Earle brothers was immersed in the slave trading enterprise. He was part owner of ships involved in 39 slave journeys, mostly to Jamaica, between 1760 and 1780, the first two of which he captained. His maiden voyage as co-owner and captain was eventful, to say the least. Earle family records state that the ship, the *Calypso*, which left Liverpool in March 1760, arrived on the Jamaican coast 'after beating off a privateer of 14 guns in a very gallant manner'.[25] A report in *The Oxford Mail* of 28th March 1761 states that 'the Prince Tom, Capt. Smith, arrived at Liverpool Wednesday last from Jamaica, brings an account of the *Calypso*, Captain Coupland [spelt as such] with 356 slaves from Bonny [Nigeria], being arrived there'. This was by no means the end of the story, however. The Trans-Atlantic Slave Database shows that the ship was captured by the French on its homeward journey, meaning that it and its return cargo were irrevocably lost.

Privateering, which involved government authorised attacks on the mercantile traffic of hostile maritime nations by private operators, was rife at this time, reaching its peak between 1775 and 1781, when Britain was at war with America, France and Spain. Three such missions left the port of Chester in 1778. There is detail within the Earle papers which shows how routes were planned to avoid encounters with enemy naval vessels but to maximise the opportunity to surprise and overpower their merchant vessels. Once on the open sea, everything was at stake and the potential loss or gain was total. Instructions were issued in advance to ships' captains to abort or re-route voyages in the event of high-value plunder being taken. An example of one such haul – the richest ever seized by a Liverpool privateer – is described in Earle family correspondence. The *Carnatic*, a French East Indiaman with a value of £135,000, was captured by Captain John Dawson of the *Mentor* on the 28 October 1778. The cargo included saltpetre, fine muslin, raw silk, coffee, tea and 'a packet of sundry things supposed to be diamonds'. It was the diamonds which greatly increased the value of the prize. The spoils were used to construct Carnatic Hall, a mansion at Mossley Hill, Liverpool, later the site of halls of residence belonging to the University of Liverpool.[26]

Despite John Copeland's misfortune on the *Calypso*, he lived to tell the tale. In November 1761 he again left Liverpool, this time at the helm of the *Mentor* – the very same ship that would later assail the *Carnatic* – bound for Ouidah in Benin. The data relating to the human cargo is particularly disturbing. The intention was to collect five hundred captives, but the actual total is calculated at 638, of whom 521 reached the destination of Kingston, Jamaica: an 18 per cent mortality rate, undoubtedly compounded by overcrowding.

These numbers, excessive by any measure, would have been driven by greed and recklessness on the part of the captain and crew. The effect would be to ratchet up the already unimaginable horror endured by the hapless victims; chained, compressed together and becoming increasingly emaciated from starvation rations in a disease-ridden environment. Another example of the rapacious and indiscriminate nature of the business was seen in the same year when William Earle of West Derby was forced to write an obsequious letter to Duke Abashy, a high-ranking West African collaborator, apologising for the capture and transportation of two of his sons amongst the generality of enslaved people aboard another of his ships.[27]

A growing awareness back home of the nature and extent of the trade fuelled abolitionist sentiment in the coming decades, but resistance amongst the powerful slave-owning elite meant that progress was slow and uncertain. A new generation of owners and operators came to the fore, including from within the ranks of established slave trading families. During this period, we see the bonds between the Earles and the Couplands further strengthened, through marriage and shared commercial interest. In 1791, William Earle of Everton married Ann Copeland, daughter of his business associate, John Copeland. The marriage settlement included an indenture acknowledging Ann's entitlement to a considerable fortune and the granting of property in Duke Street, Liverpool. These were commercial premises with a warehouse attached, round the corner from the Hanover Street base of T & W Earle & Company. Thomas Earle and Robert Norris – a member of another local slave trading dynasty – were party to the transaction.[28]

Whilst it had been fashionable for the Earles to live in this part of town, and of significant practical value given its proximity to Salthouse Dock, the area had gradually become less appealing. By the turn of the 19th century, the population of Liverpool – approximately 80,000 at that time – was expanding rapidly and would more than double again in the next 30 years. It was becoming overcrowded and insalubrious and those who could afford do so were seeking to live elsewhere. It is in this context that we see William Earle purchasing his home in Everton and Thomas land to the north of Toxteth on which he would develop Spekelands. This estate was still relatively new when Thomas Coupland mentioned it in his will in 1806.

Thomas Coupland's brother, Peter, who also features in the will, appears to have had a direct connection with the Earles himself. Later in life we see him referred to as the Reverend Peter Coupland but, at the time of his marriage in Liverpool in 1800, he was described as a 'mariner'. In 1803 he skippered a vessel called the *Governor Dalziel* on the transatlantic route, collecting around two hundred enslaved people from Old Calabar, Nigeria – a favoured and fruitful site for the Earles – before disposing of them in Havana and returning to Liverpool, a little over a year after he set off. It was not unheard of for slave ship captains to become ministers of religion, one example being John Newton, composer of the hymn *Amazing Grace*. Whether Peter Coupland experienced a damascene moment we cannot know, but it is recorded that he was ordained a priest in a ceremony at Chester Cathedral in 1814, presided over by Bishop Law. His ministry was short-lived, however, as he passed away the following year. Nine years later, his son, Richard Evans Coupland – Ann Coupland's nephew by marriage – died in The Gambia, where a colonial administration was being established.[29]

There are passing references to other Couplands embedded in slavery and plantation operations at this time. For example, William and John Coupland were in business together as Coupland and Company in Kingston, Jamaica, trading mainly in coffee and sugar in the first quarter of the 19th century.[30] They also had a base in Duke Street, Liverpool, possibly in the premises that changed hands when Ann Copeland married William Earle of Everton. These Couplands would eventually be overtaken by bankruptcy but, for a while at least, they prospered, with William in particular mixing in exalted circles. In 1818 he was a steward of the prestigious Canning Club in Liverpool, where he entertained the future peer and prime minister after whom the club was named. John Gladstone MP, father of a later prime minister, was a fellow steward. Coupland and Gladstone had traded slaves together in the early years of the century and now occupied several important civic positions, including spearheading a committee to remodel the harbour at Holyhead as a safe haven for Liverpool shipping.[31]

It is worth adding that the original will of Richard Coupland of Ormskirk, the father of Thomas and Peter, is held within the Earle collection.[32] It was drafted in August 1790, ten months before he died, and is consistent with the legacies detailed in the correspondence between his brother, Valentine, and Nic Grimshaw, Valentine's agent. The fact that the Coupland will is an integral part of the Earle Collection is further evidence of the deep and enduring personal connection between the two families. It also helps us to understand the wealth percolating through later generations.

We might now ask whether Anne Coupland née Warburton, our book club member, was aware of her husband's close acquaintance with the Earles and, if so, whether she knew the full extent of their activities. It is likely that she first heard of them in her youth.

The Warburtons had property and commercial interests in the Liverpool area at the same time as the Earles. Such was the strength of the Earle presence that they later had a street named after them. Earle Street, near their original business premises, still exists in the modern day. There were frequent references to the family's mercantile activities in the press, mostly recording arrivals, departures and cargoes. Slave journeys were reported candidly and without demur. It is hard to imagine that all this escaped Anne's attention. Whether she had concerns about it, we cannot say. We do know, however, that after her husband's death, and possibly even before, she had personal dealings with members of the Earle family beyond anything necessitated by the terms of his will.

So it was that in late 1806, Anne Coupland, scarcely a wife, found herself a widow. At 24 years of age, she was in rude health, affluent and with most of her life ahead of her. One of her first decisions would have been where to live. Her aunt's house – her former home – was nearby and Priory House may now have held painful memories for her. Indeed, an advert had appeared in the *Chester Courant* on 11th February 1806 offering Priory House for let furnished for a maximum of three years, adding that it was 'suitable for a small family'. This suggests a planned departure and a hope that Lisbon would become a long-term residence for Thomas and Anne. As we have seen, those plans were tragically frustrated.

Whilst we know Priory House would change hands several times in later decades, it seems that Anne retained a claim on the property. Where she decamped to when Earl Grosvenor occupied it in 1808 is unclear, but St John's House was an option, as were various Warburton residences.

In 1810, two eminent historians, the brothers Daniel and Samuel Lysons, of whom we will hear more, published part of their epic work *Magna Britannia*, providing a topographical account of Cheshire as part of an ambitious project to cover every county in Great Britain. In referring to St John's they state: 'Adjoining the side of the church is a building now the property and residence of Mrs Coupland, which in an old plan of the church is called "The Chambers of the Church Priests", being most probably what was formerly the habitation of the vicars choral.'[33] This is microscopic detail for a work on such a grand scale, but we are grateful for it all the same. Anne, it seems, had moved back in.

At the start of the following year, a property transaction took place involving Eizabeth Sloughter and a George Brooke of Haughton, Shropshire. It was the sale of St John's House for the sum of £3,020. Included in the sale, in addition to the house itself, were stables, a coach house, garden, orchard, courtyard and tenanted cottages in the grounds. There was a right to a pew and sittings in St John's but a reservation to Elizabeth, her heirs and assigns of the vault or burying place in which her family had been interred. She is described in the legal contract – drafted on her behalf and witnessed by 'Ph Humber-ston' and 'Geo. Mellor' – as being 'of Eccleston', a village a couple of miles south of Chester. Much of it was and still is owned by the Grosvenor family, with whom she may have come to an arrangement. We don't know her motive or whether Anne moved with her. Soon they would both be living in the heart of the city again.

Regency Chester, for those of a certain social standing, was full of excitement and promise – not on a par with London and Bath perhaps, but not without a dusting of glitz and glamour. Grand balls and concerts were a regular occurrence at establishments such as the Royal Hotel on Eastgate Street and the Albion Hotel on Lower Bridge Street. Private parties in the many substantial town houses of the landed gentry were commonplace too. One event of note was Lord Belgrave's Ball at the Royal Hotel on Wednesday 15th January 1818. For many of those who attended, this wasn't a working day, because no day was, at least in the conventional sense. These were the leisured classes.

Lord Belgrave, who would later become 2nd Marquess of Westminster, was the eldest son of Robert, Earl Grosvenor, who had occupied Priory House ten years earlier. The ball was to celebrate his return from the Grand Tour on the Continent and his coming of age. A report in the *Chester Chronicle* talks of upwards of four hundred guests, of whom a few are mentioned by name. The first commoner listed is Mrs Coupland, with Mrs Sloughter also amongst the throng. Dancing began at 6pm and was 'was kept up with great spirit till a little after twelve, when an elegant ornamental supper was served up'. This was followed by further dancing until the first departures began to take place at 2am. A great portion of the company, we are told, remained past 4am: impressive stamina, even for largely nocturnal creatures such as these.

Well-connected and socially active, it was inevitable that Anne would develop new relationships and bonds. These were by no means confined to the Chester area. Increasingly we see her corresponding and spending time with her Warburton relatives in the southeast of England. On 20th December 1823 she married for a second time, on this occasion to 'William Owen, a bachelor, one of his majesty's councils learned in the law, of the Parish of Berriew in the County of Montgomery', as he is described in the marriage register.

The ceremony took place at St Mary's Church, Hampton, Middlesex, where the Warburtons had one of their main residences. Anne is described as 'of this parish' and the accompanying marriage bond warrants that it had been her place of abode for the previous 15 days. The provision that enabled this arrangement was contained in 'the late Marriage Act', and perhaps even in the extract Dr Norris had in mind when he put together his catalogue for the book club. Also explained here is his reference to it being in 'superior law binding', given that Anne had married into eminent legal circles. What isn't clear is why she is still 'Mrs Coupland' at the book club in 1824 and not 'Mrs Owen'. It is possible that Dr Norris prepared the list before the wedding and omitted to update it.

Other detail in the marriage register suggests the event, hard upon the festive season, was a grand affair. The witnesses included Thomas Grosvenor – 2nd Earl of Wilton and younger brother of Lord Belgrave – and Harriot Legh, daughter of Sir Peter Warburton, 4th Baronet. The service was conducted by John Merewether, who would later become Dean of Hereford.

A little investigation reveals that William Owen was a member of the Owen family of Glansevern, a fine country estate situated between the River Severn and the picturesque village of Berriew, near Welshpool. Now, of course, we have another Mr Owen, distinct from the Robert Owen discussed at the start of the chapter. Perhaps he was in some way connected with a 'New Settlement'.

A useful biographical source for William Owen is *A Genealogical and Heraldic History of the Commoners of Great Britain and Ireland.*[34] Born in 1758, and therefore 24 years older than Anne, he was descended from Rhodri Mawr, the 9th century King of Gwynedd and Powys. He was the third son of Owen Owen of Cefn Hafod and succeeded to the Glansevern estate in 1816 upon the death of his brother, Sir Arthur Davies Owen, who had created it ten years earlier. In his youth he attended Trinity College, Cambridge, where he excelled academically, before becoming a member of Lincoln's Inn and being called to the bar. For several years after that he attended circuits at Oxford and Chester, which is how the opportunity to meet Anne Coupland may well have arisen. Later in his legal career he was involved with the Courts of Chancery and Exchequer before becoming Commissioner for Bankrupts and being elevated to King's Counsel.

William was a particularly prominent figure in Montgomeryshire, where he chaired the quarter sessions, as well as serving as a magistrate and Deputy Lieutenant. His sharp legal mind was complemented by a flair for oratory. Nowhere was this better displayed than in the role he played in the abolition of Welsh judicature and constitutional alignment with the English legal system in 1829. He had petitioned for this since 1817, contributing to debates in the House of Commons and addressing recalcitrant county gatherings, swaying opinion with irrefutable points of detail and respect for his professional credibility. As a proud Welshman, William may have appeared to some as guilty of a treasonable act, but constitutional arguments won the day and a defective Welsh judicial structure could not be safeguarded by nationalist sentiment alone.[35] On other great issues of the day, he supported Catholic emancipation and was regarded as a liberal and temperate reformer. He would have welcomed the Great Reform Act of 1832, philosophically and because, on a practical level, Montgomeryshire benefitted from additional parliamentary representation.

The Owen family had a noteworthy presence overseas too. To understand this fully, we need to look at the family line. There was another William Owen – uncle to Anne's husband – who distinguished himself as a naval captain in the conflict-ridden years of the mid- to late 18th century. He lost his right arm at Pondicherry, India whilst fighting in the

Seven Years' War in 1760 and returned to England the following year after the sinking of his ship, *HMS Sunderland*. In 1767 he was in Nova Scotia with the Governor, Lord William Campbell, who, as reward for William's naval service, bestowed upon him Passamaquoddy Outer Island, New Brunswick. He subsequently renamed this 'Campobello', in deference to the grantor.

There was a complication, however, in that the land comprised ten thousand acres and there was an arbitrary limit on officers of his rank receiving more than three thousand acres. He was therefore obliged to enjoin his three nephews – Arthur, David and William – in the transaction, his own two sons being in their infancy at the time.

William Owen senior, as we shall call him, continued to travel the globe pursuing his various interests, including on the political scene in Shrewsbury. It was here in 1768 that he lost an eye and was facially disfigured in an election brawl, militancy at the hustings being a particular feature of the age. Seven years later he would become the town's mayor. In the meantime, in 1770, he returned to Campobello with 38 colonists and began establishing a permanent settlement there. Restlessness got the better of him again, it seems, as he left the island in 1771. In 1776, he returned to active service as Captain of *HMS Cormorant*, which set him on a course to his death a year later, in Madras, at the age of 46.[36]

Now we do have another Mr Owen – intimately connected with Anne's husband – who was responsible for a new settlement. It was a significant milestone in the Owen family history, and it was still young and developing at the time of our book club. Some of Anne's recently acquired in-laws were settling there and it attracted some curious and quixotic characters.

A study was undertaken in 2013 by the US National Genealogical Society into the colonisation of Campobello, providing rich insights into the people and processes involved.[37] It features the strange case of Plato Denney and the pioneering ship he captained. He was one of the 38 colonists who travelled from England in March 1770 on the *Owen*, a two hundred ton vessel purchased and renamed by William Owen, who was also on board.

Denney enjoyed some status as captain and master of the ship, albeit subordinate to William himself. When William and his family left in June 1771, Denney was instructed to take charge of Campobello. Oral tradition in New Brunswick has it that Denney was pressurised by fellow settlers whose periods of indenture were coming to an end and who wanted to return to their wives and families in England. Consequently, in the autumn of 1772, they are reported to have set sail with Denney on the mother ship, only to be lost at sea and never heard from again.

This report, though it has some substance to it, is flawed. Denney – his name unchanged, apart from the occasional variant 'Denny' – was soon back in Liverpool, trading, remarrying and corresponding with a contact in Campobello. The signatures on his two marriage certificates – from before and after the Campobello expedition – and on his correspondence all tally, confirming it to have been the same man. His main business interests were now in the transatlantic slave trade, including co-ownership of the Liverpool-registered vessel *Peggy* with none other than John Copeland. His death at the age of 60 was reported in the *Lancaster Gazette* in August 1802.

So, what really happened to the *Owen* and the others who left Campobello in the autumn of 1772? An entry in *The Bath Chronicle* dated 3rd December that year reads: 'The *Campobello*, Bone [the captain], is lost in Cardigan Bay: part of the cargo is saved.' There is no detail regarding fatalities. Copious amounts of timber and part of the fractured vessel were advertised for sale by William Owen a month later and part of the sale proceeds were remitted to Plato Denney in Liverpool. Reports put out about the size of the ship suggest it was larger than the *Owen* but this, along with a different name and captain, may have been deliberate misdirection for financial gain. Sale of the timber and an insurance claim for the loss of the *Owen* could have been lucrative business, if corrupt. The evidence is indeterminate but alternative explanations are elusive.

After this episode and the death of William Owen senior, the surviving owners needed to safeguard their property. In 1787, David Owen, one of the three nephews, went out to Campobello to shore up the governance of the island and represent the family interests.

It is no coincidence that the main landing point is known as Welshpool. The early years of settlement presented significant challenges. The French military presence in North America had almost been eradicated as a result of the Treaty of Paris in 1763, which ended the Seven Years' War in favour of the British. This emboldened Anglo-American colonists, who no longer needed protection against the French from the mother country, and it was a contributory factor in the outbreak of the American Revolution 12 years later. Canada and Nova Scotia were targets for the separatists but were successfully defended, despite the loss of the 13 American colonies across the border when the war concluded in 1783. Nova Scotia was nominally loyal to the Crown, but its French Acadian population collaborated with New England and local shipping suffered attacks from American privateers. Campobello, being the nearest crossing point from western Maine, was right in the eye of the storm. Today, the island is connected to the US mainland by a causeway, despite it being across the border into Canada and a time zone away.

David Owen had to consolidate his presence there in the face of these constant threats, which he did in part by trading openly and extensively with the American rebels, in defiance of hostilities. The pattern repeated itself when Britain and America went to war again between 1812 and 1814 – this time less conclusively – with Owen still ruling the roost at Campobello.

One British acquisition during this conflict was Moose Island, just to the east, where Sir Thomas Hardy was appointed chief naval officer. Hardy and Owen were old acquaintances, and their friendship blossomed now they were living at close quarters. His was already a household name following his command of *HMS Victory* at the Battle of Trafalgar in 1805 and his inseparable connection with the ill-fated Admiral Lord Nelson at that time.

Throughout this period, long-standing residents of Campobello resisted colonial occupation and some disputes over land were settled in their favour. Owen put in place government apparatus and a legal system, unsophisticated by the standards of his homeland and no doubt informed by specialist advice from his brother William.

By now the two sons of William Owen senior – Edward William Campbell Rich and William Fitzwilliam – had reached maturity and assumed their share of the island alongside their three cousins.[38] Both men could boast singular achievements in their own right. Edward, born on Campobello in 1771, had a stellar naval career, more than eclipsing his father's. Between the mid-1820s and mid-1840s he was successively Commander-in-Chief in the West Indies, the East Indies and the Mediterranean, ascending to the admiralty in 1846. All this despite a difficult and, to some extent, disenfranchised upbringing as the illegitimate son of his father's housekeeper, Sarah Haslam.[39] Whilst living near Manchester in 1774, Sarah had given birth to a second son, also by William. This child – William Fitzwilliam – wore the badge of his illegitimacy in the prefix 'Fitz', which perhaps pricked the sides of his ambition. Orphaned at the age of four, he was boarded in foster homes in north Wales, though he and his brother enjoyed some patronage from their father's friend and naval mentor, Sir Thomas Rich.

William Fitzwilliam was an able scholar, particularly in languages and mathematics, which appeared to be an Owen family trait. He took to the seas so single-mindedly that he was described as eccentric and out of his element whilst on shore and in civilian society.[40] He was also boisterous and temperamental, which led to mutiny under his command and, at one point, dismissal from the service. This was reversed through the influence of his patrons, and he was soon in the thick of military conflict in the Indian Ocean, including a seven-month spell as a prisoner of war on the island of Mauritius. A fellow captive was Captain Matthew Flinders, who had surveyed the coast of Australia, or New Holland as it was then known. This may have provided the stimulus for William Fitzwilliam to move more directly into that field.

Some charting of the Indian Ocean and the coast of Portugal preceded his appointment, in 1815, to surveying duties in Canada, under the supervision of his brother. The primary, though by no means exclusive, focus of this work was the Great Lakes and St Lawrence River. Much of it was undertaken in winter when conditions were precarious. Simmering tensions with the Americans gave rise to a lack of co-operation and occasionally outright interference on their part.

His next major role and the one that would cement his reputation amongst the greatest ever British naval surveyors was around the coast of Africa. Here, between 1822 and 1826, he surveyed some 30,000 miles of coastline and established a chain of longitudinal distances extending from Britain to Bombay. This was despite his expedition being dogged by tropical fever, in the face of which he advocated rest, fresh air and restorative treatments that were well ahead of their time.

He and his officers witnessed first-hand and were appalled by the ravages of the slave trade, their testimony fuelling the movement to abolish it. He also captured numerous slave ships from his West African base in the Gulf of Guinea, though his superiors at the Admiralty suspected this may have been motivated as much by profit as morality. This base, created by him, was on the Island of Fernando Po, now known as Bioko. This was another new settlement attributable to a Mr Owen, but as it wasn't established until 1827 it can have no relevance to our book club. One of his early companions there was James Holman, who was famous as the 'Blind Traveller'. Undeterred by his ocular constraint, which was accompanied by limited mobility and constant pain, he visited every inhabited continent and, in 1832, became the first blind person to circumnavigate the globe.

William Fitzwilliam had a reputation for boundless energy and attention to detail which informed an unrivalled output, of infinite value to later surveyors, navigators and explorers. His personality, however, continued to be career-damaging. He was apt to overspend to get the job done, which drew some censure from the Navy Board; he was increasingly abrasive; and there was a sense that his mental acuity was giving way to instability. After a posting to South America in 1829 on more routine activities, he returned to England for four years in 1831. He became an early member of the Royal Geographical and Astronomical Societies, donating material and instruments to their cause.

At this time, William Fitzwilliam corresponded with Anne Owen, regretting her husband's unspecified illness and acknowledging proposals for the transfer of Campobello wholly to himself. There was a lack of consensus on its value, with William Fitzwilliam seeming to suggest that commercial deforestation undertaken by an agent in his absence had led to some depreciation. There were also additional land grants in the Canadian provinces, to which they were entitled under the British flag, that needed to be brought into the equation. William Fitzwilliam suggested offering them to Richard Owen of Newtown as 'it will be much better to make them available to less prosperous parts of the family'. Aside from the particulars, Anne was clearly involved in the business, probably due to incapacity on her husband's part.

By 1835, agreement had been reached amongst the surviving Owen shareholders – Arthur and David were now deceased - and full title to Campobello passed to William Fitzwilliam. He was a popular figure on the island. People tended to accept his character flaws as eccentricities and hadn't forgotten his early exploratory work in the region. He was active on their behalf too, seeking to diversify the local economy away from fish and timber, and develop amenities such as schools, roads and lighthouses. He was an advocate of the Church of England and was keen to promote the Gospel, becoming a lay preacher and welcoming missionary activity on the island. He still did some work for the Admiralty, surveying the adjacent Bay of Fundy and adding to the sum of knowledge on global tidal flows. He was promoted to rear admiral in 1842, after which he relinquished his survey work. A further promotion to vice-admiral – essentially an honorific – came in 1854, followed by retirement with a pension one year later. He died at St John's, New Brunswick and was buried on Campobello in 1857, leaving a considerable scientific legacy across vast swathes of the earth.

We are very fortunate that descendants of the Owen family have collated and deposited at the National Library of Wales an extensive collection of family documents spanning several centuries, under the title of 'Glansevern Estate Records'. Some of the correspond-ence relates to people, places and timeframes within our field of vision. Our Mrs Owen, as we can now call her, has left her stamp on it, not merely in her own correspondence but also by retaining letters to, from and about her aunt and her first husband, some of which have already been referred to. It may seem odd that Coupland material appears in what is essentially an Owen family archive, but the contents are more practical than personal and are therefore unlikely to have given Anne's second husband any cause for reflection or concern.

The Elizabeth Sloughter correspondence is particularly pertinent to Chester. Her cousin, Margaret Warburton of Hampton Court, writes to her regularly. Using the salutation 'My Dear Bessie', she addresses her letters to St John Street, Chester from 1824 onwards. This confirms that Elizabeth had moved back to the centre of the city, and to the same area that she had left a few years earlier. There is talk of the loss of a friend and creeping loneliness. Elizabeth would now be in her mid-70s, many of her contemporaries would have passed away and mobility would be a growing problem. The *Chester Directory* of 1828 lists 'Mrs Slaughter' at St John's Street. Joseph Hemingway writing in his *History of the City of Chester* in 1831 describes the thoroughfare as 'a neat and commodious street, in which there are many genteel residences, and amongst others, those of Edwd. Massy, Mrs Slaughter' and so on.[41] This was clearly a fashionable and up-market part of town.

With Anne living remotely at Glansevern, there was a need for her and her aunt to keep in touch by letter. Their communications reveal a continued close bond but also occasional discord between them. In June 1828, Elizabeth writes to Ann apparently requesting a loan and talking about going to visit a Mrs Allanson in the country, 'which will be of service to me'. A few days later she writes again, acknowledging receipt of £100 and reporting that Dora Allanson was arriving that day to take her to Broughton. She adds that she was getting the house painted; in her words, 'a very long' – and, it may be supposed, expensive – 'job'.

Letters from December of that year are more acerbic in tone. On the 17th Elizabeth writes: 'My Dear Anne, Sorry you have had the trouble and expense of sending a turkey and pheasant which in my present deep affliction I cannot partake of, coming from those who caused it.' As if to compound the rebuff, which appears to be aimed at William as well as Anne, she had passed the offerings on to friends. The nature of the offence is unclear, but a further letter dated 30th December talks of the loss of a kitchen maid, in which the Owens may have been instrumental. 'My happiness and comfort in my old age has not been considered,' she adds plaintively, smarting at perceived ingratitude. Mrs Allanson, she concedes, may be able to help.

The friend to whom repeated reference is made is Anne Elizabeth Allanson, née Whitehall-Davies, of Broughton Hall, Worthenbury near Wrexham. This was a grand Jacobean mansion, eventually demolished in 1959.[42] Oddly, there was another Broughton Hall in the possession of the family – in this case just over the border from Chester into Flintshire, which was occupied by Anne Allanson's brother, the Reverend Whitehall Whitehall-Davies. Both are mentioned in his will, proved by his sister upon his death in 1824. She inherited substantial property from him on both sides of the border. When Broughton Hall, Flintshire was offered for sale in the *Chester Chronicle* in 1790, it was described as being 'late in the occupation of Thomas Sloughter, deceased'. Perhaps mutual interest in the property is how the Whitehall-Davies and Sloughter families first made their acquaintance.

Anne Whitehall-Davies's marriage to the Reverend George Allanson, Prebendary of Ripon Cathedral, is worth a mention. It took place at the parish church in Worthenbury on 7th November 1794, with the service being conducted by Reginald Heber and witnessed by, amongst others, his wife, Mary Heber. Mary was George Allanson's sister. The Hebers' children would undoubtedly have been in attendance, one of whom – another Reginald, aged 11 at this time – would go on to achieve high ecclesiastical office and lasting renown. We will hear more about him, but, for now, there he sits, at the happy union of his aunt and uncle: pious, precocious and absorbing everything he sees.

Returning to the interaction between Elizabeth Sloughter and her niece, the start of the 1830s offers little in the way of a thaw in their relations. Elizabeth has turned to Margaret Warburton for solace and as an outlet for her emotions. Margaret expresses regret that 'the affliction weighs so heavily on your spirits' and suggests that the refusal of the game may impede any reconciliation with Anne. She refers to an ill-advised 'speech' by Anne at Broughton, which gave William, her husband, the erroneous impression that Elizabeth could care for herself. The crux of the matter may well have been the cost of medical and general domestic support. There is even a suggestion that Elizabeth is being denied access to her own resources in the line, 'The slender pittance that you reserved for yourself from the ample fortune (upwards of fifty thousand pounds) you ought to have inherited, you are most justly entitled to.'

Much of this fortune derived from leases on estates left by Sir George Warburton to Thomas Sloughter – Elizabeth's father rather than Anne's. Also included was a house in Albemarle Street, Mayfair, which has historic associations with Lord Byron, whose publisher was located there, and later, Oscar Wilde. A further revelation in the letter from Margaret Warburton is that fact that the lottery winner in 1757 was not in fact Thomas Sloughter, but his wife. For whatever reason, that escaped the attention of the *Chester Courant* and the funds found their way into Thomas's estate. There was no settled legal position on the matter but there was a societal expectation that winnings would accrue to the husband in any marital relationship.[43] Mrs Anne Sloughter had dutifully obliged.

Understandably there is a lull in correspondence between Elizabeth Sloughter and Anne Owen but, between Elizabeth and Margaret Warburton, it carries on unabated. They console each other on their deteriorating faculties – 'eyes, fingers, and mental powers' – and crave a glimpse of renewed happiness in their declining years. Elizabeth, it seems, contemplated a move to Hampton Court but was persuaded otherwise on the grounds of cost – it being 'at least twice as expensive as Chester'. She was not awash with offers of hospitality at this time, though the Allansons continued to show kindness and benevolence towards her.[44]

The Glansevern papers give us some sense of the zeitgeist and the wider preoccupations of people central to our scope, which it would be folly to omit. For example, in the early 1830s Margaret Warburton writes of their spirits being broken by numerous losses and 'the universal poverty' obliging people to 'keep quiet'. The relative prosperity of the immediate post-war years had waned as pressures driven by population growth and social upheaval took their toll. 'Even London feels it,' she adds, 'and parishes are weighed down with over-burdened poor.' Concern for the king's health, expressed in a letter of April

1830, was sadly borne out by his death two months later. The state of Ireland features too, with a reference in 1831 to 'dreadful disturbances, destroying the fruits of the earth wherever they can; digging up the ground and working up the crops so that next year, if their progress cannot be arrested, the famine will be general'. History grimly records the depth and impact of the famine of the ensuing years, though perhaps the causes were less self-inflicted than the writer suggests.[45]

Soon after this, Elizabeth Sloughter took the decision to move across Chester to Grey Friars, and it seems to have worked out well. The Grey Friars were Franciscan monks, who first established themselves in the city in the 13th century, settling close to the Water Gate for the greater ease of collecting alms from travellers as they passed through it. The property into which Elizabeth moved still stands today, occupying an enviable position with views across the racecourse to the Welsh hills beyond. This prospect would not have been unappealing to her; nor would the presence of a greater proportion of her friends and acquaintances in that part of town.

By the turn of 1832, Elizabeth and her niece were back on speaking terms. In a letter of 14th January, she writes: 'I assume you are back at Glansevern and enjoying the beauty of the place and season. I have had a very gratifying visit from my friend, Lady Brake, who was much pleased to see me comfortably settled in this bright and airy place.' There is a tacit suggestion that Anne should pay her a visit in her new abode, but this appears not to have met with a response, in the short term at least. Three months later the request was put more explicitly and by proxy, in a letter to Anne from Mrs Jacson, Elizabeth's friend and neighbour in Grey Friars. 'I hope you will come and see her on your return from town,' she writes. Anne was caught up in London and its magnetic pull.

Soon people would be drawn to Chester for a specific and momentous event. In a letter to Anne of 19th August 1832, Elizabeth effuses:

Our town has been highly gratified with a visit from the Duchess of Kent and Princess Victoria ... I trust they would be highly gratified with the Royal reception the old city paid them. The first carriage which was opened contained the Duchess of Kent, the Princess Victoria and Lord and Lady Westminster ... the new bridge was opened that they may be the first to go over ... There was great magnificence at Eaton, as the Chester papers will inform you.

The visit of the future Queen Victoria and her mother was an iconic moment in the history of Chester. Designed by Chester-based architect, Thomas Harrison, who did not live to see its completion, the Grosvenor Bridge was the longest single-span stone arch bridge in the world, then and for the following 30 years. It was deemed necessary to ease traffic flow around the city and out towards the north Wales coast. Time has not diminished its grandeur or utility, and Cestrians remain justly proud of this architectural gem in the present day.

Whilst no doubt digesting the primary content of the letter, Anne's mind appears to have been elsewhere. On the reverse she wrote, '19th October 1832, the month the will was made,' as if by way of an aide memoire. Financial issues were never far from the surface. Anne held the reins and Elizabeth continued to petition her for support. This includes her sending attested documentation to show that she had cleared debts of £10,000 and £500 respectively for Anne's grandfather and father, presumably in a further attempt at leverage. There is no evidence that this appeal bore fruit.

The correspondence thins out a little after this but revives again six months later. A notable feature of it is the extent to which Elizabeth's handwriting deteriorates, to the point of illegibility. We can see that she reflects with satisfaction on her move to Grey Friars one year after she took up occupancy, stating, 'My change of place has raised me numerous friends.' She lists a number of visitors, including Rowland Egerton-Warburton – a kinsman by marriage, inheritor and restorer of Arley Hall, and High Sheriff of Cheshire at the time of his visit. There is sadness too within the Warburton ranks at the death at Hampton Court of Harriot Legh.[46]

Most of the letters in the collection arrived at Glansevern, so it is understandable that there are few from Anne, who lived there. One exception is a letter to her aunt from

London, dated 20th May 1833. This indicates a deep rapprochement, given its tone and level of detail. Written from 3 Bolton St, Piccadilly, it talks of numerous visitors and visits, and regrets not being able to spend more time with the Warburtons and Grosvenors due to competing demands on their own time. 'Sometimes,' she says, 'we have three or four dinner invitations for Saturday and Wednesday.' These were the most popular days for socialising in London because the House of Commons didn't sit and many of the socialites had links to Parliament.

People they had seen included Mr Jervis – a judge and father of John Jervis, MP for Chester; and Sergeant Merewether, Queen Adelaide's Solicitor General and uncle of Reverend Merewether, who had officiated at Anne's wedding in 1823. Regular companions are Sir Edward Owen – 'one of the most kind-hearted men I ever knew' – and Lady Owen – 'a very obliging pleasing woman'. This is Edward William Campbell Rich Owen of Campobello, naval supremo and brother of William Fitzwilliam Owen. He was accompanied by his second wife, Sarah; his first, it seems, having been somewhat less than obliging.

Having married Elizabeth Cannon in 1802, he successfully divorced her in 1816 on the grounds of adultery with the son of the family's medical attendant. A report in *The Times* of 2nd December that year is not short on salacious detail, including the conveyance of letters through a go-between, secret trysts in a London coffee house, the adoption of aliases by both parties and the draping of a silk handkerchief over a bedroom keyhole against prying eyes. Much of this, it was alleged, took place in 1815 whilst Sir Edward was in command of a squadron on the lakes in Upper Canada. When he was told of it on his return, the accused couple immediately eloped to France, where they set up as husband and wife. Divorces were rare as they required a private Act of Parliament before the Matrimonial Causes Act of 1857. Between 1700 and 1857 only 314 of these acts were passed, mostly initiated by influential men.[47]

This unfortunate episode does not appear to have materially damaged Sir Edward's reputation professionally or personally. His naval career continued to advance and he remarried in 1829. Anne Owen's letter of May 1833 merely reports that ministers had distanced themselves from Sir Edward due to his Tory politics but that the king and queen were 'particularly affectionate towards him'. Such was the measure of trust placed in him in Royal circles that 'he brought her Majesty [Adelaide of Saxe-Meiningen, wife of King William IV] to England'.

In terms of her own social life, Anne tells her aunt of balls at St James's and weekend visits to the Zoological Gardens, now eclipsing Kensington Gardens as the most fashionable, if occasionally exclusive, place outdoors. She describes a recent visit as 'very hot' – even for the 'rich East Indian' in their company – and the thrill of seeing the birds and beasts, including an elephant and calf wandering around. A particular favourite of hers was 'a building about the size of your sitting room at Grey Friars filled with beautiful parrots and four snakes'. Other regular haunts were horticultural meetings in Regent Street and the Royal Asiatic Museum. She clearly had a taste for the exotic.

She also mentions her attendance at a flea show, at which 'two fleas dance a waltz'. 'The poor little animals,' she says, 'are educated in the same treadmill and the man feeds them upon his own blood upon the back of his hand.' Such reservations did not prevent this from being a popular form of entertainment. The letter closes with a request for her good wishes to be passed on to Mrs Allanson and her family and is signed off 'Yours affectionately, A W Owen'.[48]

Writing to Elizabeth on 12th March 1835 – this time from 14 Pall Mall – Anne tells of more glittering social occasions in the metropolis. On the previous Sunday she had been to the Chapel Royal at St James's, where the Bishops of Bristol and London – the latter being Charles Blomfield, formerly Bishop of Chester – preached before the king. He 'put on his spectacles' and 'looked very like poor George III', whom she must have seen in her youth. Much other people news is included, often of a punctilious and idiosyncratic nature. The Bishop of Bristol, it seems, abandoned his wig, taking advantage of a recent dispensation for those in his position, and the Langravine of Hesse Homburg 'is grown quite as large as Mrs Dickenson of Stanley Place [Chester], who you must well remember'. Anne exhorts Elizabeth not to leave her own fireside in the treacherous March whether, and, almost in the same breath, asks her to visit a John Morris to see if he has received the gold moulding she sent. Chester was her next intended port of call.

Elizabeth's letters to Anne in these years are equally warm. She wishes her and her husband safe travels as they divide their time between London and Glansevern and is pleased to hear any reports of their good health. Elizabeth's health, however, continues to deteriorate, as witnessed by the fact that she now dictates her letters to a Mary Weatherhead, who was in her service. There is a request in June 1836 to Anne to purchase for her 'the largest magnifying spectacles that are to be had, and also a bottle of Godfrey's Smelling Salts' on her next trip to London. There are invitations to the Owens to visit Grey Friars and to stay for as long as they liked. There is gratitude on the receipt of a birthday present in July, with which she drank the sender's health, 'which I do daily'. She begs Anne to exercise caution in London, having heard the streets are so busy that they are dangerous to cross.

Increasingly through the summer and autumn of 1836, Mary Weatherhead takes to adding her own postscripts to Elizabeth's letters, probably unbeknown to her. In June she is positive about her state of health, noting that most mornings they take a little walk together on the walls, adjacent to Grey Friars. Three months later there is significant cause for alarm. Mary's note is now the core of the letter. On 29th September she describes several visits from George Harrison, surgeon at the nearby Chester Infirmary, to treat Elizabeth's laboured breathing and 'water in the flesh'. Initially he prescribed medicine to some effect, but the symptoms persisted and grew worse, giving all observers grave concern. 'I wish you was here,' says Mary, 'but do not alarm yourself. I am going to send for some gin for her to take in water. You have no idea the size of her body, and it has come on so quick. I am going to write to Hampton Court. Do write soon.' Four weeks later, Elizabeth Sloughter's death, at the age of 87, was reported in the Chester and London press.[49]

Tributes and condolences followed, including from Thomas Grosvenor, Earl of Wilton. Elizabeth's will – drafted in October 1832, as Anne had observed – was proved in

London in June 1837 by executors John Whitehall Dod and George Harrison. The first of these was the son-in-law of Mrs Allanson and the second was the surgeon who had attended Elizabeth as her terminal condition took hold. She had died a spinster and appears to have had few close male contacts who could fulfil the executor role. There were four codicils, mainly recognising people who had supported her most directly in her declining years. One of these was Mary Weatherhead, who was left an annuity of £20 and all Elizabeth's wearing apparel. The same annuity was accorded to 'my old servant, Sarah Tomkins, now residing with Mrs Thomas at the Pied Bull Inn, Chester'. Anne Owen was the main beneficiary, however, and, in the event of her death, three female cousins of the Warburton family, including Margaret.

Despite further pecuniary gain and the often prickly nature of the relationship, Anne would have felt the loss deeply. As we have seen, Elizabeth brought her up from an early age and was a constant presence in Chester, a city which held so many memories for her. She would have turned to her husband for consolation, though he was ageing and not in the best of health himself. A letter he wrote to her as early as February 1825 states, 'I trust you will find yourself most amply provided for should anything happen to me … with the exception of the pain in my face I am well and have stood London, without air and exercise, wonderfully.' He adds, 'You are all and everything to me in this world … I hope never to visit this place again without you, unless it is for four or five days.' This last qualification tempers his expression of devotion, but there is no doubting it all the same.

A letter from Mrs Jacson of Chester to Anne Owen written in September 1834 refers to 'Mr Owen's very unpleasant accident' and a hope that he no longer feels any inconvenience from it. There are no details but it was possibly a fall from a horse or carriage, which were common and often fatal at this time.

William Owen's will was written in the same year and crystallised with his death three years later, at the age of 69, leaving Anne a widow for the second time. She was appointed sole executrix and awarded 'all my estates in England, Great Britain, America and in all the world': quite a legacy. The will also stipulated that 'my funeral be conducted in a private and unostentatious manner, unless my wife should think otherwise'. Devoted and deferential to the end. The funeral took place at St Beuno's Church in Berriew, where William was interred in the family vault, which bears the simple inscription 'Glansevern'.

Inside the church, where the walls are mostly unadorned, there is a memorial tablet in the chancel with the words:

SACRED TO THE MEMORY OF **WILLIAM OWEN** OF **GLYNGYNWYD**
AND **GLANSEVERN**
IN THE COUNTY OF **MONTGOMERY**, ESQ^r. ONE OF HIS MAJESTY'S
COUNSEL
AND A BENCHER OF THE ANCIENT AND HONORABLE SOCIETY OF
LINCOLN'S INN
YOUNGEST SON OF **OWEN OWEN** OF **GLYNGYNWYD**, ESQ^r. AND
ANNE HIS WIFE.
AN UPRIGHT AND TALENTED MAGISTRATE, CHAIRMAN OF THE
QUARTER SESSIONS,
AND ONE OF THE DEPUTY LIEUTENANTS OF THIS COUNTY.
HE DEPARTED THIS LIFE ON THE 10TH OF NOVEMBER 1837, AGED 79,
LEAVING BEHIND HIM A NAME WITHOUT REPROACH.
INCORRUPTA FIDES, NUDAQUE VERITAS
QUANDO HUIC INVENUIET PAREM
HIS WIDOW **ANNE WARBURTON** WITH THE DEEPEST FEELINGS
OF REVERENCE AND REGRET CAUSED THIS MONUMENT TO BE
ERECTED.

The Latin inscription points to his unrivalled faith and commitment to truth. Above the lettering is a chiselled profile of William, looking learned and august, and, above that, a Grecian urn. It is a fitting monument, commissioned by Anne, who continued to cleave to the Warburton name.

At the far end of the nave is another weighty memorial, this time placed by William and Anne together. It begins with Owen Owen, William's grandfather, who died in 1717, and ends with William's two brothers and a sister who pre-deceased him. The detail on David Owen, his second eldest brother, records that he was 'a Fellow of Trinity College, Cambridge and Senior Wrangler in that University in 1777', and that he died in Campobello and requested that his remains be deposited in the family vault at Berriew. 'Senior Wrangler' is the top mathematics undergraduate at Cambridge, an accolade that has been described as the greatest intellectual achievement in England. William entered that contest in 1782, coming fifth: still a highly commendable outcome, but not worthy of mention on his memorial. Both tablets are made of the finest marble and have stood up well for almost two centuries.

Support for Anne in her bereavement came from both the Warburton and Owen families. A particular source of comfort was Sir Edward Owen and his wife, now resident at Windlesham House in Surrey, whom she visited at their request. This was also an opportunity to catch up on Owen family news, including from Campobello, and to deal with practical matters relating to land ownership and management. There was contact too from William Fitzwilliam Owen and his daughter, Cornelia, direct from Campobello, expressing sympathy and regret at not having visited them that year. Cornelia adds her thanks for 'your kindness to mamma, my sisters and myself', without specifying what form that took.[50]

As a widow again, wealthy and well-connected, it wasn't long before Anne was attracting new suitors. Foremost amongst these was Sir Edward Brace, an admiral and close associate of the Owens in naval circles. A lengthy correspondence between him and Anne during the years 1838 to 1843 led to intimacy and, ultimately, a marriage proposal. This did not proceed, however, due to outside interference, including anonymous letters urging rejection on her part. She had also fallen out with Sir Edward Brace's niece, utterly and irrevocably.[51]

Another regular contact of Anne's up to the end of the 1830s was none other than William Earle of Everton. She had kept in touch with him after her first husband's death in what appeared to be a quasi-business relationship. William Earle had been widowed in 1819 and had also lost his brother and long-term trading partner, Thomas, in 1822. His primary base was now Italy, taking advantage of his family's established commercial presence there and freedom from financial worry. He was accompanied by his daughter, whose delicate health he felt warranted a near-permanent presence on the Continent. His main line was now the sourcing and exporting of fine art and ornaments to Britain. He claimed to work with and support the best artists and sculptors not in the service of the Grand Duke. Anne approved drawings he sent of merchandise and entrusted him to work within a budget that she set, mainly for the acquisition of alabasters imported through Liverpool. Many of these items would have been earmarked for the Glansevern estate, inside and out. William may also have supplied the raw material for the two Owen family memorial tablets at Berriew.

William Earle's letters are copious in length and occasionally lament the fact that Anne doesn't always reply promptly and in kind. The content ranges across their business dealings and into political, social and personal matters. There are frequent enquiries from both he and his daughter into the welfare of Mrs Sloughter when she was alive, indicating a deep and enduring interconnectedness between their families. The correspondence diminished after he collected his slavery compensation in 1837 – no doubt dulling his commercial edge – and he died in January 1839, at the age of 78. He is buried in the Protestant Cemetery in Rome, not far from the great Romantic poets, John Keats and Percy Bysshe Shelley. In death, as in life, we can't always legislate for the company we keep.

There is also a memorial to William Earle in the Walker Art Gallery in Liverpool, set by his children, extolling 'the benevolence of his heart and the integrity of his character'. Artwork from his collection is sited nearby, along with a candid recognition by the gallery of the true nature of his activities.[52] Shortly after his death, an advert appeared in the *Liverpool Albion* advertising for sale almost 2,500 bottles of choice wines and spirits at his

Everton residence, all imported by him for his own use, even though he scarcely lived there.[53]

Another property being emptied of its contents at about the same time was Priory House in Chester. A letter to Anne Owen from a Sam Gardner of Eastgate Street in the city is sketchy about a list of fixtures she requested, saying 'the grate, shelves and similar will be yours', but professing no knowledge of a clock she had enquired about. A picture had been finished – perhaps of the property – and was awaiting collection by 'the boatmen'. Most of the items would be transported by mail coach from the Feathers Hotel to Hartford, and from there by first class train to London. A new form of transport was emerging, in which Anne would take no little interest. A tenant – Mrs Thompson – had been given notice to quit Priory House and was distressed at her plight, not least because she had found nowhere else to move to. There is no indication of clemency on Mrs Owen's part.[54]

As the decade drew to a close, she appeared to be on affable terms with most of her correspondents. Happy events added to the cheer. In May 1839 there was a new arrival at Hampton Court – to Rowland and Mary Egerton-Warburton – and in July, Cornelia Owen married Captain John James Robinson, another naval man, at Campobello. The 1840s, however, started out in a different vein.

William Fitzwilliam Owen, Cornelia's father, was now in London. In January of 1840 he was writing despairingly to Anne – his cousin's widow – about his treatment at her hands. He had been unceremoniously arrested at her suit for non-payment of a debt of £500, just as he was about to settle it, he claims. His letters detail how events unfolded: 'On the 1st of January I was on my way to have the account liquidated ... when I was detained by notice from your solicitor ... and whilst begging him to explain his business, a bailiff joined him and dragged me to a sponging house with my wife, for she did not wish to quit me.' A sponging house was a privately-owned establishment where alleged debtors were held prior to a court appearance and debtors' prison, if the liability was proved and it persisted. The term is analogous to squeezing a sponge to receive its contents. They were formidable places, run by formidable people.

52

William Fitzwilliam's first letter on the matter is dated 1ˢᵗ January 1840 and written from 4 Cursitor St, Chancery Lane. This was a notorious address, in stark contrast to his lodgings on The Strand where he would have just spent Christmas. The bailiff is identified in the letter as 'Mr Sweet' – a misnomer, if ever there was one. Sweet was also the proprietor of the sponging house, which was characterised by small and stuffy rooms and a caged garden, not dissimilar to a zoo. The establishment was known to the writers Thackeray and Dickens under a later proprietor, Abraham Sloman, and informed works such as *Vanity Fair* and *Bleak House*. Inmates were charged one guinea a day for the duration of their stay.[55] William Fitzwilliam complained of an 'avoidable expense of £7 or £8', indicating that he and, presumably, his wife were confined for a week or so. During this time, Anne Owen's writ was served upon him, and he made good the debt. He also raised a counterclaim for £130, including £25 interest, on money that had allegedly been owed to him for the provision of a workman to Anne's late husband. This sounds tenuous, not least because the delay in raising the claim makes it looks retaliatory on his part.

Compounding William Fitzwilliam's indignity was communication Anne apparently had with others on the matter. In a letter of 14ᵗʰ January, he rails against her 'indecent abuse of fancied power' and has learnt that she has 'made some unworthy remarks' to his friends, which, together with the attendant circumstances, 'might become the subject of an action'. 'Your object,' he continues, 'seemed to have no other aim than offence and insult to my person … My naval pay was attachable for debt and quite security enough without subjecting my person to violence.' He had offered bail at the time of the arrest, but this was declined. Anne appears to have used the period of his incarceration to sully his reputation within his social circle, which would have been more than accomplished by the mere mention of his presence in a sponging house.[56]

As we have seen, William Fitzwilliam was prone to dispute, but he was also by this time a surveyor and navigator of world renown. His reputation counted for something, even though he was not always the first to uphold it. The series of actions that Anne set in motion do look calculated to undermine him and are entirely out of proportion with the size of the debt. She didn't need the £500 and she had far simpler and less injurious means of recovering it. Whatever the true *casus belli*, she must have had her reasons for behaving in this way as it also put her relations with the wider Owen family at risk.

Perhaps her wealth and status made her more relaxed about social niceties. Not only was there the estate inherited from William Owen, but she also had shares and dividends bequeathed by her aunt and investment properties in Liverpool from her first marriage. Members of other prominent local families in the Berriew area, most notably the Johnes, Lyon-Winders and Humphreys – the latter being distantly related to the Owens and in the line of inheritance – complained of unfounded accusations that Anne had made against them and limited their contact with her. She tried to bolster relations with the surviving Couplands but was brushed off by Thomas's nephew, Peter.

One individual who appeared unfazed by Anne's conduct at this time, including towards his brother, was Sir Edward Owen. He continued to write in genial and supportive terms, including an offer in June 1842 to see what he could do to secure professional advancement for her 'friend Lieutenant Massie' in the Mediterranean.[57] Cornelia Robinson – William Fitzwilliam's daughter – also maintained her correspondence with Anne from Campobello. Whether she was aware at that distance of the indignities perpetrated by Anne upon her father is not known. The topics they discussed varied according to the exigencies of the day, the one constant being the state of trade at Campobello, which at times was precarious. The letters trace, amongst other things, the exploitation of the Canadian interior and the push west across North America. In 1849, for example, Cornelia shares news of railway developments and the first California Gold Rush, which was then underway.

This period saw Anne taking a more active interest in business matters and the affairs of the Glansevern estate, perhaps out of necessity. She liaised with Thomas Penson, the well-known Oswestry-based architect, about new roads affecting her land; lobbied for a water feed to Glansevern from the nearby canal; and took an interest in the burgeoning railway network, particularly as it spread towards the area. Specific business transactions included a one-year deferral of a debt due from John Bernard Burke for material supplied to his

Landed Gentry – quite an indulgence on her part, but one she could afford to make – and the sourcing of seashells from a contact in South America. She still craved exotic items, it seems.

By the 1850s, she was working with a London-based solicitor called George Brace – no obvious relation to Sir Edward Brace, Anne's erstwhile suitor. Their correspondence captured the latest news – for example, concerning the Great Exhibition in 1851 and the Duke of Wellington's funeral the following year – as well as important business matters. In 1853 Brace successfully resisted what he called 'the aggression of the North Western Railway Company' by challenging an Act of Parliament to run a line through the Glansevern estate. What vexed Anne was not the fact of a railway in the area but the course of it. She saw great commercial and practical value in the general proposition and was keen to shape it as much as she could. In 1855 she approved the Salop and Welshpool line and became a shareholder in it. She was influential in appointments to key positions and the location of offices for the Oswestry and Newtown Railway.

By 1860 Government inspectors had determined and authorised the line and Anne had accepted an invitation to officiate at the opening ceremony. This significant event took place on 7th August 1861, accompanied by great rejoicing in Montgomery and the presentation to Anne of an inscribed ornamental bugle by the local militia, who attended in considerable number. In her address to them, she praised a volunteer organisation which had 'done more than any other to increase the influence of England abroad and greatly restored confidence at home ... a movement so essentially English as to give us a cheap means of defence and at the same time improve the personal bearing of every man who made himself of them'. Perhaps the fact that she was speaking in Wales, largely to a Welsh audience, had escaped her. ('England' was a commonly used, if geographically inaccurate, synonym for 'Britain' in this era, though not so much in the Principality itself.) The proceedings culminated in a dinner for 350 people at Montgomery Town Hall.[58]

During this period – on 3rd November 1857, to be precise – William Fitzwilliam Owen, passed away. His daughter Cornelia, whose husband inherited Campobello, was still in touch with Anne and continued to report on the uncertain state of trade there. By the early 1860s the island was feeling the backwash from the American Civil War – negative and far-reaching – and there was talk of selling it. Anne suggested it might be an idea to raffle it, perhaps moved by the old Warburton instinct for a flutter.

In 1866, Campobello was targeted by the Fenian Brotherhood, an Irish American organisation seeking to use it as a base for their challenge to British rule over Ireland. This was repelled but it led to an alliance between Nova Scotia, New Brunswick, Quebec and Ontario to form the political union of Canada. In 1881, Campobello was sold to a group of American businessmen, who developed it as a high-end holiday destination. Amongst the consortium was James Roosevelt – father of Franklyn D Roosevelt – who set it up as their family holiday home for many years to come.[59]

All this seems a far cry from Anne's upbringing in Chester, her brief spell at Priory House with her first husband and her attendance at our book club in 1824. Though, for the most part, physically removed from the city, it remained an important part of her life to the end. George Harrison – her aunt's executor – continued to draw dividend payments on her behalf at Dixons and Wardell's Bank on Eastgate Street, and rents still flowed through from Priory House. There were friendships and emotional attachments too, diminishing with age but still very real, nonetheless. In 1864, at the age of 82, Anne was being thanked by a Robert Temple of Chester for the kindness she showed his mother during her last illness.

Priory House had been let out to a succession of tenants over the years. One was another member of the Grosvenor family – the Reverend F Grosvenor – who prevented an attempted burglary there in 1856.[60] Thirteen years later, Lady Grosvenor would be writing to Anne, somewhat cryptically for our purposes, about more nefarious activity at the property:

Lord Westminster particularly wishes to express to yourself his appreciation of the kindness you have shown, in this the long and perplexed affair of the Priory House.

How very clever you have been just to catch the young man there on his passage to Australia! Lord Westminster begs us to thank you for your active kindness in writing to the gentleman in Sydney, which I hope we shall see crowned with success in two- or three-months' time.

What to make of this? Was this a delinquent and absconding tenant, or another prospective thief, perhaps? And who was in Sydney – an agent, an accomplice, a victim? We will probably never know. What this episode does highlight, however, is the continued close relationship between Anne and the Grosvenors and their mutual interest in Priory House. It also shows that Anne had retained some mental acuity and clarity of purpose late in life. As to the property, it, like the church beside it, had suffered some neglect. St John's would soon undergo extensive renovation, but Priory House was not within the scope of that work. It would be demolished in 1871, taking quite a story with it.

Anne's properties in Liverpool – at St Anne's Place and Rose Place – were also going to seed. Her agent there reported that the value of some places in the city had increased five-fold, but hers not all, on account of their condition. They bordered on uninhabitable, and tenants were difficult to find and unreliable. She maintained the correspondence and made decisions on rents and repairs, but they were not her top priority. Distance, advancing age and more pressing concerns all conspired against her.

On 5th January 1876, Anne Warburton Owen – our 'Mrs Coupland' – died at Glansevern. She was 93 years old. The estate, comprising 4,500 acres, was settled on Arthur Charles Humphreys, the great-grandnephew of William Owen, being directly descended from his sister, Mary Thomas, née Owen.[61] Like William, he was a barrister at Lincoln's Inn and later an MP. In 1873, he received Anne's permission to add 'Owen' to his surname and bear the Owen coat of arms.

Anne lives on in her correspondence and in a portrait painted by James Sant around the year 1850. She sits serenely in her widow's weeds, with the bust of her late husband, William, conspicuous in the background. She is clutching what looks like a letter, perhaps from him and perhaps expressing his deep and abiding love for her. This piece is further testimony of how sincerely that love was reciprocated.

Chapter Two

January

Mrs Coupland and her book-loving friends in Chester would have taken a keen interest in the news of the day and discussed topical events, great and small. Local newspapers – most notably the *Chester Courant* and the *Chester Chronicle* – were a rich source of information and, despite vying with each other – often acrimoniously – for patronage and political influence, provide telling insights into the character of the age. A fine balance was struck between global, national and parochial affairs, even if the 'news' was often diluted by delays in reaching the press, especially if it had travelled from far afield.

Despite their polarised positions, the long-standing editor of the *Courant*, Joseph Hemingway turned his coat during 1824 to become editor of the *Chester Chronicle*. His new post would have been more congruent with his views – which tended towards elitism – given that the *Chronicle* was aligned with the wealthy and powerful Grosvenor family and the wider establishment. Hemingway was also a historian, probably best known for his *History of the City of Chester*, as mentioned in the previous chapter. Even in this persona he displayed his journalistic tendencies by appearing most at ease when alluding to the present or the recent past.

He says of 1824, 'This year furnishes but few local events worthy of note,' rather like the whimsical blue plaque that proclaims nothing happened on that spot on a certain date in history.[1] We should not be discouraged by this. What may be deemed worthy of note is subjective and apt to shift with the passage of time. Indeed, events alone may not be the best prism through which to view the lives and preoccupations of our protagonists. As William Morris said, 'The true secret of happiness lies in taking a genuine interest in all the details of daily life.'

One reason for the perception at the time that not much of significance was happening may well have been the relatively benign political climate and a collective, though by no means universal, sense of comfort and wellbeing that flowed from it. This assessment appears in the *Courant* editorial of 6th January 1824:

And here, *en passant*, it may be permitted to us to congratulate our countrymen, not only on the extinction of those political convulsions, which but a short time ago threatened the internal peace of our kingdom, but on the indubitable evidences of national prosperity, which mark the commencement of the year 1824. At peace with foreign powers and sustaining a capacity for energy and greatness which is likely to perpetuate it, our commerce is extending in every quarter of the world; all branches of our manufactures are in active motion and our mechanics in full employment; the agriculturalists are also rising from the difficulties occasioned by the depression in the price of produce; public credit is sound and healthy, and government securities are approximating to the value they bore before the French war, while private capital is so abundant as to induce foreign states to seek in the metropolis of England re-sources to supply their wants and necessity.

The festive season in Chester was marked by charity, solemnity and celebration. Notable families, foremost amongst them the Barnstons, distributed offerings to the poor and a service was held at Little St John Street Chapel on New Year's Day. This was followed by a civic feast for 80 citizens at the Exchange – the forerunner to the present town hall – which fell victim to a fire in 1862. The centrepiece of the feast was a grand representation in pastry of Belgrave Lodge, one entrance to the Grosvenor estate at Eaton Hall, flanked by gothic pyramids and globes, also made with pastry. For the Grosvenor family, joy would soon turn to sadness, with the death a few days later of Gilbert Grosvenor, heir presumptive, at the tender age of nine months.

A particular highlight of the Chester social scene was an extraordinary display taking place at the Theatre Royal in Northgate Street. This featured 'Mr Barker and Co's

Peristrephic or Moving Panorama of the surrender and funeral of Buonaparte'. It boasted eight large views on nearly ten thousand feet of canvas, accompanied by a military band. The spectre of Napoleon still loomed large in the public consciousness and many Cestrians would have felt the effects of the upheaval he wrought across Europe, including personal loss. Mr Barker was therefore pandering to innate patriotism, as well as relief and schadenfreude at the defeat of the French.

The winter concert season was still in full flow, including two performances in the Assembly Room at the Royal Hotel – owned by the Grosvenor family and the previous incarnation of the Grosvenor Hotel on Eastgate Street – by Madame Catalani, the renowned Italian Soprano. This lady had performed at a concert in Brussels on the eve of the Battle of Waterloo, when she had been prevented from singing an encore of *Rule Britannia* by the Duke of Wellington, who feared his troops appearing too jingoistic in front of allied attendees, most notably the Prussians.[2] Sumptuous balls took place in the private houses of wealthy individuals, to which many of the Cheshire *haut ton* were invited. Sir John Stanley of Alderley hosted two such events in a matter of days, the first to celebrate the coming of age of his twin sons and the second an opulent masquerade. Dancing was kept up until 5am and there was partying of one sort or another for the whole week.

The business of the city was reviving too. Meetings were called amongst the Trustees of the Wrexham and Mold Turnpike Road and the Trustees of the Navigation of the River Dee, in the latter case specifically to repair and maintain the embankments on the south side of the river. The Dee remained an important though diminishing artery through the city, and concerted efforts were being made to preserve it as a commercial waterway in the face of deleterious natural forces and competition from rapidly expanding conurbations elsewhere in the region, most notably Liverpool.

Coach companies were vying for travellers and goods, the two most prominent in Chester being John Woolliscroft, operating from the Royal Mail Coach Office at the White Lion Hotel in Foregate Street, and Mercy Tomlinson at The Feathers Hotel on Bridge Street. Both trumpeted the range and pace of their services. For example, Mercy Tomlinson's Coaching Establishment's offering included daily services to London in 24 hours,

45 minutes; Holyhead, to link to the Dublin packet, in 14 hours; and Liverpool, via the Birkenhead ferry in 2 hours 15 minutes.

Regular reports were being submitted on the state of Chester Infirmary – which housed 64 in-patients at the start of 1824 – following inspections by senior medical personnel, the chaplain and select board members. Schools were welcoming back their pupils and, in some cases, soliciting more. Monsieur Louis Doré from the Italian Opera House and Theatre Royal, London announced the opening of his music academy at 43 Watergate Street for separate sessions with young ladies and young gentlemen. It appears there was some demand for his services.

The *Courant* reported that the condition of agriculture across the county was improving, especially amongst the Cheshire yeomanry. Demand for cheese was increasing and a punitive tax on salt had been removed. It added, 'Taking then, the whole of these facts together, we may speedily hope to see the English farmer resume his respectable station, though we have no wish to see him affecting in his habits of living the fine gentleman.' Here is a candid reminder of how rigidly stratified society remained in the Regency period. It is consistent with the age-old principle of the 'great chain of being', with God at the top of the hierarchy. In a deeply religious society, there were powerful forces discouraging ordinary people from questioning their place in the world. With the rise of the mercantile classes and enormous fortunes derived from trade, we see an endless jarring between the *nouveau riche* and the established landed gentry.

In 1824, national and world news was co-mingled in the press. Literate Chester residents, such as our book club members, would have consumed both as part of one seamless perusal.

In early January, amongst other things, they would have read about the grand seasonal fetes hosted at the Royal Palace in Brighton by King George IV, in whom there was often a prurient and irreverent interest. He was reported to be well and expecting several important visitors, whose identities were not disclosed. His underlying state of health, however, was affected by his indulgent lifestyle. We soon learn that he was planning a visit to the fashionable German spa town of Bad Pyrmont, to seek relief from gout and to take the opportunity to visit his Hanoverian dominions.

Physical health was also a preoccupation amongst his subjects, who were much assailed by virulent and often deadly diseases. These were not always well-understood and supposed cures were frequently ineffective or, worse still, led to further debilitation. Chester was by no means immune to such outbreaks but was generally better placed than other towns and cities of a similar size. One reason was that it was expanding less rapidly. Between 1801 and 1831 Chester's population increased by 42 per cent to just over 27,000. Though by no means trivial, this compares with rates of increase in Macclesfield of 165 per cent, Oldham of 168 per cent and Preston of 179 per cent.[3]

Migration, poverty and overcrowding were all contributors to the incubation and spread of disease. The porous bedrock of the city, meaning it was less prone to standing water, is believed to have been a mitigant against water-borne diseases. Chester also benefited from pioneering work in infection prevention and control at its infirmary, most notably by Dr John Haygarth in the late 18th century. It comes as no surprise to learn therefore that, in early 1824, Cestrians were inveighing against the inhabitants of cities such as Manchester and Cambridge for not taking the necessary measures to prevent or contain outbreaks of smallpox.

For an age associated with gentility and refinement it is remarkable how commonly violence and bloodlust obtrude. Boxing was technically illegal but it was tolerated by magistrates and allowed to flourish as a mainstream sport. At the turn of the century, prizefighters such as Daniel Mendoza and John Jackson, who also ran boxing academies in London for fashionable young men known as 'the Fancy', were household names. Their most notable successor was Tom Cribb, who had two high-profile fights with the freed Black slave, Tom Molyneux, in 1810 and 1811, winning both.[4] By the 1820s the mantle had passed to Herefordshire heavyweight and a protégé of Cribb, Tom Spring, and the Irish champion, Jack Langan. These two men met in the ring, not for the first time, at Worcester on 7th January 1824. The encounter was widely reported in the press, with publications typically castigating the activity at the outset before reporting on it in graphic –

not to say gory – detail. Respectable readers may have flinched as they read. Leading literary figures of the day were known to have attended and even become involved in boxing activities. John Keats wrote dispassionately about a prize fight he witnessed in 1819 and Lord Byron, noted for his physical attributes as well as his literary output, trained at Mendoza's academy.

Spring defeated Langan at Worcester in 77 rounds over two and a half hours, in front of a crowd of 50,000 people and surrounded by much pomp and ceremony. It was a bareknuckle fight and holds as well as punches were permitted. The time limit was merely determined by how long the combatants could remain sensible and upright. Langan was described as 'groggy and stupid' when the umpire finally stepped in, despite his second protesting that he would carry on for another forty rounds.[5] The Queensbury Rules would not appear until the 1860s.

The weather must have been a factor in the fight, as it was in daily life. In the middle of the month there were great falls of snow, locally and throughout the country. In Northampton it was six feet deep, with drifts of up to 14 feet reported. It was stormy too, causing the shipwreck of the *Hornby* near the Great Orme at Llandudno, with the loss of 14 lives. Temperatures in this period were typically two to three degrees centigrade lower than they are today and it was wetter, even in the north-west of England.[6] Rivers were frozen in the harsh protracted winters, including the Thames and the Dee, and were turned over to recreational pursuits such as ice-skating and frost fairs.

The year 1816 would remain long in the memory, for all the wrong weather-related reasons. It would be described as the 'year without a summer', due to the effects – as we now know – of the seismic eruption of Mount Tambora in Indonesia, which dramatically disrupted global weather patterns. There were frosts and floods in summer, snow in autumn and temperatures as low as minus 20 degrees centigrade in winter. In his book *1815: Regency Britain in the Year of Waterloo*, Stephen Bates writes, 'That November [1816] a dust cloud settled over Chester, causing impenetrable darkness at noon; then a few days later the fog was succeeded by two feet of snow.'[7] As most people were dependent on local fresh produce and cheap textiles, food and clothing were a challenge in extreme conditions – even to the extent that civil unrest and migrations could ensue. Eight years later, people must have wondered whether life was back to normal and when such conditions might recur.

The state of the West Indies and the enslaved population there was much reported and debated in 1824. Particularly emotive was the case of John Smith of the London Missionary Society, who was accused of breaching his duty to preach Christianity and of fomenting insurrection against plantation owners in Demerara. Central to the case were the enslaved people Quamina Gladstone and his son Jack, who were owned by John Gladstone, of whom we have already heard. In November 1823, Smith had been controversially court-martialled and sentenced to death, a judgement which required ratification by the king before being put into effect. In late January 1824, newspapers in Britian were reporting that the outcome of the trial was still awaited, against a backdrop of martial law in Demerara.

Abolitionists were outraged by the case, alleging legal malpractice and a gross miscarriage of justice. The pro-slavery group, the West India Interest, led the counter charge. In Chester, pamphlets were available on both sides of the debate from Poole and Harding, booksellers of Eastgate Street Row, including one entitled *A Voice from Jamaica, in reply to William Wilberforce, esq MP, by the Reverend George Wilson Bridges BA of Trinity College, Oxford and Rector of the Parish of Manchester, Jamaica*. At the same time – though unrelated to the Smith case – it was being reported in the Chester press that a meeting had taken place at the King's Arms to raise subscriptions to recognise John Gladstone MP for 'the important services rendered by him to this town on various occasions'. A sum of £840 – equivalent to £50,000 today – was raised for the purchase of plate. It is unclear what the 'important services' were. Gladstone was MP for Woodstock in 1824, having been rejected by Liverpool in favour of William Huskisson, and had never represented Chester. Perhaps he had used his influence in Parliament to support causes to which the subscribers were attached.

Of interest to our book club members would have been the announcement that 'the author of Waverley' had contracted to produce a new book a year for three years, in addition to the four already published, for a total sum of £30,000, which attests to the widespread popularity of his work. Only at the end of that contractual period did Sir Walter Scott, possibly having been keen to protect his reputation as an eminent lawyer, disclose his authorship. In other Arts news it was reported that the 'Lord Chamberlain has very properly issued his veto against the performance French plays in the Metropolis'. In putting his own spin on this, the editor of the *Courant* reminds us of the lingering prejudice against all things Gallic, as well as the long-established and far-reaching powers of censorship held by the Lord Chamberlain.

Random people news – not for the squeamish – included the case of Mr Dempster, a juggler, who had the misfortune to swallow a nine-inch knife at Carlisle in the course of his professional duties. He tried to get to London for treatment, but the jolting of the coach caused him intolerable pain. Having transferred to the canal network for a smoother ride, his injuries finally got the better of him not far south of Chester.

Chapter Three

Mrs Glynne
Lot 2

Tales of the Castle, *the best edition, embellished with a fine view of Hawarden Castle,*
a single volume, neatly bound

In 1793 a work entitled *Tales of the Castle* by Madame la Comtesse de Genlis was translated from the original French into English by Thomas Holcroft. Its subtitle was *Stories of Instruction and Delight.* There was narrative content, but its chief aim was didactic, aimed at instilling moral rectitude at an early age. Jane Austen had read her work and alluded to it, not always in positive terms. It is likely that book club members had been exposed to it too. In this case, the title does much of the work that Dr Norris intended, without us having to look very far behind it.

We see immediately that there is a real castle in the frame, not to mention two. Hawarden – located six miles west of Chester, across the border into Wales – has a medieval ruined castle and a fine Georgian mansion, both of which fit the bill. The older of the two was built for visibility and so bestrides a hilltop; the younger for seclusion, nestling in a hollow below. Writing in his *A Walk Around the Walls and City of Chester* in 1821, John Broster tells us that Hawarden Castle can be seen from the arch of the North Gate.[1] This may have been the 'fine view' that Dr Norris had in mind. Today we are denied the prospect by urban development and foliage.

The old castle is of uncertain origin, but it existed at the time of Edward I's military campaign against Wales in the late 13th century. Indeed, he reinforced it and used it as a base to support his conquest. Already smaller and less strategically important than Edward's coastal structures further west, it suffered considerable depletion in the Civil War of the mid-17th century. Initially possessed by the Royalists, it was wrested from them through an act of betrayal and garrisoned by Parliamentary forces.[2] This was one of the positions from which they were able to starve the citizens of Chester of provisions and force their surrender in January 1646, after four months under siege. Once it had fulfilled its military purpose, the castle was condemned to demolition by order of the House of Commons.[3] As we know, it wasn't obliterated, merely rendered ineffective as a stronghold.

This conflict also had a major bearing on the lordship of the manor of Hawarden. It had been granted to Hugh Lupus, Earl of Chester, following the Norman Conquest and passed through a succession of other owners until it became the property of the Stanleys – the Earls of Derby – in the 15th century. The Civil War was hugely punitive for this family as committed Royalists, including the execution of James, Earl of Derby, and the forfeiture of his lands in Hawarden.[4] His heir, Charles, tried in vain to recover them, finding the cost involved prohibitive. In 1652, Sir John Glynne paid Charles £9,000 for the manors of Hawarden, Mold and Hope. This superseded the contract that Charles had been unable to fulfil, which had lain unsigned for a year. That document had been drawn up by none other than Sir John Glynne, who was Lord Chief Justice during the Commonwealth.[5]

Sir John had a reputation for duplicity and sharp practice, which may not have been entirely fair. His career straddled the Civil War and Restoration and he, like many others in public office, had to steer a careful course between warring interests. He was involved in the impeachment of Thomas Wentworth, Earl of Strafford in 1641 for his conduct in Ireland but was himself threatened with the same charge and imprisoned in the Tower of London in 1645 for attempting to undermine Thomas Fairfax and his New Model Army. This was never followed through, however, and in 1648 he was released and readmitted as an MP. He petitioned for Oliver Cromwell to become king and, though unsuccessful in this endeavour, he used it to demonstrate his support for a monarchy upon the Restoration. He rode in Charles II's coronation procession in 1661 but was almost killed when he was thrown from his horse and it fell on top of him. Samuel Pepys, who regarded Glynne as a turncoat, saw this as divine retribution.[6]

Our Mrs Glynne's ancestry can be traced directly back to Sir John Glynne, though determining her identity is less straightforward than may be supposed. Sir William Glynne, son of Sir John, was 1st Baronet, and was succeeded by two of his sons – another William and Stephen – as 2nd and 3rd Baronet respectively. This pattern repeated itself in the next generation as the two eldest sons of Sir Stephen – this time reversing the name order, as the elder was Stephen – acquired the title. The 6th Baronet, Sir John Glynne, who lived from 1712 to 1777, and his children will now occupy our attention.

This Sir John is often referred to as 'of Broadlane', which is the former name of Hawarden Castle before he had it rebuilt in 1752. The main house was designed by Joseph Turner. Though a local man, still visibly commemorated in the parish church in Hawarden, Turner was an architect of no small repute. Most active in Cheshire and north Wales, his other works include the Water Gate and Bridge Gate and a fine row of Georgian houses in Nicholas Street, Chester, all of which survive to this day. Later additions were made to Hawarden Castle based on designs by the great John Nash, architect of the Royal Pavilion in Brighton, Buckingham Palace and Marble Arch.[7] All of this signals the wealth and ambition of Sir John at this time and the extent to which he had transferred his attention from another ancestral home, in Bicester, near Oxford.

Like his two times great-grandfather, Sir John didn't shy away from politics and constitutional debate. He was MP for Flint between 1741 and 1749 and from 1753 until his death in 1777. When the Jacobite Rising of 1745 was in course, he was heard drinking the health of the Young Pretender, Bonnie Prince Charlie. For this he was reported to London and imprisoned without trial. No evidence was brought, and he was discharged two months later.[8] Whilst something of a throwback to his famous forebear, his political and religious allegiances were quite different. The 1st Baronet had supported the Protestant Puritans who deposed the Stuart line, whereas Bonnie Prince Charlie sought to restore it, after it had been extinguished by the so-called Glorious Revolution of 1688. If Sir John was a Catholic sympathiser, he was well-advised not to overplay his hand, especially as the rebellion came to nothing in the end.

In Parliament, Sir John was a Tory, often speaking in opposition to the policies of William Pitt the Elder, the Whig statesman and prime minister. He had a reputation for facetiousness in the House but could also be serious and purposeful when it mattered. One example was his challenge to the Marriage Bill, which progressed unamended but would later be repealed, to the advantage of Anne Coupland and William Owen.[9]

Sir John's own marriage, to Honora Conway of Bodrhyddan Hall, Rhuddlan, had taken place in 1731. Her dowry substantially increased Sir John's estates in north Wales, most notably in Broughton and Bretton. Her impressive lineage included the Plantagenet kings, who ruled between the 12th and 15th centuries. Sir John and Honora had 13 children together – eight boys and five girls. The first of the boys died young and the second, John Conway Glynne, pre-deceased his father, dying in 1773. On Sir John's death four years later, the title passed to the Reverend Stephen Glynne, who became 7th Baronet. The Mrs Glynne who attended our book club came from this generation of the Glynne family. One of the difficulties in making this determination was the fact that it was virtually extinct by 1824. Anne Glynne was an exception.

Born in 1749 at Hawarden – the eighth sibling – she never married. This was a complication too, until the realisation that the title 'Mrs' was less rigidly applied in those days. The final challenge was the fact that her life, despite its great span, was scantly documented. There was little to officially record, it seems, other than her birth and death.

The breakthrough came with a news report in the *Chester Chronicle* from as late as 26th September 1828. Headed 'Celebration of an Event', it marked the coming of age of Sir Stephen Glynne, 9th Baronet and Anne's great-nephew, of which more will be said in due course. Buried deep in a lengthy article are the words: 'Mrs Ann [sic] Glynne, of Chester, the oldest branch of the family now living, was drunk 3 times 3 [a toast and three rounds of "hip-hip-hooray"].' The confirmation that she was still alive, the Chester and Hawarden connections, and the absence of other conceivable claimants, identify her unequivocally as our book club member.

Anne was born into a family by then firmly rooted in the landed aristocracy, whose fortunes were waxing at the time. Her father had created and stocked an extensive deer park on the Hawarden estate following receipt of the marriage settlement. Perhaps his detachment from Parliament in Anne's early years gave him the opportunity to spend more time with his wife and children.[10]

Anne was baptised at Hawarden on 29th May 1749 and would have been brought up comfortably alongside her siblings, immersed in the business of the estate and the local community. There was joy and sadness in her youth. Harry Conway Glynne, her eldest brother, died aged 15 in 1755. In 1763, her sister, Sophia, married John Yorke – son of the MP for Richmond, Yorkshire. The marriage took place at Hawarden and was witnessed by 'J Glynne' and 'H Leigh Thomas'. This happy event would soon be followed by tragedy: Sophia died at sea aboard the *Hamden Packet* whilst travelling from Lisbon to Falmouth three years later. She was buried in the port on arrival.

In the same year, another of Anne's sisters – Penelope – married William Welby, 1st Baronet of Denton Manor, Lincolnshire and later MP for Grantham. This marriage would also be fleeting, as Penelope died at Denton in 1771, at the age of 31. Anne's elder brother, John Conway Glynne, appears to have been involved in freemasonry at this time, being listed in the Grand Lodge of Freemasons of Ireland membership register in the mid-1760s. This may have been frowned upon by his father, with his alleged pro-Catholic leanings.

The 1760s and 1770s were brutal for the Glynne family in terms of their mortality. On top of the bereavements already mentioned, Anne lost her mother, aged 52, in 1769. When Stephen succeeded to Sir John's title in 1777, he was already attached to the ministry and may even have had a role at his father's funeral. Sir John left a widow, having married his second wife, Augusta Beaumont, in 1772. That wedding took place at Broadlane by special licence, witnessed by William Glynne – Anne's elder brother by three years – and, once again, H Leigh Thomas. Anne's new stepmother would have been well known to her and her siblings as she was their governess.

One of the stipulations in Sir John's will was that 'custody, government and tuition of such of my daughters as shall not have attained the age of 21' would be granted to Augusta, and that they should cohabit if it were convenient to her and 'whilst they can agree'. This suggests some discord amongst the ranks.

The property dispositions in the will were substantial. There were extensive tracts of land in north Wales, coal mining rights, turnpike dues, and stocks and shares in the River Dee Company, which had been established in 1743 to address navigation issues on the river between Chester and the open sea. Dame Augusta, as she had become, was the main beneficiary, and Paul Panton of Holywell, the Reverend John Wheler of Wareham, Lincolnshire and Thomas Boydell of Trevalyn, Denbighshire, were trustees and executors. Anne's brothers William and Francis were left generous annuities and she and her three sisters – Frances, Lucy and Mary - £4,000 each and shares in Sandycroft Colliery. Minor legacies included 20 guineas to Mr John Goldborne, wine merchant of Chester, and ten guineas to Mr Thomas of Hawarden, surgeon. A late codicil was sworn to by John Boydell of the Parish of St Martin's, ironmonger and London engraver, and John Boydell, his son, of the parish of St Swithin, London, wine merchant. The will was proved at London by the three executors on 16th April 1778.

Around this time, the Glynne family had close links with the city of Bath. This should come as no surprise: as we have seen, it was second only to London in its appeal to high society and had the added advantage of being a spa, which added greatly to its popularity. It was also accessible from Chester by means of a well-established coaching route. Two of Anne's sisters were married in Bath in 1778: Frances to the Reverend Randolph Crewe at Walcot St Swithin in August and Lucy to James Gordon at St Michael's in November. Randolph would soon become Rector of Hawarden. Frances and Lucy are both described as 'of this Parish' in their marriage records, which suggests they had the opportunity to reside in Bath. In 1780, Anne's widowed stepmother, Dame Augusta, married Peregrine Courtney at Walcot St Swithin. He died and was buried in the city five years later.

72

These events would have been significant in Anne's life in early adulthood; particularly her father's death and her sisters' marriages. We don't know whether she ever entertained the prospect of marriage, but we do know that it never came about.

Despite the attraction of Bath, Hawarden was the focal point for the family, then and for many years to come. Some of the people already mentioned incidentally in our narrative would have been familiar to Anne in her formative years. 'H Leigh Thomas', twice a witness at Glynne marriages, was Dr Honoratus Leigh Thomas. He was a Chester-based surgeon and medical pioneer, being co-inventor of the Suttonian method of inoculation. He settled in Hawarden around 1759.[11] In 1760 he married Maria Boydell, daughter of Josiah Boydell, who, according to a plaque in the church at Hawarden, was agent to Sir John Glynne for 23 years. The couple – whose wedding was witnessed by Anne's eldest sister, Penelope – occupied an elegant three-story house that the Boydells built in Rectory Lane, Hawarden, which stands to this day.

The Thomases soon started their own family and were looking for domestic support. Round the corner, in a humble thatched cottage abutting the Fox and Grapes Inn, lived a teenage girl by the name of Emma Lyon. She would answer the call. She and her mother had moved to Hawarden from Neston when she was a child to be close to her grandmother, following her father's death.[12] In later years she would scandalise and captivate Georgian society as the beautiful and enigmatic Lady Hamilton, culminating in one of history's great love stories as she came together with Admiral Lord Nelson at the height of his fame. How much more piquant must that episode have been to Anne, having known her as a child and the circles in which she had moved?

Another of Josiah Boydell's children was John, who also had a son called John. These are the two John Boydells mentioned in Sir John Glynne's will. The reference to the elder John as an ironmonger and engraver understates the case. Born at Hawarden in 1720, he was a man of immense talent and ambition, becoming a great pioneer and promoter of

British art. It was said that he was inspired by William Henry Toms' engraving of Hawarden Castle in his youth, perhaps not dissimilar to the view Dr Norris had in mind. Such was his enthusiasm that he walked to London, where he secured an apprenticeship as an engraver in Toms' business. He soon established his own presence in the field, providing a platform for him to engage the finest English artists of the age and open up an export market in prints that had so far been untapped.

As a publisher, John Boydell was responsible for bringing works by Hogarth and Milton, amongst many others, to a mass audience, but his crowning glory was yet to come. In the 1780s, after consultation with eminent artists and engravers, he committed to an illustrated edition of Shakespeare's plays, a public gallery of paintings depicting scenes from the plays and a folio of prints based on the paintings. The gallery opened on Pall Mall in 1789 to great acclaim, afterwards proving hugely popular in *fin de siècle* London. The edition of the plays, embellished with the prints, soon followed. This became John's most enduring legacy, with several reissues throughout the 19th century. However, his business fortunes, still largely dependent on foreign trade, were dramatically affected by growing conflict with France. He was forced to sell off assets, including the gallery and its contents.

John Boydell's ambition – the cornerstone to his success – also played a role in his undoing. He was well-known as a generous and genial man who lavished money on his suppliers. Artists that he worked with, such as Henry Fuseli and Benjamin West, enjoyed their share of the largesse, but those he spurned resented it. The caricaturist, James Gillray, cruelly satirised Boydell and his business ventures, his sentiment no doubt fuelled by his own rejection.

An indication of the scale of John's investment appears in a letter he wrote from London to his nephew, John Thomas – son of his sister Maria and Leigh Thomas – on 24th March 1802: 'Dear nephew … I have sent by the Chester Waggon 8 prints … to Mr Evans in Chester, desiring him to pay the carriage and send them to you on arrival. I hope they please you and all your friends. We are nearly finishing the great work of Shakespeare, which costs £150,000.'[13] With this amount invested – roughly £9 million in today's terms – it is little wonder that the business had its vulnerabilities.

John Boydell's other great lifetime achievement was in public office in London. He was Alderman of the Cheap in 1782, Sheriff in 1785 and Lord Mayor in 1790. He donated paintings from his collections to the Corporation of London, which were hung in the Guildhall. He promoted morality through the messages conveyed in the paintings and by encouraging the middle and upper classes to invest in the Arts rather than more dissipated pursuits. John was succeeded as Alderman of the Cheap by another Josiah Boydell, this time his nephew, son of his brother Samuel. Josiah was active in the business too, becoming a successful artist in his own right, contributing work to the collections and exhibiting at the Royal Society. John died in 1804 and Josiah in 1817 and both are commemorated in London; John with a monument at St Margaret Lothbury and Josiah in Hampstead churchyard.

Josiah Boydell in particular would have been well known to Anne Glynne. He was three years her junior and his mother had a hand in raising the Glynne children.[14] It is likely they played together on the Hawarden estate in their youth. The usefulness of the Boydells to the Glynnes over many years was considerable. For several generations, senior members of the Boydell family were land agents at Hawarden, starting with the first Josiah in the 1730s. In the mid- to late 18th century this role involved increased commercial exploitation of the land and managed expansion. The travel writer, Thomas Pennant, refers to a canal cut by Sir John Glynne in 1768 to transport coal from his colliery at Sandycroft to Chester via Bretton. However, the scheme proved unsuccessful, and the canal appears to have been filled in around 1775.

In 1778 an Act of Parliament was obtained, as was necessary, for the enclosing of common land at Saltney. The scope included forming a substantial riverbank on the south side of the Dee 'more effectively to prevent the inroads of tides, together with sluices to carry off the land floods and drain waters'. In line with due process, the commissioners held meetings to debate the pleas of anyone who claimed a right to the common land. A document dated 14th December 1778 records one such claim:

> We, Thomas Boydell, agent or steward to Rev Sir Stephen Glynne, Baronet, Lord of the Manor of Hawarden, and Thomas Slaughter and Bagot Tread esqs being persons having or claiming right of common etc do object to the claim of Sarah Snow, Spinster, dated 26th October last and delivered to the commissioners at their second meeting and she is not entitled to any right of common or to any allotment of the said common or marsh intended to be inclosed in respect of any ancient messuages etc described in the claim.[15]

Thomas Slaughter, or Sloughter, grandfather of Anne Coupland, owned land and property in Broughton, adjoining the Glynne estates, as previously noted.

Before this time much of the enclosure of common land was undertaken with the mutual consent of interested parties, but now it was more widespread, industrialised and enforced. Small farmers and cottagers were disenfranchised and impoverished. The cost of renting a couple of enclosed strips often made the means of working them – ploughs and grazing animals – unaffordable. They then either had to relocate to towns or work for landowners on their terms. Members of Parliament, who needed a property qualification to be there, inevitably came down on the side of the landowner. As a result, by 1800, only 16 per cent of England's agricultural land remained unenclosed and, in the 20 years after that, a thousand further Acts were passed, considerably accelerating the trend.[16] The plutocracy would argue that the system was necessary to farm more efficiently – harnessing new technologies and methods in a drive to feed a growing and increasingly urbanised population – but that would be scant consolation to the commoner, to whom no compensation was paid. As Oliver Goldsmith puts it in his classic poem of 1770, 'The Deserted Village':

> Ill fares the land, to hastening ills a prey,

Where wealth accumulates, and men decay …

Those fenceless fields the sons of wealth divide,

And ev'n the bare-worn common is denied.

What hope for Sarah Snow then in defending her patch of land in Saltney in the face of the forces ranged against her? With no detail on the final decision of the commissioners, we can't know for sure, but it's reasonable to assume that the case did not take long to adjudicate. Other objections were raised to enclosure on Glynne land, for example in Marlston and Lache in 1791, but they were defeated. This must have bred some ill-feeling towards the family amongst the general population in the area, to which Anne could not have been completely insensible.

Less than three years after acceding to the baronetcy in 1777, Reverend Sir Stephen Glynne, 7th of that ilk, died near Bridgnorth following a hunting accident. He was buried at Hawarden on 9th April 1780. Anne had now lost all three of her brothers. Sir Stephen's wife, Mary Bennett, whom he had married in August 1779, was in the advanced stages of pregnancy at the time. A boy was born in May 1780, christened Stephen, becoming the next baronet from birth. His four aunts, including Anne, would have supported Mary in his upbringing. The title Lady Glynne, informally at least, was used to refer to Dame Augusta Courtney, widow of Sir John Glynne, despite his death and her remarriage. This is how she appears in Peregrine Courtney's will of 1786, the year in which year he died leaving everything to her. She was also 'Lady Glynne' in the Bath and Chester newspapers when they published notices of her own death at Portland Place, London in 1790.

This Sir Stephen was educated at Eton and Christ Church, Oxford, before becoming something of an amateur architect and agriculturalist. In 1806 he married Mary Griffin – daughter of Lord Braybrooke and a descendent of monarchs, nobles and pre-eminent politicians – in a grand ceremony in Hanover Square, London. She could trace her ancestry back through William the Conqueror to the Emperor Charlemagne and was related to five prime ministers, including the two Pitts and, in due course, William Ewart Gladstone, who would become her son-in-law.[17] Relocating to Hawarden as the new Lady Glynne, she would have become a central figure in Anne's life. Her letter collection held at the magnificent Gladstone's Library in Hawarden provides some fascinating insights into their world.

There is joyous correspondence relating to the wedding and lots of people-news to and from fashionable resorts around Europe. As the children – there were four: another Stephen, Henry, Catherine and Mary – are born and begin to grow, they become common topics of conversation. Their health and education are paramount, and periodic concerns are expressed about both. The boys follow the Eton and Oxford route, whereas the girls are schooled by governesses and tutors, with Italian and music regarded as necessary accomplishments. In Paris, Catherine and Mary would be even taught piano by a young Franz Liszt.

Long before the children reached maturity, however, tragedy befell the family. It is clear from the correspondence that, in the winter of 1813 to 1814, Lady Glynne was in Nice with her husband, for the good of his health. He had consumption. If they had hoped for mild weather as a palliative, they were to be disappointed. Temperatures were unseasonably low and snow fell across much of southern Europe. Sir Stephen would eventually succumb to his condition in March 1815, dying on the Riviera. Anne Glynne had lost a nephew to whom she must have been closely attached.

The most immediate problem for Lady Glynne as a grieving widow, and young Stephen who was with her, was how to return home. Napoleon was reasserting control in France following his escape from Elba and all options were perilous. A tortuous route through Italy, Switzerland and Flanders eventually brought them back safely. A white charger that had been acquired from Napoleon after he rode it at the Battle of Borodino in 1812 was amongst the party. It lived on for several years before being buried on the Hawarden estate. The drama of the return journey was heightened by the fact that Lady Glynne's father had set off from England to escort her home but was intercepted and had his horses commandeered. A sea passage was ruled out for fear of the ship being seized and interned.[18]

Sir Stephen's will, dated September 1814, vested in Lady Glynne his land and property in north Wales and his house in Berkeley Square, London. There were modest monetary bequests to James Boydell – the artist's son, in the employ of Sir Stephen – and cousin, Mary Anne Gordon. Another cousin, William Welby junior, was a trustee and executor alongside Lord Braybrooke. This was an especially difficult period for Anne, because she had also lost her sister Lucy Gordon – Mary Anne's mother – in May 1814.

A major event took place on 15th August 1814 in Chester in which the Glynne family was intimately involved. Hemingway provides a succinct account:

> The citizens of Chester, anxious to show their admiration of the heroic generals, Lords Combermere and Hill, for their noble exploits under the immortal Wellington, in Portugal, Spain and France, invited them to a grand dinner at the Royal Hotel. Lord Combermere was escorted from Hawarden (coming out of Wales) by Sir S R Glynne's troop of light horse, under the command of Lieutenant S Boydell.[19]

Whilst not enjoying quite the same rank and connections as Eaton, Hawarden remained one of those estates to which visiting nobility might repair. It is questionable whether Sir Stephen, ailing and with not long to live, would have been able to play a part in proceedings.

Before long, Mary Anne Gordon, orphaned and financially endowed in 1814, was at the altar. A press notice dated 2nd December 1818 states: 'Married at Holy Trinity Church, Chester, W C Chambers of Llysmeirchion, Co Denbigh to Miss Gordon, niece of Mrs Glynne of the former place.'[20] This is a short but informative piece. It tells us that Anne Glynne was based in Chester at this time and raises the possibility that Mary Anne was living with her. The most common location for family weddings was, of course, Hawarden, so the connection with Holy Trinity must have been considerable to outdo it.

Anne appears to have retained strong ties to Hawarden, nevertheless, and continued to support activities in the area. Also in 1818, 'Mrs Glynne, Chester' subscribed three guineas towards a proposed church and two new schools for Buckley Mountain. Other subscribers included Lady Glynne, £20; James Boydell, £2; and the Prince Regent, £200. On the face of it, this latter contribution, bountiful and welcome though it must have been, looks incongruous. However, there is no suggestion of a personal connection between the acting monarch and the area, so he is more likely to have been supporting the general investment in churches and schools on a national level, as a figurehead. There are references to him in the Lady Glynne correspondence, indicating that he spent most of his time in Brighton, largely eschewing education and religion.

Some of the letters were from high profile people connected with Hawarden whom Anne Glynne would have known, or, at the very least, known about. Eleanor Butler, one of the Ladies of Llangollen – those renowned Irish emigrées and doyens of literary society – writes on behalf of herself and her partner, Sarah Ponsonby. They are unable to attend a bow meeting at Hawarden – archery being a popular pursuit at the time – and augment their apology with an exclusive recipe for ginger beer, which, it seems, Lady Glynne had sampled and commended on one of her visits to them. 'Perhaps you will permit us some quieter time to have the honor [sic] and happiness of paying you our respects at Hawarden Castle,' she adds, fishing for a less contained invitation.

A letter from Elizabeth Kenah to Lady Glynne illustrates the pleasure she derived from such a visit, commenting on 'the very many delightful days we passed at Hawarden' and the charm of the society there. The same letter gossips about her visit to Llangollen, where the Ladies afforded her bed and breakfast and 'the carved room' but commanded that her husband, 'the Colonel', 'must out at night, for we never lodge gentlemen'. He appears not to have baulked at the estrangement, returning the following day to pay his respects and with 'a little chained keepsake' as a gift for her.

In June 1823, Lady Glynne received a letter from Reginald Heber, the great hymnwriter and Bishop of Calcutta. This is the same Reginald Heber who attended the Allansons' wedding as a boy at Worthenbury in 1794. His diligence, devotion and deep intellect had enabled him to rise mercurially through the ministry, and he now occupied one of the most elevated positions within it. The bishopric covered a vast geographical footprint across British territories in Asia and Australasia, offering ample scope for the exercise of Heber's enormous missionary zeal.

His letter was written not long after his appointment and before his departure from London. In it, he expresses regret that he will not have the opportunity to visit Lady Glynne in the meantime and thanks her for all her 'kindness and particularly for this last and most flattering instance of it'. 'I can hardly tell you,' he continues, 'how much I shall prize both your book and, still more, the beautiful handwriting at the beginning of it. I am sensible that nothing I am likely to write shall deserve a place in so elegant a receptacle – yet it will be an additional stimulus to me to take all pains in my power in the hope of being able, should I have to visit England, to show Lady Glynne that her flattering present has not been neglected or suffered to lie idle.' The gift, it seems, was a journal in which he was to add his handwriting to hers.

Heber's episcopate was tragically short-lived. In 1826, after three years working inde-fatigably to fulfil his mission, he preached his last sermon at Trinchinopoly in Tamil Nadu. Returning to his bungalow, he died after plunging into an ice-cold bath. Contrasting sharply with the searing heat of the day, it was most likely the shock that killed him. As the news spread gradually around the world, there was profound public grief and a strong appetite for commemoration. Institutions were named after him and memorials set in India, Australia and England, most notably a huge marble sculpture in St Paul's Cathedral, London. In the Glynne household, the grief was palpable. Writing many years later, Lady Glynne's daughter, Catherine, makes the following disclosure:

I could not have been more than eight when Bishop Heber first visited Hawarden Castle – 1820, I believe – but words spoken of him by my mother have not faded. In 1815 she had become a widow. It was natural at this time that intercourse such as was offered should be of special value to her. For I recall the Bishop's singular gifts, his greatness, his charm, his persuasiveness. So it was through her conversation af-terwards that I recall how comforting and precious it was to her. Then I remember the deep interest on hearing he was to be Bishop of Calcutta, and the awe and sadness with which we received the tidings of his death.'[21]

Imagine being remembered for your 'greatness'. Imagine that.

In the year of our book club meeting, a young clergyman by the name of George Becher Blomfield was appointed curate at Hawarden, under the rectorship of Reverend George Grenville-Neville, Lady Glynne's brother. His elder brother, Charles Blomfield, was then Bishop of Chester, later to become Bishop of London, in which capacity he presided over the service at the Chapel Royal which Anne Owen attended in 1835. We will hear more of this family in due course.

Now we return to the coming of age of Sir Stephen Glynne, 9th Baronet, which took place in September 1818. To say it was a grand affair would be a gross understatement. The epicentre was the family estate, which hosted a lavish reception and ball, with supporting events taking place in Chester, Wrexham and Hawarden. A report in the *Chester, Cheshire and North Wales Advertiser* dated 26th September provides a graphic account of proceedings. Cannon fire was discharged from the medieval battlements at midnight and flags were visible on Hawarden Castle and nearby steeples from first light. A local holiday was declared and the community dressed as finely as their purses would permit. Five well-fed bullocks and thirty sheep were slaughtered for the enjoyment and sustenance of the local poor. The elaborate decorations on the castle entrance and a temporary marquee erected for the purpose were matched by the many adornments on visiting carriages, each of which was greeted by 'every branch of the family' on arrival. Anne Glynne would have been amongst the throng. On the lawn were most of the tenantry and a band from Buckley playing 'God save the King' and 'Rule Britannia'.

A dinner for 180 guests was 'served up in the true Old English style of baronial splendour'. Prominent families from far and wide were represented, including numerous Glynnes and Boydells. The speeches, led off by Lord Braybrooke and Sir Stephen, were replete with mutual appreciation and bonhomie. The toast to Anne Glynne – brief but venerable – was followed by fulsome praise for the Boydells, in particular James, who had run the Hawarden estate during Sir Stephen's minority. The family had also played a leading role in organising the celebration.

In the early evening, Sir Stephen observed the cutting up of an ox and the distribution of ale on the lawn before leading a glittering cavalcade of coaches, carriages, riders and pedestrians and the band to Dobshill, approximately two miles south. Here were assembled an estimated ten thousand people, who loudly cheered their arrival. Sir Stephen mounted a stage to toast the multitude, before another roasted ox was carved and served around. The return journey saw the late evening sun give way to a brilliantly moonlit sky, with the music still resounding and the receding cheers of the crowd in the distance.

The ball, brightly illuminated by lamps and a chandelier in the temporary structure, started up at 8pm to the strains of a harpist. Dancing continued until 11pm, when supper was served. This lasted until one in the morning, after which the company parted over the course of an hour or so. Order was kept by a Mr Joseph Monday, who superintended a numerous body of constables, and the household staff. Singled out for special mention were the butler Mr Whittingham, who had first worked under Sir Stephen's grandfather, and Mrs Hand, the housekeeper, 'that old and faithful servant'.

The simultaneous celebrations in Chester took place at the Royal Hotel – which had been decked in Glynne paraphernalia, including a transparency of the Glynne Arms in the front window – and at the Feathers Hotel. In the following days there was a ball and dinner for servants and their friends, hosted by Sir Stephen; a dinner for seven hundred workmen; and a gathering at the Glynne Arms, chaired by Viscount Belgrave.

Lady Glynne's correspondence includes a 'Statement of the expenses of the coming of age of Sir Stephen Glynne' from James Boydell, in which a detailed breakdown of costs is provided. The total outlay comes to £874 – over £50,000 today – roughly a third of which was spent on wine and ale, and ten per cent on butchers' meat. Such hospitality must have been warmly and widely appreciated and the impression of it must have remained long in the memory, even of the most avid socialite. For Anne Glynne, it would have been cause for reflection too: her father had been 6th Baronet and now, aged 68, she honoured the 9th as he entered adulthood. The whirl of memories and emotions must have stirred her profoundly.

There is some evidence to suggest that Sir Stephen and Anne were close, despite them being two generations apart. On 19th July 1830, the *Salisbury and Winchester Journal* reported on fashionable arrivals at Swanwick, on the Solent. Amongst them were Sir Stephen Glynne and Mrs Glynne. Sir Stephen never married and his mother would have been uniformly known as Lady Glynne. Anne, it seems, was robust enough to travel a long distance and her constitution may have benefited from the change of scene, despite reports of unfavourable weather for much of the summer season. Their arrival coincided with the death and funeral of George IV and the accession of William IV. There were events to mark the occasions and, for the Glynnes, loyal as they were, these would not have passed them by completely.

Now we revert to another royal event, this time much closer to home. In Chapter One, we saw how Elizabeth Sloughter had marvelled at the visit of the Duchess of Kent and Princess Victoria to open the new bridge in Chester in August 1832. There is a fleeting reference in Elizabeth's letter to her niece to the effect that 'I was at Mrs Glynne's to see them pass by'. Here we have evidence of a close connection between two of our book club members, albeit not directly. What must have made this occasion infinitely more thrilling for Anne was the fact that the royal party chose to visit Hawarden whilst in the area. Mary Drew, writing in 1919, tells us: 'Queen Victoria who, with her mother, the Duchess of Kent, visited Hawarden Castle so long as ago as 1832, mentioned a short time before she died to a member of her family, how well she remembered the "beautiful Miss Glynnes".'[22] These were Anne's great-nieces.

One of those Miss Glynnes – Mary – writing on an unspecified date to her mother at Butleigh Manor, a family property in Somerset, reports: 'My dearest Mama … We are just arrived from Chester where we spent a very happy day and Aunt Glynne was delighted to see us … She would be glad, I think, to spend a day with us if the horses were not so expensive.' Perhaps this was in the lean years of the early 1830s. By then it would have been well over half a century since she received her paternal inheritance, and she would have been in her ninth decade. There is an implicit plea in the letter, which may or may not have been heeded.

It is pertinent to ask precisely where in Chester Anne Glynne lived, and how it afforded a view of the Royal procession to which Elizabeth Sloughter was attracted. That information appears in a notice of her death. In late September 1835, we see the following entry in the press: 'On 7th inst at her house in Nicholas Street Chester, in the 87th year of her age, Anne Glynne, eldest surviving dau of Sir John Glynne of Hawarden Castle.'

Despite being a low-profile figure, she was of a noble family and news of her passing would have been widely noted and regretted. Soon the *Chester Chronicle* would convey this news:

> Family Mansion in Nicholas St for sale at auction at Pied Bull 12th Oct 1835. Very desirable and commodious freehold residence, on west side of street with garden and offices, lately in occupation of Mrs Anne Glynne, deceased. In thorough state of repair - entrance, stone staircase, dining, breakfast, drawing and sitting rooms, 5 bedrooms and dressing room, attics, capacious kitchens, pantries and complete servants' offices, water closets etc. Greenhouse in garden, private entrance through garden to Grey Friars. Viewing and particulars on application to Messrs Boydell and Townshend, Solicitors, Chester.

Though there may have been some spin involved to boost the price at auction, there is little doubt that this was a spacious and comfortable property. The detail also enables us to pinpoint its precise location: it still stands to this day at number 28, towards the Grosvenor Bridge end of Nicholas Street. It would indeed have provided an excellent vantage point in 1832, not least because it sits a little proud of the other properties in the row. Being adjacent to Grey Friars, it was a few short paces away from where Elizabeth Sloughter lived. Designed by Joseph Turner, the Hawarden architect who developed the castle for Sir John Glynne, the row dates from 1780 and is Grade II listed. It is possible that the Glynne family owned the property from the outset. The notice in the *Chester Chronicle* again illustrates the all-pervasive nature of the Boydells' involvement in the Glynnes' business affairs.

Anne Glynne was buried and is discreetly commemorated at St Deiniol's Church in Hawarden. Two oval silver plaques surmount a simple wooden base hung on the wall of the chancel; one carries the words, 'Anne Glynne, Daughter of the late Sir John Glynne Bart, *Obit* Sept 7 1835, *AEtate* 86,' and the other, immediately above: 'Lucia Gordon, Daughter of Sir John Glynne. Died 18 May 1814, Aged 58.' Lucy was one of Anne's two sisters who survived into the 19th century. The other was Frances, who died at Nicholas Street, also in 1814. The fact that Anne is commemorated alongside Lucy reflects the closeness of their relationship. Widowed much earlier than Frances, perhaps Lucy turned to Anne for comfort and support.

As beloved family members departed, Anne forged enduring friendships and established herself in Chester society, including as a member of our book club. At Hawarden, a new and exciting chapter was about to begin. The Miss Glynnes married – simultaneously, as it happens – and William Gladstone, now Catherine's husband, arrived on the scene. That, however, is beyond the scope of our work.

Chapter Four

February

If any of our book club members were intent on acquiring property in Chester in early 1824, there was a good tranche of it available to buy. This arose from the death of Richard Whalley, who owned numerous tenanted properties in Princess Street, Linen Hall Street and Lower Bridge Street. Pew 119 in St John's Church was also vacated and for sale. The auction took place at the White Lion Hotel on Northgate Street on 11th February.

In the same month, this establishment said a final farewell to Mercy Tomlinson as she completed the relocation of her coaching business to the Feathers Hotel on Bridge Street. It is not entirely clear why this happened, though it may have been to accommodate or more directly compete with Mr Woolliscroft, who operated the Royal Mail Coach Office from the White Lion. A letter published in the *Courant* on 3rd February praises Mercy Tomlinson as 'a humane person to her horses and a friendly and kind employer', implying that there may have been accusations to the contrary. There was also a subscription raised and the presentation of a plate to Mercy, offering further evidence of her popularity and good character.

Coaching operations were expanding rapidly at this time. London, of course, was the hub, with 1500 coaches a day leaving that city. Manchester, which had run one coach twice-weekly to London and Liverpool in 1770, now ran 20 a day to London and 60 to Liverpool. Chester departures amounted to 19 a day.[1]

An extensive and reliable infrastructure was required. The road network stretched from Cornwall to Caithness, and construction work, under the auspices of the turnpike companies, continued at a rapid rate. In Chester, the talk was of the proposed new avenue from St Bridget's – at the junction of Bridge Street and White Friars – to Chester Castle, involving the relocation of the church and the erection of a new bridge. Opinion was divided on the merits of the scheme and magistrates met to debate it. We know now that it was implemented, but the approval process was far from straightforward and at times contentious, as we will see.

Water-borne transport was on the increase too, despite Chester's diminishing importance as a port, in absolute and relative terms. The River Dee was being rendered less navigable by natural forces, and Liverpool's expansion diverted existing traffic in its direction, as well as attracting new trade. There were occasional developments that bucked the trend. For example, a steam packet was being built to work the coast between Chester to Bagillt, and timber was coming in via the Ellesmere Canal to feed shipbuilding in general.

Steam engines were proliferating, and gas was coming to the fore as a source of power, particularly for street lighting. So it is that we see the Liverpool Oil Gaslight Company advertising for a contractor to supply cast iron pipes; Manchester petitioning Parliament for gas lighting across the city; and Burnley being illuminated, much to the wonder and delight of its inhabitants.

Petty crime was an irritant on the streets of Chester at this time. A spate of thefts of lead from waterspouts was enough to put plumbers on alert and spark a move towards the use of alternative materials. Lead was even stripped from Water Gate, where it was used to fasten ornamental stones on the arch. Perhaps of more concern to law-abiding Cestrians was wanton vandalism on the city walls. Coping stones were damaged near Phoenix Tower – also known as King Charles' Tower – and between the Water Gate and the infirmary. The perpetrators appear to have struck in the hours of darkness but before the watchman came on duty at 10pm. Another anti-social issue was the 'disgusting practice of chalking walls with indecent words and sentences'. Such is the heritage of the city that any assault upon its fabric is met with the strongest condemnation.

Though it wouldn't become illegal for another 11 years, cockfighting had a dubious reputation. It remained hugely popular, however – not least amongst the race-going fraternity. A match or 'main' involving approximately 50 cocks was 'approved' between the gentlemen of Cheshire, Shopshire and Lancashire, to be fought at Chester during five days of Race Week. The admission price was five shillings a day and the venue the cockpit sited between St John's Church and the river. This had been established in 1619 by William, Earl Derby. Other places hosted the activity too, including some inns.[2] The horseracing was even delayed if the cockfighting overran, as influential men wished to attend both. Lord Grosvenor gave the nod for the contest in this instance, alongside a 'Mr Mytton'.

'Mad' Jack Mytton, a renowned Regency wastrel and gambler, had a profile in Chester. He owned a stock of racehorses which he fielded at the Roodee, and stables and a stud farm at Delamere. The epithet 'Mad' is not unfounded. From a landed Shropshire family, he was a notorious spendthrift, to such an extent that his substantial inheritance was much depleted by early adulthood. Physically robust, he was inclined to almost any exertion for the sake of a bet. On one occasion, for example, he is said to have ridden a horse through the lobby of a Leamington hotel and up the grand staircase, exiting, still mounted, from the first-floor balcony. He was a hardened drinker too, thinking nothing of despatching four to six bottles of port a day. What was left of his fortune soon evaporated and he fled to Calais to avoid his creditors. Rashly perhaps, he returned to England and imprisonment, in which state he would die, at the age of 37.[3] His presence in Chester on many sporting occasions would have brought an added frisson to proceedings.

More refined activities on the Chester social scene included the Choral Society, led by Monsieur Doré, which boasted a hundred subscribers and the patronage of Lord Belgrave. They performed the overture of *Saul* by Handel at the King's School, then housed in the cathedral complex. Madame Catalani was still in town, this time delivering concerts at the Royal Hotel Assembly Room. The supporting cast included musicians from Covent Garden and Bath, as well as the great composer and pianist, Pio Cianchettini, who had collaborated with Paganini. Before long, the Italian soprano would be offered two thousand guineas for a 30-night run at the Drury Lane Theatre in London, which would have eclipsed anything Chester had to offer. Paganini himself performed at the Chester theatre in January 1832. He cut such a striking figure – tall and lean – that one observer commented that he looked very like his own violin.[4]

The *Chester Courant* kept its readership abreast of the social scene elsewhere in the country too. In St James's Street, London, a new gaming house opened at a cost of £25,000, including the largest carpeted room in the city. On 3rd February, it reports of Brighton:

> The present has been the most brilliant winter season … ever known. The town was never so full, nor could it at any time perhaps boast of having so many persons of rank and distinction. It is scarcely possible to walk on the cliffs without being elbowed by a Peer, and coroneted equipages meet us at every turn … and as the King will probably reside here for a considerable time, gaiety will of course continue to be the order of the day.

In its next edition a week later, it shared the news that 'His Majesty is steadily recovering but it is inadvisable to come to town to open Parliament in person'. The attractions of Brighton and the king's predilection for the high life may also have had a bearing on the decision.

The King's Speech, read by the Lord Chancellor, commented on the flourishing state of commerce, agriculture and manufacture and the 'cheerful spirit of order that all classes of the community enjoy'. It addressed the question of the slave trade, but only in the most guarded terms:

> His Majesty is confident that you will afford your best attention and assistance to any proposition which may be submitted to you for promoting the moral improvement of the Negroes, by an extended plan of religious instruction, and by such measures as may gradually conduce to the same end. But his Majesty earnestly recommends to you to treat this whole subject with calmness and the discretion which it demands. It is a subject perplexed with difficulties, which no sudden effort can disentangle.

The notion of religious indoctrination as a proxy for freedom must have been anathema to the Abolitionists and could only have added impetus to their fight. The lack of appetite and energy for any meaningful change highlighted the scale of the challenge they faced.

At the same time, news was filtering through from Jamaica of an insurrection in which eight enslaved people were identified as ringleaders, convicted of engagement in rebellious conspiracy and executed. A resolution was passed by the House of Assembly on the island for the importation of more arms for the militia. Deep resentment was expressed towards Westminster for seeking to interfere in the colony's internal affairs, in particular Canning's calls for bans on the flogging of females and driving with a whip. Palmerston proposed an increase of 5,000 men in the regular army, on top of the 73,000 already in service, in anticipation of further trouble in the West Indies.

The case of Missionary Smith still occupied space in the newspapers, but there wasn't much to say. Early in the month it was reported that the colony was tranquil, and nothing further had been done. There was some misinformation that Smith had been executed, the fallacy of which provoked renewed calls for a fair trial. Another mistaken account advised readers that, following conviction, he had been exiled from the West Indies and that Christianity was beginning to quell the urge amongst the enslaved to rebel. By the end of the month, little reliable news of the case had been disseminated. The reality was that Smith had died in prison on 6th February, too weak to cope with the conditions in which he was confined. At 4am the following morning, he was buried surreptitiously in an unmarked grave, to avoid arousing further disquiet. Back home, and for some weeks to come, he remained a hot topic of discussion as a living man.

The state of Ireland, where approximately one-third of the British Army was deployed, was another intractable concern for the Government. It too was mentioned in the King's Speech and, in the debate that followed, Viscount Lorton likened the condition of the Irish people to a state of slavery. Much blame was attributed to absentee landlords, who drew £2 million a year out of the country and made little effort to appoint effective agents to manage their estates. This was devastating for the local economy and provoked great resentment.

Religion was a perennial source of friction in Ireland, where the Roman Catholic majority felt marginalised and oppressed. Adding salt to the wound was the unrestrained evangelism of the Protestant Church, driven by the London-based Society for Promoting Christian Knowledge. A report presented in February 1824 declared that 1.4 million books – bibles and religious treatises – had been distributed by the society over the course of a year. There was also a grant of £6,000 for 'the propagation of the gospel in foreign parts', earmarked for Reginald Heber, the new Bishop of Calcutta.

In Greece, the struggle for independence from the Ottoman Empire, begun in 1821, was at its height. Corinth had been occupied and Missolonghi blockaded, under the command of Lord Byron, who had fled scandal in Britain and committed fully to the Greek cause. Such were his exploits there that he became a national hero and remains so today. At his base, he received literary figures and military men, whom he kept at his own expense. Despite inheriting a title and estate, most of his considerable wealth came from his poetic output. His role in the conflict did much to popularise the cause in Britain, where subscriptions were raised in support of it. In Liverpool, the mayor led a particularly successful fundraising campaign.

Also in Liverpool this month, an unsavoury incident illustrated widespread tensions in the workplace. A sawyer was bludgeoned to death, purportedly by colleagues who stood out for better wages while he continued in his role. Any activity by workers to combine for improved pay and conditions was severely circumscribed by law, though there was a growing feeling in influential circles that this should be reviewed. There were restrictions too on the export of machinery and a complete ban on mechanics leaving the country, based on the same protectionist thinking that gave rise to the Corn Laws. Taxes were another bone of contention – in Chester, for example, tobacco manufacturers petitioned the House of Commons for relief from crippling duties.

As ever, snippets of news from near and far found their way into the press. Despite the exertions of people like William Fitzwilliam Owen, there was still much exploration to be done. In the same spirit, one Captain Cochrane was traversing Russia and Siberia on foot in search of a land bridge between Asia and North America. Soon he was able to confirm that no such bridge existed, though the channel he discovered – the Bering Strait – was frequently blocked by ice for much of the winter.

Closer to home, Spring and Langan were readying themselves for another prize fight, having resolved their differences on the size and structure of the ring and pledging £500 on each side for the victor. Langan, still bearing the scars from the previous encounter, was keen to restore his professional reputation and cashflow.

In Manchester, bodies were snatched for medical dissection and a huge fire substantially damaged Marsland's cotton mill in Oxford Road. People news in Chester included the grave condition of Mrs Richard Baker after giving birth to a stillborn – her 22nd child – and the elopement of a married doctor and publican's wife who were dramatically apprehended in London. The marriage of Robert Hughes 'at the mature age of 16' to Jane Davies, 'a youthful widow of 70', was felt to be newsworthy too.[5]

Chapter Five

Mrs Humberston
Lot 3

Contributions to Natural History, containing some very fine specimens of the Cotton plant, and an interesting sketch illustrative of the mineralogy of the banks of the Humber; 2 vols., bound in Russia

The first point to make about this entry is that there is no extant work entitled simply *Contributions to Natural History*. This appears to be a device on Dr Norris's part to lead into his references to 'the Cotton plant' and 'the mineralogy on the banks of the Humber'. The second of these is easiest to explain because it requires no further knowledge or research. It is merely a play on the words 'Humber' and 'stone', 'Humberstone' being an occasional variant of 'Humberston'. We then need to ask why the letter C has been capitalised in 'Cotton' and what significance there may be in two volumes and the Russian binding.

Let's begin with the question of identity. If we consider Cotton as a possible surname, that becomes relatively straightforward. The *Reading Mercury* of 21st May 1798 contains this marriage notice: 'Philip Humberston, esq; to Miss Cotton, eldest daughter of the Dean of Chester'. It is unclear why this was reported in Reading and not conspicuously elsewhere. The marriage had taken place at St Oswald's Church – then housed in the south transept of Chester Cathedral – on 8th May.[1] The Reverend George Cotton, who must have presided over the ceremony, was Dean of Chester from 1787 until his death in 1805. He was a reactionary figure, for example in his appeal to Parliament on behalf of the local clergy in 1790 not to repeal the Test Acts, which denied Catholics, Jews and dissenting Protestants access to public office.

Dean Cotton had three daughters: Catherine Maria, Frances Hester and Mary Philadelphia. Our 'Mrs Humberston' was the eldest of the three. The middle name of the youngest

– Philadelphia – is an echo of the Cotton family's colonial links. This takes us back – not for the first time, and by no means the last – to the grim reality of the transatlantic slave trade.

Catherine's two times great-grandfather was a man called Thomas Lynch, who was Governor of Jamaica on three occasions between 1663 and 1684. He had sailed with William Penn and Robert Venables in 1654, under orders from Oliver Cromwell to seize the island of Hispaniola – Haiti in the modern day – from Spain. The expedition failed, with a costly loss of men on the British side, as a punishment for which Penn and Venables were briefly imprisoned in the Tower of London on their return to England. This was despite them having sailed on and successfully taken the island of Jamaica, which was less well defended by the Spanish.

Lynch's governorship began at the height of the age of piracy in the Caribbean, a practice which he supported wholeheartedly for patriotic and personal gain. One of his associates was the notorious Welsh-born buccaneer, Captain Henry Morgan, who attacked Spanish interests in the region without remorse. Lynch was forced to relent under diplomatic pressure, after which he pursued a campaign against the pirates with equal vigour. On land, he unsuccessfully attempted to defeat the Jamaican Maroons – communities of free Black people in the mountainous interior who had managed to escape enslavement under the Spanish after transportation from Africa. He developed sugar plantations and reputedly sent the first consignment of sugar back home from Jamaica, as well as generally encouraging colonisation and exploitation of the island's resources, including slave labour. By the time he died in 1684, Lynch had enslaved people of his own, 12 of whom were included in the property disposed of in his will.[2] The legatee was his daughter, Philadelphia – named after the city then being founded by William Penn, son of the Jamaican invader, in what would become the state of Pennsylvania. She married Sir Thomas Cotton, 2nd Baronet of Combermere in Cheshire, producing a fruitful stem of the 'Cotton plant' to which Dr Norris whimsically refers.

George Ormerod, whose expansive three-volume *History of the County Palatine and City of Chester* was published in 1819, cites a memorial in St Marcella's Church near Denbigh relating to this branch of the family:

Sir Robert [Cotton, 1st baronet Combermere, who died in 1712] is succeeded in honour and estate by his fourth son, Sir Thomas, who married Philadelphia, sole daughter and heiress of His Excellency Thomas Lynch kt, a person remarkable for his valour and loyalty. Having been three times Governor and Captain General of Jamaica, in which government he died, leaving his daughter a vast fortune Honestly Gotten, well-bestowed and prudently managed. This lady has brought forth a numerous issue to preserve the memory of their worthy progenitors.[3]

The Cottons paid the piper and called the tune, without letting the facts get in the way of a good story. Indeed, it could be argued that the inscription protests a little too much about Thomas Lynch's virtues and the manner in which his fortune was amassed. Interestingly, Ormerod offers no qualification, perhaps out of deference to his patrons and subscribers, which included members of the Cotton family. The slavery interests continued to percolate through and enrich later generations, until Catherine's cousin, Lord Combermere – who made the triumphal entry into Chester from Hawarden in 1814 – cashed them in when compensation claims were settled in the 1830s.

Catherine was born at Combermere Abbey, a sprawling former Cistercian monastery in South Cheshire, in 1777. Three years earlier, Dr Samuel Johnson, visiting with Mr and Mrs Thrale and their daughter, had described it as the best house of its kind that he ever saw. Catherine's father, George, was the third son of Sir Lynch Salusbury Cotton, 4th Baronet. The fact that he moved into the ministry, and achieved high office within it, does not run counter to his kinship with slave owners. As noted in the previous chapter, the Anglican church was immersed in colonial affairs and saw itself as agent towards a more enlightened future. Her mother was another Catherine Maria, her maiden name being

'Tomkinson'. There was money on this side of the family too: her grandfather, James Tomkinson, a successful Nantwich lawyer, had accumulated sufficient wealth to buy nearby Dorfold Hall in the 1750s and commission the renowned architect, Samuel Wyatt, to make alterations to it.

The Cottons had long-standing connections with Chester, and Catherine would have been well acquainted with the city, particularly from the age of 10, when her father assumed the deanery. It is likely that she met her future husband, Philip Humberston, in Chester, where he was establishing himself in legal circles. He had ties with the cathedral and may have known Dean Cotton before he knew his daughter. The Humberston family haled from Gwersyllt and Holt, near Wrexham. They worshipped at All Saints Church in nearby Gresford, where Philip was baptised in 1771 and where some of his ancestors are memorialised.

We know that he was practising in Chester in the 1790s as a partner in the law firm Massey & Humberston, based at The Friars, at the junction of White Friars and Weaver Street.[4] We have encountered him before with his legal hat on, acting in the sale of St John's House on behalf of Elizabeth Sloughter. In December 1797, he was witness to the marriage at Holy Trinity Church of 'Charles Morral ye Younger and Elizabeth Boates'.[5] Catherine is likely to have been with him and perhaps even caught the bouquet, as she and Philip would marry six months later.

Philip's business premises at The Friars soon became the marital home. This robust Georgian building in its own grounds, dating from around 1740, survives and is Grade II* listed in the present day. It is located on the former site of a friary belonging to the Carmelite order, whose white cloaks account for the street name, 'Whitefriars', or 'White Friars', as it was then known. Fragments of the original building are still to be found in the brickwork of the property. With a footprint of approximately eight thousand square feet across two main floors, the accommodation it provides is ample. This would have mattered to the Humberstons as they started a family. There was also the need to house domestic staff and the growing business. Philip and Catherine had ten children between 1799 and 1818, nine of whom were girls. The first born – another Catherine Maria – died in infancy, as did the fourth – Mary – in 1806. The names Catherine and Mary would be adopted for other children born after these bereavements.

In a wider context, the turn of the new century was characterised by the threat of war, as Napoleon's forces ravaged the Continent and made extensive preparations to invade England. People wanted to play their part in the defence of the realm, including Philip Humberston, who was appointed as one of four Volunteer Officers for Chester in September 1803.[6] An extract from George Lee Fenwick's 1896 work *A History of the Ancient City of Chester* encapsulates the military build-up on the home front.

> In early 1803 it became apparent that hostilities between England and France were again inevitable and an invasion of England was carefully planned on a giant scale. 'Let us be masters of the Channel for six hours,' said Napoleon, 'and we are masters of the world.' … When he assembled one hundred thousand men and brought together an immense number of flat-bottomed boats at Boulogne to transport them across to the White Cliffs of Dover, he had left out of his calculations the Englishman's love of his country. The threat of invasion aroused people, and armed men sprung up as if England had been sown with dragon's teeth. In a very brief period, 400,000 volunteers were raised and armed. The proposal for a levy en masse was superfluous. At Chester on 27th July a public meeting was held at the Exchange and in short time a regiment of volunteers 1,300 strong was raised and armed.[7]

Tensions heightened and mobilisation continued throughout 1804, but the threat to British shores was never carried through. Whilst Catherine may have been comforted by her husband's willingness to fight, she, and the nation at large, would have been immensely grateful for her cousin's actual combat with Napoleon overseas. Stapleton Cotton, as he was known before his elevation to the peerage, commanded British forces in the Peninsular Wars in Portugal, Spain and France between 1809 and 1814, scoring a number of notable successes. Perhaps foremost amongst these was the victory at Salamanca in 1814, which Wellington attributed almost entirely to Cotton's courage and gallantry. These qualities were his hallmark, along with the sartorial elegance he displayed on the battlefield. Coupled with his achievements against a formidable enemy, it is little wonder that many people cast him in the mould of national hero. It is said that he would have occupied a prominent role alongside Wellington at Waterloo had the king not intervened after Cotton indiscreetly gossiped about one of his numerous affairs. Not that he was in a position to speak, being a notorious philanderer himself.[8] No doubt people winked at this, and at his dealings in enslaved people, on account of his exploits in the national interest. He would certainly have been a great source of family pride, not least in Chester, where the Humberstons would have enjoyed the acclaim he met with in 1814. By that time, they had remembered him in the christening of their only son, Philip Stapleton Humberston, born in August 1812.

The make-up of the family continued to change through death as well as birth. Philip lost his mother in 1800 and his father in 1808, both of whom are buried at Gresford. The years 1805 and 1806 were particularly punishing, with the respective deaths of Dean Cotton and the infant Mary. By the end of the decade, a further three children had arrived – Hester, Anne and Sophia – in addition to the two eldest survivors, Frances and the second Catherine.

In 1809, we get a glimpse of the social life and connections of the Humberstons in the diary of the Reverend Sir Henry Poole as he recorded his journey from London to his old family seat of Poole Hall, near Hooton on the Wirral.[9] His entries during his stay include:

26th June – Afternoon tea with the Cottons

28th June – Went to the seaside in the morning with Mr and Mrs Blundell from Little Crosby. Mr and Mrs Gladstone dined with us.

11th July – Went in canal boat with Cottons to Chester and spent day with Mr and Mrs Humberston, Mr Cotton's son and daughter, Mr and Mrs Jones from Wales with us.

13th July – The Cottons from Thornton and Miss Majendie, Mr and Mrs Humberston from Chester dined here, and spent a very pleasant day, and the servants had a dance in the evening in the hall.

It is not entirely clear who all the Cottons are here – it was a big family, scattered around the region. Less clear still is the identity of Mr and Mrs Jones from Wales. Miss Majendie was the daughter of a former Bishop of Chester, at that time Bishop of Bangor. The following year she would marry James Henry Cotton, Catherine Humberston's younger brother. The Blundell family had been lords of the manor at Crosby Hall since the Middle Ages, and nearby Blundellsands took its name from them. We don't know categorically whether 'Mr Gladstone' was John Gladstone, but there is a good chance it was. He and William Blundell, then head of the family, moved in the same business circles, for example as members of the committee which put the construction of the Runcorn Bridge into effect.[10] Even though John Gladstone's six brothers followed him to Liverpool, he remained the most high-profile sibling and could therefore be referred to without the necessity of a Christian name. Visits to the banks of the Mersey and leisure cruises on the recently completed Ellesmere Canal – the Chester and Ellesmere Port branch opened in 1797 – were popular at that time.

On 25th October of the same year, Philip Humberston was socialising again, but this time without his wife. He was one of the Vice Presidents on the organising committee to mark the Golden Jubilee of King George III in Chester. For him and about eighty others amongst 'the most respectable men in the city and neighbourhood', the celebrations culminated in a sumptuous dinner at the Royal Hotel.[11] There is a report in the *Courant* that 'a great quarrel' arose, tactfully qualified with the words, 'On further enquiry we understand the only ground of difference was who should show the most lively feelings of respect for the day and love for the King.' Out on the streets, the rejoicing was unrestrained, including the ceremonial parading and roasting of an ox. Sentiment ran deep in favour of this amiable, ageing and afflicted monarch amongst the people of Chester, ancient and loyal as the city was.

In the 1815 edition of the *Commercial Directory of Chester*, Philip Humberston is noted as the sole proprietor in his legal practice. He was forging ahead with his business and may have taken on additional premises close to the family home. There are references in various sources to his trading address being 'White Friars', rather than simply 'The Friars' and his nameplate on the north-east side of the street.[12] Through this period, Philip and Catherine completed their family with the arrival of Maria in 1811, Philip Stapleton in 1812 and the second Mary in 1818.

Catherine had lost her mother shortly before Mary's birth, inheriting £1,500 in her will, a similar sum having been advanced to her at the time of her marriage. She had lost a brother too, in 1814 – the career soldier, Thomas Davenant Cotton, of the Royal Fusiliers, who were involved in sundry campaigns overseas. One of these had led to his marriage in 1810 to Mary Brinley in Halifax, Nova Scotia, in a ceremony conducted by the bishop of that province. Mary was descended from a wealthy Bostonian family who were forced to flee as loyalists during the American War of Independence. Thomas's death occurred at the Battle of Nivelle in the French Pyrenees during the Peninsular Wars. Wellington's troops, amongst whom he was fighting, were surprised by the enemy at the outset of the battle but defeated them and suffered fewer fatalities, though, sadly, Thomas was one of them. Two weeks later, Mary gave birth to their son, George Edward Lynch Cotton, in Chester.

A more distant relative who was beginning to achieve some notoriety at this time was the Reverend Horace Salusbury Cotton. He was part of a branch of the family, based in Reigate, who were keen retain and promote their eponymous links with the Combermere line. His father was called Robert Salusbury Cotton and he named his sons Lynch and Stapleton. In 1814, he was appointed Resident Chaplain in Newgate Prison by the Court Aldermen of the City of London; this was despite his own confinement in the Fleet Prison for debt five years earlier. He was a fire and brimstone preacher who offered little in the way of salvation to the condemned, in this world or the next.

An example of his approach can be found in the case of Eliza Fenning in 1815, which is covered in some detail in Ian Mortimer's encyclopaedic *The Time Travellers Guide to Regency Britain* as a palpable miscarriage of justice.[13] She was a servant to a family named Turner in London and was accused by them of attempted poisoning after she and they fell ill following the consumption of food prepared jointly by Eliza and Mrs Turner. They all made a full recovery, but she would soon die on the gallows once the accusation had been prosecuted against her in court. No substantive evidence was offered, and no meaningful defence could be procured. Appeals for clemency were ignored by the highest authorities in the land. In his condemnatory sermon, Cotton, a friend of the Turners, proclaimed that she was so wicked that even Satan had deserted her.[14] Attendance at these services was enforced for prisoners on death row, including being required to stand alongside their empty coffin as a reminder of where they were bound. Cotton remained in post until 1839. Charles Dickens visited Newgate during his tenure and wrote about the barbarism of his methods.[15]

Perhaps the Cottons and Humberstons in Cheshire were able to distance themselves from any malpractice within the family that took place elsewhere. Often, they had more pressing concerns closer to home, and this was certainly the case for Philip Humberston as elections loomed in 1818. At this time, they were notoriously riotous and litigious affairs, as candidates touted shamelessly for votes, by fair means or foul. Money talked and those who could lavish most on the electorate usually came out on top. The two Chester seats in 1818 went to Richard and Thomas Grosvenor, under a Whig banner. The defeated parties were the independent candidates, Sir John Grey Egerton of Oulton Hall and John Williams, a Chester-born barrister. Philip Humberston was involved in presenting a petition to Parliament in early 1819 on their behalf, citing illegal treating and bribery on the part of the Grosvenors. An inquiry was implemented, and the result was upheld, albeit by no means unanimously.[16] Later in the year, Catherine's widowed sister-in-law, Mary, married clergyman, Ralph Simpson, at St Mary's-on-the-Hill in Chester.

The following year – 1820 – the Duke of Wellington was in town. We can't be sure that Catherine and Philip met him, but it's likely that they did, not least because of his visit to Combermere, where Stapleton Cotton was his host. Once in Chester, he stayed and attended a great public dinner at the Albion Hotel on Lower Bridge Street, which then rivalled the Royal Hotel for grandeur and opulence. It must have been a truly momentous occasion for the city, with an added festive twist as Christmastide came on.[17]

In 1823, Catherine lost two of her cousins in their 20s – brothers Robert Salusbury Cotton and Rowland Edward Cotton – both of whom were on military service, the latter in Jamaica. Two more of their brothers – Sydney John Cotton and Hugh Calveley Cotton – soon began to make a name for themselves in the Antipodes. Sydney was also an army man and Hugh a surveyor and engineer. Both found their way to Australia via India.

In 1824, Sydney was in Hobart, Van Diemen's Land – now Tasmania – where he was responsible for stores at penal settlements and the allocation of convict gangs to settlers. After a spell in Burma, he returned to New South Wales and Queensland to oversee penal colonies until free settlement came about in the 1830s. He then saw out his military career with distinction in India once again, most notably on the North-West Frontier in the 1840s and 1850s. He was amply decorated for his services and became governor of Chelsea Hospital.

Hugh arrived in Hobart a little later and did some valuable engineering work there before clashing with other senior figures in the field. This damaged him reputationally and financially to the extent that he was reliant on government support when he too relocated to India, in his case in the 1850s. Here, he was able to practise unhindered, which he did to great effect in the field of irrigation. The honorific rank of colonel was conferred on him by way of recognition.[18]

In book club year, another of Catherine's cousins, Henry Tomkinson – this time on her mother's side – married Harriet Phillips at the Collegiate Church in Manchester, which would later become Manchester Cathedral. One of Harriet's nephews was Thomas Jodrell Phillips Jodrell, who had literary connections. Whilst at Cambridge, he was friendly with

Christopher Wordsworth, William's nephew, and holidayed in the Lake District with him. As a young lawyer in London, he co-habited with Henry Edgar Austen, nephew of Jane. Later in life, in 1877, having made his mark in legal and educational circles, he hosted fledgling American novelist, Henry James, for dinner at his Mayfair home. James described him, perhaps ungraciously, as 'a very pretty specimen of a fresh-colored, blue-eyed, simple-minded yet cultivated (two things which go together so much here) old English gentleman'.[19]

Also in 1824, there were more elections in Chester, this time for mayor and sheriff. Mr George Harrison – not to be confused with the surgeon of the same name – was sworn in as mayor, despite rowdy opposition. The post of sheriff was more keenly contested, between the fancied Mr Shearing and a Mr Whittakers. The voting lasted several days, and dubious tactics were once again employed, in which Whittakers' camp was most implicated. One example was that of a Lieutenant Sage – a brewer, apparently on sick leave from the East India Company – who threatened to withhold supply from an independent publican on Frodsham Street if he didn't vote advisedly. The publican promptly settled his bill and ordered his stock elsewhere.

More pertinently for us, it was reported that the Clerk of the Dean and Chapter sent an imperative order to a man in Dee Lane to vote for Mr Whittakers, the suggestion being that this was not a one-off. The clerk was Philip Humberston. The dean – now Peter Vaughan – disowned the action. Philip's motives are unclear, but the report is consistent with his stance at the 1818 general election and the challenge to the Grosvenors, who also dominated the Body Corporate in the city of Chester. There were no obvious consequences for Philip as a result of his apparent insubordination. Perhaps it was subsumed in the wider election mayhem. He remained sufficiently embedded in the local establishment to be invited onto the committee for the Chester District Society for Promoting Christian Knowledge, presided over by the bishop and the dean.

When Catherine sat down with her fellow book lovers in 1824, her family circumstances were relatively stable. Her household included her husband and their six surviving daughters, spanning a 17-year age gap up to their early twenties. Philip junior would have been at boarding school. This stability would soon be interrupted, however.

In 1825, Catherine junior married into the church and relocated with her new husband to a rural parish in Cambridgeshire. The following year, Hester – the third eldest daughter – died in Chester and was buried at St Bridget's, a few paces from the family home. Philip senior continued to run the legal practice as a sole proprietor, which was unusual, and demanding for him, but at least earnings stayed within the family. His most prominent line of business was in property and conveyancing. His name appeared in the local press regularly as agent for the sale or let of private dwelling houses and commercial premises. One example was the letting of an elegant town house in King's Buildings in centrally located King Street in 1828.[20]

As the 1820s drew to close, a febrile atmosphere was building around the prospect of parliamentary reform. The great and the good of Chester nailed their colours to the mast. It was a traditionally conservative city, small, but with long-established representation in Parliament. Now the process that had delivered that was under threat. An open letter from 'Noble, Gentry, Freemen and Clergy of the county palatine of Chester' published in the *Chester Chronicle* in April 1831 – the year before the Great Reform Act was passed – rails against the direction of travel:

> We regard the measure late before the House of Commons as so dangerous in its principles, and in its tendency so destructive to the welfare and prosperity of the Country, that we are resolved to use every means in our power to prevent a Bill founded on such unconstitutional grounds passing into a law.

Viscount Combermere's name appears towards the top of the list of signatories. The letter does not elaborate on what the 'unconstitutional grounds' were, as the draft Bill aimed to introduce greater democracy. The aristocracy feared disruption to a social hierarchy that they headed and controlled. Revolutions throughout Europe in the preceding decades had challenged absolutist monarchies, most notably in France. Convenient analogies were drawn with the Britain of the early 1830s, in which the reform movement was characterised as seditious. The monarchy, the Anglican Church and the landed gentry conspired in favour of the status quo. Combermere's vested interest was strong indeed – recently enobled and with estates at home and abroad.

Another of Catherine's cousins was Sir Willoughby Cotton, who had a controversial public profile. In his youth he had been expelled from Rugby School for leading a group of disaffected boys in a quite literally explosive attack on the headmaster, which was only quelled by the reading of the Riot Act and the involvement of the local militia. He was still able to enter the army, where he also excelled in the Peninsular and Belgian campaigns under Wellington's command.

In the early 1830s, he led the British forces in Jamaica, where he suppressed a major slave revolt involving an estimated 60,000 rebels. Despite their numbers, they were no match for heavily armed British troops. Cotton further drew their sting by threatening captured rebels with immediate execution and making a tactical offer of amnesty to any who abandoned their positions and returned to work. One place that experienced significant bloodshed in this episode was a plantation known as 'Chester Castle'.

The consequences of the rebellion were far-reaching. The financial cost of the military response is estimated at £130 million in today's terms; the human cost is incalculable. When the events were reported in Britain – often with reactionary editorial spin – racial prejudice was reinforced and the pro-slavery lobby emboldened. A government-appointed committee tasked with examining the state of slavery in the West Indies comprised 25 peers, six of whom were slaveholders. One of the six was Viscount Combermere.[21]

Catherine would have had some awareness of colonial matters, though her main focus was domestic life at home. More Humberston children married and flew the family nest. In 1836, Sophia wed William Eccles of Davenham, near Northwich. Their marriage was cruelly attenuated, however, as she died three years later, leaving behind a husband and a one-year-old son, William Hall Eccles. Her widower remarried in 1841, to the daughter of the Prebendary of Carlisle, and young William would grow up in the company of his stepmother and three stepsiblings.

Still a teenager, he distinguished himself in military service. At 16, he was appointed to the Rifle Brigade, following an approach by Viscount Combermere to Prince Albert, no less. Between June and September 1855, he played a leading role in the Battle of the Great Redan against Russian forces in the Crimea, during the Siege of Sevastopol. Though twice severely injured, he was never far from the front line and returned to Davenham the following year to a hero's welcome. For the rest of his life, he was widely known and feted as 'Redan Eccles'.

William also excelled in a more innocuous pursuit, as a member of the travelling orchestra, The Wandering Minstrels. The orchestra's 40 or so members were drawn from the military and aristocracy, including links to the Egerton and Grosvenor families. They undertook innumerable charity concerts in the last four decades of the 19th century and were immensely popular, though in their later years they were eclipsed by the rise of Victorian music hall entertainment.[22] When Wiliam died in Folkstone in 1900, obituaries talked of the Redan, his minstrelsy and his Cheshire connections through the Eccles and Humberston families.

The next Humberston daughter to marry, in 1838, was Maria, to Vincent Roger Corbet, third son of the late Shropshire baronet, Sir Andrew Corbet. The service, led by the Bishop of Bangor, took place at St Bridget's Church. Vincent is variously described in census records as an 'annuitant', 'landed proprietor' and 'JP [Justice of the Peace] for the County of Cheshire'. He appears not to have had a settled profession, which was by no means essential on account of inherited wealth. Perhaps this was also influenced by another significant factor in his life: he was blind from birth, according to the 1861 census.

This may also explain why he is often recorded as being accompanied by others, well into adulthood. For example, in 1829, aged 25, he stayed with his parents at the Mostyn Hotel in Parkgate on the Wirral, a favourite summer haunt for affluent families from Chester and elsewhere.[23] In 1832 he was visiting Cheltenham with a Mr Domville. Maria became a lifelong companion for Vincent, outliving him by 17 years. Her death occurred in Leamington Spa in 1902.

Vincent's cameo in our story would be incomplete without a reference to the 'Shakespeare Walnut Tree'. An entry in *The Cambrian News* of 26th December 1879 tells us of just such a tree in a nursery at West Felton near Oswestry, not far from where Vincent was born and brought up. Until the middle of the 19th century, when ill-health was a constraint for some, it was the annual meeting place on Shakespeare's birthday of numerous literary friends who shared a love of the Bard's work. Poets, painters, actors, doctors, musicians and divines were amongst them, as was Vincent. The origins of the ritual are unknown. Perhaps the tree dated back to Shakespeare's time; perhaps it mimicked the walnut tree that thrived on John Shakespeare's doorstep when his incomparable son was born. The West Felton tree decayed and was removed in 1874, though a wine bottle and inscription beside it remained in place, for some time at least.

In 1840, Philip Stapleton Humberston, the only son of Philip and Catherine, married Elizabeth Henrietta Hughes at Holy Trinity, Chester. She was the daughter of Hugh Robert Hughes of Kinmel Hall, Abergele. He also owned Bache Hall in Chester, which would become their marital home. Hugh's wealth, embodied in these properties, derived from his family's interests in the Parys Mining Company on Anglesey, which at one time was the largest copper mine in Europe. By the time of his marriage, Philip Stapleton had qualified in the law and joined his father in the firm at White Friars. This would have been a considerable boon to Philip senior, who was 70 years old when his son married and who only had another four years to live.

Catherine was widowed on 20th August 1844, her husband being buried at St Bridget's, alongside their daughter, Hester. She soon took the decision to vacate The Friars, which may have had an empty and melancholy feel now the family was depleted. She moved with her unmarried daughters and domestic staff to Newton Hall, a substantial late 17th century property in its own grounds, approximately two miles north-east of Chester. For Catherine, now in her late sixties, it offered the prospect of repose, away from the considerable bustle of the city. The hall and much of the area around it was owned by Earl Kilmorey, into whose family her aunt, Sophia Cotton, had married half a century earlier.[24]

Another significant occurrence around this time was the marriage, in December 1847, of Frances Humberston to the Reverend Robert Yarker. Neither had been married before and both were on the cusp of their fifties. Robert had been born in Ulverston but had practised in Chester since the 1820s. He was appointed curate at the old Viking church, St Olave's, on Lower Bridge Street, Chester, in 1827 and was one of the members of the clergy who signed the open letter resisting parliamentary reform in 1831. He wrote on ecclesiastical matters, one example being his 1834 publication *The Gospel the Rule by Which Christians will be Judged!* The title page describes him as 'Perpetual Curate of St Olave's and Evening Lecturer at St Peter's, Chester'. His curacy was perhaps less perpetual than he anticipated, as the parish of St Olave's was dissolved by order of the Council in 1839 and absorbed into St Michael's.[25]

Robert was also a minor canon at Chester Cathedral, before being becoming Vicar of Neston, approximately 11 miles north, in 1846, a move which may have influenced the timing of his proposal to Frances. He developed the church at Neston and established another at nearby Willaston, where he and Frances are commemorated, respectively on the font and in a stained-glass window on the east side of the nave. Robert's death in 1853, and especially Frances's in 1855, would have hit Catherine hard; she had already mourned the loss of four daughters and a husband.

Another close family member who entered the clergy, and excelled in that line, was George Edward Lynch Cotton. He would have been well acquainted with his Aunt Catherine and his Humberston cousins in his youth. He was born to his newly widowed mother in the family home, Brook House, in Chester. This was an ample, four-storey, six-bedroom house in Brook Street, perhaps half a mile from The Friars, directly across the city centre. Mother and child would have needed support, of both an emotional and practical nature.

George was six when his mother married Ralph Simpson, and a year later they were living in the London area due to Ralph's work, which was also in the ministry. George was educated at the King's School, Chester, Westminster School and Trinity College, Cambridge, where he stood out academically, taking a First in the Classical tripos. The *Dictionary of National Biography* describes him as remarkable at school and university for 'force of character, accompanied by a quaint and grotesque humour, very industrious and methodical in his work, and earnestly religious'.[26] In 1837, he was appointed to the post of assistant master at Rugby School by the pioneering headmaster, Dr Thomas Arnold, by whom he was greatly influenced. George's career, it seems, was not impeded by the ancestral vices of Sir Willoughby Cotton, whose target at Rugby had been one of Arnold's predecessors. His stepfather is listed as a clergyman at the school in the 1841 census, which may have helped George to settle and progress there. In Thomas Hughes's classic 1857 autobiographical novel, *Tom Brown's Schooldays* – based on his own time at Rugby – George is 'the young master'.[27]

In 1845, whilst still at Rugby, he married Catherine's grandniece, Sophia Tomkinson, in a ceremony at Acton, Cheshire, near the Tomkinson family seat at Dorfold Hall. Their first child – a boy, born two years later – was christened Edward Thomas Davenant Cotton, in memory of the father whom George never knew. George and Sophia appear to have been ambitious for their son, as he appears in the 1851 census as a three-year-old 'Scholar at Rugby School'. Any such sentiment would not have been misplaced: Edward grew to become a lieutenant colonel in the British Army and conservative MP for Wirral, ultimately being knighted for his services. In 1889, he inherited the considerable fortune of his great-uncle, Thomas Jodrell Phillips Jodrell, of whom we have already heard.

George, well-established at Rugby, applied unsuccessfully for the headship there in 1852, but was instead appointed into that role at Marlborough College. At that time, it was limping through its first decade and was in urgent need of redirection. George brought with him a reforming zeal that touched all areas of the institution and, after a transformational six years at helm, left it as one of the highest-ranking public schools in the country.

His next appointment was in the ecclesiastical sphere, as Bishop of Calcutta, 32 years after the death of Bishop Heber. This was a particularly sensitive time, as the Indian Mutiny of 1857 – suppressed by military force and the promise of greater freedoms from the British overlords – still cast a long shadow over the subcontinent. George landed at Madras with his family on 8th November, the very day Queen Victoria's proclamation was read declaring a new form of government, directly from Westminster, rather than through the discredited and moribund East India Company.

He had the delicate task of balancing the interests of those who supported the spread of Christianity and education, which were inseparable in Victorian times, with those who saw it as an imposition and resented it, such contention being a major factor in the Mutiny. George steered a careful course, introducing a more secular style of education and making it widely accessible to the poorer classes, whilst at the same time engaging closely with the missionary cause. To this day there are Bishop Cotton Schools in Indian cities such as Shimla and Bengaluru.

Like his illustrious predecessor, he travelled widely around his vast episcopate, seeking understanding and influence, which greatly enhanced his popularity and effectiveness. Also like Heber, his life ended tragically and prematurely during the fulfilment of his duties, in his case on 6th October 1866, at the age of 53. Whilst returning to a steamer after consecrating a cemetery at Kushtia on the Ganges, in modern-day Bangladesh, his foot slipped on an uncertain gangplank, and he plunged into the river below. Caught by the strong undercurrent, he disappeared from view and was never seen again.[28]

George was widely praised and lamented, including by the Indian Government, who commented on 'his great knowledge, his sincerity and his charity'. The most profound sense of loss, of course, would have been felt by his wife and family, including the surviving Humberstons. One apparent legacy resides in the expression 'to bless one's cotton socks'. The story goes that George introduced a rule that children in his schools should be issued with socks, first to be blessed and then worn during lessons. Over time 'Cotton's socks' became corrupted to 'cotton socks' and enshrined in the idiom.

In widowhood, Sophia soon returned to Cheshire, living with her brother, Henry, at Reaseheath Hall, near Nantwich. She died at her own home in Berkeley Square, London in 1907, aged 78, leaving a sizeable estate to her daughter, Ursula. Two decades later, Ursula was the donor of a stained-glass window in the west walk of the cloisters in Chester Cathedral, which she dedicated in the following terms:

In thankful remembrance of
George Edward Lynch Cotton, 1813-66. Born in this
City. Headmaster of Marlborough College.
Bishop of Calcutta and Metropolitan of
India. Drowned at Kooshtea, Assam.
These windows are dedicated 1926.[29]

George's express wish in his will was that he should be buried in the cathedral in Calcutta, but this wish could not be fulfilled. Commemoration in Chester is just as fitting. His grandfather had been dean there, his early education had taken place there, and he was a deeply devout Anglican all his life.

When George Cotton was making his mark in India, his Aunt Catherine was in her declining years. She and her daughters Anne and Mary had settled into Newton Hall and, from 1854, had begun to worship at a new church in nearby Upton-by-Chester, which had been built as a chapel-of-ease to St Mary's-on-the Hill. Her son, Philip Stapleton, his wife, Elizabeth, and their son, Philip Hugh, worshipped there too. Their properties, variously on Northgate Street in Chester, at Bache Hall and, later, Mollington Banastre, were all within reach of the church.

The Humberstons were becoming part of a growing community in the Upton and Newton areas, attracted by improved transport links fostered by the railways. Wealthy merchants and industrialists were escaping from increasingly cramped and congested urban areas to more congenial surroundings. Land was being bought up and grand residences built. Incomers gravitated to the church, and it was here that new acquaintances were made.

Despite advancing age, Catherine appears to have been active during the middle and later years of the 1850s, exhibiting produce at horticultural shows and serving as a patroness for the annual Chester Infirmary Ball at the Royal Hotel. Doubtless she continued to take great pride in the achievements of her children, including Philip Stapleton's election win in April 1859, ushering in a six-year stint as MP for Chester. Soon afterwards, time would take its toll, firstly on Catherine junior, who died in Cambridgeshire in June, and then on Catherine senior, who passed away two months later, aged 82. It is possible that grief at the loss of her daughter hastened her own demise.

Catherine died peacefully at Newton Hall amongst close family, who were at pains to ensure she was appropriately commemorated. There is a plaque in the church in Upton which reads simply 'In pious memory of Catherina Maria Humberston' – 'Catherina' perhaps being used to differentiate her from her daughter Catherine. This tribute was augmented in the 1870s with a fine stained-glass annunciation window created by the renowned Victorian exponent of this art, Charles Eamer Kemp. It is dedicated to Catherine and to her daughter-in-law, Elizabeth Henrietta Humberston, whose widower – Philip Stapleton – commissioned the work. A further tablet in St Mary's-on-the-Hill in Chester includes both Catherines on a more substantial Humberston family memorial. Philip senior features, as do three daughters who died in infancy and the four who reached maturity but pre-deceased their mother. The tablet was originally in the relocated St Bridget's Church, near Chester Castle. This was demolished in 1891 and its jurisdiction transferred to St-Mary's-on the-Hill.

Though more affluent and well-connected than most families of the age, the Humberstons were not atypical in terms of family size and exposure to infant mortality and premature death. The survivors met with some distinction. Only the men could excel professionally, and they did. Philip Stapleton built on his father's successful legal practice to the extent that he was able to step away to focus on public life. In addition to his parliamentary career, he served as JP and Deputy Lieutenant for Cheshire and Denbighshire and became an Honorary Colonel in the Cheshire Regiment. His son, Philip Hugh, seemed destined to follow a similar path until his life too was cut short when he collapsed and died suddenly in 1883, at the age of 44, whilst chasing a tram in City Road, Chester.[30]

The Humberston daughters were closely involved with church activities, in some cases marrying into the ministry, and were great subscribers to charitable causes. In Upton-by-Chester alone, they were generous benefactors towards the church – where several family graves are to be found in an intimate grouping – and they funded a new school building at Upton St Mary's, which opened in 1884. Philip Stapleton died in 1891, Anne in 1894 and Mary in 1906, the last of a generation of siblings which began before the 18th century had come to a close.

Two questions remain before we bid farewell to Mrs Humberston: firstly, is there any significance in the fact that her offering from Dr Norris was 'bound in Russia'? Nothing obvious is revealed by the biographical data. She had relatives involved in travel and conquest, heroically and disreputably, but not conspicuously in that part of the world, at least not in or before 1824. We should probably not try to look beyond the fact that Russian leather was regarded as one of the finest leathers in the world, due to an elaborate curing process, and was becoming even more distinguished as cheaper cloth-based bindings were introduced to cater for growing demand. It was a compliment to Catherine that she would have recognised and appreciated. The second question is why there were two volumes. One inference is that there was a second, undisclosed Humberston presence in the room – perhaps too young and immature to merit a full seat at the table.

Chapter Six

March

Business in Chester and the surrounding area was brisk at the start of March. We see Philip Humberston acting as the agent for a large timber sale at Norton, and for the enclosure of land at Congleton and the resulting sale of seven private plots. The innkeepers of Chester, supported by some landowners, were concerned about the impact of beer duties on their trade and had enlisted the support of Lord Grosvenor to petition the House of Lords for their repeal. The Town Clerk, Mr Finchett-Maddock, was advertising for a matron and a turnkey for live-in roles at the city gaol, the former to be a widow and the latter an unmarried man. Crime, great and petty, went on unabated, including more thefts of water pipes from buildings. Mr Jones of Brook Street reported just such a felony outside his own dwelling house.

Public health concerns abounded too. There were calls for Chester magistrates to follow the example of their counterparts in Liverpool in ordering all dogs found at large to be destroyed, as a safeguard against rabies. Cases of several children and a horse being bitten had been reported. Rewards were suggested for the delivery of a dead dog to a tanner. Smallpox was also endemic; here again, Liverpool led the way – 2,500 women and children had been vaccinated in 12 months under the auspices of a lying-in charity – and Chester was urged to follow suit.

The state of the road network to the west of Chester continued to be a focus of intensive lobbying. A meeting at the Town Hall on 16th March commended the improvement in the Shrewsbury line of road in 'perfecting the route from the Metropolis to Holyhead'. However, the commercial importance of the Chester line was considered paramount, given its location as the gateway from Ireland to the expanding cities in the north of England and the Midlands. Now there was a practical problem too: the departure time of the

Dublin Packet from Holyhead had been brought forward by two hours to coordinate with the London Mail via Shrewsbury, meaning that the Chester Mail would miss it.

The Mayors of Chester and Dublin were liaising on the need to remove defects on the roads on the Chester route and were appealing to mayors in other affected areas to exert pressure on the legislature to that end. At the Town Hall, the text of a petition was read, agreed upon and left open for eight days, during which time more than six hundred people signed it, including Philip Humberston. The resolutions, imploring the House of Commons to order preliminary surveys and estimates, were forwarded for publication in Irish and British regional newspapers. Dublin merchants added a rejoinder, asking for 'better-powered steam packets from England' (even though they were mostly from Wales) and proclaiming that the road near Conway was 'the most dangerous and hilly mail coach road in Great Britain'.

The Chester press joined in the chorus of appeals. Editorials pointed to the financial support granted by Parliament to the Shrewsbury line of road and insisted that Chester be looked upon in the same manner, not neglecting the need for a new bridge over the Dee. 'The landed proprietors and gentry of the Principality ... especially in the counties of Flint and Denbigh', many of whom included the *Courant* and *Chronicle* in their weekly diet of newsprint, were exhorted to 'institute public meetings in furtherance of the efforts which have now commenced, and give the whole weight of their influence to measures promising incalculable advantages to themselves and the public at large'.[1]

At the same time, correspondents were criticising construction work already underway. One letter complained about the slow progress being made on Thomas Telford's Conway Bridge, then partly completed, which, it suggested, was more reflective of a French work ethic than a British. The way in which this initiative was funded – by means of an increase in the cost of postage – was cited as a model for further road improvements in the area.

In the city centre, the walls were in urgent need of repair. Around 2pm on Sunday 28th March, a serious chasm resulted from the foundations suddenly giving way between the infirmary and the nearby Water Gate. A section of the wall amounting to ten square yards collapsed into the timber yard of Alderman Williamson. Mercifully, there were no injuries, despite it being a popular time for promenading.[2] This is just one example of the fragility of an age-old structure which Cestrians have cherished and preserved, by one means or another, throughout its long antiquity.

Having touched on transport links to Ireland, we should talk more about who the travellers were and what awaited them on arrival. Many were soldiers, reinforcing troops already stationed there. More dragoons were sent from Manchester to counter what were reported as 'daily atrocities and disturbances'. In the House of Commons, John Hobhouse, a Whig, tabled a motion proposing £9,000 be set aside for the educating of Catholics in Ireland and £90,000 for new barracks for the soldiers who kept them in subjection. His speech met with a chorus of approvals.[3]

There was an acceptance that Irish schools were under-funded, but there was a more fundamental flaw in that Catholics were being taught by people whose religious opinions were diametrically opposed to their own. Some politicians, such as Sir John Newport, another Whig, argued that total eradication of religious differences was the only way quell disquiet and get Ireland to pay its way. Poorer Catholics, mostly from rural areas, who had organised themselves into a clandestine movement known as the Ribbonmen, were at the forefront of resistance and clashed with Protestant factions from the British mainland.

The citizens of Chester were in expressive mood, particularly on issues which were seared into the collective consciousness, such as slavery. There was another meeting at the Exchange and another petition, on this occasion asking Parliament to better the conditions of 'negroes in the West Indies'. Various abuses were highlighted, including the treatment of enslaved people as chattels, the enforced separation of families, the practice of flogging enslaved women, and non-observance of the Sabbath. Indeterminate references to the 'ultimate' abolition of slavery and the need to have regard to the interests of West Indian proprietors had a diluting effect. The petition even thanked 'those benevolent West Indian proprietors who have made the temporal and spiritual welfare of the slaves the subject of their attention and care'. As we have seen, there were powerful vested interests within the local community.

By this time, news of Reverend Smith's death in Demerara, before the king was able to pronounce a final judgement in his case, had reached home shores and was widely regretted and condemned, including in the petition. However, it was mealy-mouthed on this issue too, referring to the 'intrigues of missionaries in Demerara' and a backlash against Methodists amongst the powerful elite in Barbados. The press even reported, without foundation, that Smith had been kept in good conditions and had been well looked after by his keeper.

The petition was ordered to lie at the Commercial Newsroom – Thomas Harrison's elegant structure at the foot of Northgate Street – for signature and, afterwards, for presentation to the House of Lords by Earl Grosvenor and the Bishop of Chester.[4] Cestrians were essentially endorsing Parliament's general position on the matter, rather than offering challenge or dissent. What did it hope to achieve, therefore? Many towns and cities – Shrewsbury was another in the same month – hosted meetings which opined on this topical and emotive issue. Chester would not have wished to be an outlier, mute and detached from a question of such intense public debate. The petition was a useful way keep political influence alive and exert soft power, even in support of the status quo.

Abolitionist sentiment was being aired in other spheres of life. The much-derided Window Tax, which had been in place since 1696, had achieved the desired effect of increasing tax revenues but it had also reduced the prevalence of windows, which people bricked up as a form of avoidance. It was discussed in the House of Commons, both as a recognition of public feeling and to explore how any resulting hole in the exchequer may be filled in the event of repeal. The debate was rhetorical: the legislation stayed in place until 1851.

There was a petition from Liverpool 'praying that bull and bear baiting, and other cruel sports, might be abolished'. These activities were supposed to have been curtailed by the Police Act of 1803, but they remained commonplace throughout the country, including in Chester.[5] In 1827, the German traveller, Prince Hermann Pückler-Muskau, attended a shady venue on the outskirts of London, where he witnessed and later reported on the exploits of 'the illustrious Billy', a terrier that had been trained to savage anything that lay in its path. On this occasion, in a ring surrounded by tiered seating thronged with spectators from all walks of life, Billy despatched a hundred rats in under ten minutes and then dealt with a badger in the same manner. Bear-baiting followed, in which other dogs were used. Cockfighting took place in the same arena, with bets of up to £50 being laid for a single encounter.[6] The Liverpool petition was unsuccessful, and decisive action would have to wait until the Cruelty to Animals Act of 1835.

Our readers, as well as keeping abreast of the newspapers, would have welcomed the arrival of popular publications in town. Messrs Poole and Harding were now stocking, *inter alia*, Ann Radcliffe's seminal gothic novel, *The Mysteries of Udolpho*; parts of Oliver Goldsmith's *Vicar of Wakefield* and his complete essays; and a new edition of Part IV of *Rasselas* by Dr Johnson. There was also a new compendium entitled *The Mirror of Literature and Amusement*, which included a map of Captain William Parry's discoveries around the Northwest passage and professed to be 'pregnant with instruction and amusement to all ranks, from the peer to the cottager'.

On the sporting front, further improvements were made at Chester Racecourse, including the upgrading of the grandstand and relocation of the distance chair. Large scale inter-county cockfights were reported at Shropshire and Warwickshire, but it was boxing that was coming under most scrutiny. At the Worcester Assizes a judge severely censured the magistrates for allowing the 'late brutal fight between Spring and Langan', observing that 'no expectation of pecuniary advantage could justify their conduct'. There may have been some cant in this, as nothing preventative was done. A famous pugilist who was punished at the assizes was John Carter of Oxford, who had sought to supplement his earnings in the ring by stealing a parcel from the Banbury Mail. He was captured and sentenced to transportation for seven years.

There were other snippets of news of possible interest to our book club members, including confirmation from Calcutta, six months after the event, that Bishop Heber had arrived. Theatregoers would have been alarmed to hear that Mrs Siddons, the greatest tragic actress of her day, was gravely ill and reportedly at the point of death. Though long retired and known to be in ill-health, she would live on for seven years.

Another great celebrity, Lord Byron, was in the news again. He had sold his manorial property in Rochdale to swell the coffers of the partisans in Greece. It was a noble gesture, which further endeared him to the people in that country.

Though infant mortality rates were high, as we have seen, there were instances of great longevity too. One such was the Scottish Highlander, Patrick Grant, who died peacefully and apparently quite suddenly in his 111th year. In his youth he had fought at Culloden and Falkirk, and was in the company of Bonnie Prince Charlie during his spirited venture south and when he embarked, vanquished, on his return journey to France.[7]

People news closer to home included actions against women who had refused to marry a suitor. In one case a William Collier obtained £50 from a 'faithless nymph' for a breach of promise of marriage.[8] Two Cambrian societies had recently been founded in Chester: one for the perpetuation of the Welsh language and one to support the children of destitute families in Wales. Some people sought to relieve their own poverty by plundering the wreck of the *Hornby* off the north Wales coast. They came in gangs of a hundred or more from up to sixty miles away and could only be deterred by the militia and the threat of severe punishment. At the other end of the social spectrum, new holiday properties were available at Hoylake and West Kirby, reflecting the increasing popularity of the west side of the Wirral, including and beyond Parkgate, amongst the leisured classes.

In early March the weather was adverse, with reports of a hurricane and lightning storms around Chester and the Wirral, and sub-zero temperatures as cold as they had been all winter. Ladies' 'Fashions for March', both morning dress and ball dress, were advertised in elegant and graphic detail, though perhaps they were not so well-adapted to the cold. Personal appearance was of great importance in the Regency period and was a powerful indicator of wealth and status.

Finally, the people of Chester, including those in whom we have a specific interest, would have been mindful of the following instruction – counterintuitive to our modern way of thinking – as they went about daily lives:

KEEP TO THE RIGHT: There is perhaps no subject of public inconvenience less attended to than that of the proper direction of foot passengers in passing each other on crowded streets. Few are ignorant that carts and horses, in the carriage road, must be on the near or left side of the way they are proceeding in; and as the driver of a cart must of necessity, when on the footway, be on that side of it which is nearest to his horses, being his right hand in the way he is going, this gives the law for the passengers, which is simply that everyone is to pass on that side of the footpath which is on his right hand in the way he is going and the left of the person he passes, moving either in the same or in the opposite direction. Attention to this simple rule will render the passage of the footways much more convenient than they now are; will avoid that pressure and jostling which is a continued interruption to those whose avocations require despatch; and prevent much annoyance to those who are little able to contend with an opposing force. An observance of this rule would remove much of the inconvenience often experienced in our rows, especially when they are crowded.[9]

Chapter Seven

George Johnson, Esq.
Lot 4

Johnson's Rasselas. *- A valuable edition, by mistake in common law binding. Letter'd*

Here we have the most common name we have yet come across, and probably in the whole Club, which could make identification difficult; but, first, let's deal with the offering. A work by Dr Johnson may simply have been logical as a namesake – we have already seen how Dr Norris played on names where he could – and the choice of *Rasselas* may have been prompted by topically, based on the knowledge that a new edition was available. The one in question, however, is valuable and lettered, suggesting he had an original in mind. A lettered volume is usually one of 26, aligned with the alphabet, and is therefore, by definition, rare.

The main theme of *Rasselas* – the pursuit of happiness and its illusory nature – may have had some relevance to George Johnson and his mindset, but we have no means of knowing that. The reference to the book being 'by mistake in common law binding' is a whimsical *mea culpa*, teasing the recipient and paying a backhanded compliment to Mrs Coupland, whose offering is in 'superior law binding'. It is also a useful pointer to the fact that George worked in the law.

There were indeed many Johnsons in the area around the time of our book club. It is worth first considering one or two of the more convincing 'pretenders'. George Fenwick in his *History of Chester* makes passing reference to a G Johnson, an honorary surgeon of the city in 1767, but this is too early and the profession doesn't fit.[1] In the 1780s, the landlord at The Elephant and Castle Inn in Northgate Street – one of two of that name in Chester at the time, the other being in Foregate Street – was called George Johnson.

This hostelry stood behind the Exchange and to the left of where the entrance to the market is today. The emblem of the Elephant and Castle had strong associations with Chester. It was the crest borne by the company of carvers in the city and a carved figure broadly in this shape features in a stall-end in the choir of the cathedral.[2] The cathedral carving, recognisable but dysmorphic, with an elongated head and horse's hooves, was the work of a 14th century craftsman who had never seen an elephant and was taking its appearance by report. Inaccuracies aside, it is a figure of the most exquisite artistry and charm.

The landlord could not have been our George Johnson because he was also too old to fit. The *Chester Courant* of 31st October 1780 talks about it being 14 years since 'a person of this city' – Mr Johnson of the Elephant and Castle – lost a favourite daughter, aged four, by sudden death; this was deemed newsworthy because a lock of her hair was said to have kept growing after the event.[3]

Two more George Johnsons who can be ruled out on account of their age are one whose seat was at Timperley Hall in east Cheshire in the 1780s and one who served as under-alderman in Chester in the 1790s. On the north wall of St Peter's Church in Chester is an elaborate marble mural monument, written in Latin and translated as: 'Here is buried George Henry, son of Joseph Johnson ... He lived 16 years, 10 months and 9 days, departed this life at the King's School, Shrewsbury 6.11.1818.' Joseph Johnson was a wine merchant and Sheriff of Chester in 1807; it is possible that our George – though clearly not the one commemorated at St Peter's – was related to him in some way. A Francis George Glynne Johnson was baptised at St Michael's, Chester in 1780. Perhaps he had a family connection with the Glynnes, elevating him as a candidate. However, on closer inspection, it seems he moved out of the city in his youth and was more prone to breaking the law than prosecuting it.

Another person of interest was John Johnson of Netherleigh House. Sheriff of Chester in 1792, he became mayor in 1815 and was knighted the following year. However, there was no obvious 'George' in his lineage, and for most of his life he was known as John Cotgreave, having succeeded to the estates and arms of his cousin, Thomas Cotgreave, in

1795. This John Johnson is not to be confused with 'a man of colour', as Hemingway describes him, who bore the same name and was publicly executed for burglary in Chester in 1819.[4]

The most telling clues to the identity of George Johnson, Chester Book Club member, are his profession and business associates. A document held at the Shropshire Archives contains a recital of a mortgage contract for a property in Ruabon near Wrexham, which was being sold due to the bankruptcy of one of several mortgagors. One of the solvent parties was Henry Potts of Chester. Witnesses to the recital in 1825 included Dorring Rasbotham, clerk to Messrs Potts and Johnson, solicitors, Chester, and George Johnson. George was in partnership with Henry Potts, and therefore scarcely an independent witness. However, the document tells us what we need to know.

This George Johnson's close connection with the Potts family ties him to the book club, of which 'Mrs Potts' was also a member. From 1823 onwards, there are numerous references in the local press to Messrs Potts and Johnson, solicitors, trading from premises in Northgate Street. Most of these relate to their agency in property transactions. They would have been in direct competition with Philip Humberston, but in a market that was comfortably able to sustain both firms.

The *Chester Courant* of 18th May 1824 carries this marriage notice: 'On 13th inst. at Lymm by the Rev M D Taylor, George Johnson, to Elizabeth, daughter of Robert Taylor, Esq of Lymm Hall, in this county.' Though by no means a trivial affair, the wedding was somewhat upstaged by another entry in the same edition headed 'MARRIAGE IN HIGH LIFE', referring to the union of Augusta Swinfen and the Reverend John Peel, son of Sir Robert Peel, then Home Secretary and later twice prime minister.

A valid question is why Mrs Coupland was allocated a copy of 'the Late Marriage Act' rather than George Johnson, whose wedding took place in the same year as our book club meeting. Perhaps the meeting took place in early 1824, when a wedding in December 1823 would have been more relevant than one the following May.

The presiding minister was the Reverend Mascie Domville Taylor – younger brother of Robert Taylor, George Johnson's new father-in-law. Reverend Taylor inherited Lymm Hall, east of Warrington, on Robert's death in 1835 and owned it until his death in 1845. This was a substantial six hundred acre estate that had been in the Domville family since the 14th century, although the hall dates from late Elizabethan times. Around the turn of the 17th century, ownership passed from William Domville to his nephew, William Mascie, and from him to his sister, Anne Taylor. From then on, their three surnames appear repeatedly in the family line, and sometimes coalesce in one individual, as was the case with the Reverend Mascie Domville Taylor. His rectorship was at Moreton Corbet in Shropshire, seat of Vincent Corbet's family. Mr Domville, who accompanied Vincent to Cheltenham in 1832, would have been related to the Lymm Hall dynasty.

We will return to the Domville-Mascie-Taylor connection, because of the way their story intersects with ours, but first let's consider George's family circumstances more directly.

In the 1851 census, George declares his birthplace as 'Wilmslow, Cheshire'. This helps us to ascertain that he was one of the children of the rector of that parish, the Reverend Croxton Johnson. Croxton was also born in Wilmslow, in his case in 1761, and, in 1788, he married Frances Houghton Peters in Liverpool. Croxton appears to have been an influential figure in the Manchester area, with interests extending beyond the church. In 1795, he was Vice President of the Manchester Agricultural Society, involved in the petitioning of Parliament in favour of 'an act of general enclosure for the cultivation and improvement of waste and unproductive land in the kingdom'.[5] Though perhaps well-intended, this was more bad news for the commoner.

Croxton was an innovator too. Twelve years later, the same society awarded him a silver cup, valued at seven guineas, for inventing a machine to sow wheat.[6] It is unclear whether Croxton's invention ever reached a mass market. He was already well-off, however, because of what his wife had brought to the marriage.

Frances's father – and therefore George's maternal grandfather – was known as 'Ralph Peters of Platt Bridge [near Wigan]'. This was to differentiate him from other men of the same name in the same family, one of whom was her brother, Ralph Peters of Southport. Historians looking through a broader lens, refer to them in chronological terms as Ralph Peters II and Ralph Peters III, as I shall now do.

Ralph Peters II married Elizabeth Entwistle, the sister of a man called Bertie Entwistle, whose wealth and influence would accrue to several generations of the Johnson and Peters families, especially after his death in 1803. The Peters family was not without some pedigree itself. Particular interest centres on an important artwork that they owned, entitled *View of Liverpool in 1680,* also known as 'the Peters painting'.[7] It is unclear who the artist was or how it found its way into the Peters family, but we know that it was presented to Liverpool Town Council in 1818 by Ralph Peters III and that it was in his father's possession in 1766, when John Eyes produced an engraving based upon it. It is now a priceless exhibit at Merseyside Maritime Museum and almost certainly the oldest surviving image of the city's waterfront.

It is reasonable to assume that the painting was owned and perhaps even acquired by Ralph Peters I. He was the grandfather of Ralph Peters II and George's two times great-grandfather. He served as Liverpool Town Clerk from 1702 until his death in 1742, living initially in Castle Street and later John Street, as well as maintaining a family home in Platt Bridge, or 'Platbridge' as it was then called. He was a subscriber to Liverpool Blue Coat Hospital in 1709 and, three decades later, a trustee.

It is in Liverpool in the late seventeenth and early eighteenth centuries that the stories of the Peters and Entwistle families begin to intertwine. John Entwistle, of Foxholes in Lancashire, is a key figure. Born in 1633, he was involved in civic office for most of his adult life, including occupying the post of Recorder in Liverpool from 1662 until old age precluded it in 1709. One of his early duties was to proclaim Charles II as king from the market cross in Ormskirk.

John's second son, Bertin, followed him into the Recorder role, serving in it until 1722. He is not to be confused with several Bertie Entwistles, who mostly came later, though there may have been some confusion within the family itself. The name they were keen to recall was 'Bertine'. Their illustrious ancestor, Sir Bertine Entwistle, had been amongst the happy few who fought for Henry V at the Battle of Agincourt, ultimately dying at the Battle of St Albans in 1455 under his successor, Henry VI.

Bertin's son was another John Entwistle, who departed from family tradition by becoming a merchant and seafarer, operating out of Liverpool in the early to mid-18th century. This was George's great-grandfather on his maternal grandmother's side. We know that this John was particularly close to the Peters family because he was a trustee of the Blue Coat Hospital at the same time as Ralph Peters I and was a witness to his will.

Almost inevitably, a Liverpudlian dignitary associated with oceangoing activities in this period was involved in the slave trade. Our source material – *An Account of the Oil Painting 'Liverpool in 1680'*, written by R Stewart-Brown in 1909 – for all its wealth of data, merely informs us that John Entwistle was party to 'the lucrative trade to and from the West Indies'.[8] There is no mention of the brutal and exploitative way in which such returns were made possible.

Onshore in Liverpool, John was a partner in several businesses, including a sugar house, a brewery and a fledgling whaling enterprise. In addition to commercial premises, he owned residential properties in central Liverpool, amongst which were two large gardens and a summer house fronting onto Water Street.

Before returning to two of John Entwistle's children – Bertie and Elizabeth, born in the early 1730s – another sibling, Richard, merits mention. He is recorded as having part-owned and captained slave ships in the 1760s, taking the triangular route to West Africa and the West Indies – in his case Jamaica and Guadaloupe – before returning to port in Liverpool. He was in partnership with the notorious slave trader, John Tarleton, and their ships bore the cynically misleading names 'Friendship' and 'Hope'.

It was against this background that Bertie, John Entwistle's eldest son, entered 'the family business'. He moved it to another level entirely by becoming a major owner-operator of slave plantations across the West Indies, primarily in Antigua, St Vincent and Dominica. He was joined in Antigua, his main place of abode, by his brother, William.

In 1766, Bertie, in his early 30s, was paying tax on 40 enslaved people in St John's on the island, though he hadn't yet acquired any land there. This would soon change, however, and he would continue to accumulate human chattels. In 1780 he paid tax to St John's Church, Antigua – where he and William each owned a pew – on 74 enslaved people and 533 acres of land. By 1788, he had added a further 708 acres of land to his estate, this time at Jolly Hill, just south of St John's.[9] Barnacle Point on Antigua and plantations on St Vincent and Dominica were further additions to his holdings.

About the time Bertie was first making his mark in the West Indies, the Entwistle and Peters families converged directly, through the marriage of his sister, Elizabeth, to Ralph Peters II. These were George Johnson's grandparents on his mother's side. A year later, in 1766, their union was blessed with the birth of his mother. It seems that Frances Houghton Peters grew to become a famous Lancashire beauty, immortalised in the 1782 poem 'Preston Guild' by the Reverend Thomas Wilson.

> All the world is at Preston Guild, the multitude spreads,
> So thick through each street 'tis a pavement of heads …
> But who's the first toast and the favourite belle,
> Must a secret remain, for no mortal can tell.
> All agree in the praise of the delicate features,
> The person, and manners, and airs of Miss Peters.[10]

Mentioned in the same poem is Nic Grimshaw who, as well as being Preston-based bailiff, handled the financial affairs of the Couplands in the late 18th century, as we saw in Chapter Two.

When the Reverend Croxton Johnson married Frances in 1788, he would have considered himself a lucky man: not only was she a society beauty, but she had resources too. By this time, her Uncle Bertie was ageing and heirless with very considerable assets. Properties he owned in Liverpool, which had already been placed in trust for Frances's benefit, were converted to a life interest for the married couple and would remain in the family after their death. The sum of £1000 was also paid over to them.[11] When Bertie died in April 1803, after a short illness, the Johnsons – now with young children, including six-year-old George – would be further enriched.

Bertie's will, drafted on 16th April 1802 and proved on 23rd July 1803, runs to 25 pages.[12] Written in an ornate and stylised script, it is almost completely bereft of punctuation, which was common legal practice to avoid clauses and sub-clauses being open to prejudicial misinterpretation by the courts. Enough can be deciphered, however, to reveal an accumulation of assets and divestments. There are some intricate and prescriptive arrangements for maintaining the portfolio and establishing a family legacy. George Johnson is mentioned frequently within the will, though as a contingent legatee in the event others predeceasing him.

The first references are to Bertie's ownership of properties in England. He is described as 'late of the island of Antigua but now Tavistock Street in the parish of St Paul, Covent Garden' in London. He has other houses in Irby and Arrow on the Wirral and is mortgagor on 'certain houses, shops and other buildings and hereditaments in the City of Chester'. It is not clear where the Chester properties were, but they were previously owned by a man called George Ball, whose family had connections with Boughton. Servicing a mortgage on such a portfolio would have been one way of converting a regular and substantial income stream from the West Indies into valuable assets back home. Here we see hard evidence of the proceeds of slavery being invested in Chester.

Bertie's English-based properties are placed in the trust of Samuel Martin of Marylebone and Thomas Jarvis of Winchester, both late of Antigua. They are used to fund annuities to Ellen Entwistle – one of his unmarried sisters – and three other ladies, with whom his relationship is unknown: Mary Hunter of Limehouse, widow; Elizabeth Williamson of Wavertree; and Ann Summers of Liverpool.

The first member of the Johnson family mentioned in the will is Bertie Entwistle Johnson, the second son and the testator's godson, who was then eight years old. His education and maintenance are amply provided for, and he stands to inherit the properties and related annuities in Irby at the age of 21. Should he die before that, the fourth son – Henry Entwistle Johnson – is next in the ranking, followed by a daughter, Clara Entwistle. The eldest sibling, Croxton, and the third son, George, bring up the rear. Henry is first in line for the Arrow properties and annuities, followed by Bertie, Clara, George and Croxton junior. It is as if Bertie Entwistle is favouring the children whose names most closely resemble his.

Croxton senior was already involved in the day-to-day running of the Entwistle empire, as he directed the management of the properties in Irby and Arrow and received rents and profits from them on Bertie's behalf. In the will, he is charged with the same responsibility *vis a vis* the Chester properties and is awarded five per cent of any receipts from Irby and Arrow. He appears to have been undeterred by any considerations of morality, taking comfort perhaps in the broader involvement of the Anglican Church in the business of slavery.

The status of the Chester properties at the time the will was drafted is indeterminate. They were still mortgaged and there seems to have been some dispute over title. George Ball had died insolvent with creditors at the door. Assuming resolution of the dispute and discharge of the mortgages, Clara would be first in line to inherit, followed by the four Johnson sons, in the same order as Irby. In the event of title not passing, the will stipulates that £1,200 should be laid out for the purchase of other properties in Chester for the Johnson children. It is not clear why Bertie was so keen to have a property portfolio and family presence in Chester, except that it was a popular and fashionable place to live. However, there was an ancestral connection with the city too, as we will soon discover.

Now comes the sting in the tail: 'Whoever becomes entitled to the property in Irby, Arrow and Chester shall henceforth take and use the surname "Entwistle".' On the face of it, this looks narcissistic. Bertie would have viewed himself as a hugely successful businessman and may have been reluctant to pass on his gains without preserving something of himself in posterity, if only vicariously in a family name. His favouring of Bertie Entwistle Johnson makes sense in this context. This was not an uncommon practice at the time: a name could confer status in a rigidly hierarchical society, and possibly even a coat of arms, which had privileges attached to it, such as the right to vote and trade. Bertie's will, contrived and lop-sided as it was, could have given rise to envy, and perhaps even enmity, amongst the Johnson brood. George stood to gain less than most.

To maintain his plantations across the Atlantic, Bertie appoints two additional trustees, the Antigua-based John Burke and Daniel Hill the Elder. It would be their job to manage the estates for 20 years 'in such a manner as shall be most conducive to the advantage of persons interested therein or intitled thereto'. Those persons – granted 'a moiety', or half, each – are two more nephews: Entwistle (that name again) Hague and Ralph Peters III, sons of Bertie's sisters, Dorothy and Elizabeth respectively. As well as the net proceeds, rents, issues and profits from the plantations, Entwistle and Ralph are awarded a half-yearly allowance of £100 each. Both men were in their late twenties at the time. Bertie even goes so far as stipulate the agents to be used for the importation of sugar and rum into Britain: Blacke and Kemble of London and Ewart Rutson & Co of Liverpool. A partner in the latter firm was William Ewart, a close associate of John Gladstone, who named his famous son after him. Entwistle Hague's moiety in the West Indies would crystallise after 20 years and be conveyed to him, lock, stock and barrel.

Ralph Peters III had more to consider. Bertie describes him in the will as 'bred to law', and consequently sets an expectation that he will go to Antigua, as soon as he qualifies as a barrister, to practise there. He is required to attend to and look after the Antiguan estates and, once a year, travel to and 'see to the proper running of' the plantations on St Vincent and Dominica. Perhaps sensing that there may be some reluctance to do this, Bertie offers a financial incentive of £800 a year plus expenses, reducing to £300 if Ralph neglects St Vincent and Dominica.

Minor legacies in the will are granted to other godsons born in the West Indies, including the sons of two of his trustees, Samuel Martin and Thomas Jarvis. Frances Johnson, George's mother, receives a further £500, the reference to which is accompanied by a reminder of the marriage settlement and the more recent transfer of a share in tenements at Chorley Street, Liverpool. These had previously been owned by Bertie's brother, William, who had died in 1798. Chorley Street was laid out on the former site of John Entwistle's property near Water Street and was almost certainly named after his mother, whose maiden name was Chorley.[13] It is probable that these tenements were also bought with the proceeds of slavery.

Almost the last entries in the will relate to individual members of the enslaved population:

- to William son of Mary Richardson a mulatto woman of Antigua a £40 annuity
- to Frances a mulatto daughter of Cathy a negro woman belonging to my late wife and Cherry a negro woman also belonging to my late wife a £40 annuity
- to my negro manservant Arno a £20 annuity
- I hereby liberate and make free the said Frances Cherry and Arno

We might speculate on why some have been singled for special treatment in this way. More telling is the fact that most of those enslaved by him – by now running into many hundreds – get no mention at all. For them, the continuity that he seeks to achieve in his will represents an ongoing tragedy, personally and collectively.

Ralph Peters III appears to have embraced his legacy. Having practised as an attorney in Britain for a mere three years, he gave it up shortly after Bertie's death. He sold his property in Platt Bridge and bought a more palatial one in Southport, soon disappearing from the local directories until 1834, the year after the Slavery Abolition Act was passed, when compensation was on the agenda for slave owners.[14] This implies that he was in the West Indies, as per his uncle's wishes, although the plantations were still being accounted for in Bertie's name by his trustees. One example is a slave return for September 1817 which identifies 464 slaves on the Antiguan estates, with ages ranging from three months to eighty years. It is signed with the mark of John Burke, which suggests he was illiterate, despite his huge business responsibilities and the volume of assets under his control.[15] Between November 1835 and February 1836, Ralph Peters III claimed a total of £7,076 for 518 slaves on the estates in Antigua and St Vincent, no mention being made of Dominica.[16] In modern day terms, this equates to more than £1.2 million.

Ralph Peters III did not live long after that. He died in 1838, leaving behind three sons – George's cousins – and around £30,000. When these three sons passed away in the final quarter of the 19th century, they left estates valued at between £61,000 and £172,000 – completely out of proportion with anything they had achieved in their lifetimes. Indeed, one of them – Ralph Peters IV – appears to have been certified a 'lunatic', dying at Southall Park, a private asylum in west London in 1879. The other two, William Henry and the Reverend Thomas – for who whom Ralph Peters III had bought the advowson at Eastington in Gloucestershire – left substantial properties in Exeter and Bath: a demonstration, if needed, of how money begets money and how the proceeds of slavery cascade down the generations.[17]

Entwistle Hague was similarly enriched and aggrandised. He is associated with Parkfield Hall, Hayfield, a stately home of the early 19th century to the east of Manchester. A story appears to have been put about that his father was a self-made millionaire who started out in business hawking articles from a basket around the local area.[18] Quite how he made such a startling transition is not stated. More likely – though more prosaic – is that the hall was built, or at the very least acquired, out of Uncle Bertie's legacy and that the true source of the funds was suppressed to prevent Entwistle from being stigmatised by it.

He doesn't feature in slavery compensation claims because he died ten years beforehand, in dramatic circumstances. It appears that the Luddite movement was particularly strong around Hayfield, and Entwistle's manor, amongst others, was targeted. So alarmed was he about the prospect of attack that he built a dungeon at the hall in which to hold any captives. As a member of the local gentry, he continued to be vilified by disaffected textile workers and was eventually forced to flee his home. Whilst making his way to his town house in King Street, Manchester, he was attacked by rioters and flung them his purse, containing five hundred guineas, as a decoy. His hope that avarice would blind them to their principles paid off and he escaped. However, he was so shaken by the experience that he died in Manchester shortly afterwards, at the age of 53.[19]

Brief mentions should be made of members of the Peters and Entwistle families who distinguished themselves in more wholesome ways, on either side of the Atlantic. Two sons of Ralph Peters I – the Reverend Richard and William – emigrated to Pennsylvania in 1735. The catalyst for this, in which Richard may or may not have been culpable, was a bigamy scandal. Having married a servant in Westminster, he later proclaimed her dead and married a second time, only for his first wife to soon present herself, very much alive and well. This was no barrier to Richard's progress in America, where he quickly ingratiated himself with the Penn family and became highly active in religious, civic and educational affairs. He served on the Pennsylvania Governors' Council from 1735 to 1775 and collaborated with Benjamin Franklin on the foundation of the College of Philadelphia, which would later become the University of Pennsylvania.[20]

William Peters – who was George Johnson's two times great-grandfather – also numbered Franklin amongst his social circle, alongside George Washington and James Madison. He built the stately Belmont Mansion in Philadelphia, which still exists today and is widely known and visited. William's son, another Richard, was a lawyer and, at the time of the Revolution, a captain in the Continental Army, led by Washington. In 1779, in the thick of conflict, he gave Washington a draft design for the Continental flag, which was a precursor to the Stars and Stripes. Richard went on to become Speaker in the Pennsylvania House of Representatives and Senate in the late 1780s and early 1790s.

Edmund Entwistle, born in 1660 and third son of John Entwistle of Foxholes, made his mark somewhat closer to home. He entered the clergy and rose to the rank of Archdeacon of Chester, a post he held from 1695 until his death in 1707. According to Ormerod, he was an early patron, if not founder, of the charity for the relief of clergymen's widows and orphans within the Archdeaconry of Chester.[21] In this, he followed the charitable lead of his bishop, Nicholas Stratford, who founded the Blue Coat School in the cathedral grounds in 1700, before its move to purpose-built premises by the North Gate 17 years later. Together they were instrumental in establishing a lending library at 'Namptwich', which was very much ahead of its time. Edmund married the bishop's daughter, Grace, by whom he had two daughters. After Grace died, he married Priscilla, the daughter of Thomas Bunbury, 1st Baronet of Stanney, by whom he had two sons. The bishop and archdeacon were staunchly Anglican. In 1696, they signed an oath of allegiance to King William III, swearing to take revenge on his enemies – 'papists' and adherents to the former King James II – were he to be killed.

Bishop Stratford's Deputy Registrar, Henry Prescott, kept an illuminating diary at this time. When the bishop died suddenly from apoplexy in February 1707, Henry walked four laps of the Roodee, on which Chester Racecourse stands, to digest the news. When Edmund Entwistle died six months later, Henry found his consolation in the company of Edmund's brothers, who were lodging at the White Lion, Chester. On the following day, they took 'a turn on the walls', before drowning their sorrows. After the funeral at the cathedral, the widow, Priscilla, raised an altruistic objection. She wished the body of Edmund's first wife to be brought to his grave to be by him. Two weeks later, after receiving the necessary approvals, Grace's coffin was removed and relocated in line with Priscilla's request.[22]

The bishop and archdeacon are commemorated conspicuously on tablets on the south wall of the nave of Chester Cathedral, close to the great west door. Their inscriptions, both in Latin, provide biographical data and enlarge upon their selfless charitable work amongst the poor and needy. The bishop is commended for his vigorous defence of the Reformed faith against the Church of Rome. Edmund's memorial is the marginally smaller of the two, but no less ornate. A crest beneath combines motifs from the Entwistle, Stratford and Bunbury coats of arms, and there is a bust above which can only be a representation of the man himself: a handsome, moustachioed fellow, wearing a hat at a jaunty angle, with his improbably long outstretched left arm securing it on his head. Such an image must have had profound meaning to the commissioner – almost certainly Priscilla – but eludes our understanding, over three centuries later.

With such strong ancestral connections with Chester, the Wirral and Liverpool, perhaps it is natural that the Johnson family gravitated from east to west Cheshire after Bertie Entwistle's death. Croxton senior even bought his own estate at Irby and was soon mixing in exalted Cheshire circles.[23] In 1803, for example, he collaborated with the heads of the Warburton, Stanley, Cholmondeley, Legh and Leycester families on an address to the king to express their relief at his surviving an assassination attempt, which became known as the Despard Plot.[24]

Croxton senior died at little over ten years later, at the age of 54, when George was 18. The family had retained a home in Knutsford. George's sister, Elizabeth, married there in 1817 and, shortly afterwards, his mother put it up for sale. Elizabeth's husband was the Reverend George Shiffner of Combe Place, Sussex – the son of an MP and heir to his father's baronetcy. Croxton junior, George's eldest brother, remained a confirmed bachelor until his early forties and was accustomed to mixing in high society. In 1815, in his mid-twenties, he held the prestigious position of steward at Manchester Races and, in 1824, he was listed in the *Morning Post* as one of the fashionable arrivals at Marshall Thompson's Hotel in Cavendish Square, London.

In 1819, Bertie Entwistle Johnson was ordained a priest by the Bishop of Chester at a grand ceremony at St James's Church in the capital. By this time, he had come into his inheritance and, by rights, should have been Bertie Entwistle Entwistle. A name change – and a tautologous one at that – may have raised some awkward questions. People were starting to distance themselves from all things slavery related, especially within the clergy.

139

In 1827, Bertie married Isobel Legh of Lyme Park, from of one of the oldest landed families in Cheshire.

George Johnson, less preferred than some of his siblings by his great-uncle Bertie, worked his way into the legal profession and began to establish a reputation. He and Elizabeth started a family not long after their marriage: Robert George arrived in 1825, Frances Jane in 1827 and Isabel Eleanor in 1829. Frances's birth was registered at Holy Trinity in Chester on 10th October 1827. This shows that the family was becoming more rooted in Chester, though we know that George was in the city for a few years prior to that, including attending the book club in 1824. Also in that year, he was noted as a 'fashionable arrival' at Parkgate, in the company of members of the Potts family and Mr Boydell.[25] This is presumed to have been Mr James Boydell, son of Josiah, the engraver.

The *Directory of Cheshire* for 1828, listing nobility, gentry and clergy, has 'Potts and Johnson' at Northgate Street, though it erroneously describes them as 'chymists'. This is the same Chester thoroughfare in which Philip Stapleton Humberston would soon locate his solicitor's practice. In his 1831 history, Hemingway lists tenants on the main streets who were exempt from the duty of serving on open juries, amongst whom were Messrs Potts and Johnson, on account of their professional involvement in the legal process.[26] Also in 1831, George's father-in-law, Robert Taylor, was appointed Sheriff of Cheshire and was combining with other landowners to resist the growing spirit of reform which threatened their interests. One of his collaborators in this was Rowland Egerton-Warburton of Arley Hall, who was related to Anne Coupland, as we have seen. Robert died in 1835, aged 62, leaving all his possessions to his widow, Jane, in a crisp, businesslike will. Soon afterwards Potts and Johnson would be advertising Lymm Hall for let.

Four of George's siblings – Croxton junior, Frances, Eleanor and Edward – married in the early 1830s. Eleanor's marriage in 1830, at Burton on the Wirral, is the most relevant to us, because her husband was Richard Corbet, elder brother of Vincent Roger Corbet, who would marry Maria Humberston four years later. Eleanor's was another grand society

The remaining portions of this Document shall be given in a week or two. Meanwhile, it will be seen, on reference to the HOLME Pedigree in Ormerod's *History of Cheshire*, 1st ed., vol. ii., p. 253, that what I already print qualifies some of the statements in that interesting family tree.

T. HUGHES.

Notes.

[1096]   THE CHESTER BOOK CLUB, 1824.

THE CHESTER BOOK CLUB consisted of twelve members, who, after circulating the books, sold them by auction, at an evening party, at one of their houses in turn, Du. NORRIS usually being the Auctioneer: it was he also who drew up the following playful catalogue, descriptive of the members of the Club. He had apparently just issued a List of the Books then in circulation, and the one now printed he calls a

"SUPPLEMENTARY CATALOGUE, 1824.

Lot 1.

A brief sketch of Mr. Owen's *New Settlement*, with notes, and an abridged extract of the late Marriage Act, neatly bound together in superior law binding...................................[Mrs. Coupland.]

Lot 2.

Tales of the Castle, the best edition, embellished with a fine view of Hawarden, Flintshire; a single volume, neatly bound ....[Mrs. Glynne.]

Lot 3.

Contributions to Natural History, containing some very fine specimens of the Cotton plant, and an interesting sketch illustrative of the mineralogy of the banks of the river Humber; 2 vols., bound in Russia ....[Mrs. Humberston.]

Lot 4.

Johnson's Rasselas.—A valuable edition, by mistake in common law binding. Letter'd............
[George Johnson, Esq.]

Lot 5.

The Art of Social Life, imperial quarto, splendidly bound in Russia, gilt extra; a fine copy, in the highest preservation, and worthy a place in the best collection ....[Mrs. Mainwaring.]

Lot 6.

The Guide to Domestic Happiness, 2 vols., beautifully bound in purple Morocco. Scarce; only 18 copies extant, exclusive of this .....[Mrs. Massie.]

Lot 7.

Flora Britannica, 2 vols., 8vo, richly bound in green Morocco, gilt extra; the 2nd vol. embellished with a highly finished drawing of that beautiful plant Magnolia-Hibernica, faithfully copied from nature ....[Mrs. Nicholls.]

Lot 8.

The Sisters, a popular tale of Lepanto, but translated from the Welsh; 2 vols., crown 8vo, handsomely bound in red, gilt, and letter'd ...
[Mrs. Panton.]

Lot 9.

Caleb in Search of a Wife, a new edition, corrected after the manner of Bowdler's Shakespeare, the objectionable passages omitted, the good only retained. 1 vol., curiously printed in black letter..
[Rev. Geo. Pearson.]

Lot 10.

The Comforts of Human Life, a fine folio edition, particularly well bound, and in excellent preservation ....[Mrs. Potts.]

Lot 11.

Illustrations of Country History, 2 vols., embellished with 2 two fine portraits; handsomely bound in blue Morocco. Very choice copies................
[The Misses Townshend.]

Lot 12.

The Balance of Comfort, a new edition, interspersed with original poetry; a handsome copy in high preservation, embellished with an expressive title page ....[Miss Venables.]"

The names given within brackets are supplied from a list left in MS. by Dr. Norris on the copy from which I transcribe this for THE SHEAF.

Newton.   H.

[1097]   THINGS I REMEMBER.

No. 12.

A CHESHIRE COUNTY ELECTION.

Perhaps some of the readers of "THE SHEAF" may like to know something about the way in which County Elections were conducted about 60 years ago in CHESTER. I well remember one of these taking place about that time in the Shire Hall, as it was called, at Chester Castle. The High Sheriff of the county, the returning officer, stood in the place usually occupied by the judge; on his right stood the late Mr. WILBRAHAM EGERTON, of Tatton Park, and on his left Mr. EDWARD DAVIES DAVENPORT, of Capesthorne, the late Members for the whole County. After the legal and customary formalities had been gone through, and a crowded audience had settled down into something like order; the two candidates were severally proposed and seconded by their friends, in brief complimentary terms, with scarce a word in reference to the politics of the day. For a moment there was a buzz of expectation, while the High Sheriff asked if anyone else had a proposition to make.

A very curious incident then occurred, that is indelibly fixed on my memory. An elderly gentleman, Mr. W. Folliott, well known in the city for his eccentricity, standing near me, made sundry demonstrations of impatience, and, looking round him, asked would no one propose another candidate? Finding no answer to his query, he said aloud, drawing himself up in stately form, "If no one will propose a member, I will propose myself!" Of course there was a great laugh at the proposal, which enlivened an otherwise rather dull programme.

The extract from *The Cheshire Sheaf* upon which this book is based

Anne Warburton Owen
(née Coupland), by James
Sant, c1850
Reproduced with the kind per-
mission of The National Li-
brary of Wales

Glansevern, Montgomeryshire – home of Anne Warburton Owen

St John's house (rear) – home of Elizabeth Sloughter

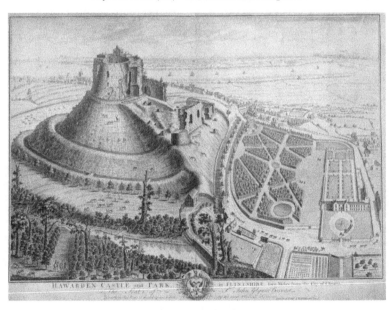

Hawarden Castle and Park in Flintshire by W H Toms (c1740) – childhood home of Anne Glynne

Anne Glynne's house in Nicholas Street, Chester   Anne Glynne memorial, St Deiniol's Church, Hawarden

The Friars, Chester – home of the Humberstons – and the spire of the former Holy Trinity Church

George Edward Lynch Cotton (1813-1866), Mrs Humberston's nephew

Edmund Entwistle memorial, Chester Cathedral

View of Liverpool in 1680 – 'The Peters' painting'

Llanrhydd Hall, Ruthin – George Johnson's home

Mainwaring House in Watergate Street by John Romney (1785-1863)

Oteley Hall, built by Charles Kynaston Mainwaring, demolished 1959. Credit *www.lostheritage.org.uk*.

Mainwaring family memorial,
Welshampton Church

Lord Byron on his Death Bed by Robert Seymour

Mrs Hester Lee Massie

The Reverend Richard Massie

Massie portraits reproduced with the kind permission of Julian Armitstead

wedding, with the newlyweds' arrival at the Corbet family seat in Shropshire being greeted with cannon fire, the ringing of bells and a decorated ceremonial arch for them to pass through. There was much generosity towards the local poor and a huge family celebration that encompassed the Corbets, Johnsons, Domville Taylors, friends and tenants. One report describes wedding music, dancing and an elegant supper for nearly two hundred people, concluding poetically:

The votaries of terpsichore soon returned to the ballroom, but many gentlemen remained, who preferred indulging in the more substantial pleasures of the bottle. Time was not thought of, and it was only on the several parties returning home from this scene of festivity and delight, that they were convinced, by the ploughman whistling at his work, that they had trespassed largely on the succeeding day.[27]

These families were tight knit, genetically as well as socially. A further indication lies in the fact that Richard and Vincent Corbet's mother was Mary Taylor, who was the sister of Robert Taylor of Lymm Hall. As Lady Corbet, she and her husband, Sir Andrew, enabled and presided over the wedding celebrations, which rippled through the local community in much the same way as Sir Stephen Glynne's coming of age.

Sir Andrew Corbet, in drafting his will in 1831, mentions his ancestral seat in Shropshire but identifies his dwelling as being on the west side of Nicholas Street in Chester, a property he purchased from Henry Potts, George Johnson's business partner. He and his wife were therefore near neighbours of Anne Glynne, Elizabeth Sloughter and Catherine Humberston. His wife is the main beneficiary, followed by Vincent, whose blindness may have made him more dependent and deserving of support than other close family members. Sir Andrew also leaves her the residue of the estate bequeathed to her under the will of her late uncle, Mascie Taylor of Chester: a reminder of the tenuous nature of a married woman's right to property at this time. Eleanor Corbet, née Johnson, is recognised with a legacy of £50. The will was proved by Sir Andrew's widow following his death in 1835.[28] Vincent is listed in the 1837 *City of Chester Poll Book* as living at the Nicholas Street address.

In 1834, Frances Johnson – George's eldest sister - married the Reverend John Bingham of Great Gaddesden in Hertfordshire. His brother, Arthur Bingham, who had drowned off Ecuador four years earlier, was a captain in the Royal Navy. Arthur had commanded a ship called *Little Belt*, which was involved in a hostile encounter off the coast of Virginia with *USS President* in the lead up to the outbreak of war between America and Great Britain in 1812. It was unclear which ship had fired first, but *Little Belt*, by far the smaller of the two, took the greater losses, amounting to nine killed and 27 injured. Bingham was exonerated by the Admiralty and rewarded with a promotion, despite his role in what would become known infamously as 'The Little Belt Affair'.

The death of George's mother-in-law, Jane, at the end of the decade was transformative for him and his family. She was co-heiress to a number of properties in Denbighshire – courtesy of her late father, the Reverend John Foulkes – which George's wife then inherited. There were unspecified financial assets too, apart from £8,000 which was to be held in trust for George and Elizabeth's children; half earmarked for Robert George and a quarter each for Frances and Isabel. The trustee was none other than the Reverend Bertie Entwistle Johnson, then of Lymm, who must have stayed close to George and Elizabeth and ingratiated himself with the Taylor family.

George was the sole executor of the will, which he proved in London a month after Jane's death in August 1839.[29] The *Chester Chronicle* dated the 23rd of that month informs us that she died in Stanley Street, Chester – not far from where some book club members lived, but, more importantly, close to her daughter and son-in-law. In her will, George is described as 'of Eccleston'; however, his practice was a stone's throw from Stanley Street, and this address may have been a residential option for him and his wife, especially during Jane's widowhood and declining years.

George and Elizabeth had a home in Eccleston because George had been appointed principal land agent to Robert Grosvenor, 1st Marquess of Westminster. They are likely to have been living at one of the Marquess's grace and favour properties in the village. George's new role represented a significant achievement on his part, as well as illustrating the circles in which he moved and the esteem in which he was held. Elizabeth's inheritance from her mother included a fine country estate called Llanrhydd Hall, near Ruthin, which the Johnsons soon chose to occupy, for part of the time at least. It would stay in the family until the middle of the 20th century.

George's capacity for work and willingness to take on additional responsibility is impressive. The size of the Grosvenor estate runs to approximately 140,000 acres, including three hundred acres of the most valuable land in the world in London's Mayfair and Belgravia districts. These holdings were in the family long before George took up his position with them.[30] In November 1845, alongside this role, George became Clerk of the Peace for Cheshire upon the death of his former business partner, Henry Potts. The appointment was in the gift of the Lord Lieutenant of the County, none other than the Marquess of Westminster.[31] George continued to serve in this capacity well into the 1850s.

It was the 2nd Marquess of Westminster who conferred the clerkship upon George, as his father had died earlier that year. The funeral, which took place on Tuesday 25th March 1845, was grand and grave. Condolences were received from Buckingham Palace, and the people of Chester were given the opportunity to view the coffin at the premises of Mr Gardiner, cabinet maker in the city, on the Saturday before. On the morning of the funeral, shops closed, bells tolled and union jacks were set at half-mast. People made their way in droves to Eccleston, where the funeral took place. The hearse and four mourning coaches – undecorated at the deceased's request – were supplied by Mr Nickson of the Royal Hotel. George joined a select group of invitees who breakfasted at Eaton Hall. He then travelled in the funeral cortege in the second of the mourning hearses, the first being occupied by close family members. He was also part of the procession into Eccleston Church, where the service was conducted by the Reverend George Becher Blomfield, by then Canon of Chester Cathedral, having graduated from the rectorship of Hawarden. In the early afternoon, the family and mourning party returned to the hall, the crowd dispersed and business as usual resumed in the city. The funeral maintained a tradition stretching back four centuries – and now six – in which Eccleston Church has been the last resting place of members of the Grosvenor family.[32]

Through the 1850s there is evidence of the Johnsons dividing their time between Eccleston and Llanhrydd. George was a member of the Eccleston Association for the Prosecution of Felons, alongside the Marquess and others. This was a standard approach to keeping the peace in more rural areas, where a police presence was limited or non-existent. A sliding scale of rewards was offered for the apprehension and conviction of offenders, with the value of the reward differing according to the severity of the offence. Damage to property and theft were targeted in the main, horses being particularly prized. There was even wording to the effect that 'members of this Association are engaged to each other to set out on horseback, on the shortest notice, in parties of 12, [on] different routes, in pursuit of any stolen horse to the distance of at least 50 miles', which approximates to the maximum distance a single horse can ride without rest.[33] There is no record of the frequency with which such pursuits took place.

At Ruthin, the family became involved in the local community in various worthy and charitable ways, including Robert George Johnson serving on the district Board of Guardians of the Poor. In the summer of 1857, a Grand Fancy Bazaar was held in the grounds of Ruthin Castle, in aid of the restoration of the local church. Amongst the patrons were Mrs Johnson of Llanrhydd and Mrs Humberston of Newton Hall. It seems the two families had remained in close contact since the days of the book club, a third of a century earlier. In 1858, Isabel married Edward Davies, the local curate at Llanrhydd, and a year later their first son was born, whom they christened George.

By the late 1850s, perhaps through George's work and contacts at Eaton Hall, the Johnsons had acquired a fashionable address at 5 Cadogan Place in the West End of London. It was here in 1860 that George died, at the age of 63. Despite having been born into a privileged, if tainted family, he had worked hard and achieved much.

In the 1861 census, Elizabeth is listed at Cadogan Place with daughter, Frances, and son Robert, both unmarried. Precisely when she died is unclear, but it appears to have been within the next decade. In the 1871 census Frances is lodging at Doughty Street, London – where Charles Dickens resided for a time – and Robert is visiting Robert Mascie

Taylor at his home in Merionethshire. In both cases, Robert is shown as a non-practising barrister and owner of farming land approaching two hundred acres.

In December 1874, at the age of 49, Robert married Cecil Mary Diana Wynter, daughter of the Reverend Philip Wynter, Dean of St John's College, Oxford. Her mother was Diana Taylor, daughter of the Reverend Mascie Domville Taylor of Moreton Corbet and elder sister of the Robert Mascie Taylor, whom Robert Johnson had recently visited. Mascie Domville Taylor was cousin to Robert Johnson's mother, which means that he and his new wife had great-grandparents in common. The marriage would soon be ripped apart by tragedy. In October 1875, Cecil died in childbirth at Llanrhydd. The remote location and difficulty in summoning medical help may have been a factor. A healthy baby boy was born, whom Robert named Bertie Cecil Johnson.

Perhaps still grieving over the loss of his wife, Robert died in London in 1883, at the age of 58, leaving Bertie a seven-year-old orphan. This Bertie, who had ample means and property left to him in the UK, chose to spend much of his adult life owning and running a ranch in Mexico.[34] The setbacks of his early life may have left him feeling rootless, and with a thirst for far-flung adventures somewhere in his genes.

In 1889, a 'numerous and brilliant gathering' was reported in the press. It was to celebrate the marriage of Croxton Scutt Johnson and Emily Shiffner, near the Shiffner family seat at Combe Place in Sussex.[35] The groom was George Johnson's nephew – son of his brother, Edward – and the bride his great-niece, being the granddaughter of his sister, Elizabeth. As if to emphasise the calibre of the occasion, invited guests included Mr, Mrs and the Misses Best and the Reverend, Mrs and Miss Perfect. Of more consequence to us, there was a Major and Mrs Bertie Shiffner – brother and sister-in-law of the bride – and a Mrs Bertie Johnson, widow of George's brother, who had died in his Shropshire parish in 1873. This is a reminder of the all-pervasive nature of the Christian name 'Bertie' – plain and uncontracted – through every branch and generation of the Johnson family.

Before closing out on George Johnson, it is necessary to add a footnote on his kinsfolk, the Mascie Taylors, and their Chester connections. Robert Mascie Taylor, whom Robert George Johnson was visiting in 1871, was an officer in the British Army. Born in 1818, he saw most of his active service overseas. In 1842 he married Elizabeth Garland in Cape Town, before moving on to India, where they started a family together. By 1851 he had left the army and was living with his family as a 'fundholder' – on investments, in other words – in Christleton, near Chester. The next three censuses have them at their home in Merionethshire, before we see a significant change in the census of April 1891. Here we have Elizabeth as a 68-year-old visitor at her daughter and son-in-law's home in Reading and 72-year-old Robert visiting a Sara Hester Jones, an unmarried 65-year-old living on her own means at 13 Stanley Place, Chester. Another visitor at the latter address is Frances Jane Johnson, George's daughter.

Of course, visiting family and friends is perfectly normal and explicable. It's what happened next that raises questions in this case. Firstly, Elizabeth died at the Taylor family home in Wales in May 1891 – one month after the census was taken. This is confirmed by her gravestone at Overleigh Cemetery in Chester. Later that year, Robert commissioned a mural brass in Chester Cathedral – positioned above where his mother and father were laid to rest in the north aisle – but to Sara Hester Jones, rather than his late wife. The wording reads:

To the glory of God and in loving memory of Sara Hester Jones, a benefactress of this Cathedral and this city, born July 8th 1825, fell asleep Dec 1st 1891. This tablet was placed here by her lifelong friend Robert Mascie Taylor of Tyn Llwyn, Merioneth.

Sara entrusted £500 to Robert which he conveyed, in line with her wishes, to Chester General Infirmary, where her father, Dr Llewellyn Jones, had been an honorary physician.[36]

Whilst all of this was unfolding, Robert Mascie Taylor sprang another surprise: he married again. The wedding – to Harriet Bentham, 15 years his junior – took place at Lancaster Gate in London on 21st January 1892. They set up home together nearby at 53 Gloucester Place, Hyde Park, where Robert died in 1904, at the age of 86. He was buried alongside his first wife at Overleigh, with no mention on the gravestone of his second wife, who survived him by almost 20 years.

Chapter Eight

April

The approach of Easter in the middle of the month and the sense that spring was in the offing seemed to awaken and invigorate the city. The latest fashions were arriving in abundance, William and Henry Brown having 'just returned from town with new and beautiful articles'.[1] Miss Bryan and Miss Coker had even crossed to Paris to obtain a stock of new millinery and dresses for the season. Newspaper columns were replete with advertisements for such merchandise and detailed articles about what was considered *à la mode*.

There were stirrings on the sporting front too, particularly as the horseracing season approached. A new steam packet was preparing to be launched from Chester to work the north Wales coast, ideally in time for the first race meeting. A grand sale of carriages and bloodstock at the White Lion was being touted for Race Week and a new trophy to the value of a hundred guineas was presented to the Racecourse on behalf of the Chester trades. This was first known as the Tradesmen's Plate, later becoming the Chester Cup, which is still competed for today. Interest in the hunt was building, with the Chester Harriers turning out their quarry at the Oak Inn in Hoole at 11am every Thursday morning. Pugilism was again on the agenda and all eyes were on Manchester, where Spring, Langan, Crib and others were gathering in ominous pursuit of each other.

For the sportingly inclined, all that was required was an upturn in the weather, which was unseasonably cold. Hail, snow and thunderstorms were experienced early in the month, and a 14-inch snowdrift was recorded in Leicestershire.

Public works continued to dominate the business of the city, most notably the proposed new bridge and its environs; the upgrading of the road network along the north Wales coast; and the condition of the city walls. The first of these polarised opinion. The committee reported that permission had been granted for a bill to be presented to Parliament for the relocation of St Bridget's Church and the forming of a new thoroughfare from Bridge Street to the castle. The cost was to be mitigated by arrangements that were already in place. The city magistrates had committed to granting land and money, and the dean and chapter were surrendering their affected land at little more than nominal value. Earl Grosvenor had gratuitously offered his premises which intersected the proposed line of the street. A shortfall of £3,000 remained, which would be covered by an appeal from the bishop to church commissioners and by public subscription. Ratepayers were urged not to object.

However, they did. There was innate resistance to change and disruption, but also a reaction to the way in which the matter was being handled. No public meeting had been held to debate the issue and it was felt that the rateable inhabitants of Chester, a city of modest size and means, were already sufficiently burdened by their parish dues. Such was the strength of feeling that several hundred citizens put their names to a petition, also for presentation to Parliament, which sought to countermand the proposals. The committee responded by arguing that there was no intention to ignore or defy the will of the people, which could be elicited after Parliament had given their approval, and that the sequence of events had been determined by the parliamentary timetable. Now came a legal challenge to the magistrates' grant, which would delay proceedings in any case. Somehow, over the following weeks and months, these opposing factions had to be reconciled.

The progress of civil engineering work already underway had come in for criticism too, as we have seen. The suggestion that there was a lack of haste to upgrade the Holyhead road and complete the bridges at Conway and Menai was met with a robust response by Thomas Telford's chief engineer, Mr Provis. In a letter published in the *Chester Courant* on 6th April, he details the work done, the size of the workforce engaged – never dropping below a hundred – and the level of official scrutiny.

Work on the city walls was under the microscope too. The promenade was blocked and stones which had been dislodged were at risk of being stolen. There were calls for rewards to catch delinquents and a public subscription to effect repairs. This was deemed by many to be a better use of public funds than a plate for the races or the roasting of oxen at civic events, such as the king's birthday celebrations. A police enquiry was com-missioned into the collection and application of murage duties, to establish how the state of the walls and the funding of remedial work had become such a cause for concern.

The condition of some churches was a further bugbear, particularly St Bridget's, though that matter would be resolved if the relocation plan were to come into effect. At St Os-wald's, repairs were required but politics were getting in the way. Appended as it was to the cathedral, the parish had received a mandate from the bishop for the work to be car-ried out. Questions were then asked as to the division of responsibility between the two institutions and a five-man church committee was appointed to confer with the dean and chapter and report back.

In the legal arena, local trials were reported in detail. Conviction on flimsy grounds followed by severe punishment – to our minds at least – was by no means uncommon. John Jones was transported for life for allegedly burgling the home of a magistrate, though the evidence was circumstantial at best. Elizabeth Fenn was sentenced to 12 months hard labour for stealing a piece of cotton and Charles Burrows to seven years transportation for pilfering two pairs of stockings. Charles was the hangman's son, and at least escaped his father's noose. Even the police weren't above the law, with Constables Hyatt and Peers receiving a guilty verdict and a reprimand for neglect of duty.

Another trial featured the well-known Chester silversmith, George Lowe, the founder of a family business which operates on Bridge Street to this day. The action in *Lowe v Booth and others* was an attempt to recover the value of items which had been entrusted to a carrier and not delivered. A box of valuables, including gold and silver coins, had been handed to the Golden Lion coach office in Foregate Street by Thomas Lowe, George's son, for conveyance to London. Such transactions between the two parties had been com-monplace for the preceding ten years, without any difficulty arising.

In this case, the Lowes were notified a week later of non-delivery and checks via the coach firm showed that the box had not progressed beyond Newcastle-under-Lyme. In their defence, they argued that the culprit had not been identified and that the Lowes had not paid the premium required to ensure extra security on the part of the carrier. The case turned on whether a notice regarding the premium had been adequately displayed in the coach office and, if so, whether it was defeated by precedent as far as the Lowes were concerned. The defence was successful. The plaintiff was left to bear the loss and with the quandary of how best to transport such goods in the future.

A criminal trial at Chester that had particularly gripped the imagination of the public was that of 19-year-old Joseph Dale. In the autumn of 1823, he had been convicted of murder by stoning a man to death in the Peak District, even though he had been in a group and the identity of the assailant who dealt the fatal blow could not be established. The execution was set for Wednesday 21st April. Proceedings started at 5am, with Dale, lightly manacled, being escorted by cart from the castle to the city gaol. Despite the early hour, an estimated three thousand people lined the route, many of them deep in lamentation – moved by the youth, stoicism and dignity of the condemned man. The remainder of the morning was occupied by breakfast and much religious ritual, including Dale being privy to his own death sermon, just like Eliza Fenning nine years earlier. At 12 noon, he was led to the drop at the east front of the gaol, granting the executioner forgiveness and giving him a few shillings for his pains. A cap was drawn over his face and the rest was the work of a moment. His remains were dissected for medical science by the surgeons at the infirmary next door, in accordance with the terms of his sentence.[2]

There was trouble elsewhere in the county, as industrial unrest broke out in the silk trade in Macclesfield. In the face of competition from France, employers had taken the decision to increase the working day from 11 hours to 12 – a regime already in force in some neighbouring towns. The Cheshire Yeomanry were called in to counter a 'mob' of 12,000 people in the marketplace, reinforced by dragoons from Manchester the following day. Such was the strength of feeling, however, that the silk masters were forced to back down and leave the working hours undisturbed. The press criticised the workers for violence and intimidation and called for more respect for the yeomanry, who were commended in a letter from Robert Peel, then Home Secretary. Though not openly expressed, fears of a repeat of the Peterloo Massacre in Manchester in 1819 must have been at the forefront of the mind.

Business in Parliament was deemed to be so advanced that MPs gave themselves an extended 17-day break. This decision was perhaps bolstered by some smugness at the latest Quarterly Revenue report, showing both a reduction in taxation and increase in revenue. 'Every Englishman rejoices at the cheering prospect which this country presents at the present moment ... with happiness and prosperity pervading the whole land,' trumpeted the *Courant*.[3] For some, it may have been the best of times; for others, it was arguably the worst. In Ireland, for example, people would have begged – quite literally, in many cases – to differ.

The burning down of an English-owned property in Tipperary was one of many acts protesting against what was perceived to be an iniquitous and overly burdensome tithe system. This, in turn, fuelled sectarian tensions, despite calls on both sides of the religious divide for an end to inflammatory marches. The desire for peace was widespread, but the means of achieving it elusive. Some influential commentators in England called for an even stronger line against Irish lawbreakers, as a means of restoring confidence and re-spect in central government. Others were more conciliatory, suggesting that Catholic emancipation may be part of the solution, and pointing to the fact that a model that en-tailed a predominantly poor Catholic population of seven million supporting four Angli-can archbishops and 18 bishops was fundamentally flawed. If force were to be used, they argued, an occupying army of 50,000 – twice the government-approved figure – would not be enough. A motion in the House of Commons for pro-Catholic legislation was defeated, with the prime minister – Lord Liverpool – contending that Ireland already dis-proportionately benefited from the strength of the English constitution, lower rates of taxation and a ready market for export goods.

The prospect of finding common ground was further diminished by the conduct of English troops in Ireland. A long complaint was published in the *Dublin Evening Mail* about officers from the 10th Hussars who were accused of ogling Irish ladies at the theatre and generally behaving insolently in social settings. There was an arrogance and aloofness attributed to the 'Dandy Hussars', which gave rise to much resentment. Moves were afoot to relocate the regiment to the interior of the country and an investigation had been ordered by Lord Combermere, then Commander-in-Chief in Ireland. When he subsequently undertook a troop inspection, he dismissed two commanding officers summarily.

The statute book was updated, including renewal of the Alien Bill of 1816, which prevented free entry into the country.[4] This reflected a lingering mistrust of post-revolutionary France, though this was less real than imagined since the defeat of Napoleon, and deportations had slowed to a trickle. Other legislation included a tightening of the Game Laws, which vested property in game in the owner of enclosed land, or lords of the manor where the land was unenclosed. Licences were required to hunt game, and penalties were mandated for trespass. A motion to allow persons accused of felony access to counsel was defeated in the Commons. All of this left ordinary people vulnerable to the whims of landowners and the vagaries of the law, which, of course, were far from separable.

Slavery continued to be a topic of energetic debate in Parliament, with a Slave Trade Piracy Bill and agreed convention with America high on the agenda. Earl Grosvenor attempted, somewhat presciently, to introduce the question of compensation for slave owners in the event of manumission and recommended that a fund be established for that purpose. Earl Bathurst, Secretary of State for the Colonies, acknowledged the general sentiment towards manumission but pointed out that little had been done in practical terms to that end. As to compensation, there was devil in the detail. For example, there was the issue of how to price in the planter's right of ownership of the children of enslaved people, which the law recognised. Though not part of the debate, there is a chilling aspect to the notion that the planter would be rewarded financially for the propagation of his enslaved population. Petitions urging the abolition of slavery continued to be received from around the country in both Houses, including two from Chester: one to the Commons presented by Lord Belgrave, and one to the Lords presented by the bishop.

Meanwhile, Britain's colonial footprint across the globe continued to expand. Companies were formed to develop a million acres of land in New South Wales for sheep farming and to cut a canal across the isthmus of Darien, despite the dismal failure of previous schemes of this nature in Central America. Ongoing support for the Greeks in their struggle for independence and open conflict with Algeria both sought to protect British interests in and around the Mediterranean. Domestic shipbuilding had reached such a pitch that hands were hard to come by. New financial institutions and instruments were being created in line with the scale and trajectory of Britain's overseas trade. At home, churches were being built at a rate of knots, with a further £500,000 approved for that purpose on top of the £1.2 million already spent. The proposed new St Bridget's Church in Chester was a potential recipient, though initial applications had not borne fruit. Charity and philanthropy were in evidence too, not least in the founding of a new bank by Elizabeth Fry, the great social reformer, which would lend at an interest rate of ten per cent on pledges, compared with the 20 per cent or more applied by pawnbrokers.

There was literary news for the discerning reader too. The Royal Society of Literature had elected ten individuals to each receive a £100 annual allowance for life, including the poet Samuel Taylor Coleridge and the economist Robert Malthus. Horizons were broadened by the arrival from China of a traveller by the name of Mr Morrison, who brought back a rich collection of literature from that country. One domestic publication that should never have seen the light of day was a handbill which was widely posted in the Oldham area. It announced the forthcoming ascent in the town of the celebrated Italian aeronaut, Signor Francisco Paulini, at a specified date and time. An estimated ten thousand people arrived for the spectacle, but not the good signor or his apparatus. The crowd finally dispersed after several hours of waiting, well past nightfall. The hoaxer, rightly or wrongly, was identified as 'an Irishman'.[5]

Chapter Nine

Mrs Mainwaring
Lot 5

*The Art of Social Life, imperial quarto, splendidly bound in Russia, gilt extra, a fine
copy in the highest preservation, and worthy of a place in the best collection*

Dr Norris is always highly respectful towards his subjects but in Mrs Mainwaring's case
his language appears exceptionally effusive. She is clearly an important figure within the
group, and the use of the words 'in the highest preservation' – once more taking the
description of the book as being analogous to the person – implies some seniority in years.
'Imperial' may hint at regal connections, and the combination of the book title and the
assertion of worthiness creates the impression that here is someone who would be at ease
in the most elevated social setting. Indeed, the title *The Art of Social Life* appears to be
entirely of Dr Norris's contriving, making it peculiarly pertinent to Mrs Mainwaring. We
again see the reference to Russian binding, which echoes the compliment paid to Mrs
Humberston.

'Mainwaring' is a prominent name in Cheshire and has been for many centuries. The family descends from Ranulph de Mesnilwarin, who lived at the time of the Norman Conquest and in whom the manor of Blacon, north-west of Chester, was vested in 1086.[1]
Members of the family were active in political and constitutional affairs down the generations, at both a local and national level. A Randall Mainwaring is recorded as a Royal
Commissioner involved in the asset stripping of churches at the time of the Dissolution,
donating the spoils to charity as well as to the Crown.[2] Another ancestor was the Jacobean
pirate, Sir Henry Mainwaring, who defied Admiralty orders in 1610 by ignoring his commission and plundering Spanish galleons in the Caribbean for personal gain. Such was his

success against the Spanish, including rescuing British shipping from pirates of their own, that his reputation was restored, and he was rewarded with a knighthood and senior naval ranking.[3]

Later in the 17th century, Mainwarings took up opposing positions in pivotal historical events, such as the Civil War and the Monmouth Rebellion. They variously occupied the highest civic positions in Chester – alderman, sheriff and mayor – and represented the county in Parliament for several terms of office. In Chester Cathedral – a few paces away from Edmund Entwistle – is a still more ornate tablet commemorating 'the Eminently Loyal Sir William Mainwaring, Chancellor of the County Palatine of Chester' who 'died in the service of his Prince and Country in the Defence of the City … Wherein he merited singular honour for his Fidelity, Courage and Conduct … He died honourably but immaturely in the Twenty-ninth year of his age October 9 1644'. Sir William's demise came after Prince Rupert fell back on Chester in the wake of the Royalist defeat at Marston Moor in July of that year and as Parliamentarian troops readied themselves for the encirclement and besieging of the city.

Sir William belonged to a branch of the family which had settled in Peover in East Cheshire. This branch failed in 1798 with the death without issue of Sir Henry Mainwaring, who willed his name and title to his uterine half-brother.[4] This new Sir Henry Mainwaring – more commonly known as Harry – will feature not a little in our story.

Other branches of the family developed in Chester and at Bromborough on the Wirral. George Mainwaring, who was born in London, married and settled in Chester in 1672, becoming mayor in 1681 and MP in 1689. On 9th September 1682, the Duke of Monmouth arrived in Chester, staying with George at his house in Watergate Street and being confirmed as godfather to his daughter at a service at the cathedral the following day. There was a great tumult surrounding this visit, as people protested in favour of his claim to the throne.[5] As the son of Charles II, albeit illegitimate, he was regarded as a buffer against the future James II, who was Catholic. The duke's rebellion after James was crowned three years later was suppressed and he was executed.

In 1690, George Mainwaring and Roger Whitley lost their parliamentary seats to Sir Richard Levigne and Sir Thomas Grosvenor, whom they accused of expediently creating new freemen and paying them for their vote. Petitions presented to the House of Commons to overturn the result appear to have been ineffectual and the Mainwarings reverted to local politics.

George's son, James, was an alderman in Chester, becoming sheriff in 1696 and mayor in 1708. He inherited the manor of Bromborough through his mother's line. His son, another James, was born at Bromborough in 1702. He became a Baron of the Exchequer – a senior judicial post – and married Mary Kynaston, the daughter and co-heir of Charles Kynaston of Oteley Park. This beautiful estate at Ellesmere, Shropshire, which was reputedly first planted in the 14th century, remains in the Mainwaring family to this day. There followed, in succession, Charles and James, both of Bromborough. The younger brother of this last James was yet another Charles, who entered holy orders and inherited Oteley Park. On 24th June 1800, he married Sarah Susanna Townshend at Holy Trinity in Chester.

A little over three years later, Sir Harry Mainwaring of Peover, married Sophia Cotton at Wrenbury. Some of this detail may sound familiar: Combermere Abbey is in the parish of Wrenbury and Sophia was the younger sister of Stapleton Cotton – later Viscount Combermere – and cousin of Catherine Humberston, née Cotton. These two ladies – Sarah Susanna and Sophia – are the only two possible claimants to the identity of our Mrs Mainwaring at the Chester Book Club in 1824. On closer inspection, the die falls decidedly on the side of Sarah – more commonly known in her lifetime by her middle name, Susanna – because of her presence in the city and the use of the salutation 'Mrs'. Given that Sophia had married a knight of the realm, she was 'Lady' Mainwaring, so we have the same distinction that helped us to differentiate between Mrs Glynne and Lady Glynne.

Susanna was born in 1772 to John Townshend and his wife Anne, née Bennett, at Trevalyn, between Rossett and Gresford, just over the Welsh border from Chester. We have heard of this place before because it was the homestead of Thomas Boydell, beneficiary and executor to the will of Sir John Glynne, whose Hawarden estate was a few short miles away.

Susanna was distantly related to the Cottons, as her great-grandfather, Nathaniel Lee, had married Sydney Cotton, daughter of the first Combermere baronet. Her family was associated with Hem House – now the site of a farm – and Trevalyn House, both near Rossett. This latter property is a magnificent 18th century structure which still stands, and, for many years, served as a hospital. It was bought outright in the early 19th century by Susanna's brother from the Reverend Robert Twiss. Though incidental to our narrative, it is perhaps worth mentioning that he was the father of Sir Travers Twiss, an eminent professor and international lawyer, who scandalised late Victorian society by marrying a purportedly respectable lady who later fled the country amid allegations that she was in fact a prostitute.[6]

The Townshend family derived its pedigree from Sir Robert Townshend, who fought on the Royalist side in the Civil War, having land confiscated as result and only returned once the conflict had abated. Upon the Restoration, he became the first knight created by Charles II on his return to London.[7] A tablet in All Saints Church, Gresford, neatly traces his lineage down to his two times great-granddaughter, our Susanna:

Sacred to the memory of Sir Robert Townshend knt and Anne his wife ..., of Anthony their only son, of John the only son of Anthony ..., of Frances, the wife of John ..., of John their son and Anne his wife, daughter and coheir of Henry Bennett esq of Moston in the County of Chester ..., of Susannah [sic] Townshend, youngest daughter of the above John and Frances Townshend.

The Bennetts are an old established Cheshire family, associated with Barnston on the Wirral and well represented in the merchant and professional ranks down the centuries. The Henry Bennett mentioned in the inscription was Mayor of Chester in 1734 and is personally memorialised at St Peter's Church in the city, having 'left the sum of Twenty five Pounds the Interest to be given to Twelve Poor Widows of this parish on Christmas-day for ever'. John Townshend is described as 'of St Peter's' in the register at Holy Trinity in respect of his marriage there to Anne Bennett in 1760, suggesting that he had a town house in that parish. Susanna's betrothal to the Reverend Charles Mainwaring in the same church four decades later may have stemmed from a neighbourly acquaintance; the Mainwaring mansion occupied a generous space on the north side of Watergate Street on the short stretch between the two churches.

Their union was blessed with three children, born in relatively quick succession – Charles Kynaston in 1803, Susan in 1804, and Townshend in 1807 – all of whom survived into adulthood. The widespread appearance of 'Kynaston' in family Christian names reflects pride in Charles's father's maternal line. Not only was it fruitful in terms of land and possessions, but it also boasted a number of noteworthy individuals within it. Perhaps chief amongst these was Sir Francis Kynaston, who was a squire of the body of Charles I and a celebrated scholar and poet, translating Chaucer's *Troilus and Criseyde* into Latin verse.[8]

As a married couple, Susanna and Charles divided their time between Oteley Park, Bromborough Hall and Chester, until fate intervened with the death of Charles in May 1807 at the Shropshire estate. He was 37 years old. His will, drafted a little over a year before his death, is light on detail, especially for a man of such ample means. In it, he expresses a wish for a decent, low-key burial in the church at Welshampton – adjacent to Oteley – 'in case I die in Co. Salop'. Otherwise, he was content to be buried in the parish in which he died, despite there being a family vault at Welshampton and the likelihood that his body could be readily transported there.

A memorial to Charles features obscurely in the vestry of St Michael and All Saints Church, Welshampton. This was built by the Mainwaring family in the 1860s, on the same site as its predecessor, and was designed by the great English Gothic Revival architect, George Gilbert Scott, who was also highly instrumental in the Victorian restoration of Chester Cathedral. A verse on the memorial talks of 'the widow's swollen eye' and 'the terror of the orphan's sigh', capturing something of the feeling at Charles' untimely death.

Susanna inherited everything, apart from amounts of £1,000 granted to each of the younger children, who stood to benefit more generously were Susanna to remarry. It is not clear why the eldest child, Charles Kynaston, was omitted, but it is reasonable to assume that he was already provided for, perhaps through a trust fund. Amongst the movable property bequeathed to Susanna were 'all my plate, household goods, books, bedsteads and bedding, linen, carriages, live and dead stock and other furniture'. Susanna – described misogynistically to our modern sensibilities as 'the relict and sole executrix' – proved the will in the month in which the death occurred.[9]

She maintained a presence in Chester thereafter, supporting charitable causes, including acting as a patron in the fundraising effort for William Barth, a former draper, and his destitute family.[10] Such philanthropy is in keeping with the ethos of this branch of the Mainwarings, who, Hemingway tells us, founded alms-houses in Trinity Street for three poor widows, supported by a modest annuity. Susanna would have been attracted to the city by her familiarity with it, her social contacts and, of course, the enviable property she had at her disposal. A print by John Romney from the early 19th century shows a half-timbered, four-bay, gabled house above undercrofts, including a partial row either side of the main doorway. This property was pulled down and, in 1852, replaced by a line of gabled brick buildings which still feature at numbers 58 to 66 Watergate Street today.[11] Chester would also have offered greater educational opportunities for Susanna's children, who were still at a tender age in the early years of her widowhood.

After a respectful period of mourning and as the children grew, Susanna began to acquire a reputation as a socialite and hostess of the highest order. Her annual masquerades became the talk of the town. The first of these reported in the Chester press took place at the start of 1822, and the coverage was extensive and effusive. On 11th January, the *Chester Chronicle* ran an article spanning two columns, which described a masked ball at the house of Mrs Charles Mainwaring at which the costumery was studied and ingenious. She and her family, who were well represented amongst the 90 or so guests, set the tone for the evening. Her brother John Stanislaus Townshend – of whom more anon – mimicked her to greet arrivals, whilst she appeared in the character and demeanour of a demure charity schoolgirl. Her schoolfellow was none other than Mrs Humberston. Her daughter, Susan, by now 17, wore a costume half black and half white with a disk bearing two dazzling spots, which observers recognised as a partial eclipse of the sun.

Some costumes played into other forms of entertainment. For example, Miss Mary Hesketh – granddaughter of Henry Hesketh, Watergate Street wine merchant and associate of Thomas Sloughter – attended as a ballad singer. In this guise, she eulogised the company with a song crafted for the occasion, while other Heskeths threw in humorous catches and minuetted to the music. Five masked figures, decorated with wreathes and knots of holly, tripped around the wassail-bowl – from which hot, mulled punch was drunk at Yuletide – before presenting their hostess with a Christmas box containing 'a fair mince pie'.

Some outfits that would meet with opprobrium today were not merely acceptable but were the source of the utmost mirth and theatre back then. Charles Kynaston Mainwaring and a friend went as Jews, salivating over a young lady in the character of a pig, excited either by the temptation of forbidden fare or the ruby that adorned her snout. Another lady represented Wouski, a voluptuous Black woman who shares a hammock with the future King William IV in a Gillray print of 1780, apparently inspired by rumours of the prince's dalliances during a trip to Barbados. There was a Chinese Mandarin, seven feet tall, and a Mohawk chief, accompanied by war-whoops and skeletal trophies, who somehow simulated a scalping as part of the proceedings. Other appearances that reflected cultural stereotypes included Scottish highlanders with kilts and bagpipes, an Irish balladeer and a Turkish executioner.

Some masqueraders were inspired by literature. Examples include Lady Pentweazle, an unprepossessing though vain character from Samuel Foote's 1752 play *Taste*, and Dr Syntax, a comic figure created by William Coombe in 1809, who travels the country looking for picturesque landscapes to sketch and share with the wider world. Another is Tabitha Bramble, who features in Tobais Smollett's 1771 novel, *The Expedition of Humphry Clinker*. A proud but deeply flawed woman, her shortcomings include an unswerving ability to mangle the English language and superciliousness towards the poor and downtrodden. These characters were well-known and recognised at the time, even if they have since melted into obscurity. They satirised hypocrisy and pretention in Georgian society in way that clearly struck a chord with our partygoers.

The revels continued late into the night. 'At four in the morning,' we are told, 'Miss Hesketh gave the signal for departure, in an appropriate poetical acknowledgement of thanks to the amiable hostess, and each party returned home to dream of the pleasures of the past, and to devise fresh frolics for the future.' If it were not the case already, Susanna Mainwaring was now at the centre of the Chester social scene. Perhaps only she could better what she'd started.

The following winter, Susanna hosted a series of grand occasions. We are again grateful to the *Chester Chronicle* for reporting on them. The first took place in early December 1822 and consisted of 'an elegant ball and supper' for more than a hundred members of the local gentry. A week later she hosted 'about 50 distinguished individuals' at dinner. These appear to have been little more than a warm-up for the next masquerade, which would take place on an unprecedented scale. Approximately 300 tickets were issued in advance of the event, set for 15th January. Interest would not have been hindered by the description of Susanna in a press trailer as the person 'who may fairly be considered the leader of fashionable circles in this city'.

'Possessing the advantage of a cultivated and ample fortune, this highly respectable lady uniformly characterised her entertainments with liberality, and a boundless desire to see her guests happy and "at home",' gushed the reporter. Comparisons were made with St James's or The Mall on Gala Day, as all manner of coaches, carriages, chariots and chairs clattered across the cobbles of Chester's main streets towards the appointed place.[12] On this occasion, other houses were thrown open to offshoots of the main event, delivering 'a miniature masquerade in almost every quarter of the town' and 'affording the absentees almost as much enjoyment as the main actors in the principal scene'. It is easy to imagine Elizabeth Sloughter and Anne Glynne welcoming such roving revellers. The arrival of the 'lovely and grotesque' at the Mainwaring mansion was complete by 10pm, which was the cue for full use to be made of the splendid suite of rooms within.

Susanna's character could not have contrasted more sharply with the previous year. She was a gouty old man, confined to a chair and tended upon by one her two sisters who, somewhat confusingly, were called Frances Anne and Frances Sarah. Two Mr Townshends, Mr Cunliffe and Charles Kynaston Mainwaring presented themselves with song and dance as Apollo and the Graces. Miss Susan Mainwaring sported a crimson velvet dress lined with satin, worn by Lady Anne Coventry at the coronation of George II, surmounted with a gold coronet. Another Mainwaring who wore a dress conspicuously was Townshend, Susanna's younger son, who imitated an old lady. Other family members attended variously as the King and Queen of Hearts, a 'blooming Welsh girl from the Vale of Clwyd' and a Polish nobleman. There were clowns, gypsies and shepherdesses, the latter being portrayed by two Miss Humberstons, who are imprecisely identified amongst the six alive at the time. Their mother had recreated the style of the 1750s by imitating a respectable old lady of that period called 'Mrs Grub', whose *sang froid* was challenged by her frolicsome granddaughter, played by a friend, Mrs Wintour. George Johnson was there as quack doctor, and the real doctor – Dr Norris – as Thomas Testy, a quarrelsome Gloucester baronet.

It was not uncommon for guests to change costumes two or three times during the proceedings, and Susanna made a point of discarding hers part way through, to more directly focus on her hosting duties. Miss Catherine Humberston teamed up with a Miss Cotton and Colonel Egerton in the form of two rival cooks and a scullion, whose acrimony towards each other heightened in pitch as the evening progressed. They then transformed into Peter Palaver, the wandering showman, his wife and daughter to present a peep show, thrilling onlookers with miniature histories of heroic figures, such as Admiral Benbow and Marshall Blucher. Mrs Palaver and her daughter embellished the scene with music from an organ and tambourine, along with fitting vocals. Another party was a troupe of Morris dancers, providing alternative entertainment in a highly animated style.

Even the announcement of supper at midnight had a strong element of performance about it. It was the cue for masks to be removed and for the bearers to marvel at each other in mutual recognition. There were more songs – whimsical and exhilarating – and resounding toasts to 'the munificent founder of the feast and her lovely daughter'. Once more, the carousing continued through the night, until the hardiest constitution could no longer withstand the need for rest. The next visitor would be Mr Jefferies, the upholster, to remove the lavish decorations that he had been called upon to supply.[13]

It is now clear why *The Art of Social Life* was such an apt choice for Mrs Mainwaring at the Chester Book Club. Indeed, she and her gatherings could have been the very subject of such a work. By the time the club met in 1824, however, the masquerades appear to have become a thing of the past. The newspapers, which took such delight in reporting them, contained no such matter beyond the festive season that straddled 1822 and 1823. Who knows why this might have been? As we have seen, they were no small undertakings, so it may have been more of a case of whether to repeat them rather than whether to discontinue them. Susanna was entering her fifties, at a time when life expectancy in wealthy families was in the early forties, and health issues may have crept into the equation.[14] All three of her children had reached adulthood and their focus had shifted elsewhere. Relationships were forming and, before long, wedding bells were sounding. Susan married in 1825, followed by both her brothers a few years later.

There is also a sense that Susanna had handed on the baton. On Monday 5th January 1824, almost on the anniversary of her last masquerade, great festivities began at the magnificent Alderley home of Sir John Stanley, in east Cheshire, to celebrate the coming-of-age of his twin sons. As mentioned in Chapter Two, these spanned the whole week and touched not just the estate and neighbourhood but the entire county, as far as the higher orders were concerned. Tuesday featured a 'fancy ball' for around 200 people, followed by a masquerade on the Thursday for the same assemblage. These people knew how to party. Susanna was in attendance, as were members of her family on both the Mainwaring and Townshend sides, as well as another two unspecified 'Miss Humberstons'. Mrs Johnson from Knutsford was there, accompanied by her daughters and sons – one of whom would have been George – as well as Miss Taylor from Lymm, whom he was soon to marry.[15] In the later 1820s, 'Grand Fancy Dress Balls' were taking place annually at the Royal Hotel, much according to Susanna's blueprint. Such imitation, elevated to a corporate level, was a sincere form of flattery.

In August 1825 Charles Kynaston came of age and, although 'great rejoicing' at Oteley Park was reported in the press, there is no underlying detail. It seems he went on the grand tour of continental Europe and returned with ideas for the redevelopment of Oteley. The work done between 1826 and 1830 included a neo-Elizabethan mansion – replacing an earlier half-timbered Tudor property – and magnificent terraced gardens in the Italian style. Susanna would have lived just long enough to see this in the making. The house was pulled down in the mid-20th century, but much of the terracing remains.[16] Another major family occasion during this period was Susan's marriage to the Reverend Edward Duncombe at Holy Trinity, Chester, in November 1825. This would have been celebrated in fine style too, probably at the Mainwaring home a few yards up Watergate Street from the church.

A melancholy occurrence of the following year was the death of Susanna's brother, John Stanislaus Townshend, at Trevalyn. His will had been witnessed by George Johnson, most likely in a professional capacity. John's widow, Dorothea, was the main beneficiary and Charles Kynaston Mainwaring was a trustee. His three sisters, including Susanna, were left ten guineas each for mourning rings. John's striking middle name is to be wondered at. It was associated with 18th century kings of Poland, who may have been a source of inspiration. John owned the patent to operate the Theatre Royal in Chester and was of a strong theatrical bent. We see this in his dramatic and protean appearances at the masquerades.

In 1828, Susanna suffered another bereavement with the loss of her sister, Frances Sarah Townshend. Frances Sarah co-owned another property in Watergate Street, which she and her other sister, Frances Anne, had bought from the Bamford-Hesketh family of Gwrych Castle near Abergele.[17]

The Mainwarings appear to have been expanding their footprint in Chester during this period. The *Directory of Cheshire, 1828* includes 'Chas Mainwaring' at Eastgate Street and 'Mrs Mainwaring' at King's Buildings, King Street, under the heading 'nobility, gentry and clergy'. Are these definitively Charles Kynaston and Susanna? Whilst we can't be absolutely certain, it is unlikely that other Mainwarings in Chester would have been categorised and referred to in this way. 'Mrs Mainwaring', it seems, was so well-known in the city that a Christian name was superfluous. Her reasons for moving, or for dividing her time between two Chester properties, can only be speculated upon. King Street was new and fashionable, whereas, at Watergate Street, perhaps the timbers were starting to creek. It also had better views, east and west, assuming the stairs were navigable for her.

In January 1829, a ball was held at the Royal Hotel at which fancy dress was compulsory. Strict instructions were issued on how carriages and chairs should traverse the streets – single file up the south side of Eastgate Street and the east side of Bridge Street, for example. Traffic control in the city centre remained a concern. This event required a fee 'in aid of the funds for alleviating the deplorable state of distress and destitution to which the Spanish and Italian refugees now in this country are reduced'.[18] The hardship stemmed from Napoleonic colonisation of their homelands. Attendees included Susanna's eldest son, daughter and sister; Mrs Humberston and two of her daughters; George and Mrs Johnson; Anne Owen, née Coupland; and Mad Jack Mytton, whose behaviour did not excite comment on this occasion.[19] Conspicuous by her absence was Susanna, whose health may well have been failing.

On 6th December of the same year, she passed away in Chester, having lived just long enough to see Charles Kynaston appointed High Sheriff of Shropshire. She had drafted her will at the start of 1826, so there are monetary bequests to the brother and sister who pre-deceased her which were never revoked. Two late codicils were added, however – in late December 1828 and mid-January 1829 – suggesting that she knew death was approaching and had detail to attend to. The first of these denies a sum to Charles Kynaston because he was 'so amply provided for elsewhere' and the second deals with specific items that were of either practical or sentimental value. Jewellery and clothing of various descriptions – including lace that Frances Anne had brought back for her from Brussels – were left to her daughter, nieces and surviving sister. There was much ermine fur and items made of black velvet, including a hat with white feathers, as well as an orange India shawl and a ring containing a lock of her brother's hair. Taken together, these confirm an impression of affluence, elegance and, perhaps, occasional showiness.

Townshend Mainwaring was the main beneficiary of the will. There was also a £50 gift to the 'school of Blue Girls near the Infirmary' and £5 to 'the present matron, Mary Elizabeth Parry, should she continue to give satisfaction to the Ladies of the Committee at the time of my death'. It is presumed that Susanna was one of these ladies and that this was how she, and others like her, dispensed philanthropy and served the wider interests of the city.

She was interred quietly, in line with her wishes, in the Mainwaring vault at Welshampton on 12th December 1829. Her elegant signature in the will was verified by two men local to Ellesmere, including James Taylor, her son's butler at Oteley. Charles Kynaston proved the will on 22nd April 1830.[20] Her name appears on a tablet in the church in Welshampton, amongst several generations of Kynastons and Mainwarings. Whilst her age is quoted accurately at 57, the year of death is stated as '1820' – nine years out: more evidence that whatever is cast in stone is not always synonymous with fact.

A letter of 14th January 1832 from Anne Owen to Elizabeth Sloughter conveys the news that Mr Mainwaring – Charles Kynaston – is to be married to Miss Fanny Salusbury, daughter of John Lloyd Salusbury of Gaelltfaenan Hall, Denbighshire. This union took place at nearby Henllan the following October, with the service conducted by the Reverend Duncombe, who was now based with his wife, Susan, in Selby, Yorkshire. Five years later, Townshend Mainwaring married Fanny's elder sister, Anna Maria Salusbury, who, by that time, had inherited Gaelltfaenan. This was a platform for further social elevation on Townshend's part: he acquired the Marchweil Hall, near Wrexham, in the year of his marriage and became High Sheriff and Conservative MP for Denbighshire at the turn of the 1840s. He instituted the playing of cricket at Marchweil, a tradition that would continue into the early 20th century, when the property was owned and occupied by Sir Alfred McAlpine, the construction magnate.[21]

From an early stage, the Mainwaring brothers became heavily involved in the development of the railway network across a wide area. In 1839, Charles Kynaston joined the Committee of the Shrewsbury and Birmingham Railway – connecting Shrewsbury, Oswestry, Chester and Midland railways running into north Wales – and in 1845 Townshend followed suit.[22] Townshend used his influence as an MP to help steer the Chester to Holyhead Railway Bill through Parliament. By the mid-1850s, they were both patrons of the Rhyl Convalescent Home for the Working Classes, where the honorary manager and secretary was none other than George Johnson of Llanrhydd. Sir Stephen Glynne, great-nephew of Anne, was a regular visitor.[23]

In August 1857, there were large-scale celebrations in and around Denbigh to mark the cutting of the first sod on the Vale of Clwyd Railway, which Townshend had been highly instrumental in promoting. His wife was handed a ceremonial silver spade and carved oak wheelbarrow, whereupon she 'cut a few sods, put them in the wheelbarrow and wheeled it a few yards to great cheering'.[24] The opening of the line 14 months later was a local holiday and was attended by further rejoicing, during which Townshend and his fellow directors boarded the first train from Rhyl to St Asaph.

In 1861, Charles Kynaston died at his town house in Cavendish Square, London. Townshend outlived him by 22 years and continued to be involved in great schemes aimed at the public good. In 1868, he was appointed President of the National Eisteddfod of Wales, using his acceptance speech to emphasise his Welsh credentials through lineal descent from the Kynastons and intermarriage between the Mainwarings and the Salusburys of Lleweni and Mostyn. So determined was he to make this point that he went back as far as a Norman ancestor who was reputedly first to jump from his boat onto English shores, proclaiming what translates as 'Foremost, if I can'.[25] This became the Mainwaring family motto, and well describes Susanna's position in Chester society almost eight centuries later.

Townshend's death at Gaelltfaenan on Christmas Day 1883 was widely reported in the press. He was praised for his professional achievements and philanthropy, including the erection in nearby Trefnant of a school and the church where he was buried. His considerable musical ability was commented upon, extending to the composition of a hymn that was sung at his funeral. The railway network and the considerable benefits it brought to the communities in which he was active are also part of his legacy.

Before closing this chapter, we should briefly consider a couple of offshoots of Susanna's family who were foremost in their field.

The 1851 census for Trevalyn lists John Townshend – Susanna's nephew – living with his wife, Priscilla, and George Bennett Townshend, a 14-year-old born in Australia. He turns out to have been the son of George Townshend and grandson of the late John Stanislaus. George, the father, had travelled out to the Hunter Valley region of New South Wales in 1826, with Charles Boydell, to take advantage of free land grants and the prospect of making a fortune from the fertile but, as yet, uncultivated expanses. They named the locality Gresford, the nearby river the Allyn and their homesteads Trevallyn and Camyr Allyn. Another Boydell – William – arriving later, called his Caergwrle. These place names – transposed directly from north-east Wales, where a double 'l' is used in 'Allyn' – still feature on the map of this spectacularly beautiful area to this day.

The expatriates worked hard and realised their ambitions, at least until a drought and resulting economic depression occurred in the 1840s. This forced George – by now a family man – to sell land to Dr Henry Lindeman, who renamed it Cawara. Lindeman's is now one of the most recognisable names in the wine-producing world, and Cawara one of its top brands. Boydell's and Camyr Allyn also still survive and prosper amongst the esteemed vineyards and wineries of the Hunter Valley Region.[26]

Susanna had a great-grandson, Colonel Sir Watkin Randall Kynaston Mainwaring, who was Quartermaster General in Egypt between 1916 and 1919 and High Sheriff for Flint in 1924. His son, Hugh Salusbury Kynaston Mainwaring also distinguished himself in military service, in his case in World War Two. He was captured in north Africa and imprisoned in Italy in 1942, but obtained his release when Italy signed the Armistice with Allied powers in September 1943. He assisted over five hundred fellow prisoners of war to evade pursuit by the Nazis, who placed a 2,600 lire bounty on his head. Pretending to be an Italian soldier returning south – which endeared him to farmers and peasants, who provided what food, shelter and clothing they could – he eventually completed a precarious journey to Algiers, where Field Marshall Montgomery secured his return home.[27] He was honoured with a CBE in 1944 for his heroics.

Finally, we return to Sir Harry Mainwaring, who, as we have seen, had greatness thrust upon him. His main preoccupation in adulthood appears to have been hunting, leading to his appointment to the prestigious post of Master of the Cheshire Hounds, which he held from 1818 to 1837. Undeterred by short-sightedness, he embedded an eyeglass in his hunting crop and hunted four days-a-week over a wide area.[28] He was a member and, at one time, chair of the Grand Jury at the Cheshire Assizes, even attempting to relocate the process from Chester to Knutsford – a move which was swiftly averted by a powerful Chester lobby, led by the Grosvenors. In June 1811, he was amongst the official party who attended the opening of Thomas Harrison's Grand Entrance, or Propylaea, to Chester Castle, and his name appears on a brass plate commemorating the laying of the first stone. Beneath that stone was placed an urn containing several coins from the reign of George III, which was then giving way to the Regency.[29]

He was also involved with Chester Racecourse and, in 1816, suggested the building of a grandstand – a scheme which found favour and was implemented. When the Duke of Wellington was welcomed at the Albion Hotel in Chester, Sir Harry was part of the organising committee and an attendee at the great public feast that was held in his honour.[30] He was soon organising a great celebration of his own, when his son – another Harry – came of age at Peover in 1825, surrounded by around 250 of the great and the good. The poor were not disregarded, receiving offerings of beef and ale. This was not out of character for Sir Harry, who supported initiatives to relieve the poor and distressed of East Cheshire and was a regular visitor at Knutsford House of Correction.

He was, however, a staunch defender of the established social order. A member of the Nantwich King and Constitution Club, alongside Viscount Combermere and other members of the Cotton family into which he had married, he lauded the Protestant ascendancy, field sports and country life. In April 1831, he appended his name to the petition to the House of Commons deploring the 'Proposed Alteration of the Elective Franchise of these Kingdoms', branding it 'dangerous and destructive to welfare and prosperity'.[31] As mentioned in Chapter Five, the resistance was towards the Second Reform Bill, which would be defeated in the House of Lords later in the year, to much public outcry. The bill passed on its third iteration in 1832.

During the mid-1830s, Sir Harry and Lady Mainwaring maintained their lifestyle, attending the best balls, being noted as 'fashionable arrivals' in one place or another and procuring the best amenities for themselves and their family. Sir Harry, by now, had invested heavily in the Cheshire Hounds and its infrastructure, which was an expensive business. The upshot was bankruptcy.

By 1838, he and his wife had fled the country to avoid creditors and were living in Boulogne. Tragically, Lady Mainwaring died and was buried there in May that year.[32] Sir Harry would soon return to face justice, leading the itinerant life of a bankrupt. In November 1841, he was called for trial as an insolvent debtor at Chester Castle, where he had so recently held such sway, and his estates were assigned to his principal creditor. He was described in the *Chester Chronicle* of the 5th November as 'Sir Henry Mainwaring, late of Marbury, in the County of Chester, Baronet; previously of Boulogne, in the Kingdom of France; then of Nantwich in the said county of Chester; and formerly of Over Peover'.

He returned to Marbury, adjacent to the Combermere estate, to live out the remaining 18 years of his life in a cottage with his daughter, Hester. He was still able to trade a little on his name and title, for example by endorsing Bowers's Cough Lozenges, which, according to their advert, 'he finds very efficacious for relieving his cough'. Towards the end, he appears to have enjoyed some social rehabilitation, becoming involved in a committee to prepare for the 1858 Royal Agricultural Show at the Roodee, other members of which included Philip Stapleton Humberston and Sir Stephen Glynne. When he died suddenly in January 1860, the obituaries were not unkind, *The Daily Post* providing one example:

In consequence of his too ready hospitality, and from a desire to increase the estates which he acquired with the name of Mainwaring, Sir Harry became involved in pecuniary difficulties, which brought ruin on himself and others. For many years he has resided with his amiable daughter in the romantic village of Marbury, near Combermere Abbey, beloved and esteemed of all who knew him.[33]

Chapter Ten

May

We saw in Chapter Eight how the city was readying itself for Race Week, and, at the start of May, the final preparations were being made. Houses, shops and the Rows were being trimmed up and racegoers were starting to arrive en masse. A main of cocks was being openly advertised, to be fought during the races at the Close Pit, St John Street. The theatre was crowded, and a travelling circus did a brisk trade. The Race Balls held at the Royal Hotel were described in the press as the most brilliant in living memory and demand for beds and stabling at the Albion Hotel far outstripped supply. Amongst the guests at the Royal were four lords, seven knights of the realm – including Sir Harry Mainwaring and Sir Andrew Corbet – and Mad Jack Mytton. At the head of the guest list at the Albion were Prince and Princess Sapieha of Poland, who joined approximately two hundred others at The Tradesman's Ball in the new assembly room, now the largest in the city. This was part of a recent investment that had resulted in an 'immense pile of a building', stretching from Lower Bridge Street to the eastern section of the city walls.[1] Book club members would have attended one or other of these gatherings.

The weather, it seems, was variable. On the one hand it was described as mild – giving rise to the hope of a full season at Parkgate – but, on the other, there were reports of damaging frosts and floods around the country. A decision on whether to install warm baths at Chester Infirmary – arguably a necessity in any conditions – was much debated. Local newspapers heard from correspondents on both sides, including a passionate and eloquent plea in favour of the proposal from 'A Governess of Chester Infirmary'. The counter argument, largely based on cost, was equally strongly put. The institution continued to be subject to regular weekly inspections, including by the eminent physician, Dr William Makepeace Thackeray, who shared a great-grandfather with the novelist of the same name. Dr Thackeray was a much-loved figure in Chester. When he died at the age of 80 in 1849, there was an elaborate funeral and the unveiling of a tablet in his honour at Chester Cathedral. Boys from the Blue Coat School, in whose education and welfare he had taken a keen interest, were amongst the chief mourners. A prominent monument to him was also sited at Overleigh Cemetery.[2]

In early May 1824, a successor to the recently deceased Bishop of Bath and Wells was announced – it would be George Henry Law, the incumbent at Chester. With equal alacrity, Charles James Blomfield was appointed into that vacancy. As we have seen, he was the elder brother of George Becher Blomfield of Hawarden and was later Bishop of London. His credentials for the Chester post included serving as Rector of St Botolph without the Walls in Bishopsgate – where a nearby street is named after him – and as Preceptor to the Earl of Wilton at Eaton Hall.[3]

Whatever important developments were taking place in the city, the spectre of crime was never far away. Whether it was coincidence or not during the race season, horses were very much the prey. There were thefts at Hatton Heath and Great Boughton and a general warning was issued that horse gangs 'at present infect this part of the country'.[4] Henry Hesketh – grandson of the Henry who had associated with Thomas Sloughter – fell victim to highway robbery in his capacity as Distributor of Stamps for Chester and District. Such a quantity of his stamps was stolen from the Chester to London mail coach that the Bow Street Runners were called in to investigate. At about the same time, George Lowe was appealing the verdict following the loss of his merchandise in similar circumstances, but without success. One miscreant who had been apprehended was Dr Trigg of Hawarden, the surgeon who left his wife and absconded to London with Mrs Newton, also married. He was tried, convicted and sentenced to six months hard labour. Against this rising trend in crime, Mr George Burgess, previously a constable at Chorlton Row in Manchester, was appointed to command the police establishment in Chester.

Commercial activity revolved mostly around the property sector. The Pied Bull Inn, scene of many a property auction, was itself up for sale, through Messrs Potts and Johnson. Opposite Mrs Mainwaring's house on Watergate Street, two shops, which came with pews at Holy Trinity, were on the market, as were two on Lower Bridge Street and two on Foregate Street. Businesses being advertised included a druggist's; a whitesmith's; skin houses in the leather trade; and a timber yard and adjacent warehouse. In a thriving economy, these were more likely to have been opportunist rather than forced sales. One exception was William Read, proprietor of the Iron Bridge Tavern in Egerton Street, who had been declared insolvent and his stock in trade deposited at Messrs Snape and Co Brewery in King Street.

In the Commercial Rooms on Northgate Street, another petition was open for signature. It called for an inquiry into the case of Missionary Smith, the outcome of which was now widely known and condemned. Reports appeared of his hastily arranged funeral, his wife being denied access to it and her pitiable return to England. The supervening concern was for the safety of other Christian missionaries, who were penetrating all corners of the globe. In Demerara – so often the first powder keg to ignite – there were calls for the missionaries themselves to be shackled and expelled. The Demerara colonist newspaper proclaimed: 'We shall not suffer you to enlighten our slaves, who are by law our property, till you can demonstrate that when they are made religious and knowing, they will continue to be our slaves'.[5] As an aside, there was heated argument, led by Wilberforce, about whether such property encompassed those of mixed race, whose paternity was almost certainly white European and, in many cases, the plantation owner himself. The master was effectively enslaving his own child. As we saw in the case of Bertie Entwistle, the same legal status attached to them as to other enslaved people.

In parallel with the pressure being brought to bear on preachers in the colonies, the London Missionary Society and the British and Foreign Bible Society boasted widespread conversions to Christianity through the dissemination of the New Testament to regions and in languages as diverse as Eskimo and Indo-Pacific. The god-fearing citizens of Chester were deeply invested in this cause.

Closer to home, the state of Ireland continued to be vexatious. The population there had risen to around seven million, exacerbating problems relating to poverty and religious tension. There were only a million Protestants on the island, of whom half were Dissenters. Calls in Westminster for sectarian groups, such as the Orangemen, to be banned were resisted, on the basis that public officials were often their patrons or grand masters. Population growth and land management practices led to the subdivision of tenancies, which then became an even less viable means of subsistence. Protests and disturbances broke out, particularly in the south and west of Ireland.

Whilst there was some industrial unrest in mainland Britain – such as arson attacks on silk mills in Macclesfield – and huge divisions in society, many people enjoyed a level of prosperity that enabled them to re-invest in the economy. Shares in railways did particularly well, with an application pending to link Birmingham, Liverpool and Manchester, for which £100,000 had already been subscribed. Steam ships and coaches were upping their game too. The St George Steam Packet made the quickest ever recorded passage from Dublin to Liverpool in 10 hours 40 minutes, and a coach covered the 125-mile route from London to Bristol in 11 hours, prompting the suggestion that travellers should insure their lives.[6] Over 150 steam ships plied their trade around the British coast, the busiest sea lanes being Leith to London, Liverpool to Greenock and Liverpool to Dublin. Progress on the Conway Bridge was now reported to be rapid, and a lighthouse was under construction at New Brighton.

The investment in infrastructure was partly borne out of economic success, and the confidence and ambition it engendered, but it was also a response to population growth. Liverpool, an extreme example but by no means a complete outlier, had seen its population rise from 5,000 to 130,000 over the previous century and was home to 9,500 sailing vessels, compared to six barques in Elizabethan times.[7] Immigration was a factor too. France had released their Spanish prisoners of war but provided no safe haven for them, so many came to England, dependent on relief. As we saw in the previous chapter, Chester was sympathetic to their cause.

The state of the king's health was almost as great a source of enquiry as the state of the nation, and, of course, they were inextricably linked. At the turn of the month, the king had been indisposed for five weeks by attacks of gout and coughing fits, leading to his confinement at Windsor and the cancellation of his drawing rooms. These were events at which he received mostly ladies from the upper echelons of society who were coming out, moving abroad or entering royal service.[8] Now, not only was he well enough to reinstate them, but he had new rooms at St James's Palace in which to host them, with which he was apparently very pleased. On one typical occasion, as the king readied himself within, crowds of fashionable ladies in carriages lined the street, surrounded by a vast array of onlookers. They pressed into the palace and presented themselves and their compliments to him in a highly curated manner throughout afternoon. Amongst the visitors were the Bishop of Chester, Lady Warburton and 'Miss Townshend', according to the Chester newspapers.[9] Again, a Christian name would have been helpful, but there is a good chance that this was one of the Misses Townshend that feature elsewhere in this book.

At Knutsford, east of Chester, a hot air balloon landed in a field. In it was Windham William Sadler, an aeronaut of some repute, who had commenced his flight in Salford. After some complications, including the need to disappoint a potential passenger in the interests of greater buoyancy, he had taken off alone at around 5pm. On completion of the flight, with the help of the good people of Knutsford, the balloon was safely stowed, and he retraced his twenty-mile journey by post-chaise, arriving at an inn in Salford at 11pm. Despite some concussion from a bumpy landing, he repeated the feat at Rochdale two weeks later.

Having heard a good deal about Mr Sadler, Chester folk would soon be able to see him at first hand. On 27th May – fittingly Ascension Day - he staged a flight in his home city of Liverpool. He was accompanied by Mr Peel of the 3rd Dragoon Guards, who was a cousin of the future prime minister and the passenger who had been left on the ground at Salford. Strenuous preparations had been made, including the erection of a 40ft tent in Cattle Market Square, Lime Street, to contain the inflated balloon, which was periodically displayed to an awestruck local populace. Much care was taken to ensure an adequate supply of gas. Inflation began a day or two in advance under the watchful eyes of physicists and gas engineers, Mr Sadler himself being one by trade. On the morning of the attempt – for an attempt it always was – huge crowds descended on the city, including carriages from Chester, where notice of the event had been circulated. Flags and streamers decked towers and steeples, bells were rung and signals fired. Roofs and even chimney tops were amply tenanted.

Some confusion and anxiety mingled with the intense expectation when an inferior hoax balloon rose from the gasworks in Dale Street, its occupants risking life and limb in the interests of their jest. Messrs Peel and Sadler soon entered the car, almost casually, not to say inadequately, dressed in unadorned jackets and trousers. The ascent began in clear and bright conditions, amid a great tumult, taking a southerly course. Crowds followed as if invisibly tethered, until the balloon disappeared from their view almost an hour later. Rising majestically above the Mersey, the sun picked out its red and crimson silken flanks. The two airborne companions, in these rarified conditions, drank the king's health and raised three cheers to him.

Soon the descent began, with some speculation about a landing in the Hoole area of Chester, where residents prepared assistance and entertainment for the intrepid travellers. Spectators lined the eastern section of the city wall and, here too, churches and chimney tops were not neglected in pursuit of a prime vantage point. The balloon's trajectory towards the city was averted by an easterly turn in the wind, which resulted in it coming to ground inoffensively in a field at Bridge Trafford, some five miles away. The few people nearby approached eagerly and a quest for reflective glory began in Chester. Mr Tomlinson of the Feathers and Mr Willoughby of the Royal Hotel both bolted out of the city in their respective chaises in the hope of recovering the celebrities and showing them appropriate hospitality. Mr Tomlinson edged the contest and returned with them and their apparatus in mid-evening. Mr Sadler was gracious in thanking and rewarding all those who assisted.[10] He had so captured the imagination of the Chester public that there was an appetite for more of the same, but this time closer to home.

Balloon flight was not new but the first craze in the mid-1780s quickly subsided and was only revived in the 1820s when hydrogen gave way to gas – more cheaply and abundantly available due to wider municipal use – as a source of power. The celebrated balloonist, Vicenzo Lunardi, visited Liverpool and Chester in the autumn of 1785. Whilst he was constrained by injury, recorded flights were undertaken by his collaborators, George Biggin and local man Thomas Baldwin. After landing safely in Warrington, Baldwin returned to his native city the following day to much acclaim. In some ways, he eclipsed his contemporaries by adopting a scientific approach to flight and detailing his experiences, making him something of a pioneer in the fields of aerial cartography and travel writing.[11]

For older Cestrians in 1824, these events would have been tinged with a nostalgic glow; for the younger generation, they were the stuff of folklore. So it was that Mr Sadler's skirting of the city quickly evolved into a full-blown invitation to ascend from it. A deal was struck with the mayor and magistrates and a date set: Monday 7th June. The castle esplanade and military band were readied and the Gas Company on Cuppin Street was co-opted to provide free gas. Publicity was generated and anticipation grew.

In the meantime, reports from overseas were dominated by news from West Africa and Greece. In Sierra Leone and the Gold Coast, the Ashantee had surprised and routed British troops, killing the Governor, Sir Charles McCarthy, and provoking fears of an end to British control of the region. There was speculation that there was some agency on the part of European slave traders who resented attempts by His Majesty's ships to obstruct their business.

In the middle of May, news arrived of the tragic death from fever, almost a month earlier, of Lord Byron. This was a loss in the moment militarily but, in literary terms, for all time. As one commentator put it: 'Thus has perished, in the flowering of his age, in the noblest of causes, one of the greatest poets England has ever produced.' This must have affected our book club members, who would have been acutely aware of his genius and celebrity, arising from his appearance and behaviour, as well as his poetic output. Perhaps they had just picked up the newly released Cantos 15 and 16 of *Don Juan*, which were criticised by many for their moral turpitude. In Greece, where the struggle for independence was at a high pitch, Easter festivities were deferred and a 21-day period of mourning put in place. Symbolically, Byron's heart was retained there, whilst the rest of his body was returned to England.

Byron bequeathed his memoirs to his friend, the poet Thomas Moore, who struck a deal worth £2,000 with publisher John Murray. *The Sun* newspaper reported that Moore considered the content scandalous and agreed to meet 'a near female acquaintance of Byron', who burnt the papers entirely in his presence. This is regarded as possibly the greatest literary crime in history. There were some attempts to defend his reputation in the aftermath of his death, a task undoubtedly eased by the destruction of his memoirs.

There wasn't much in the press of a lighter nature to set against this sombre news. Readers may have had their curiosity piqued by the arrival in London of the King and Queen of the Sandwich Islands – or Hawaii as it is now called – and accounts of their stay at the Adelphi Hotel. Here they played whist in the lobby and gave a press conference that was rendered futile by the ineptitude of their interpreter. Much was made of their great size, dark skin and florid clothing, in reporting that would be roundly condemned in the modern day. Despite an element of theatre around them, the reason for their unprecedented visit was deadly serious: they were on a diplomatic mission to cede their possessions to the Crown in return for protection from hostile invasion, potentially by Russia.

Chapter Eleven

Mrs Massie
Lot 6

*The Guide to Domestic Happiness, 2 vols., beautifully bound in purple Morocco.
Scarce; only 18 copies extant, exclusive of this*

The surnames 'Massie' and 'Massey', which derive from the same root, are deeply in-grained in the history of Cheshire and are found throughout the county in the modern day. An old ditty, which prizes the conveyance of information above the consistency of rhyme, proclaims:

In Cheshire there be
As many Leighs as fleas,
As many Lowes as sloes,
As many Masseys as asses,
As many Davenports as dog's tails.[1]

Despite this, the identification of this book club member is more straightforward than most, partly because 'Massie' is less prevalent than 'Massey', and partly because of the detail that Dr Norris provides. There are also emerging connections with other members, which help with the verification process.

An account of Mrs Mainwaring's masquerade in January 1822 tells us that 'Mrs Massie looked so cross as an old maid, that we really should not have remembered her, had she not now and then forgot herself'.[2] In 1827, a Hester Lee Massie witnessed the will of

Frances Sarah Townshend – sister of Mrs Mainwaring – implying a close connection with the Townshend family. The other sister, Frances Anne, in her will of 1830, bequeathed 'to my cousin Hester Massie my hair bracelet with emeralds and pearls and £5'. A little genealogical research confirms that she was the daughter of Edward Townshend, brother of Susanna Mainwaring's father, John.

Hester Maria Townshend was born in Hoole, Chester in 1776. She would lead a remarkable life. Her mother was Anne Baldwin, the daughter of John Baldwin Rigbye, who built Hoole Hall in 1760. His wealth came through his maternal line, including inheriting Harrock Hall near Parbold, Lancashire, in 1787, which carried with it the obligation to adopt the family name of 'Rigbye'. When he died in 1793, Anne's brother, Thomas Baldwin, succeeded to his estates. This was the renowned Chester balloonist of whom we have just heard. What pride and trepidation Hester must have felt as a nine-year-old girl as her uncle rose above Chester Castle on 8th September 1785.

Hester's father, Edward, was the son of John Townshend of Trevalyn. Her eldest brother, Edward Venables Townshend, who will feature further in our story, was born at Wincham Hall, near Northwich. Like other families we have seen, the Townshends had a strong presence not just in Chester, but in other desirable locations radiating out from it.

Mixing amongst leading county families, it would not have been difficult for Hester to come into contact in her youth with the Massies of Coddington, not far south of Chester. Indeed, there is reportedly a Royalist Civil War song that mentions this family alongside the Townshends and the Mainwarings, suggesting not just that they go back a long way together, but that they shared the same allegiances.[3] In October 1796, at the age of 20 – necessitating parental consent – she married the Reverend Richard Massie, five years her senior. He was the eldest son and heir of Thomas Massie, who owned considerable residential property at Parkgate, as well as the family seat at Coddington. The wedding took place in the parish of Neston, which served Parkgate, Hester being described as of that place in the marriage bond. This may not have reflected her permanent place of abode, as only four weeks' residence was required to meet the qualifying criteria. Such was the Massie presence in the area, however, that Richard's mother, Elizabeth, was dubbed 'Old

Madam Massie' by local people and remembered for her charitable deeds there well into the 1880s – some seven decades after her death.[4]

The Massies claim ancestry as far back as Hamon de Masci or Massey, born in Normandy in 1056, who became the first Baron of Dunham – hence the Dunham Massey estate south-west of Manchester. According to Ormerod, Coddington descended to the Reverend Richard Massie from John Massie of Broxton, who was born in the time of Henry VIII.[5] Richard received it somewhat diminished by the excesses of his eccentric uncle, another John Massie – colloquially known as 'Black John' – who burnt down Coddington Hall. There are references to another Richard Massie who, during the reign of Elizabeth I, made an ill-advised trip to Rome which aroused the suspicions of Sir Francis Walsingham, the queen's spymaster. This is one of several indications of Catholic sympathies on the part of the Massies, which carried the risk of the gravest consequences for many generations.

The fearless forebear of Civil War renown was Edward Massie – son of John Massie and Anne Grosvenor – who fought for the king, before turning to Cromwell so committedly that he gained a seat in his Parliament. Perhaps pricked by old family loyalties, he turned again to the Royalist cause, leading to imprisonment, escape and exile in Holland. He returned to fight at the decisive Battle of Worcester in 1651, where he sustained severe injuries and was captured. This was followed by another spell of imprisonment and escape, this time to Ireland, where he died.[6]

In 1642, as the Civil War began, there were accounts of Catholic recusants being apprehended in the Broxton Hundred on Massie land. In the 1670s, the Masseys of Puddington – a branch of the family which took that spelling of the name and were long settled on that part of the Wirral – harboured the Catholic priest, John Plessington. He was betrayed to the authorities, convicted of high treason and executed at Boughton in 1679. Today, his name appears on an obelisk in Boughton, as counterpoint to the name of George Marsh – the Protestant martyr burnt at the stake nearby in the Maryan purges of the 1550s – which features on the opposite side. Mary Davies, mentioned in Chapter

One as a source of the Grosvenors' great wealth, became close to the Masseys of Puddington after her marriage and move to Chester. She was converted to Catholicism by
them, resulting in some estrangement from her family.[7]

One of the Reverend Richard's aunts was Maria Sobieski Massie, who has a given name
which appears to have been a nod to a scion of the Polish royal family. Maria Sobieski
was the granddaughter of King John III Sobieski, wife of James Francis Edward Stuart –
the 'Old Pretender' – and mother of Charles Edward Stuart or Bonnie Prince Charlie –
the 'Young Pretender'. Maria Sobieski Massie was born in 1737, two years after her namesake's death and eight years before the Jacobite Rising, which adds weight to the suppo-
sition around her moniker.[8] The Stuart claim to the throne was well-founded on their
lineage but denied on the basis of their Catholicism. These facts also argue in favour of
Massie leanings towards the Church of Rome, investing some irony in the Reverend Richard's lifelong immersion in the Church of England.

Over time, we start to see evidence of a Massie presence in Chester. In 1748, Anne Massie
– widow of William Massie of Coddington – stated in her will that she had a house in
Chester, where she then lived. She left money for the release of debtors from prison and
for their sustenance thereafter, and to 'twenty poor housekeepers of Chester'.[9] Other beneficiaries included members of notable families with strong connections to Chester, such
as the Needhams – ennobled under the title 'Kilmorey' – the Leches and the Barnstons.
This Anne's nephew – another William Massie, uncle of the Reverend Richard – became
an eminent surgeon in London but died at the home of John Lloyd in Watergate Street,
Chester in 1808. At the turn of the 19th century, Thomas Massie – father of the Reverend
Richard, whom we shall call simply 'Richard' from now on – contested the manorial rights
at Waverton, near Chester, reaching an agreement that allowed the land to be enclosed
and benefit to be derived from the rising price of agricultural produce.[10]

By the time Thomas died in Parkgate in 1802, Richard and Hester had blessed him with
five grandchildren. Hester would continue giving birth almost annually until 1820, whereupon she would boast of having brought 22 children into the world, or even 24, because

she was not coy about two early miscarriages.[11] Now we begin to understand Dr Norris's wry selection of *A Guide to Domestic Happiness*, the two volumes presumably representing the long-suffering parents and the 18 extant copies their surviving children in 1824. This certainly tallies with genealogical data. The pertinence of the title is reinforced by stories passed down the family line of difficulties in finding domestic staff to take the children in hand and a consequent reliance on the older ones to support the upbringing of their younger siblings. With such a host of characters in play, this narrative needs to take care over whom it features and to what extent. Some, however, should not escape without comment.

The Massie children mostly appear to have been born in Holy Trinity parish, Chester, and the address '3 Stanley Place' quickly comes to the fore. The street appears regularly in births, marriages and deaths columns and the house number in later censuses and reminiscences. It would have been fashionable and pristine, having been built only in the 1770s and occupying a prime location between the Linen Hall and the city walls. Richard was Rector of St Bridget's, and so needed a base in the city, and Hester would have valued being close to relatives and friends who lived nearby.

Richard also held the rectorship at Aldford, a village south of Chester, adjacent to Eaton Hall, but appears to have regarded that as more of a sinecure than his parishioners did. He would pick up Eccleston in due course too. He had considerable inherited wealth but would have welcomed the income from these livings, with a growing family to support. One of his earliest clerical duties, whilst still curate at Coddington, was to officiate at the wedding in 1800 of Charles Mainwaring and Sarah Susanna Townshend. He appears to have been popular and successful at St Bridget's, where the size of the congregation rose from approximately 80 in 1778 to 140 under his tenure.[12]

In 1813, three of the Massie children - Harriet Vyse Massie, Watkyn and Anna Maria - were baptised together by their father at St Bridget's, alongside Maria and Philip Stapleton Humberston, all five being in their infancy at the time. These economies of scale are understandable in the context of such large families. The year 1815 saw the first fatality amongst the younger generation of the Massies, with the death of George, who was still a baby. Cornelia Lee, Mary Mackenzie and Henry – the 8th, 21st and 22nd children respectively – succumbed in successive years from 1818 to 1820. The family would have mourned these losses deeply. Studies have shown that large family sizes and high mortality rates in the Regency period did not diminish the grief occasioned by each individual loss.

Another bereavement, in the middle of the decade, came with the death of Richard's mother – 'Old Madam Massie' – in Parkgate. She left her considerable wealth in trust to Richard and Hester's children and appointed as trustees Edward Venables Townshend, John Stanislaus Townshend and Philip Humberston. The will was drafted in 1807 and shows the three families of Townshend, Humberston and Massie interacting closely some 17 years before our book club meeting. John Stanislaus Townshend is noted as being 'of Gayton', which suggests that he was living not far from Parkgate at the time. 'I give and bequeath to my said son Richard Massie,' continues the will, 'whatever money he may find in my inlaid cabinet.'[13] There may have been an earnestness on his part to conclude the search once the document had been read.

The oldest child, Eliza Anne, married William Theophilus Buchanan, an Ulsterman, at Holy Trinity in 1823. He was from a landed family who owned estates in Staffordshire and Donegal. As a young soldier, he had fought in the Peninsular Wars under Lord Hill, distinguishing himself in several campaigns and being decorated for his services. His brother, also a soldier, achieved even greater lasting memory, largely through the presence of a plaque in his honour at Chester Cathedral:

Sacred to the memory of John Phillips Buchanan of the 16th or Queen's Regiment of Light Dragoons who, in the glorious and decisive Battle of Waterloo, on the 18th day of June 1815 was killed by a musket shot in the HOUR of VICTORY in the 27th year of his age ...

By the mid-1830s, William was on the Grand Jury of Chester Assizes, alongside Sir Harry Mainwaring, and, in 1837 had the stately Ravenscroft Hall near Middlewich built for himself and Eliza. He died in Bristol in 1865, leaving effects valued at approximately £70,000 to his widow, who outlived him by 20 years.

Eliza would have been one of three 'Miss Massies' listed as attendees – in the company of their parents, Mrs Coupland and Mrs Sloughter, amongst others – at Lord Belgrave's Ball at the Royal Hotel in 1818, as described in Chapter One. Here they danced quadrilles and mingled with army officers, one of whom may have been William Buchanan. The other two 'Misses' are likely to have been Susan Hester and Frances Maria, their ages overall ranging between 18 and 21.

Three years later, Susan married the Reverend John Armitstead of Sandbach and, in 1827, Frances married the Reverend George Becher Blomfield, formerly curate of Hawarden, as we have seen, but by this time Rector of Coddington and Tattenhall.[14] These families were intimately connected with the Massies. For example, after Frances died in 1837 at the rectory in Stevenage, where the Reverend George was then incumbent, Richard and Hester went to stay with him. Indeed, they are both shown at that address in the censuses of 1841 and 1851. The Blomfields have their own story to tell, to which we shall briefly return. Susan lost her husband to a stroke in 1865, the same year in which William Buchanan died. She would live on into the 1880s.

The eldest son, confusingly, was another Richard who became a man of the cloth. We will call him Richard junior. In 1834, he married Mary Anne Hughes, daughter of Hugh Robert Hughes, of Bache Hall, Chester, who was a man of ample means, as mentioned in Chapter Five. Richard junior is described as 'a gentleman of wealth and leisure' who 'devoted himself to literature'.[15] In 1854, he published a translation of *Martin Luther's Spiritual Songs* and in 1860 *Lyra Domestica: Translated from the Psaltery and Harp*, which contained some popular hymns. 'Lyra domestica' means 'domestic lyre', which reminds us of Dr Norris's book choice for Hester and the notion of home comforts, one of which would have been music.

A Massie family source notes a touch of eccentricity on Richard junior's part. It seems he liked to wear a red wig and tall beaver hat and carried a crutch on account of some lameness from which he had long since recovered. The source adds that 'he and his mother and his sisters are remembered as remarkable for their quiet spirituality and saint-liness'.[16] Perhaps this demeanour was easier to maintain once the children had grown up and dispersed.

Richard junior, who later in life became a JP, settled at his estates at Wrexham and Pulford Hall, south of Chester. In 1873, he attended Philip Stapleton Humberston's wedding at Henllan, showing that the close friendship between the families had endured through another generation. Corbets and Cottons were on the guest list too. In 1886, he donated £10 towards a memorial fund for Dean Howson, the indefatigable restorer, not to say rescuer of Chester Cathedral, who is buried and fittingly commemorated in that place. Richard passed away at Pulford the following year. Two of his unmarried sisters, Barbara and Sidney, also died there, in 1882 and 1891 respectively. Sidney was a talented artist and produced several studies of buildings in and around Chester in her younger days, including a sketch of Saighton Grange of circa 1830. Their current whereabouts are un-known.[17]

Richard junior's younger brother by two years was Thomas Leche Massie. His home ad-dress was the family town house at 3 Stanley Place, Chester, but, as a naval man, he was away for extended periods of time. His career was illustrious, including service in Crimea and Alexandria, where he is credited with building the strategically important harbour. He achieved the rank of admiral in 1866 and became known as 'the Father of the British Navy'. When he died in Chester 1898, in his 97th year, obituaries cited his ultimate profes-sional status as well as an intriguing episode from when he was still a rookie in the service. We have heard much of the demise of Lord Byron in 1824 – it appears that Thomas was on the scene:

Admiral Massie formed one of the boat's crew that went ashore to bring off Lord Byron to a British man-of-war during his last illness in Greece. The admiral stated that when they reached the harbour they were informed by the medical men that the poet was too ill to be removed, and he died shortly afterwards.[18]

Being so close to possibly the greatest celebrity of the age at the moment of his death must have left a deep and abiding impression on young Thomas. His own longevity provided the opportunity for some years of retirement in Chester, during which he was Chairman of Governors at Chester Infirmary and a member of other philanthropic organisations. He would have been comfortably off, especially after inheriting Richard junior's estates.

With his wife, Charlotte Hester Townshend – a first cousin and the daughter of Edward Venables Townshend of Wincham Hall – he had three children. One of these was called Maud Cleopatra Massie. She was born in 1849, baptised at the new St Bridget's Church and also lived much of her life at 3 Stanley Place. She merits mention here because of her extraordinary life, which included eventually marrying the stepson of Edward, her elder brother. Edward was a military man who, at the age of 21, met and married an Austrian noblewoman called Olga Maria, Baroness von Wessenberg-Ampringen. She had a six-year-old son called Peter – better known as 'Pello' – and professed to be a widow. This claim has been challenged by research which shows her to have been the mistress of a top-ranking member of the French Government.

Edward and Olga had three sons together, one of whom died in infancy. He left the army to avoid a distant posting, and the family settled in the south of France. When Olga tragically died in a train crash in 1878, the two surviving sons were sent to Maud in Chester. Pello, now 19, went to Austria where he served in the army and, being a talented writer and artist, was reputedly a tutor to the Hapsburg family. He married, but when his wife died in 1914, Maud travelled to Austria and quickly filled the vacancy, she being 65 years old and Pello 55 at that time. They returned to Chester to live, along with Pello's daughter, Helen, from his first marriage. War soon broke out and Pello was monitored as an alien.

Some months later they were sent back to Austria, where Pello re-enlisted as a colonel and fought against the Allies. Maud was now in enemy territory and subject to considerable privations herself, leading almost to starvation. They both survived the war, returning to live in Kent, where Maud died in 1928. Despite these upheavals – or perhaps because of them – the Austrian side of the family were close to the Massies in England and had a particular affinity to Chester.[19]

Turning again to the immediate offspring of Richard and Hester Massie, we find Edward – uncle of the Edward just alluded to. Almost inevitably now, he was another churchman, following the Massie trend of acquiring livings in east Cheshire, which would have been influenced by the Armitstead presence in Sandbach. Indeed, in 1832, Richard relinquished St Bridget's and Aldford in favour of Eccleston and Goostrey, the latter being in the gift of John Armitstead, his son-in-law. Edward became rector of nearby Gawsworth and, in 1845, married Sophia, the daughter of the Reverend Charles Mytton Thorneycroft, his father's predecessor at Eccleston. His main focus was the restoration of Gawsworth Church, for which considerable funding and expertise were required. To this end, he entered into some astute partnerships, including engaging the irrepressible George Gilbert Scott. As his services didn't come cheap, innovative methods were required to meet the cost. On 21st August 1852, *The Staffordshire Advertiser* carried the following notice:

North Staffordshire Railway. Excursion to the gardens and pleasure grounds of Elvaston Castle, near Derby. The Right Honourable the Earl of Harrington has kindly granted access for a day to the far-famed Gardens and Grounds of Elvaston Castle, the fees for admission to be appropriated in aid of the fund for the RESTORATION of GAWSWORTH CHURCH, near Congleton … special trains from Macclesfield, The Potteries, Birmingham, Tamworth, Burton & c … The day appointed for this delightful trip is Monday, September 6, and the manager earnestly invites the public to a participation of the privileges and objects of the excursion. All particulars are published in handbills, which may be had on application to the Rev E Massie,

GAWSWORTH Rectory, Congleton, or the manager of the trains, T Cook, Leicester.

This somewhat understated manager was none other Thomas Cook, whose global travel business sprang from these modest shoots.

The tendency for the Massie men to enter the military or the church was embodied in the 10th child, William Henry, who did both. He was born at Stanley Place in 1806. He was educated first at Overleigh Hall in Chester, which was another casualty of infrastructure work on the Grosvenor Bridge, and then Macclesfield Grammar School. Overleigh had been built by the Cowper family and was steeped in Royalist history, going back to the Civil War. Bonnie Prince Charlie is said to have been entertained in the Macclesfield building by Sir Peter Davenport during his ill-fated venture south in 1745. This exposure may have fired young William's imagination and given rise to his lifelong interest in all things antiquarian. He was a talented artist too and sketched wherever he went.

In 1826, Richard was offered a cadetship for one of his sons in the Indian Service, which was William's cue to join the 39th Bengal Native Infantry. The climate and disease-ridden conditions took a severe toll on his health, however. This was so apparent on a visit home that he was persuaded to stay and turn to the ministry. He excelled in his studies at Trinity College, Dublin, before being ordained in Chester by Bishop Sumner in 1834. He was first granted the curacy at Goostrey, through family patronage, and then the rectorship at St Mary's on the Hill, Chester, by the Marquess of Westminster. He later became a minor canon at Chester Cathedral and was the prime mover in the foundation of Chester Archaeological Society.

Like his father at St Bridget's, William invested deeply and effectively in church and parish life at St Mary's. During a cholera epidemic in 1849, he ministered fearlessly to the afflicted, and, in 1854, he provided great spiritual support to the garrison and regiment of the 23rd Royal Fusiliers, for whom he was chaplain, when they suffered substantial losses at the Battles of Alma and Inkerman in Crimea. His religion, which bore no vestige of

Catholic sympathies, was interwoven with his historical interests. He translated and pre-sented on the charter of St Werburgh from the time of the first Norman Earls of Chester and used the anniversary of the Gunpowder Plot as a pretext for preaching Anglican su-premacy. His sermons and lectures met with much acclaim, including from the Society of Antiquaries, whose offer of a fellowship he declined. His work on the history of seals and in arguing that Chester was not an established British city before arrival of the Romans was particularly highly commended. Through his determined efforts, Chester Archaeo-logical Society attracted interest and support from the bishop, the Marquess of Westmin-ster, Viscount Combermere and Sir Stephen Glynne, amongst others, ensuring a blueprint for success.

William recognised that his parish, with six townships and a growing population, was unsustainable with a single church in its midst. He therefore instigated the erection of two churches, which would lead to the creation of new parishes at Saltney and, in due course, Upton. He engaged the services of the architect James Harrison – no relation to Thomas – even though he had demonstrated his own capability in this field by designing a church at Byley, whilst in post at nearby Goostrey. As was his wont, he took an assiduous interest in the construction, walking between the churches on a regular basis to monitor progress.

Whilst returning from Upton in heavy rain 1855, he caught a chill but went straight out again to attend to a distressed parishioner. This led to what proved to be a fatal illness on his part, his death occurring on 5th January 1856, at the age of 49. Perhaps the debilitation he had suffered in India had weakened his constitution. Despite his energy and vigour towards an array of worthy causes, it was said that he looked older than his years. He was buried at St Mary's with semi-military honours, given his chaplaincy at the garrison. In the region of a thousand people were reported to have thronged the tight space around the rectory and church. Amongst the chief mourners were his brother Richard, and Lawrence and the Reverend John Armitstead, whose son – another Reverend John – was a pall-bearer. William left an indelible mark on Chester, in his churches and in his theological and antiquarian output. An obituary in the *Chester Chronicle* suggested that his disposition had been so charitable that 'he didn't have a shilling to attract a wife'.[20] The principal subscribers to memorials in his honour in the three churches over which he had presided included Messrs Dixons and Wardell – the Chester bankers – and Philip Stapleton Humberston.

The life of the next child – Townshend Massie, born in 1808 – is less well documented, but we do know that he died on 25th April 1836 whilst bathing in a rough sea at Bahia in Brazil. The fact that this was reported in the *Manchester Times* on 16th June is a reminder of the pace at which news travelled the globe, no doubt compounding the grief of his family upon its arrival. Townshend was probably on naval duty. Bahia was on a trade route which was still afflicted by Portuguese piracy and slavery, having been the site of a major slave revolt the year before his death.

John Bevis Massie, born in 1809, was indisputably a naval man. He was mostly a midshipman in British, Irish and Mediterranean waters, before becoming a 1st Lieutenant in the Pacific. In the early 1840s, he was aboard two ships which bore the flag of Sir Edward Owen. In December 1847, the *Kentish Independent* reported that he was being transported home from Rio de Janeiro, as the British attempted to mediate hostilities in the River Plate area, as an invalid. His death a little over three years later may well have stemmed from injuries sustained in combat.

His younger sister by a year, Harriet Vyse, married Lawrence Armitstead of Cranage Hall, who was the elder half-brother of John. The ceremony took place at Holy Trinity, Chester in 1829, the year in which Lawrence was High Sheriff of Cheshire and in which he completed the rebuilding of Cranage Hall with the help of the noted architect, Lewis Wyatt. The union ended less than seven years later with Harriet's untimely death.

Watkin Massie, born in 1812, followed the lead of his brother, William – unhappy though it was – by entering the Indian service, in his case with the Bombay Artillery, which he joined in 1840. His experience was equally unfortunate in that he was invalided out the following year. The 1841 census shows him as still in the army but staying in Sandbach with his sister, Susan, and the Reverend John Armitstead. This is a reminder of the closeness between some of the Massie siblings, despite – or maybe even because of – often large age gaps. It was 15 years in this instance.

It is likely that Watkin never returned to India, and later censuses have him in the Croydon area, including as head of The Priory, a boarding school for boys, in 1881. He died that year, unmarried and intestate. His brother Richard advertised for claimants to his estate, valued at £2,300, before inheriting it himself. Family records suggest that he emigrated to Australia at one point, supported by his modest army pension and money from an aunt.[21] This benefactor is likely to have been Mary, widow of Watkin Williams Massie, a cousin of Richard senior. When she died in 1861, she left £20,000 to the Massie children.

It is reasonable to ask why this generous bequest – approximately £1.2 million in modern day terms – was made to relatives who were not lineally distant but not particularly close either. There appear to have been two reasons: firstly, these two branches of the family had a strong relationship and, secondly, Mary was not short of money. Watkin Williams, who was baptised at St Mary's on the Hill in 1768, was three years older than Richard, and both were only children brought up in the Chester area. Watkin Williams joined the East India Company as a civil servant, becoming chief judge and magistrate of the Zillah – or region – of Nuddeah in West Bengal by the time he was 30.[22] The city is now called Nabawip and is the seat of an ancient university and a place of pilgrimage. It is highly likely that he was instrumental in securing a post in the army in Bengal for William Henry Massie in 1826.

Watkin Williams used the wealth he acquired in the service to buy, successively, homes at two of the most desirable addresses in Britain: at 6 Charlotte Square, Edinburgh in 1814 and later at 2 Lansdown Villa, Cheltenham, where he died in 1838. When Mary passed away in 1861, in Bath, she left the modern equivalent of more than £10 million overall. Her late husband's work in India would have been lucrative but perhaps could not account for the totality of this wealth. If we look at her own background, we find that she came from the landed family of the Mackenzies of Fairburn, Ross-shire. It is no coincidence that one of Hester and Richard's daughters was christened 'Mary Mackenzie'.

Mary Massie, née Mackenzie, was the sister of General Sir Alexander MacKenzie, 10th Baronet of Fairburn. He died in Bath in 1853, close to where Mary then lived, leaving nothing to her other than a reminder of the 'affectionate regard I have ever felt' and acknowledging her 'independent position in life'. His assets were substantial, however, and beneficiaries included a range of other family members and charitable institutions, especially in Scotland. Set against the philanthropy was the disreputable source of much of this largesse. In 1834, he had lodged a successful compensation claim amounting to £10,358 – on a par with William Earle – for 385 enslaved people at his Tourama estate on St Vincent, one of the islands on which Bertie Entwistle once plied his malevolent trade.[23]

Details of the life of Anna Maria Massie, who was baptised in 1813 with two of her siblings, are sketchy. She appears not to have married. There is a record in *Slater's Directory* of 1855 of a music teacher of that name based in Egerton Street, Chester, but it is not definitively her and it is questionable whether she was still alive at that date. The next child was Charles, presumably named after an uncle of Richard who died in 1810, having been a surgeon in Wrexham; he is commemorated in the church at Bangor-on-Dee. Young Charles appears to have entered the ministry, before his adult life took another course.

When the census was conducted in 1841, Charles was listed as a clerk at Sandbach in the company of the Reverend John Armitstead, his sister Susan and brother Watkin. Ten years later, however, there is a note of a 'C.M.', a Church of England clergyman born in Chester as a patient at Tuebrook Villa in Liverpool. This was a private asylum, to which words such as 'lunatic' and 'insane' were casually and unashamedly attached. We can reasonably suppose that this is Charles because of a burial record of 1895 at nearby West Derby Cemetery which gives his full name and address at the asylum. This means he was there for most of his life, which spanned eight decades. Presumably, the family chose this asylum over Chester, which was opened in 1829, because it more directly met his needs.

Charles was one of 43 patients at Tuebrook in 1841, surrounded by former merchants, physicians, attorneys, senior servicemen and others from the upper echelons of society. What set him on this course, when so many of his siblings were excelling in their chosen fields, is beyond our conjecture.

Charlotte, born in 1815, reached adulthood but didn't marry. When the census was taken in 1841, she was with the Blomfields, her mother, father and a number of her siblings at Stevenage Rectory. She died at Eccleston five years later.

The Massie children that remain to be mentioned are Robert George and Hugh Hamon, born at Stanley Place respectively in 1815 and 1817. For greater transparency, we should deal first with Hugh Hamon, who retained in his middle name a link with his Norman ancestor. He won a scholarship to Corpus Christi College, Oxford, graduating in 1838. Some time after that, he decided to seek his fortune in Australia and appears to have been successful in that regard. In 1852, the *Australia and New Zealand Gazette* described him as the Assistant Commissioner at the National Gold Commissioners' Department. Hugh stayed and continued to prosper, dying at the Australian Club, Macquarie Street, Sydney on 3rd October 1893. He is buried at the Waverley Cemetery in the city, reputedly one of the most beautiful in the world.[24]

Robert George followed the same path, travelling to Australia in 1839, and, after experiencing mixed fortunes in agriculture in the Hunter Valley – in common with George Townshend – moved into colonial administration. He was one of the first members of the Queensland Legislative Council and was later elected to serve in the New South Wales Legislative Assembly. He and his brother, Hugh, were amongst the Commissioners of Foreign Countries and Colonies who attended the Sydney International Exhibition in 1879.

In 1854 Robert George married Annette Browne, daughter of Major Sylvester Browne, a former East India man who had relocated to Sydney aboard his own barque in 1830, after first delivering a cargo of convicts to Tasmania. Major Sylvester built two impressive houses – 'Newtown' and 'Enmore' – after which suburbs of the city were supposedly named. His son, Thomas Browne, was the author of several Australian classic novels under the pseudonym Rolf Boldrewood. Robert George died in Parramatta in 1883, leaving a widow and seven children. One of these was another Hugh Hamon Massie, who achieved fame in both hemispheres.[25]

Hugh junior was born in Victoria in April 1854 – three weeks before his parents' marriage. He excelled at cricket, which led to his selection for New South Wales and Australia. In 1882, he played a pivotal role at The Oval in what became recognised as the first ever test match, scoring a quick-fire 55 runs out of a total of 127, in a seven-run victory. The press lamented 'the death of English cricket' and dubbed the next English tour of Australia 'the quest to regain the ashes', giving rise to one of the most famous sporting contests in the world.

A hard-hitting batsman, Hugh featured in some of the finest teams of the age, including a select 11 at Lords called 'The Gentlemen' alongside W G Grace and C B Fry. Grace later reminisced that 'besides being a good cricketer, Massie was one of the best fellows who ever visited England'. Whilst in the country, he took the opportunity to call on his relatives in Cheshire, on one occasion delighting locals by turning out in a village cricket match between Harthill and Aldersey, near Coddington. In 1895, he was made an honorary member of the Marylebone Cricket Club. He also achieved success in business, becoming a director of the Commercial Bank of Sydney. When the *Chester Chronicle* lamented his passing in 1938, at the age of 84, he was described as 'a man of exceptional charm'.[26]

A British periodical boldly entitled *Truth* contained some reflections on Hugh junior late on in his life. Besides describing him quirkily as 'one of the slashingest batsmen' Australia ever brought forth, it identified him as 'grandson to a 22er': 'To wit, old Grandmother Massie of Pulford Hall in Cheshire, who not only brought her husband … 22 children, but lived to 98 [in fact, it was 96] in so full vigour that she never needed spectacles nor ear trumpet, as well as keeping every one of her natural teeth, including wisdom teeth, up to the end of her days.'[27]

Hugh junior was 19 when Hester died in 1873. She had survived her husband by almost two decades, Richard having breathed his last at Eccleston in 1854. They are buried next to each other and some of their children in quiet, leafy surroundings by the ruined church in the village. Her lichen-crusted inscription can still be made out:

Also in memory of Hester Lee Massie (Born Dec 7th 1776. Died October 1st 1873.). Widow of the Rev Richard Massie and mother of 22 children of whom eleven survived her. 'Her eye was not dimmed nor her natural force abated. Having lived by faith, she died, in faith; giving glory to God. Her last words were, 'In you, O Lord, do I put my trust.'

Hester clearly took immense pride in her family and showed incredible resilience in creating it and in surviving so long and in such rude health. It seems her children were a life force in themselves and that she possessed an implacable faith and optimism to buoy her up. Remarkably, she carved out time for other wholesome pursuits, our book club being a prime example. She and her husband were at the heart of the community, which is what the city of Chester essentially then was.

Richard was Chaplain of Cheshire Penitentiary and a great supporter of educational institutions, which were founded on the fundamental precepts of the Anglican Church. One example amongst many is his involvement in an inspection and prize-giving dinner at the Earl and Countess Grosvenor's Schools, which housed a combined 460 pupils, on New Year's Eve 1827. He and Bishop Blomfield presented children with bibles printed the by the Society for Promoting Christian Knowledge. In 1830, Richard was an award recipient himself, in the form of a plate in recognition of his services to St Bridget's, which by this time had relocated to its new site closer to Chester Castle.

In 1832, Richard and Hester moved to the rectory at Eccleston on his appointment there. It is likely that the younger children accompanied them, though the Stanley Place town house remained within the family, becoming the home of Thomas Leche Massie, as we have seen. The role at Eccleston was out of all proportion to the size of the village because of its attachment to Eaton Hall and its eminent inhabitants. When Robert

Grosvenor, 1ˢᵗ Marquess of Westminster, died in 1845, Richard presided over the funeral. George Johnson, we recall, was one of the more prominent attendees. The *Chester Chronicle* reported that the coffin was lowered into a vault and that the Reverend Massie 'closed it with an impressive distinctness, somewhat painfully broken by his feelings on the consignment to his last earthly resting place of the remains of his old and valued friend and benefactor'.[28]

During his tenure, Richard's name appeared alongside that of 'Lord Westminster' and, for a time, 'Geo. Johnson' at the top of the list of members of the Eccleston Association for the Prosecution of Felons. Richard junior was a licensed gamekeeper. The notion of these two men of the cloth brandishing firearms in pursuit of miscreants may appear incongruous to us today; it was not uncommon then, when religion was bound up with law and order and policing was in its infancy and largely confined to urban areas.

Richard passed away in 1854. An auction of household goods was held at the rectory, as Hester began the process of vacating it. The vast array of lots included around a thousand volumes of books, which must have been a wrench for our bibliophile, newly attired in her widow's weeds, mourning her beloved husband of almost 60 years. Practicality must have been the driver. By 1861, Hester was at nearby Pulford Hall, with her son Richard and daughters Sidney and Barbara, where she would live out the rest of her days. By the time she died, at such a staggering age, she had divested much of her wealth to her children, leaving her remaining £4,000 to her sole executor, Richard junior.[29] She would have been 48 at the time of our book club meeting, still with half her life ahead of her.

We are fortunate that two fine miniature portraits of Hester and Richard, featured individually, were painted and survive to this day, in the ownership and care of one of her direct descendants. Both are seated at an angle but looking directly at the artist, their attire formal and their gaze serious. Though the depictions may be stylised, there is no doubt that they would have made a handsome couple. Richard's hand is resting on an open book, perhaps one from his copious collection.

Finally, we turn to the Blomfields. George Becher Blomfield, widowed upon the death of Frances Maria in 1837, remarried in 1842, this time to Mary Anson, daughter of Frederick Anson, Dean of Chester, who preceded Dean Howson and who initiated the work to substantially recover and adorn the cathedral. George's second marriage was even briefer, as Mary died in 1845. In 1854, he married for a third and final time, on this occasion to Elizabeth Fielden of Mollington Hall, near Chester. By now he was an established canon at Chester Cathedral and a leading light in the church missionary society in the city, alongside the Reverend William Massie. He also contributed greatly to the Chester Archaeological Society. He was able to maintain his living at Stevenage in parallel, only fully relocating in later life to Mollington, where died in December 1885. It seems he had caught a chill at Dean Howson's funeral, which quickly developed into a fatal bronchial condition.[30]

Of the five children of George and Frances Maria, one – Charles George Blomfield – became Police Commandant in Madras, and a second – Richard Massie Blomfield – became a rear admiral and was knighted for his services to the Royal Navy. A third son – Reverend George James Blomfield - had himself a son called George, who is shown in attendance at Watkin Massie's school in Croydon in 1881. In effect, Hester Lee Massie's great-grandson was being educated by her son.

George Becher Blomfield's elder brother, Charles James Blomfield, was the eminent churchman who presided successively over the bishoprics of Chester and London, as noted. His son, Arthur William, born at Fulham Palace in 1829, excelled in the field of architecture. The family's strong affinity with Chester must have extended to Arthur, because he completed some important commissions in the city, including designing the fine monument to the celebrated Bishop Pearson in the north transept and mosaics at the east end of the cathedral.[31] The Royal College of Music and Bank of England Law Courts are amongst his other works, as is Holy Trinity Church, Stevenage, which he built for his Uncle George. He was amply decorated during his illustrious career, culminating in a knighthood in 1889. One of his early protégés and lifelong friends was Thomas Hardy, who studied architecture before devoting himself so brilliantly to the art of the novel. Sir Arthur Blomfield died in 1899.

His two daughters, Mary and Eleanor, from his second marriage, achieved fame – some might say notoriety – in an entirely different field. On 4th June 1914, they gained admittance to the Throne Room at Buckingham Palace and appealed directly to King George V on behalf of the suffragette movement. Their most immediate motive was to plead for the cessation of forcible feeding of imprisoned protesters.

Beneath the byline, 'The violent demand for the vote by the militant suffragist movement continues in full fury,' one newspaper reported on 'a handsome young woman on her knees … with her hands stretched towards the King'.[32] Lady Blomfield, who was also present, refused to condemn the action and may well have been complicit in it. On top of widespread outrage in the press, London police officers were ordered to adopt harsher measures in dealing with campaigners. One publication reported that 'The Misses Blomfields are not related to the Rear Admiral Sir Richard and Lady Massie Blomfield'.[33] In fact, they were his cousins.[34]

Chapter Twelve

June

Early summer brought hot, dry conditions, interspersed by occasional light rain. This fuelled a growing appetite for sea bathing, which led in turn to the operation of a new coach service from Chester to Barmouth: a 26-hour round trip. Monsieur Doré was offering music and dancing lessons in Parkgate for the duration of the season and Philip Humberston was hopeful of selling a 34-bed hotel in Hoylake, which included 6 bathing machines – essentially beach huts on wheels. In Liverpool, the heat was a stimulus to the outbreak and spread of malignant diseases, including typhus.

By now, Chester Races were in full swing and had attracted the attention of the renowned commentator, Nimrod, of the *Sporting Magazine*. He suggested they were less convivial and less well-attended by the gentry than in former days but that the sport had greatly improved. He commended the range of silverware and associated prize money on offer, pointing to Sir Thomas Stanley's winnings of a thousand guineas the previous year. He took an even keener interest in the attendant cockfights and the theatricality that surrounded them. 'Admirers of airs, attitudes and postures of the human body would have had a high treat in the Chester cockpit,' he observed. The cockers, who animatedly hurled the combatants into the arena, wore turned-up hats, fustian jackets and red waistcoats. All that was lacking, Nimrod felt, was a new Hogarth to capture the scene on canvas.[1]

June was a busy month in ecclesiastical circles too. News that the king had approved the appointment of Dr Blomfield as the Bishop of Chester was greeted with long and loud peals of bells. The fifth anniversary of the Church Missionary Society was celebrated at the Town Hall in self-congratulatory style. Every year was bringing 'nearer to view the blessed prospect of evangelising the world'. England stood 'elevated as the great moral lighthouse of the Universe … and distinguished as the source of all good'. The minds of Christians were stirred up 'to labour for the spiritual emancipation of 600 million of our fellow men', including 75 million women in India 'who by their superstitions and degra-dations were sunk below the level of brute creations'. In that country, colonial authorities associated indigenous religions with witchcraft, and, in the previous 30 years, a thousand women had been executed on those grounds. Sierra Leone had been home to 'rude bar-barians and gross idolaters' who, until their recent conversion, had 'worshipped in devil-houses alone'. The rhetoric was powerful and penetrating to devout Anglican ears. Ex-hortations to fundraise and fight the good fight did not go unheeded.

There was praise for the work of the missionaries – including for governors such as Sir Thomas Brisbane in New South Wales and the late Sir Charles McCarthy in West Africa, who saw evangelism as an important aspect of their role – but there were cautionary ref-erences too. A motion was passed deploring the loss of missionaries around the world, and the fate of John Smith in Demerara was never far from their thoughts. Obituaries were starting to appear in the press, mostly exonerating Smith from any blame and la-menting the fact that his royal reprieve had arrived too late to take effect. Abolitionist MP, Henry Brougham, led the condemnation of Smith's treatment in a heated debate in the House of Commons on 2nd June, which had to be swiftly suspended when around a hundred MPs left the chamber to catch a glimpse of a balloon overhead, piloted by Mr and Mrs Graham.

The business of the House contained more petitions for the final abolition of slavery and calls from Roman Catholics in Ireland for their emancipation, citing the injustice of 90 per cent of a largely impoverished population contributing to a church from which they derived no benefit. Another petition – from the mariners and watermen of Greenock – sought an end to impressment into the navy but was defeated on the basis that it was deemed to be the only way to maintain the fleet and British domination of the seas. A private bill was tabled pleading for the reform of the House of Lords, where corruption was regarded as endemic. The Lord Chancellor, Lord Eldon, was accused of 'carrying 40 proxy votes in his pocket', which he shamelessly deployed on questions great and small. This bill, too, was defeated.[2]

Whilst Ireland remained a contentious adjunct to the Union, dissent in Scotland was being mollified. The king had paid a visit in 1822 – the first by a Hanoverian monarch – and, in June 1824, returned the Scottish earldoms that had been seized by the Crown during the 1745 rebellion. He was now preparing to receive some royal visitors himself, in the shape of the King and Queen of the Sandwich Islands. This king's name was revealed to be 'Tirahee Tirahee', or 'Dog of Dogs' in translation. The queen's name was not disclosed. They had with them for interment the remains of Captain Cook, who had been killed on their shores in 1779. The general feeling towards them of respectful curiosity was not universally held. The *John Bull* newspaper railed against 'the copper-coloured islanders … with a navy of five canoes and an annual revenue of five pigs and 15 plantains' being placed 'on a footing with the enlightened sovereigns of Europe'.[3] Such blatant racism was not widely endorsed, but it was voiced without let or hindrance, nonetheless.

Overseas, Greece was still very much in the headlines. There was optimism that independence could be achieved, despite setbacks such as the death of Lord Byron and imperialist pressure from Russia, who proposed partition and a protectorate under its control. The destroyer of Byron's memoir was revealed as his half-sister, Augusta Leigh, and a decision had been taken to inter his remains in Poets' Corner, Westminster Abbey. Conflict and instability continued to prevail in Spain too, where there were rumours of a coup and further colonial ambitions towards Chile and Peru. A treaty had been struck between the British and Dutch governments to partition the East Indies, which further eroded the vestigial power and influence of the East India Company.

There were less weighty items of news which may have impressed themselves upon the reader in June 1824. For example, the misplaced skull of Sir Thomas More – separated from his body on the orders of King Henry VIII almost three centuries earlier – had been found by workmen in St Dunstan's Church, Canterbury and removed to a more suitable resting place. In keeping with the speculative spirit of the age, the jockey, James Robinson, placed a bet that he would win both the Derby and the Oaks and be 'married by Sunday'. In the event, he won both and married on Saturday.[4]

Men who gained physical strength from their work often turned it to their advantage in a sporting context. George Thacker and Abraham Storr, two canal diggers, fought each other in the River Witham, Lincolnshire – the venue adding to the danger and novelty of the bout. Both boxers, beaten and exhausted, were pulled from the water by spectators, after which Storr was declared the winner. Spring and Langan met again in more conventional, though no less punishing, circumstances. This encounter, just outside Chichester, set a record for the longest match – 77 rounds – and the largest purse – a thousand sovereigns, which Spring carried off. Langan was left insensible.

Some occurrences that were reported in the press may have been experienced first-hand by book club members. Female Friendly Societies were becoming more established as a means of charitable support in times of need. The Chester Original Female Friendly Society celebrated its third anniversary with a procession to, and service at St John's, followed by tea at the Union Hall. The more established Flookersbrook, Hoole and Newton society, to which Cottons and Townshends were known to belong, met in similar style.[5]

Anyone who was in the city on Monday 7th June, and the days immediately preceding it, cannot have failed to notice what is probably best described as the circus surrounding Mr Sadler.

The committee assembled for the purpose had moved swiftly to put preliminaries in place, including the installation of a pipe from the gas works to the portico of County Hall, and the erection of huge sails and tarpaulins to conceal the balloon pre-flight. Flags were displayed on prominent structures for promotional purposes, including on the shot towers of Messrs Walker and Mellor, and church bells pealed with uncommon regularity. Thousands of people visited the Castle yard on Sunday to witness the build-up to the event. Many more still attended the following day, arriving in their droves from 9am by every conceivable means of transport; chaises, gigs, carts, waggons, horses and asses amongst them. Lift-off had been set for 2pm. Soldiers of the 53rd Regiment kept order, and the militia band entertained from an early hour.

An account of what was happening behind the scenes is given in strongly negative terms in the *Courant*, which may have been partly justified and partly influenced by a delay which meant their reporting deadline for the whole event was missed. The *Chronicle*, which had no such challenge, was more sanguine about proceedings. Whatever their respective stances, there are certain facts which cannot be contested.

Mr Sadler had arranged to meet two committee members at the gas works at 10am on Sunday so that the pipes could be secured in accordance with his instructions. He got there early, whereupon an unfortunate exchange with the manager and staff led to him leaving swiftly and in high dudgeon. His requirement that the pipes be pinned down had given way, without consultation, to the positioning of sentries along their line to protect them, which he deemed inadequate. When the committee members arrived, his whereabouts could not be established. Three hours later a messenger returned to say that 'he had taken to the water and was not expected back until late evening'. This action was prompted less by pique and more by logic, in that his absence beyond reach would place the onus entirely on the committee and the gas works to remedy the matter. When he reappeared at 10pm, no one in authority was on hand, so he retired to his accommodation at the Albion Hotel. Soon afterwards, he snubbed an appeal by the secretary of the committee – who was now available to receive any instructions he might choose to offer – with the words, 'It will be time enough to see him in the morning.'

As dawn broke gloriously on Monday – the day of the scheduled flight – Mr Sadler and the committee remained at odds. Perhaps now lacking the time or resources to follow the instructions to the letter, the committee resorted to persuasion. Public disappointment and reputational damage to Mr Sadler were put forward as arguments for proceeding unless it was utterly impractical to do so. With so many people descending on the city in anticipation of a spectacle, there was also a risk of unrest.

Mr Sadler held his line and declared that he would not bring out the balloon until the pipes had been properly secured. There were more heated words, which was his cue to again retreat to his hotel. When the secretary of the committee arrived at 5.45am, he was informed, in the words of the *Chronicle,* that 'Mr Sadler had inclined to inflate himself instead of his balloon'. This time, the secretary's intervention bore fruit, and the aeronaut snapped into action, possibly feeling that he had made his point and that a complete non-event could still be avoided.

The balloon was soon tethered to the gas supply and inflation commenced, though with a minimum duration of 12 hours, this process could not be completed within the agreed schedule. By midday, little inflation had occurred, yet the crowd was swelling and the heat was beginning to sear. Seats were placed in the shade under the armoury and portico for some of the ladies. Others preferred the view from the roof of the armoury - precarious though it was - which afforded imposing views of the Castle esplanade and the vast hordes assembled at other vantage points. Much favoured, though equally vertiginous, were the towers of St Mary's and St John's, as well as any number of lofty rooftops elsewhere in the city. In the near distance, people gathered on the hill at Brewer's Hall and in the far distance at Beeston and Hawarden. The townsfolk of Wrexham were out in force, as the wind appeared to pull in that direction. The city walls were densely populated, despite some dilapidation.

A sixty-foot ladder placed in the Castle ditch allowed illicit access through a barrack house window: a transgression largely ignored, presumably on the basis that such a risk merited some reward. There was no danger of Mr Sadler being short-changed, with entry tickets for the Castle Yard, priced at three shillings and sixpence per head, subject to voracious demand. Pilot balloons released from the gas works provided a much-needed diversion as the main attraction continued to falter. Tactical approaches were adopted, including weights and the might of 50 men to bring the balloon closer to the ground to improve the rate of inflation. Three, four and five o'clock came and went, and impatience grew. As time elapsed, the role of the militia in both containing and entertaining the crowd took on added importance.

At 5.30pm, a cannon crack announced the emergence of the car and triggered a press amongst spectators. Mr Sadler appeared, insouciant in his blue jacket, trousers and skin cap. Ballast bags were removed, cords taken down and the balloon relocated to a distant part of the yard between the gateway and the barracks. He entered the car alone, having rejected the company of a committee member, which may have had the potential to rea-waken antipathies in a confined space. Lady Stanley and Mrs Barnton escaped the throng to present the colours – richly emblazoned flags bearing the arms and motto of the city – after which the signal, 'Let go,' was pronounced.

The words 'grand', 'beautiful', 'gorgeous' and 'sublime' were used in contemporary ac-counts to describe the ascent. As Mr Sadler glided majestically above the castle, the air thrilled to the thunder of cannon and cheers of spectators, to whom he doffed his cap and flourished his flags. The wind, having changed course, took him first in a southerly direction over Eaton Hall and then further east, towards Beeston. The heat of the sun – still powerful in the early evening – swelled the balloon to its full extent and propelled it to an impressive height of three miles. Visibility enabled distinct views of the River Ribble and Derbyshire hills. Closer at hand, steamboats scudded busily between Liverpool, Tran-mere and Birkenhead. The solitude could not have contrasted more acutely with the clam-our on the ground.

Still in clear view of Chester, he reduced the gas and began his descent in the direction of Tarporley, a little over ten miles away. Country-dwellers scurried to greet him. At 7.20pm, he threw out his drag, which was caught by an awestruck local who helped guide him and his equipment to their rest, unimpeded and unscathed. His balloon was loaded onto a carriage as he was elevated again – this time onto the 'shoulders of the peasantry', who bore the 'bold adventurer' to the Swan Inn in the village. He met with much acclaim from the hundreds who managed to gather there. Church bells pealed their own appro-bation.

Fortunately, according to the *Chronicle*, a landau containing Mr Gunning, an insurance broker, accompanied by two unidentified ladies from Liverpool, arrived there soon after-wards. Mr Tomlinson, still flushed by his successful pursuit of the week before, was not far behind. With him in a chaise was the secretary of the organising committee. On this occasion, Mr Willoughby was nowhere to be seen. Faced with the two alternatives, Mr

Sadler chose to return to Chester in the landau, his flags streaming from it, reaching journey's end at 10.45pm. The chaise followed with the balloon.

Thousands of people still lined the streets of Chester, affording him another hero's welcome. He addressed them briefly, thanking them for their kindness and apologising for the delay, for which he hoped he had provided some compensation. He then entered Mr Tomlinson's establishment at the Feathers Hotel, which was also the scene of a grand celebratory dinner the following evening, at which he was roundly lauded by local worthies.[6]

A week later the *Courant* and *Chronicle* reflected more soberly, but with no greater accord, on proceedings. The *Courant* praised the spectacle but argued that Mr Sadler's behaviour in the run-up to it had been unreasonable, avoidable and knowingly consequential for a great mass of people. In their view, not only should he not be invited back, but it would be in his own best interests not to entertain such a possibility. The *Chronicle* castigated this line, pointing to the gratification that the ascent had brought to the city, without completely dismissing what they termed as the petulance and obduracy preceding it. They felt strongly that he would be welcome back and at no great interval either, with all parties fortified by the wisdom of recent experience. Here they declared a vested interest by naming Mr Fletcher, their proprietor, as chair of the organising committee and a prime mover in securing the event. Also named was Mr Hanshall, their editor, as secretary.[7] Alongside this role, he was a noted historian, responsible for works such as *The Stranger in Chester* and the *History of the County Palatine of Chester* – not to be confused with George Ormerod's magnum opus. Neither of these refer to his close encounter with Mr Sadler because they pre-date it, having been published in 1816 and 1823 respectively. This chronology is unfortunate.

A final question before closing out on this brief but momentous episode in the story of the city, is the extent to which the book club members we have met experienced it. It is possible that Mrs Coupland was out of town, perhaps at Glansevern, but her Aunt Elizabeth may well have been on hand. She and Anne Glynne may have viewed it together, as they did Princess Victoria's visit eight years later. Their homes were nearby, and the

Humberstons were closer still. Mrs Mainwaring had two properties in the city, as we have seen, and the Massies had their town house at Stanley Place and links to St Mary's, adjacent to the castle yard. With multi-storeyed properties at their disposal, they may have watched from the comfort of their own homes, preferring not to immerse themselves amongst the crowds outside.

Chapter Thirteen

Mrs Nicholls
Lot 7

*Flora Britannica, 2 vols., 8vo, richly bound in green Morocco, gilt extra; the second vol.
embellished with a highly finished drawing of the beautiful plant Magnolia-Hybernica,
faithfully copied from nature.*

The overwhelming impression created by this offering is of the pastoral and horticultural.
The green and the gold, alongside the reference to 'Hybernica', establish a link with the
island of Ireland. The *Hedera Hibernica* is the Irish Ivy and *Juniperus Hibernica* is the Irish
juniper, for example. There appears not to be a *Magnolia Hibernica*, so it could merely be a
device on Dr Norris's part to add a further layer of flattery by implying that a plant is
being named on Mrs Nicholls' behalf. This was at a time when species of vegetation were
being discovered and newly christened around the world, following the lead of pioneering
botanists such as Joseph Banks, who had died in 1820. Words such as 'richly bound',
'embellished' and 'highly finished' add to the unctuous feel of the passage. The book –
Flora Britannica – did exist, having been first published in 1800 and claiming to have made
great progress in the taxonomy of plants. It is possible that Mrs Nicholls had a genuine
interest in horticulture and would therefore have been even more receptive to the blan-
dishments.

In this instance, we are fortunate not to have to make inferences to arrive at an identification. The 33rd volume of the third series of *The Cheshire Sheaf*, published in 1935, provides some biographical notes on a man called William Nicholls, accompanied by the
words: 'In 1824 Mrs Nicholls presented two handsomely bound volumes to the Chester
Book Club.'[1] This is based entirely on the 1880 reference to the club in the *Sheaf*, which is

the wellspring for this book, but the contributor misread it. Mrs Nicholls presented nothing, as we know. The connection made between William Nicholls and our Mrs Nicholls, however, is reliable.

William married Dorothea Russell at St John's, Chester on 30th May 1791. He was 31 and she 21 years of age. His genealogy is indistinct, obscured by a profusion of people with the surname 'Nicholls' in Chester for generations. Dominant male Christian names include Peter and other Williams, one of whom was Dean of Chester from 1644 to 1657 – albeit under the variant spelling of 'Nichols'. Another was a minor canon at the cathedral and perpetual curate of Holt from 1748 to 1763.

The brother of this last William – Benjamin – is believed to have been the father of the William in whom we are most interested. After attending Jesus College, Oxford, in the 1730s, Benjamin became chaplain to the Earl of Uxbridge and occupied clerical posts in the Manchester area. He also held a curacy at Holy Trinity, Chester – where he was a signatory to many marriages, including amongst the Bennett and Townshend families – from 1750 to his death in 1765.[2] In June 1755, he was listed in the *Chester Courant* as a subscriber to Chester General Infirmary – alongside the elder Thomas Sloughter and sundry Mainwarings and Massies. These facts point to him having been settled in Chester, other than in his middle years.

Dorothea's line is clearer. She was the daughter of Reverend William Russell, of Lidley Hayes in Shropshire, and Elizabeth Byrne. This is where the Irish connection comes in: Elizabeth was daughter of Sir John Byrne, 3rd Baronet of Timogue, in Leinster. The Byrne's – or O'Byrnes in earlier generations – could trace their ancestry to the first kings of Ireland. Staunch patriots, they defended their national interests against waves of invaders, including the Danes and Anglo-Normans. They were particularly persecuted during William III's campaign in 1698, when one of their number – William Byrne – was notoriously hanged in front of the Newgate in London whilst negotiations for his release were in course.

216

Over time, the Byrnes became more integrated into the British establishment. In 1728, Sir John Byrne married Meriel Leicester, the daughter of Sir Francis Leicester of Tabley in Cheshire, and became High Sheriff of Cheshire in 1840. There was wealth on both sides of the family. Sir John Byrne's great-grandfather was an affluent clothier in the middle of the 17th century, which led to the creation of the baronetcy. The Leicester baronetcy was a product of the service rendered to the Royalist cause by Peter Leycester during the Civil War and was created soon after the Restoration.

Peter was a noted antiquarian and book collector. He wrote about the early history of Cheshire, with reference to the Domesday Book, and amassed a library of over 1,300 volumes – a colossal number for the time. He married Elizabeth Mainwaring, daughter of Randle Mainwaring, who was four times great-grandfather of Charles Mainwaring, husband of Susanna. Peter researched and wrote about the Mainwaring pedigree, raising sensitive questions about legitimacy which set the parties at odds. Following a vituperative exchange of pamphlets between him and Sir Thomas Mainwaring, the dispute was settled in favour of the latter at Chester Assizes in 1675.

The Leicester title became extinct after three generations but was revived when Sir John Byrne's descendants adopted the surname and the family seat at Tabley. Dorothea's cousin and contemporary, Sir John Fleming Leicester, 5th Baronet in the Irish line, was created 1st Baronet de Tabley in 1826. He was an active soldier in the Napoleonic Wars and became colonel of a regiment raised for home defence, later known as the Cheshire Yeomanry. He was also an MP, amateur artist and patron of the arts. His presence in London, where he had a fine town house and gallery in Berkeley Square, brought him into contact with the Prince Regent, who became a personal friend.[3]

After William and Dorothea married, they appear to have lived initially in the centre of the city. The *Chester Directory* of 1792 – part of Broster's *The Chester Guide* – has 'W Nicholls, Deputy Registrar of Wills' in Abbey Court, by the cathedral. We know this is our William because he held that role, then and for a time to come. Such lists were selective, perhaps too arbitrarily so, and we can't infer from Dorothea's omission that she wasn't there.

Also mentioned in the directory is a Mrs Russell of King Street, who was most likely Dorothea's mother. She was newly widowed, her husband having passed away earlier in the year. According to probate records, he had been a clerk of the city of Chester, although precisely where has not been established. In the updated list of 1795, William Nicholls is shown as having moved round the corner to Northgate Street. By 1800 game duty records had him at Chorlton, four miles north-east of Chester.[4]

A curious incident from this period concerns William Nicholls' sister, who was reported in the *Chester Courant* of 21st February 1792 as having married a Mr Skerrett, surgeon, of Malpas, at St Oswald's. In the very next edition, a week later, there was a complete retraction. No rationale was given. On the same day as the retraction, there is a record of a marriage taking place at St Oswald's between Robert William Skerratt and Sarah Nichols.[5] There are discrepancies in the spelling of the surnames but there is too great a convergence with other data for this not to have been William's sister and her betrothed. The reason for the deferment, if there was one, is unknown.

Details of the Nicholls' move to Chorlton come from no less an authority than George Ormerod, who tells us that 'the Stanleys of Hooton sold the estate to William Pownall of Chester in 1791, who sold an alienated portion to William Nicholls, Deputy Registrar in the Archdeaconry of Chester'.[6] Ormerod would later acquire the property himself and engage in much of the compilation of his *History of the County Palatine and City of Chester* there.

In 1800, William appended his name alongside 31 others – including the mayor and members of the Townshend and Barnston families – to the formation of the 'Chester Self-Denial Union', whose published aims were these:

We whose Names are Subscribed do agree not to give or accept any set Dinners, or Suppers, from the 1st Day of November to 1st Day of May next (this agreement not to extend to Entertainment of Strangers). That no pastry whatsoever, nor hot Rolls, Muffins, Cakes or Bread of a finer Quality than Household be used in our Houses, unless in Case of Illness. That no Cream shall be used in Cooking Dinners, or Suppers, or Meat Stewed to Gravies. That we will discontinue as much as possible the use of Butter.[7]

It seems the lifestyle of these worthy gentlemen, and its consequences, had stirred them into collective action. They understood which food items were most culpable. Being so formal and so public in their declaration may have offered an added incentive not to waver, though there was still a loophole or two to be exploited. We should not read too much into the lack of follow-up reporting and credit them for this bold initial step.

Soon we see evidence of William acting in his official capacity. In the National Archives there are letters from the early 1800s which he issued around the diocese, on behalf of the Bishop of Chester, Henry Majendie, requesting crop returns. There are also records of him becoming a regular house visitor at Chester Infirmary for inspection purposes. In 1803, he was selected to represent St Oswald's parish in soliciting subscriptions towards a fund for 'such of the Chester Volunteers as may be unable to provide for themselves'. The target of £3,500 – more than £200,000 in modern day terms – indicates the extent to which the city, in line with the country as a whole, was being placed on a war footing, to counter any attempt at invasion by Napoleon's forces across the Channel.

The victory that removed that threat took place on 21st October 1805 – at the Battle of Trafalgar. On 29th November, Bishop Majendie put out a circular on behalf of the Patriotic Fund to all churches in the diocese urging a collection 'for the Relief of the Widows and Orphans of those brave men who gloriously fell in the late naval action'. Any sums raised were to be passed to William Nicholls for onward transmission to the central committee.[8] It is not known what the response was, but the national mood was strongly disposed to the cause.

This year also saw the death of Dorothea's mother. William lost his mother – residing in Abbey Square – early the following year. These events may have enabled them to spend more time at Chorlton and created the opportunity, through inheritance, to acquire the property. There is indeed a record of William buying Chorlton House, after a period of tenancy, in 1806.[9]

On 13th May 1807, William was present in Chester for the proving of a will. This was a regular professional responsibility of his, except that on this occasion he may have known the subject of the document. It was Thomas Coupland, and the two men who stood before him to attest to the will were the slave-owning brothers, William and Thomas Earle.

In late 1806, a list was published of attendees at 'the Music Festival and those of the City who appeared at the Assemblies at the Royal Hotel'. 'Mrs Nicholls, Chorlton' was there and, amongst others, several Humberstons – including Mr and Mrs – several Townshends, ennobled members of the Glynne and Mainwaring families, and Mr Johnson.[10] We see here the nucleus of the book club socialising together 18 years before it met.

Chorlton was mentioned to differentiate Dorothea from at least one other Mrs Nicholls living in Chester at the time. As early as 1789, a Mrs Nicholls was posting notices in the local press about her school for young ladies. Almost 40 years later – in 1828 – the *Directory of Cheshire* was listing academies run by Mrs and Miss Nicholls at 50 Nicholas Street and at the 'Ladies' Building', King's Buildings, King Street. By this time, however, the school was in transition. A notice placed in the *Leeds Intelligencer* on 29th March 1827 reads:

Establishment for young ladies, King's Buildings, Chester. The Misses Green respectfully soliciting a share of public patronage, beg Leave to inform those Parents and Friends who are interested in the Education of Young Ladies, that having passed several years as private governesses of Families of the highest respectability, they intend, at Midsummer next, to enter (for the reception of Boarders exclusively) on the Establishment in King's Buildings, so long and so satisfactorily conducted by Mrs and Miss Nicholls, whose sanction and introduction they hope to justify, by unremitting exertions in establishing the Morals and promoting the Mental Improvement of those Young Ladies who may be confided to their care. The most eminent Masters are engaged.

Now we turn to William's activity and undoubted prowess as a historian. He was a collector of historical artefacts on no small scale, though many of the items he amassed have long since dispersed. It is reported that he possessed coins and a Roman fibula – a pin which was used to fasten garments – which Pennant speculated was part of a good collection.[11] Ormerod described him as an 'FSA [Fellow of the Society of Antiquaries] and a gentleman of great zeal in the investigation of local antiquities', adding that his 'assistance in circulating enquiries and collecting information for the account of Cheshire in *Magna Britannia* has been acknowledged by its learned and ingenious editors'.[12]

The editors in question were the brothers Daniel and Samuel Lysons, who, between 1806 and 1822, endeavoured to compile 'a concise topographical account of the several counties of Great Britain'. In reality, there was nothing concise about it and the ambition of the project, commendable in itself, proved to be its undoing. Taking each county in alphabetical order and having produced several weighty volumes, they were unable to progress beyond Devon. Samuel's death in 1819 left Daniel to plough on doggedly, but forlornly, with the remainder. We are fortunate that Cheshire arrives early alphabetically, in that the record that the Lysons brothers have left us is incomparable in its detail on the economic and social structure of the county at that time. The credit that William Nicholls can take in this achievement cannot be understated.

The John Rylands Library in Manchester holds an immense collection of William's documents and correspondence.[13] These include original armorial papers used by Sir William Dugdale in his visitation of Cheshire, compiled in 1663 and 1664, as well as many other notes and catalogues in William's own hand on Cheshire manors, parishes, churches and topography. From 1806 to 1809, William corresponded extensively across Cheshire in his effort to collate data for *Magna Britannia*, despite his awareness that the task was herculean. As early as February 1806, Hugh Cholmondeley, Dean of Chester, was voicing strong reservations:

Before I quit [London], I will endeavour to see Mr Lysons. I am sorry to hear he does not meet with the encouragement he could wish but I fear this is to be attributed in some measure to the vastness of the work which he has undertaken, which I'm afraid will preclude that minuteness and accuracy desirable in all county history.

The same letter included an indication that William's health was failing. He was in Bath for a prolonged stay and the dean expressed his hope that the waters would be serviceable to him. He also encouraged him and 'the ladies' to visit him at London or his college at Oxford – Brasenose – if his health permitted. The fact that the letter ends with the words, 'With best compliments to Mrs N and Miss Russell,' suggests that the ladies in question were Dorothea and her as yet unmarried sister, Philippa.

An example of the minuteness that was captured in the research is found in a letter from the Reverend Thomas Armitstead in January 1809. He was married to William's sister, Jane, and was not obviously connected with the Armitsteads of East Cheshire, mentioned in Chapter Eleven. He reports on the number of ash trees in Delamere Forest, which stood at eight thousand; a reduction of two thousand on its skirts from its original extent. Quite how or by whom these were counted is not stated. There is much people news in the same letter and a fervent hope that William's recent silence on his own condition was an indication of his recovery. Unfortunately, this was not the case. With this in mind, along with the related fact that he moved between Chester and Bath, where he occupied a fashionable residence at 7 South Parade, it is remarkable that he maintained the correspondence so assiduously.

It seems that William was well known and well connected in his prime, perhaps by association with the Lysons brothers – Samuel being antiquary professor at the Royal Academy and Keeper of the Records in the Tower of London – or perhaps on his own account.

In November 1806, he wrote directly to the famous playwright, Richard Brindsley Sheridan, in Sheridan's alternative capacity as Treasurer of the Royal Navy, recommending a 'Mr Fish' of Chester to his service.

On one occasion, Daniel Lysons was unable to fulfil an arrangement to travel to Chester from his family seat in Gloucestershire because his wife was ill. He wrote to William stating that, 'My friend Robert Smirke expected to meet me at Chester this week ... If you should see anything of him looking about the cathedral or elsewhere, I shall be much obliged to you if you will have the goodness to mention the reason of my not going to Chester, then if he should have time I shall be much obliged to him for sketches of the elevation of the different parts of the cathedral and chapter house which were not done by Mr [John] Nash from his having misunderstood me.' Smirke and Nash, referred to so casually here, were amongst the foremost architects of the age.

The thanklessness of William's task is brought home by the profusion of excuses and apologies in the letters he received. Delays or shortfalls in providing information are blamed on the writer's own ill-health, the weather, a lack of transport in the form of road-worthy horses, and misunderstandings. Mr Heron of Bartington went so far as to dismiss his housekeeper for placing the correspondence in a drawer instead of forwarding it directly to him.

So immersed was William in his work that he may have been neglectful in other areas of his life. There are letters to and from him regarding outstanding bills with wine merchants, including one in 1806 from Daniel Smith, who was based at the White Lion, Chester, and had been another self-denier in 1800. In May 1809, William wrote from Bath in the following terms: 'Dear Sir, I really have to apologise for not attending to your favour sooner – have been from home and indisposed and much engaged in that I scarce thought upon, private concerns.' He adds, 'My friend the Dean of Chester has lately had wine quite secure by the canal, which induces me to adopt the same mode of conveyance in the present instance.' The canal ran just below his Chorlton home and so was highly convenient for him, once he had settled his account and released the merchandise from bond.

At other times, William was inclined to cut out the middleman, especially when he bought his wine in bulk. A letter of October 1808 from Robert Markland – a Manchester industrialist, whose family was enmeshed in the transatlantic slave trade – talks of a consignment of Madeira wine having landed from Jamaica and arrangements for a delivery by Markland's Liverpool-based agent direct to William at King Street, Chester. This address may have been the property inherited from Dorothea's mother.

Perhaps over-indulgence was responsible for, or at least a contributory factor in his decline. It is reasonable to suppose that his involvement in the Chester Self-Denial Union did not have the desired effect. A graphic letter of 1807 from Paul Panton – a friend whom William was trying to entice to Bath for the good of his own health – indicates that gout was present, describing the way in which William's legs had to be swaddled in flannel or held in a horizontal position. Reassuringly, he continues, 'I know from repeated experience how far your friendly disposition will carry you.'

Writing from London in March 1809, Philip Humberston was focused on his own condition. He had delayed his return to Chester by five days until he was 'calmer' and in a fitter state to travel but was still confined to the house on his arrival. 'Under these circumstances,' he states, 'we must again postpone the pleasure we had hoped for in visiting upon you and Mrs Nicholls.' He wished to take the waters at Cheltenham during the first three weeks of April and suggested a get-together in Bognor in the summer, should it be practical for William, Dorothea and her sister. It is highly improbable that this ever came about, because William continued to deteriorate and died on 19th August 1809. For a while longer, correspondence addressed to him came in and Dorothea, in her distressed state, did her best to deal with it.

Ormerod, who had spoken to friends of William, suggested that his death 'had been accelerated by the assiduity with which he devoted his leisure hours to an employment which varied so little from his official pursuits'.[14] When the Cheshire volumes of *Magna Britannia* were published in 1810, the Lysons brothers acknowledged 'the exertions and enquiries of William Nicholls of Chester' and regretted the fact that he was unable to review the draft and witness the end product.[15] A lasting memorial to him appears on a pillar in Chester Cathedral, on the south side, where the nave meets the transept. It reads:

In the vault near this place lieth the body of William Nicholls, Esqr, FSA, many years Deputy Registrar of the Diocese of Chester, a situation he filled with superior ability and unsullied integrity. A Kind and Affectionate Husband Whose Virtues were Conspicuous, in Piety truly Christian, in Charity Liberal, in Friendship sincere. Benevolent to All. He lived Beloved and died Lamented. August 19th 1809. Aged Forty nine Years.

The funeral took place at the cathedral on 25th August. William's will, drafted in March 1807, leaves all his real and personal estate to his 'dear wife Dorothea'. Also mentioned are his sisters, Sarah and Jane, and brothers-in-law Robert William Skerrett and Thomas Armitstead. Here is final confirmation that the marriage between Sarah and Robert did take place and that it lasted. There was a deceased sister, Ann – wife of Alexander Daniel – whose children are remembered too. When Dorothea proved the will at Chester on 31st August 1809, it must have been a singularly poignant occasion for her, knowing the pivotal role her deceased husband had undertaken in that process.

In late October and early November, the *Courant* advertised the sale of a wide range of high-quality household furniture, previously belonging to William Nicholls esq deceased, on the premises in King's Buildings. This tells us that their property was not just in King Street but in the elegant row of six three-story Georgian terraced houses in the north-west corner of it. This strengthens the possibility that William was related to Mrs and Miss Nicholls, who ran their ladies' school from there.

Dorothea opted, for a time at least, to live in the less clamorous surroundings of Chorlton House, which she and her husband had developed from the farm that they had purchased a few years earlier. In early 1811, she decided to offer the house up for sale. A notice placed in the *Chester Chronicle* of 19th April shows the extent and make-up of the property:

For sale. Very desirable residence, good dwelling house, excellent coach house, stables, other offices, outbuildings, gardens with wall and fruit trees, shrubs in high
perfection; hot house, greenhouse, 83 acres at Chorlton, 4 miles from Chester near
the branch of the Ellesmere canal leading from Chester to Liverpool. Also two neat
well-built cottages, and cow houses to each, between the dwelling house and the
canal. The lands and one of the cottages adjoin the canal at Caughall Bridge, where
the packet boats between Chester and Liverpool pass daily. To be sold on the 18th
May at the Pied Bull.

The purchaser was George Ormerod, who had access to the papers that William had collated for the Lysons brothers.[16] As well as Chorlton House being intrinsically attractive,
the knowledge of its connection to another insatiable historian may have given it added
appeal.

It seems that Dorothea moved back into the city – and possibly to King Street – again.
In 1814 she was a patroness in a charitable assembly, alongside Mrs Mainwaring, which
met at the Exchange to generate support for destitute fellow-citizens.[17] Hemingway writes
of a terrible storm that occurred in December 1822, one casualty of which was Mrs
Nicholls' chimney, though this wasn't categorically Dorothea.[18] We know she was firmly
rooted in Chester in 1824 because of her involvement with the book club. The *Chester
Directory* of 1828, which informs us of Mrs and Miss Nicholls' whereabouts, has a separate
entry for 'Mrs Nicholls, King Street'. It looks as though Dorothea had settled back into
the town house she had shared with her late husband.

There were changes in the composition of her family through this period, for good and
ill. In 1827, her brother-in-law, the Reverend Thomas Armitstead died at the vicarage in
Cockermouth, to which he had moved following a long spell at Backford. He had also
been a magistrate in Chester for many years. In his younger days, he was rector at St
Martin's and master of a private school in the city, quite possibly the one run by the

Nicholls family. Thomas and Jane had called their daughter 'Dorothea', presumably as a tribute to her aunt.

In 1828, Dorothea's sister, Philippa, married William Richards of Kinnerton Lodge, formerly Town Clerk for Chester, at Holy Trinity Church. Both parties were well into middle age, limiting the time they would have together as a married couple.

Dorothea was ageing too, and on 13th August 1835, she passed away. Fittingly, there is a tablet on the south wall of the nave of Chester Cathedral, squinting across to where her husband is commemorated, which reads:

Sacred to the beloved memory of Dorothea widow of the late William Nicholls esq and the eldest daughter of the late Rev William Russell and Elizabeth his wife, died XIII August 1835 aged LXV years

Nearby is another memorial:

To the memory of the Reverend William Russell MA Late of Lidley Hayes Salop who died 29.11.1792 Aged 59 years and of Elizabeth his Relict who died July 6th 1805. She was the youngest daughter of S John Byrne of Timogue in Queens County Baronet and Meriel his wife was the only child of S Francis Leicester of Tabley in the County of Chester Baronet. Erected as a tribute of filial affection by their daughters Dorothea and Philippa.

The sisters had chosen to immortalise their lineage too. In an edition of *The Cheshire Sheaf* from 1935, there is reference to a memorial window to William and Dorothea in the cathedral. If it was sited close to their tablets, it would have fallen victim to wartime bombing a few years later.[19]

Philippa, who had been so close to William and Dorothea that she accompanied them up and down the country, would have felt their losses severely. A few years later she would suffer another bereavement. When William Richards died in the early 1840s, he left properties in Kinnerton, Dodleston and Christleton to Philippa, along with any interest he may have had in her late sister's property, and cash in Williams and Jones's Bank in Chester. One of the witnesses to his will was George Johnson. Dorothea had left a house on the west side of Nicholas Street – close to where Anne Glynne lived – to Philippa, who chose to sell it under a trust arrangement to a local solicitor and lease it back.[20] The sums involved were nominal: it appears to have been a device used to allow married women access to assets independently of their husbands, at a time when their rights to ownership were severely constrained. When Philippa died in 1851, she was devoid of close relatives. Her beneficiaries were nephews of her late husband and friends of hers in Chester.

Finally, we return directly to Dorothea, thinking not just of how she supported her husband in all his great endeavours, but the way in which she supplanted him when his illness took hold, fatally in the end. She undoubtedly did more for him and the Lysons Brothers than she has ever been given credit for. Perhaps the only plaudits she got were buried away in the book club. If we look again at her offering, we see that *Flora Britannica* and *Magnolia Hibernica* are riffs on *Magna Britannia* – a work she was intimately attached to – and we appreciate the full extent of Dr Norris's conceit.

Chapter Fourteen

July

The great Chester Midsummer Fair officially ran between 5th and 23rd July – signalled by the age-old tradition of hanging a glove from St Peter's Church – although there was some anxiety about illicit trading either side of it. The *Chronicle* railed against horse dealers from Yorkshire and elsewhere who did business on the outskirts of the city on Sunday the 4th, declaring that they should be placed in the stocks for not observing the Sabbath. The *Courant* highlighted the fact that some incoming manufacturers of cotton goods lingered in the halls beyond the 23rd, which disadvantaged regular traders who paid their dues to the Corporation. The malpractice didn't end there; for example, one Chester farmer was duped into buying his own horse back after it was stolen and its coat trimmed. On the positive side, the range and volume of goods for sale was commended, as was the quality of the horses and cattle, many of which were imported from Ireland. People flocked to Chester, where the markets did brisk business.[1]

The weather, which continued to be glorious, would have helped, not just in Chester but further along the estuary too. Mrs Nicholls and Mr Humberston were amongst those who arrived at Parkgate early in the month for the bathing season, perhaps also keen to escape the hubbub of the fair on their doorsteps. Whilst Parkgate was far from quiet either, the demographics there were different. There was a growing feeling that more should be done to attract the young and able-bodied, and events such as dances and re-gattas were under consideration. Lord Grosvenor arrived at Eaton Hall later in the month, where the pleasure grounds were described 'as a complete arcadia'. For him, this had the added advantage of escaping the 'parched and arid impurities' of the London air, which Prince Hermann Pückler-Muskau so derided. On his arrival, Lord Grosvenor took the opportunity to lay the first stone in the construction of the new bridge over the Dee at Aldford.[2]

Whilst, for some, the river was a blessing, for others it was a curse. A tragedy at Lower Ferry, six miles downstream from Chester, claimed the lives of 11 people. What began with a convivial gathering at the Ferryhouse Inn spiralled into something very different when a group of revellers tried to cross the Dee at 10.30pm against a strong head tide. After one arduous but successful crossing, the boatmen aborted the second attempt but were overpowered by two men the worse for drink who seized the oars. Ten other men and three women boarded, overloading the boat and adding to the peril. When it capsized soon afterwards, other boats came to the rescue but could only save four of the passengers.

As bodies were recovered in the ensuing days, there was criticism of the River Dee Company and 'opulent individuals of the neighbourhood' for a lack of earnestness and financial support for the search. One man who bucked the trend was the Reverend George Grenville-Neville, who put up a reward, mindful of the fact that several of the deceased were amongst his Hawarden parishioners.[3]

Safe travel was a concern on *terra firma* too. The Chester and Hereford Mail coach was upset by roadworks near Wrexham, leaving a lady passenger with a broken leg. There were complaints in the press about 'the shameful mode of Driving of Opposition Coaches between this City and Manchester', which further endangered travellers. Journey times were central to the marketing pitch and, as we saw in the race to recover Mr Sadler, competition between Chester-based carriers was fierce. Road improvements were underway through the turnpike companies, which could generate appreciable income. For example, the Boughton toll gate – in the process of being re-let – collected the modern equivalent of £40,000 a year. Thomas Telford reported positively on improvements in the Chester line of road along the north Wales coast, and on progress made towards completion of the bridges at Conway and the Menai Strait. In Chester, further work was required on the city walls, following a breach in the steps by Morgan's Mount.

Other construction projects included the raising of the wall at Chester Gaol by four feet to comply with new legislation and the upgrading of facilities at the infirmary, which the board was keen to keep on the agenda, despite opposition. Alterations at the gaol entailed a new location for executions above the west doorway, where a strong iron railing protected the apparatus of the drop. The infirmary, meanwhile, was dispensing free cow-pox vaccinations every Wednesday. This was proving highly effective in countering small-pox.

At the cathedral, there was praise and gratitude – mingled with some regret – for the outgoing bishop, the Right Reverend George Henry Law, now translated to Bath and Wells. Special mention was made of his exertions in collecting large sums of money for repairing the 'venerable fabric' of the building. The fact that this endeavour would span many years to come is an indication of the extent of the dilapidation. Sketches from the early part of the century by George Cuitt and others illustrate the scale of the challenge perfectly.[4] On 18th July, the bells – cracked, but no less melodious for it – pealed loudly for the third anniversary of the king's coronation, though celebrations in the city were more muted. This may have been because George IV, whilst revered as the monarch, was mocked for his excesses and lacked the popular appeal of his father, George III. What's more, the coronation had been a blighted affair, not least because of the exclusion of Queen Caroline, who had been long estranged from her husband and who died, much lamented, soon afterwards.

Crime reports feature the newly installed chief of police, Mr Burgess, in connection with two incidents. In the first, he arrested a man called David Jones on suspicion of stealing a horse from Dunham Massey, which was later found in a field at Flookersbrook, Chester; his enquiries were ongoing. In the second case, he was punched in front of the bench by one Gabriel Roberts, who was in the course of being tried for affray. A stiff custodial sentence followed. A Mr Williams was convicted for practising as a tanner whilst not being a freeman of the city, and a young pickpocket by the name of Warring responded to the pronouncement of his sentence of transportation for seven years with the words, 'Thank you, sir, that's just what I wanted.'

The most egregious crime that had come to light was an alleged homicide at Peck Mill, near Dunham-on-the-Hill, to the east of Chester. William Parkinson, aged 70, was accused of killing Joseph Fletcher, who had long been on terms of intimacy with Parkinson's daughter, but without his blessing. An inebriated Fletcher had left the local inn one evening and made his way to Parkinson's house, undeterred by the daughter's intimation that he wasn't welcome there. Parkinson seized a musket with a bayonet and Fletcher became abusive. In the ensuing fracas, Fletcher received a fatal wound, dying at his own house nearby following the intervention of a neighbour. Surgeons were summoned but no attempt was made to secure Parkinson, who made off in the direction of Manchester.

Almost immediately, Burgess began placing notices offering a 10-guinea reward for the apprehension of the offender, with five guineas added if he were to be conveyed to Chester Castle. The description carried Parkinson's age alongside other particulars: five foot, eight inches tall; grey hair; features pitted with smallpox; blind in one eye; lame in one arm; slender and upright. He had on a snuff-coloured coat, light breeches and white yarn stockings. A sighting had been made at The Swan with Two Necks inn at Shrude Hill, Manchester, but after that the trail had gone cold.

The balmy, settled weather being experienced in Cheshire was not replicated across the country. In London, thunderstorms were so severe that they caused loss of life as well as damage to property. At Plymouth, there was a tidal flux several feet high which bore the hallmarks of a tsunami. Moderate rain in other areas was seen to be further enriching the harvest.

A general sense of national pride and prosperity continued to be broadcast in the press, at times spilling over into jingoism. On 30th July, the editorial in the *Chester Chronicle* enthused:

When we look backward into the pages of history we perceive no power equal to Great Britain … However the British Isles may sink or degenerate in future times, the prowess and deeds of our ancestors – the glorious and important events of the days in which we live – the victories of a Nelson and a Wellington, will be read in their native language to the furthest ages, and by admiring millions, in distant and immense portions of this earth. In Europe, over all North America, over New Holland [Australia], and probably in Southern Africa, the English language will become the language of the population to the most distant periods of time.

Not everyone across His Majesty's dominions would have identified with these sentiments: many people were too focused on self-preservation and trying to make ends meet. They saw the skull beneath the skin. Rabies was abroad again – in Liverpool and London stray dogs were being destroyed in their thousands. Whilst the Treasury boasted a balance of payments surplus of £6.7 million and oats were routinely imported from Ireland, two hundred families in Galway faced starvation for want of food or the means by which to acquire it. At the other end of the social spectrum, lords and ladies attended the sumptuous Caledonian Ball at Almack's in all their finery, including jewellery to the value of £700,000 worn by the Duchess of Argyll.

Diseases which are often innocuous in the present day stalked their prey, indifferent to background or class distinction. At the start of the month, it was reported that the King and Queen of the Sandwich Islands had contracted measles; by the middle of the month, lacking any natural immunity from previous contact, both had died of it. The body of the king, who was only 28 years old when he passed away, was placed in an inscribed lead coffin and put on public display, arousing much curiosity and a heavy footfall. The British monarch expressed his regret that their scheduled meeting had never come to pass. The diplomatic mission had been frustrated too, leaving the Sandwich Islands more vulnerable to Russian intervention than ever. In similar circumstances and at almost the same time, reputedly the first Chinese lady to visit Britain – You Fung Queon – succumbed to consumption in Pall Mall. Grief was co-mingled with casual racism. 'Three interesting Foreigners have paid the debt to nature this week,' warbled the *Chronicle*, for example.[5]

Another coffin being viewed in London, albeit privately, was that containing the body of Lord Byron, now repatriated. A family decision had been taken to lay him to rest at his ancestral seat at Newstead Abbey, perhaps in response to objections from Westminster Abbey based on his questionable morality. Byron's estrangement from the Establishment and animosity towards the country of his birth was further exemplified by a £5,000 bequest in his will to a young Venetian lady, 'provided she did not marry a British subject'. The fact that many English officers abandoned the Greek cause upon his death is testament to his charisma and force of character.

Elsewhere in London – at Westminster – there were rumours of dissention in the Cabinet and Lord Liverpool's retirement as prime minister. The king, wishing to prevent it, headed over from Windsor. There was business to be done too, not least in respect of Portugal, where military aid was requested to shore up the regime.

A French newspaper, *Pandoré,* reported that 88 women had been sold by their husbands in public markets in London in the first five months of the year. This opprobrious practice – famously depicted more than 60 years later in Thomas Hardy's *The Mayor of Casterbridge* – was perfectly legal and continued into the early 20th century. In Sheffield, searches were underway for around 40 runaway husbands, who had used an alternative means to escape the bonds of matrimony and the obligations that went with it.

North of the border, in Edinburgh, Mr Sadler was in action again, making best use of the favourable weather and long summer days. His smooth two-hour flight from the green at Heriot's Hospital across the Forth estuary to Leven in Fife was likened by *The Scotsman* newspaper to a jubilee celebration. Soon afterwards, he was in Dublin, the city of his birth and scene of his greatest triumph, when, in 1817, 100,000 people had cheered his ascent at the first ever airborne crossing of the Irish Sea. On this occasion he departed from Cobourg Gardens, landing approximately 20 miles away at Skerries, again without incident. The people of Chester, so recently witness to such a display, would have read of his ongoing exploits with considerable interest.

Overseas, the colony of Demerara continued to be in a state of ferment. Sir Benjamin D'Urban, a seasoned colonial administrator had assumed control and proclaimed that any attempt at insurrection by 'the Negroes' would be put down by military force. Another missionary by the name of Austin was being persecuted, including by means of a petition raised by the planters to suspend him from the ministry. Meanwhile, perhaps in anticipation of a perceived need to replace slave labour, three hundred convicts were being transported to Bermuda to improve the port facilities there. At the same time, a treaty was signed with America towards the suppression of the slave trade.

The British continued to splay around the world of their own volition, as new opportunities were created for them to do that. Faster sailing ships had been deployed to New South Wales and Van Diemen's Land and the duration of the passage to India had been slashed by a new route via Marseilles, Malta and overland across Egypt. The Reverend James Henry Cotton, Precentor of Bangor and brother of Catherine Humberston, received a letter from the Bishop of Ohio pleading for more Welsh ministers to serve a growing expatriate community in his episcopate. Costs to émigrés were subsidised and employment was guaranteed.

The world, however, was a no less dangerous place. In Europe, France had received intelligence of the possibility that Britain would send military aid to Portugal and, interpreting it as a bellicose move, threatened to retaliate. In parallel, they were preparing to invade St Domingo – which was becoming more commonly known as Haiti – with every expectation of success. The Spanish, meanwhile, were faring less well, as the last remnants of their army in South America were defeated. Russia, already accused of harbouring malign intentions towards Greece and islands in the Pacific, was pushing through Asia towards Britain's prized possessions in the Indian subcontinent.

For every news story that gave concern, there seemed to be one that lightened the mood. The body of a deceased woman was reported at Bache Pool, Chester, but the investigation that was immediately raised found her seated at the nearby Egerton Arms, holding a pitcher and smoking a pipe. A deaf man entering the local militia, in attempting to repeat the initiating oath, swore that he was an elephant rather than a Protestant. The Earl of Orford, on being offered the role of President of the Norwich Bible Society, declined on the grounds that he was addicted to blasphemy and gambling, doing little to enhance the image of the nobility in the process. In the same East Anglian city, a man called Townsend – a pedestrian – collected 300 equally-spaced stones with his mouth, depositing them in the same basket, during which he walked 52 miles in a little under his target time of 11 hours. The following week, he walked backwards for 40 miles in the same time frame.[6]

Chapter Fifteen

Mrs Panton
Lot 8

The Sisters, a popular tale of Lepanto, but translated from the Welsh, 2 vols., crown 8vo, handsomely bound in red, gilt, and letter'd.

In late 1824, a public appeal was made for financial support for James Forshaw, a former shopman at Broster's booksellers and stationers at the Exchange, who lost any eye when a turnip was thrown through the shop window during a riotous outbreak on the last day of the local elections. Already almost blind in the other eye, he was unable to continue to work and support his family. Earl Grosvenor, the sitting MP, contributed £25, whilst amongst the many who subscribed £1 were the 'Mrs Pantons'. In 1827, funds were being raised for the establishment of Chester Female Penitentiary, 'the object of which shall be to afford an Asylum to females who, having deviated from the paths of virtue, are desirous of being restored, by religious instruction, and the formation of moral and industrious habits, to a respectable station in society'.[1] Donations of £10 each were received from Mrs and Mrs E M Panton, alongside Mrs Nicholls and Mrs Mainwaring.

The presence in the city around the time of our book club of two ladies by the name of Mrs Panton, acting in concert and associating with other members of the club, strongly suggests that they are the sisters we are looking for. Only one of them features in the brackets set down by Dr Norris, implying that the elder sister was the primary attendee, initials conventionally being used to identify a younger sister with the same surname.

Lepanto was the scene of a major naval battle of 1571 when a coalition of Catholic states defeated the Ottoman fleet near its base on the west coast of Greece. It may have penetrated the public consciousness again in 1824 because it remained an Ottoman stronghold and was in Lord Byron's sights when he died at nearby Missolonghi. Indeed, there is a canto in his epic poem *Don Juan*, entitled 'The Battle of Lepanto', which recalls the 16th century conflict. The Panton sisters may have had a particular interest in Byron, but it's more likely that Dr Norris was simply indulging in more wordplay, recognising the similarity in form between 'Lepanto' and 'the Pantons'. As to the reference to Welsh and the traditional national colour of red, we need to go a little deeper to fully appreciate that.

The Pantons in whom we are interested are said to descend from Thomas Pontfract – secretary to Henry de Lacy, who lived in the late 13th and early 14th centuries and whose titles included Earl of Lincoln and Constable of Chester.[2] Jane Panton was born at Pentraeth, Anglesey in April 1757, the daughter of Paul and another Jane Panton. Her younger sister, Elizabeth Maria, followed her into the world a little over six and a half years later. By the time of their births, Paul was a well-known figure in north Wales. Born in Bagillt, Flintshire, and later lord of the manor of nearby Coleshill, he was a notable antiquary and traveller, in which capacity he became acquainted with the seminal travel writer, Thomas Pennant. He was also a barrister and took a keen entrepreneurial interest in lucrative mining projects in the Holywell area. He was described as 'mine mad'. As an antiquarian, he was an avid collector of Welsh manuscripts and a proponent of early Welsh literature. It is reasonable to suppose that his Celtic leanings rubbed off on his children.

Paul moved further west upon his marriage to Jane Jones in 1756, which brought with it a fine property called 'Plas Gwyn', near Pentraeth on Anglesey. Jane died at the age of 39 in 1764. By this time there were two sons – another Paul, who would eventually inherit the estate, and Jones. Paul senior remarried in 1770, to Martha Kirks, a Chester widow, and, from this point on, we see the Pantons strengthening their links to the city. Two children from this union – Thomas and Bulkeley Panton – were born and baptised in Chester in the early 1770s. This completed the new family unit in which Jane and Elizabeth spent most of their formative years.

Both Paul Pantons developed Plas Gwyn and were keen agriculturalists. In 1764, an old manuscript called *Idea Agriculturae,* by Henry Rowlands, was published with a dedication to Paul senior, describing him as 'an encourager and admirer of the no less pleasing than useful Art of Husbandry'. As we saw in Chapter Three, the land that he had at his disposal increased in 1777, when he was granted estates in the will of Sir John Glynne, a Flintshire neighbour and presumed good friend. This raises the likelihood that the Panton sisters were acquainted with Anne Glynne from an early age, albeit she was eight years older than Jane and 14 years older than Elizabeth.

For many years, Paul junior was one of the most active members of the Agricultural Society on Anglesey.[3] Educated in part at the King's School, Chester, he was called to the bar at Lincoln's Inn, before returning to Anglesey, where he became Deputy Lieutenant and Colonel of Volunteers from 1803, and High Sheriff in 1807. As we have seen, this was a critical period for the military on the home front, as Napoleon extended his dominance across mainland Europe. Paul junior's other responsibilities included being Distributor of Stamps for north Wales – an important fiduciary position - and on the bench of the Merioneth Court of Great Sessions. He had legal practices in Anglesey and Caernarvon and, in 1815, became High Sheriff of Flintshire, the county of his father's birth.

Paul junior was also a prolific writer and lobbyist, corresponding regularly in the Chester press under the pseudonym 'Monensis'. In 1781, he published an influential piece entitled 'Free Thoughts on the Continuance of the American War'. A committed loyalist, he played a leading role in raising a parliamentary petition against Catholic emancipation and added his name to the sympathetic address to George III following a failed assassination attempt, as mentioned in Chapter Nine. Like his father, he was a great collector and patron of Welsh literature, as well as being adept at music, the violin being his instrument of choice. In 1794, he even invested in his own printing press, which would soon need to be licensed under an Act of Parliament of 1799.[4] It was in this highly literate, politically charged environment that the Panton sisters were brought up. It is little wonder that the book club – with its opportunities to read, debate and contribute positively to society – appealed to them.

Paul senior's second son, Jones Panton, married Anne Whitaker in 1789. The wedding took place in St Michael's Parish, Barbados, where the couple were described as 'English settlers'. Little is known about her family except that her father, Thomas, had married on the same island and in similar circumstances in 1757. It is possible that they were connected with William Whittaker (a variant spelling of the surname), of Bromley, Kent, who died in 1759 after building up substantial ship-owning interests and plantations on Barbados. Jones and Ann named one of their daughters 'Lauretta Maria', which were the Christian names of William's wife. Whatever the nature of their business in the West Indies, they were soon back in Anglesey, as their first son – another Jones – was born there in 1790.[5]

In 1797, Paul senior died at the age of 70. His will, drafted two years earlier, included a provision of £2,300 each for Jane and Elizabeth, leaving them comfortably off. By contrast, his son – Bulkeley – was left only £100 'as his conduct has been very shameful and undutiful'. His precise misdemeanours were not recorded. He was, however, enlisted in the army – perhaps to instil discipline – but he died of a brief illness in this service a year later. Paul junior was the main beneficiary of his father's will, inheriting Plas Gwyn, whilst widowed Martha was granted a house and all its contents at Holywell for the remainder of her natural life.[6]

Martha lived on until 1814. Her will is sketchy and haphazard, and could perhaps have served as a warning to other family members of the importance of orderliness in such matters. It is also illuminating in terms of her Chester connections and possessions. Her main beneficiary – her stepson Paul – received 'all messuages, dwellinghouses with brewhouse and malt kiln, gardens and other appurtenances thereto belonging situate in fforegate street in the City of Chester'. The rents and profits from the tenancies were to go to her namesake Martha, daughter of Jones Panton, despite this Martha having an older brother and sister. Her stepdaughters, Jane and Elizabeth, were left a pair of silver candlesticks at Plas Gwyn.

Of interest amongst the monetary legacies are one of £2,300 to the Reverend Thomas Armitsted [sic] and another of £1,100 'to be divided between Mrs Skirrat [sic] and her two nieces whose names are Daniel'. 'Jane the wife of Thomas Armsted [sic]' was granted an interest in any residue. This Reverend Thomas is appointed as the sole executor and is shown to have proved the will.[7] The name 'Nicholls' is not mentioned, but these are William and Dorothea's kith and kin. We don't know the exact detail of all the relationships but, clearly, these families were close. As we have noted in William Nicholls' correspondence, he and Paul Panton junior were on friendly terms. Paul and his sisters attended the Chester Music Festival in 1806, at which Mrs Nicholls was present, alongside other future book club members.

In June 1821, the wedding took place in Beaumaris between William Peploe Hamilton – a 38-year-old Chester-born minister – and the inheritrix, Martha Panton, nine years his junior.[8] He was related through his three times great-grandfather to Samuel Peploe, Bishop of Chester from 1726 to 1752. The bishop's house on the banks of the Dee, below St John's Church, was eventually occupied by William's father, Peploe Ward, before he purchased Hoole Old Hall in the early 1800s. It was William who assumed the surname 'Hamilton' in place of 'Ward'.[9]

William and Martha settled in what would become the Hoole area of Chester, where they acquired extensive land holdings over the next two decades. William was soon involved in the administrative affairs of the city. In 1824, he was part of the committee that reviewed plans for the upgrading of the infirmary, drafted by William Cole, protégé of Thomas Harrison. He was granted a gaming licence in the same year, undeterred by any moral contention with his calling. In 1825, he presided over the Anglesey marriage between Jane Elizabeth, daughter of Jones Panton, and the Reverend Bulkeley Williams.

In 1822, Paul junior died at Plas Gwyn. He was unmarried, so his younger brother, Jones, inherited. Some legacies were granted to Jane and Elizabeth, further augmenting their wealth, and consequently their scope to live where and how they pleased. In the late 1820s

241

there is evidence of their precise whereabouts in Chester. *The Directory of Cheshire* for 1828, lists 'Mrs Panton' at 4 Northgate Street. When subscriptions were being raised in early 1829 for a new church at Boughton – subsequently named 'St Paul's' – 'Mrs Panton, Northgate Street' and 'Mrs E M Panton' donated £5 each. Around the same time, they attended the charity ball at the Royal Hotel in aid of Spanish and Italian refugees, in the company of Anne Owen and members of the Mainwaring, Humberston and Johnson families. Once more, their address was given as Northgate Street.

During this period, there were more marriages amongst Jones Panton's children. Two significant occasions were the weddings of Lauretta Maria to Thomas Williams in 1828 and William Barton to Ann Rumsey Williams – no relation to Thomas – in 1832. The latter union was celebrated with unprecedented fervour in Caernarvon and Beaumaris, the hometowns of the bride and groom respectively. Ceremonial guns were fired, beacons blazed, and locals were plied with gratuitous food and ale.

Set against these happy events were the deaths in 1830 of two other Panton nephews – another Jones and Thomas Whitaker – both of whom were enlisted in the Royal Navy. It must have been acutely painful for the sisters to experience members of the younger generation pre-deceasing them.

Three years later, Elizabeth Panton died. Her will, first drafted in 1829, describes her as being 'of Upper Northgate Street, Chester', which forms a junction with King Street, where Mrs Mainwaring and Mrs Nicholls lived for spells. The main beneficiary was her sister, Jane. There were shares in property, mines and the Ellesmere and Chester Canal Company. The last of these investments went to Martha Hamilton, along with £2,000, 'a diamond hoop ring and ffrench books'. Poignantly, there were bequests of '£3,000 and my English books' and £1,000 to nephews Thomas and Jones respectively which had to be redistributed by codicil after their deaths. A further '£1,000 and my Italian books' were left to cousin Josepha Corbett of Longnor Hall, Shropshire and £1,500 to cousin Thomas Panton, formerly of Leghorn. There was a well-established branch of the family, including three successive Thomases, who were merchants in Leghorn, just like the Earle brothers.

Perhaps this explains Elizabeth's collection of Italian literature. 'China jars I bought at Hastings' were left to Anne, wife of nephew Paul Griffith Panton. The south-east coast may have been a place of resort for the sisters because of the connection with the Whittakers, who were based in Kent.

A niece, Jane Elizabeth, had died in Chester in 1829, having given birth to a daughter, also christened Jane, who lived for five days. A total of £5,000 was left to the niece's surviving children, Bulkeley and Anne, the latter being Elizabeth Panton's goddaughter. Bulkeley died at Northgate Street aged eight in 1835, suggesting that the sisters may have had a hand in caring for the children after their mother's death. Jane Panton, by now in her late seventies, was minded to place a tablet on the north wall of the chancel in Chester Cathedral:

SACRED

TO THE MEMORY OF

JANE ELIZABETH

THE BELOVED WIFE OF THE

REV^D BULKELEY WILLIAMS

OF BEAUMARIS

SECOND DAUGHTER OF JONES PANTON ESQ^R

OF PLASGWYN ANGLESEY

DIED ON THE SIXTH OF APRIL MDCCCXXIX

AGED XXXIII YEARS

ALSO

JANE THEIR INFANT DAUGHTER

AGED V DAYS

ALSO

BULKELEY PANTON THEIR SON

DIED ON THE ELEVENTH OF MAY MDCCCXXXV

AGED VIII YEARS AND VIII MONTHS

TO THE GREAT GRIEF OF HIS FATHER AND
ONLY SISTER AFTER A SHORT ILLNESS WHICH
HE BORE WITH CHRISTIAN MEEKNESS
Of such is the Kingdom of Heaven

Monetary gifts alone in Elizabeth Panton's will amount to over £15,000. A good portion of the balance is in charitable donations, including £20 each to Bangor Dispensary, Chester Infirmary, Anglesey Bible Society and Chester Penitentiary. There is £50 for the Blue Girls' School in Chester and £100 to the poor of Pentraeth. The nature and distribution of Elizabeth's assets exemplify the sisters' values: family first, but charity an important second. They retained strong interests in Anglesey and Chester; and religion, education and moral rectitude mattered deeply to them. The will was witnessed by two leading surgeons at Chester Infirmary, both of whom we have encountered before: William Makepeace Thackeray and George Harrison. Nephew, Paul Griffith Panton, and niece, Martha Hamilton, were executors and proved the will in London on 3rd July 1833, exactly one month after Elizabeth died.

Though Jane was to live another seven years, she drafted her will on 10th June 1833, moved by intimations of mortality following the loss of her sister. Marked 'Northgate Street, Chester', it begins with the words 'Trusting to enter heaven with my beloved brother and sister'. Cash amounts are left to nephew Paul Griffith Panton (£10,000), niece Martha Panton (£5,000), great-nephew Bulkeley Panton Williams and great-niece Anne Elizabeth Williams (£2,500 each). Jane of course had no inkling that Bulkeley would pre-decease her. The books that she bequeaths – including to Bulkeley and Anne, despite their tender years – provide an insight into her reading tastes and whom she felt would most cherish them after her death:

Bulkeley Panton Williams

   'Eustace's Travels' [John Chetwode Eustace, *A Classical Tour Through Italy*, 1819]

244

'Mrs Opie's works' [Amelia Opie, 1769-1853, writer and abolitionist]

Anne Elizabeth Williams

'All the works of Mrs Edgeworth' [Maria Edgeworth, 1768-1849, Anglo-Irish novelist and educationalist]

Reverend Bulkeley Williams

'Hewlett's sermons' [Rev. John Hewlett, *Sermons on Different Subjects*, 1786]

Anne Barton Panton – wife of Paul Griffith Panton

'All Sir Walter Scott's works that I have'

Mary Panton – great-niece, daughter of Paul Griffith and Anne Barton Panton

'Dr Johnson's works'

'Blair's sermons' [William Blair, Presbyterian preacher, sermons published 1777]

Josepha Corbett – cousin

'Alison's sermons' [Published 1763-1771. Francis Alison was a Presbyterian preacher and educator, who moved to Philadelphia and taught three of the signatories to the American Declaration of Independence.]

Lucy Panton Corbett – wife of cousin, Panton Corbett

'Scott's Life of Napoleon' [Sir Walter Scott, *The Life of Napoleon Bonaparte, Emperor of the French*, 1827]

Richard Corbett – son of Panton and Lucy

'Dr Clarke's Travels' [Edward Daniel Clarke, *Travels in various Countries of Europe, Asia and Africa*, 1811-1823]

Edward Corbett – brother of Richard Corbett

'Walpole's letters' [Correspondence of Horace Walpole, 1717-1797, writer, antiquarian]

Apart from the sheer extent of this reading matter – the 'works' of the writers mentioned and the letters of Walpole were particularly voluminous – there are some interesting specifics within it. The overriding themes are history, travel, education and religion, as well as classic literature. Women writers feature prominently, as does Presbyterianism, with its

Puritan leanings. The travel books may have been left to the young men, Bulkeley and Richard, with a future Grand Tour in mind. Earlier Panton males had enjoyed that experience as part of their cultural upbringing, and it had led to the foothold in Leghorn being established.[10]

On the face of it, leaving material on abolitionism to Bulkeley, then aged six, looks heavy. It was topical, however – slavery was about to be outlawed in the British Empire, though it would take many years to implement the legislation. There was activism in the family too. Joseph Plymley Corbett (1759-1838) was Archdeacon for Shropshire and married the sisters' cousin, Jane Josepha Panton, from the Leghorn branch of the family. He was the foremost abolitionist in that county, chairing the Society for Effecting the Abolition of the Slave Trade and travelling widely to garner evidence and support for the cause. He was personally acquainted with the great champion of the national campaign, Thomas Clarkson, who had visited the family home at Longnor in 1791.[11] Jane Panton may also have heard candid first-hand accounts of conditions in Barbados from her brother, Jones, following the time he spent there in early adulthood.

A further gift in the will to Anne Barton Panton is 'the two views of Matlock in the drawing room, as they are my own'. This suggests she was a talented artist, as well as a voracious reader. An amount of £100 is left to 'the Rev P Hamilton of Hoole Lodge as a small proof of grateful affection for all the kind attention I have received from him since he has become my nephew'. There are generous sums for all the daughters of the Archdeacon and sundry other female family members and friends, including Mrs Nicholls, who would also pre-decease her.

Like her sister, she leaves charitable donations to Chester Penitentiary and Infirmary, the Blue Girls and Boys Schools – across the road from where they lived – and the Anglesey Bible Society. In addition, she endows the Lying-in Charity, perhaps mindful of her niece's death in childbirth and the loss of her great-niece a few days later. The distribution of her assets overwhelmingly favours the women and girls to whom she was close, providing them with some degree of independence at a time when societal odds were stacked against them.

In common with her sister, Paul Griffith Panton and Martha Hamilton were appointed executors. Two members of the Corbett family acted as witnesses. In 1836, some small additional bequests were included in the will: to servants and £100 to Archdeacon Panton 'as a small proof of gratitude and esteem'. He would never receive this however, as he died in 1838, whereas Jane lived on until 1840, just as she turned 83 years old. Perhaps as notable as the inclusions in Jane's will are the omissions. There is no mention of her brother, Jones, or his surviving children Barton Panton or Lauretta Maria Williams, all of whom feature in her sister's will.[12] This may be evidence of a growing rift in the family through the 1830s, which culminated spectacularly in a trail at the Old Bailey in 1838.

The catalyst was the death of Jones Panton senior on 26th May 1837 and a dispute that arose almost immediately concerning his will – or wills, as the case may have been. Although 76 years of age, Jones must have been in reasonable health until his final weeks because he had arranged to attend Chester Races at the start of May, only withdrawing at short notice. Jones' funeral and the reading of a will followed hard upon his death. This will, drafted in 1829 and revised by codicil in 1831 and 1833, appointed his youngest son, Barton, as sole executor and heir to almost his entire estate, valued at between £55,000 and £70,000 – approximately £3 million to £4.2 million in today's terms. This was on top of considerable property that had been gifted to Barton by his father during his lifetime. Bequests of £7,000 to Martha Hamilton and £400 to Lauretta Maria Williams were reduced by means of the codicils to £10 and £200 respectively, with the difference further adding to Barton's share.

There had been a serious falling out between Jones and his eldest surviving son, Paul Griffith, in 1828, which explains his complete exclusion from the will, and perhaps from Jane's will too. There had also been bad blood between Jones, on the one hand, and Lauretta Maria and her husband Thomas Williams on the other. This related to a breach of promise of marriage case brought against Lauretta Maria by a surgeon of Beaumaris which, it seems, Jones had been forced to settle. The acrimony must have subsided, otherwise Lauretta Maria would have been denied any inheritance. However, Jones, the testator, was closest to his son Barton and his family, who lived with him at Plas Gwyn. The arrival of a granddaughter in the household in 1835 was a singular source of delight for Jones.

It is not known whether Jane Panton attended her brother's funeral on Anglesey in 1837, but she surely would have done had her health permitted. What is known – crucially in the context of the lawsuit – is that Lauretta Maria and Thomas Williams did not. Nor did they attend the ensuing family gathering at which the will tabled by Barton Panton was read. Instead, Thomas immediately produced an alternative will which he claimed had recently been signed by Jones and witnessed in his presence, purporting to disinherit Barton and instead endow his wife and, by extension, himself. This was the pretext for the case *Panton v Williams*, which was played out in the highest profile court in the land and involved leading judicial figures for both the prosecution and defence. Martha Hamilton stood alongside her brother Barton in the bringing of the suit.[13]

The hearing lasted several days and was reported in microscopic detail in the press. On the face of it, Thomas Williams' position was precarious: the version of the will he produced bore classic hallmarks of a forgery – it appeared to have been written on a map drawn in pencil and signed in ink by Jones, with pencil marks remaining despite an attempt to erase them – and he faced the prospect of transportation if convicted. The verdict reached, however, was not guilty. This may have been influenced by the judge's summing up, which envisaged the possibility that Jones had produced a pre-eminent final will, deliberately and in sound mind, which not only confounded Barton's hopes but also kept him in the dark as to its existence.

On top of this, Williams commanded considerable public sympathy. Although far from impoverished himself, he may have been perceived as an underdog challenging the consolidation of a fortune within old-established landed family. There may also have been a feeling that, even if he was culpable, he did not deserve the fate that awaited him in the event of a guilty verdict – a fate that would have been far less severe had Barton not decided to by-pass the ecclesiastical court, in which such cases were commonly tried, in favour of the criminal court. So it was that the jury took a mere 30 minutes to clear him. Williams emerged from the dock and the courtroom to a rapturous public reception.

The matter rumbled on, however. After further legal wrangling on both sides, Barton succeeded in an appeal based on a reappraisal of the evidence, some of which post-dated the initial trial. This appeal concluded in 1843 and had the effect of reinstating the original will and condemning Thomas Williams and his wife, albeit to a remarkably light penalty of a £100.[14] In the wake of an arduous and expensive litigation process, perhaps it was felt that such a judgement was fair.

Sadly for Jane, who was in no way implicated in the matter, she would have died knowing that the Panton name had been besmirched by the lawsuit and that it had inflicted a punitive defeat on her brother and her niece. Her personal legacy was beyond reproach. The most tangible reminders of the family in modern-day in Chester – apart from memorials in the cathedral – are street names in Hoole. These include Panton Road, Panton Place and Hamilton Street, reflective of the long-term presence in that area of Martha and William Peploe Hamilton.

Chapter Sixteen

August

Gentle rain greeted the month of August, providing some relief to Cestrians who had suffered the sharp heat of the preceding summer months. The prospects of a good harvest remained positive. Elsewhere, Mother Nature was less forgiving: there had been violent storms as close to home as Liverpool and heat-related deaths in France, Spain and Portugal. Added to this, there were earthquake shocks in Paris, Lisbon and, less palpably, in Perthshire.

High profile figures passing through Chester included General Sir John Byng, whose reputation had been tainted when his delegation of responsibility to an ill-prepared deputy contributed to the Peterloo Massacre (Byng had two horses running at York that day); the great Shakespearean actor, Edmund Kean, on his way to Ireland; and Thomas Telford, returning after conducting surveys into a proposed ship canal from Bristol to the English Channel, or 'British Channel' as it was then called. Byng and Kean were guests at the Royal Hotel.[1]

Perhaps Telford was consulted on proposals for the new bridge over the Dee, which remained very much on the agenda. A letter addressed to the mayor and signed by William Peploe Hamilton, amongst others, urged further public consultation on the matter. At an amply attended meeting which followed a few days later, there was robust debate as to the merits of the scheme. Funding was an issue, and the concerns of Chester ratepayers were being sympathetically heard. Tolls were proposed, with possible concessions for Chester inhabitants. Tolls would be required on the old bridge too, partly to increase capital and partly to ensure adequate use of the new bridge.

The committee was now well-established and Mr Finchett-Maddock – a popular local man – was appointed solicitor to the enterprise. Even the newly installed bishop spoke up in favour of it, praising the architecture of the city and observing that the plans he had seen from Mr Harrison, including for the approaches to the bridge, represented aesthetic enhancement as well as new commercial opportunity. He described the financial support being received – including an advance of £15,000 from one individual – as 'Christian charity'.

Opposition remained. A memorial, signed by 70 people, objected to any increase in rates and to tolls on both bridges, calling for the complete abandonment of the scheme. Instead, they argued, the old bridge should be developed, at a projected cost of £4,000, compared with potentially ten times that amount required for the new bridge. Proponents expressed disappointment that city traders who had supported the proposal at its inception in 1819 had now set their faces against it, especially as nothing had fundamentally changed. If anything, arguments in favour had been bolstered, for example by an increase in the population of the city of four thousand between 1810 and 1820 and more intense commercial pressures. The continued silting up of the Dee and rapid expansion of Liverpool meant that coastal shipping which had previously been bound for Chester was now by-passing it almost completely. Additional road traffic had to be accommodated somehow, and funnelling more of it across the old bridge, even if reinforced, was not the answer. The width and gradient of Lower Bridge Street would simply become more of a constraint. What's more, a new bridge would complement the redeveloped castle frontage – also the work of Thomas Harrison – and attract even more visitors to admire the beauties and curiosities of the city.

Plans and cost estimates for work on the old bridge were requested but were unforthcoming, in stark contrast with the new bridge, for which Harrison's colour impression was displayed to the loudest approbation. Challenges were put as to how Lower Bridge Street would be reconfigured and what would replace the Bridge Gate, which would have to be demolished despite it being a mere 45 years old. Nor was there any confidence that the old bridge was strong enough to support an enlarged structure. Gradually, point by point, committee members skilfully unpicked the counterproposal until it was recognised as wafer thin. When a vote was taken on it, it was soundly defeated. A resolution in favour of the new bridge was adopted almost unanimously. This was accompanied by commitments to relocate St Bridget's Church, which was now in a dilapidated state, and to push ahead with tolls on both bridges.

Steps were then taken to co-opt the advocates of the old bridge scheme onto the committee for the new bridge, but not without them first renouncing their opposition publicly at the meeting. Given the weight of sentiment expressed verbally and by vote, this was something they could scarcely refuse to do.

With this hard-won consensus, proceedings drew to a close. The will was firmly established, and the impetus was there. The committee was now broadly based, recognising the scale of the task ahead and as a bulwark against further dissent. Members with whom we are already familiar included Earl Grosvenor; Sir Henry Mainwaring; George Johnson; Dr Norris; Philip Humberston senior; John Townshend; Reverends George Grenville-Neville, Thomas Armitstead, Richard Massie senior and William Peploe Hamilton; John Boydell; and William Makepeace Thackeray, MD.[2]

Other gatherings were mentioned in the press this month. One was the inaugural sermon preached before a packed cathedral by Bishop Blomfield, at which even non-conformists were present. At the Exchange, Earl Grosvenor chaired a meeting of the local branch of the Society for Promoting Christianity amongst the Jews, which had been founded in London in 1809. In a more social vein, the Chester Innholders Company, comprising 60 members, held their AGM at the Coach and Horses, time being 'spent with that good humour and conviviality which always characterises this jolly company'.[3] Competitive rivalries were suppressed, for one evening at least.

Meanwhile, at St John's, elders and parishioners met for a more sinister reason: a hole had been discovered in the accounts. John Pritchard, Assistant Overseer of the Poor, had allowed arrears of £395 to accumulate, which he ascribed to illness on his part. He added that he was now paying that sum by degrees, implying borderline embezzlement. He was under some pressure, as the meeting was four to five hundred strong and solicitors were present. The main victims were the House of Industry, or workhouse, which now had a funding shortfall, and ley-payers who had acted in good faith. Despite this, there was sympathy for Pritchard, whose job of collecting dues was known to be a difficult one, and some appetite to keep him in his post. At one point, as Pritchard pleaded mitigation, the minister bridled at supportive cheering. The investigation continued.

Back at the cathedral, services were suspended after the bishop's address to allow workmen to fit up the casing for a grand new organ. Perhaps the primary concern should have been the state of the bells, which one correspondent in the local press described as 'disgraceful to the church and city', though urging retention of 'the beautiful great bell, the grandeur of the music of which is so generally admired'.[4]

Other noteworthy events in the city this month included the launch, to much public acclaim, of the new brig *Belem Castle* – named after a landmark in Lisbon – from Mr Wilson's boatyard on the Dee, bound for the Mediterranean trade. Work on foundations in Eastgate Street uncovered a Roman hoard, comprising coins and a fibula, which, somewhat haphazardly, were 'distributed in various hands in this city'.[5] The recipient of this fibula was recorded as John Lowe, the silversmith.

The city's institutions continued to evolve. The architect, William Cole, produced plans for the new St Bridget's Church, described as 'chaste and elegant', as well as for improvements at the infirmary. A ladies' boarding school on White Friars was under new management as Misses Taylor and Broomhead filled a void created by the death of the previous proprietor, Mrs Halston. This operated in the same market as the Nicholls establishment on King Street.

The courts were busy too, mostly with crimes of a physical nature. George Hannon and Thomas Spencer were bound over for fighting over the affections of a domestic servant, whilst George Edge and Richard Rowlands were severely reprimanded for bathing naked in the Dee. According to the *Chester Chronicle* of 6th August, 'two apprentice tailors, Charles Meacock and Thomas Youde, slipped out of their master's house in St John Street at 12.30am on Saturday night to fall in with a night-nymph in the depraved purlieus of St Olave's churchyard'. A row broke out, upon which 'Honest Charley [a policeman], being on the alert, arrived with his lanthorn and left with the parties charged'. They too received a severe reprimand. Mary Hancock was threatened with the termination of her tenancy at one of Earl Grosvenor's alms houses after she slandered a married neighbour by suggesting she had been to Liverpool to consort with soldiers.

Mr Burgess, Chief of Police, had arrested an impressive haul of eight pickpockets, two assaulters and two robbers at Knutsford Races. Unfortunately, he was also the victim of assault and was now sporting a conspicuous black eye, courtesy of a bludgeon. Other alleged offenders remained at large, most notably William Parkinson of Dunham-on-the-Hill. Repeated appeals were made for his capture and action was being considered against any party who had failed in their duty to apprehend him before he took flight.

The place to which Parkinson had reportedly absconded – Manchester – was literally a hive of industry at this time. Contemporary data suggests there were 30,000 textile looms in operation in the region and 500,000 people employed on them, compared with almost nothing a decade earlier. The road infrastructure was being improved there too, including the recent macadamising of Mosely Street and King Street in the city centre. Plans had been laid down by George Stephenson for what was termed a 'railroad' to cover the 33 miles from Liverpool to Manchester, at a projected cost of £300,000. There had been delays in obtaining parliamentary approval and resistance from canal proprietors, but there was cause for optimism. A similar scheme to connect Stockton and Darlington had been sanctioned and others, such as Liverpool to Birmingham, were under consideration.[6] Also in Manchester, a new society of Christians had been formed who had pledged to live solely on vegetables.

In Liverpool, there was a stark reminder of the dangers of steam-powered travel when the boiler on the Earl of Bridgewater Steam Packet blew up as passengers disembarked from Chester and Ellesmere Port, with two fatalities. A gentleman from Liverpool called Rees Davies safely negotiated a different mode of transport when he joined Mr Sadler in Hull for another successful flight. Over on the Wirral, a boxing match took place at Tranmere between two other Liverpudlians: Boscow, a butcher, and Morison, a glassblower. The crowd of approximately 15,000 was more than half made up of people who had crossed the Mersey to spectate. Boscow won in 29 gruelling rounds, but both fighters were the object of derision in the press on account of their amateur status. At the same time, Spring and Langan, and others of their ilk, were lauded, despite their questionable, not to say illegal, choice of career.

Conflict on a grander scale was taking place around the world. Following the lead set in Demerara the previous year, insurrection had broken out amongst the enslaved people of Jamaica and the militia had been mobilised to some effect. One of the estates targeted was called Chester Castle. In parallel, bishops had been appointed to Jamaica and Barbados, further exemplifying the view that Christianity was the route to peace, reconciliation and enlightenment.

British military action elsewhere had subjugated the Dey of Algiers and the Ashantees, reasserting control in North and West Africa respectively. The need to provide troops to Portugal had subsided but concerns were escalating over other parts of the world. Russian ambitions towards the Sandwich Islands appeared to have been confirmed by further intelligence from overseas, and there were even rumours that the Tsar had assembled a fighting force of a hundred thousand men to conquer South America, now the Spanish were no longer in command. There was a tangible reminder of the threat from Russia when six of their ships were sighted passing up the Channel.[7]

Britons continued to travel the world in the interests of exploration. Captain Lyon's ship was berthed at Stromness in the Orkneys, kitted out and ready to set sail for the North Pole. Meanwhile, news arrived dramatically in a published letter from Sir Stamford Raffles, founder of Malaysia and Singapore, that priceless artefacts from another previously unexplored region had been lost. Raffles had been returning to Britain on the ship *Fame* with his family and treasures when it caught fire and sank. He and his family were saved but much recorded history and topography was destroyed. Worse still, they were travelling with rare and previously undiscovered animals, which also perished in the disaster.[8]

Once again there were curiosities in the press which may have caught the reader's eye. A visit by a group of Cestrians to a church for the blind in Liverpool returned a heartwarming account: the place thrilled with music and song, and church members effortlessly made rope and engaged in needlework, including one woman who threaded the needle with her tongue. The town of Carmarthen in west Wales was all but abandoned for a day because an ancient and highly specific prophesy by Merlin suggested it would be laid waste by a flood. All parties were mistaken, including the magician, and the townsfolk returned to business as usual the following day. The timing coincided with Carmarthen Fair, which was thinly attended as a result.

Two more criminal trials had contrasting outcomes. In Oxford, John and Grace Simmons, husband and wife, were tried and convicted of bigamy on the same day – both had seen fit to wed a second time when their original marriage was still in force. Closer to home, Charles Thompson was up in front of Chester magistrates for leaving the Mostyn Arms in Parkgate without paying for his food and drink. The landlady, Mrs Briscoe, had managed to seize his hat but not him, and he was later apprehended in Chester. In his defence he presented an incredible riches-to-rags account of his life, having been born into a noble family and educated at Rugby School before venturing across the Atlantic and returning in a state of complete destitution. This appears to have hit home because, not only did Mrs Briscoe return the hat and drop the charges, but he was awarded £3 to relieve his immediate wants by the mayor and magistrates, one of whom was Mr Finchett-Maddock, who was a Rugby man himself. Thompson was deeply moved by these acts of kindness.[9]

Finally, recent discoveries made by the esteemed astronomer, Professor Gruithuisen of Munich, after whom a crater on the moon is named, were widely reported. He had published the third part of his essay on 'the many plain indications of Inhabitants in the Moon, and especially of a colossal building'. He had set out to address key questions, including the extent to which there are indications of animated beings and the location of the greatest and plainest traces of art on the moon. He had concluded that vegetation grew on the surface between 55 degrees latitude north and south, and that there was evidence of living beings between around 50 degrees north and 47 degrees south. Three places had been detected in which the moon's surface had been altered artificially, leading to an inference that there were roads and 'great colossal edifices resembling our cities on the most fertile part, nearing the equator'.[10] His essay, which was accompanied by several plates, concluded with a suggestion that the inhabitants worshipped the stars and considered the earth as a natural clock.

Chapter Seventeen

Rev Geo Pearson
Lot 9

Coelebs in Search of a Wife, *a new edition, corrected after the manner of Bowdler's Shakespeare, the objectionable passages omitted, the good only retained. 1 vol., curiously printed in black leather.*

Coelebs in Search of a Wife was a popular novel of 1814 by Hannah More which would have been well known to the membership of the Chester Book Club. It was highly moralistic, with Coelebs on the lookout for a wife who met the exacting behavioural standards laid down by his late mother. There was a swift follow-up, *Coelebs Married*, but Dr Norris makes no mention of this. To suggest that *Coelebs in Search of a Wife*, of all books, needed bowdlerising is a comic masterstroke that the assembly surely appreciated, with the possible exception of George himself.[1] This and the choice of black leather binding paint him as a bachelor, presumably not intending to remain that way, and a stiffly puritanical man of the cloth. It is worth noting that the book came out in two volumes, yet Dr Norris stipulates only one; perhaps this was sufficient once the work of the censor had been done.

Delving into George's biographical data, we find that he held posts at St Peter's, Chester, in 1817, and St Olave's between 1819 and 1822, before becoming a minor canon at Chester Cathedral until 1825. He is also recorded in parish registers as having conducted baptisms at Holy Trinity during this period, alongside Robert Yarker and Richard Massie senior.

George was born in Lichfield on 8th September 1791 to the Reverend John Batteridge Pearson and his wife, Elizabeth, née Falconer, and was baptised in the cathedral in that city by his grandfather, the Reverend James Falconer. There were connections with Chester and north Wales through the Falconer family, including a great-grandfather who had been born in Chester and his mother's aunt – also Elizabeth – who had married the aforementioned travel writer Thomas Pennant, of Downing Hall in Flintshire.[2] As we will see, this was by no means the most notable literary connection in the family. George attended Charterhouse and gained his Bachelor of Divinity at Cambridge University before moving to Chester, his ties to Lichfield perhaps diminished with the death of his father in 1808.

We are fortunate that the year in which George's life is best recorded is 1824. He was a prominent figure at the meeting at the Exchange in March that year which aimed to petition Parliament 'for bettering the conditions of negroes in the West Indies', as referred to in Chapter Six. A Mr Granville, reflecting on recent salutary events in Demerara and Barbados, called specifically for a ban on the flogging of women, observance of the Sabbath and – 'looking forward to the ultimate abolition of slavery' – regard for the interests of West Indian proprietors. George rose to second the motion, emphasising the need for 'temperate language' and 'a moderate tone' in the petition. His views, he said, coincided exactly with the measures adopted by His Majesty's Government and stopped short of those of the likes of Wilberforce and Buxton, who wished to take 'a wider field'. Now George was warming to his task:

> Our greatest object is to procure for the slaves those privileges which *humanity itself* dictates should be extended to them and which, through the benevolence of many West Indian proprietors, they are enjoyed by *many*, yet are secured to *none* by sanction of law; to provide for their religious instruction … to inform their minds, to correct morals, to accustom them to … the care of a family and the comforts of domestic life; to improve and advance their condition gradually, *as they are able to bear it*, and to secure for them those advantages which are necessary, in order to enable them to appreciate the blessings of liberty, when they can be safely extended to them …

He closed on a jingoistic note:

It is a fine reflection that almost in every place wherever British valour and British enterprise have penetrated, we can trace the triumph of British benevolence, and that we have repaid to all the countries which have been subjugated under our sway, the advantages that we have received from them, by returning to them the blessings of our liberties, our laws and our religion ...

This is impressive oratory – one of the signal delights of the age – but we should look beyond it to the substance of what he says. In 'seconding' the motion, he dilutes it by urging caution and avoiding any mention of abolition. He also contradicts himself by alluding to the lack of legal protection afforded to enslaved people before expounding on the 'blessings' brought by 'our liberties, our laws and our religion'. This is at best naïve and, at worst, reactionary.

So why does he do it? However sincerely held his views were, he was echoing a widely supported establishment position. There was a reluctance to do anything too radical too quickly, which is why abolition took so long to come about and why those with a stake in the slave trade, some of whom may have been at the meeting at the Exchange in Chester, were given such a soft landing in the form of massive compensation payouts. The question must have given rise to lively debate within George's social circle. Jane Panton for example, with her abolitionist leanings, would surely have been exasperated at such conservatism. The meeting closed and the resulting petition was signed and submitted to Parliament.[3]

In August 1824, George was involved in an altogether more benign activity: singing in the choir at the cathedral on the occasion of the bishop's inauguration.[4] In September, he was signing another petition, this time in support of 'the establishment of a society upon a plan of the Royal Humane Society for recovery of persons apparently drowned or dead'.[5] Recent drownings in and around the Dee estuary may have given impetus to this cause, which was not so much about prevention and as the belief that bodies should be buried in consecrated ground.

In October, the Chester District Committee of the Society for Promoting Christian Knowledge met to advance its aims. This was another prodigiously attended session, at which the bishop took the chair. A primary purpose was to supply 'the poorer inhabitants of this city and neighbourhood with Bibles, Common Prayer Books and Religious Tracts', either gratuitously or at reduced prices. The Reverends George Pearson and Thomas Armitstead were appointed secretaries and Philip Humberston found his way onto the committee. A long list of subscribers, paying their annual dues of one pound and one shilling, included George Johnson, William Peploe Hamilton, Richard Massie senior and Elizabeth Sloughter.[6]

1825 was an important year for George too, because, happily, his search for a wife bore fruit. On Saturday 16th September he married Catherine Humberston, second surviving daughter of Catherine and Philip, at St Martin's Church in Chester. The bishop presided over the ceremony. We don't know for a fact, but there is likely to have been a good sprinkling of book club members in attendance. It is possible that a fledgling relationship was developing when Dr Norris presented his catalogue, making the tease more apposite and any embarrassment on George's part more acute.

At the time of their union, George was 34 and Catherine 22. He clearly carried the approval of Catherine's parents, god-fearing people that they were. He played his part in the civic and religious affairs of the city and was well-connected in ecclesiastical circles. He was also independently wealthy. Upon his father's death in 1808 he had inherited land and three houses in Lichfield. He had probably further benefited from the generous estate of his grandfather James Falconer, who died the following year.

The source of his father's wealth and network in the Lichfield area bear scrutiny. John Batteridge Pearson was well acquainted as a young man with Lucy Porter, stepdaughter of the great man of letters, Dr Samuel Johnson. An extract from James Boswell's *The Life of Samuel Johnson* shows just how strong that acquaintance was: 'This lady [Lucy], whose name frequently occurs in the course of this work, survived Dr Johnson just 13 months. She died at Lichfield in her 71st year, on January 13th 1786, and bequeathed the principle part of her fortune [derived from her late brother, an army officer] to the Rev Mr Pearson of Lichfield.[7] A review of Lucy's will confirms that this included a house in Tamworth Street, Lichfield, which was later passed on to George. John even won a legal case against the Bank of England concerning the transfer of disputed stock to him under the terms of Lucy's will.[8]

There is also evidence in Boswell's *Life* that he and Dr Johnson were personally acquainted with John. Boswell talks of the two of them having supped with him and Mrs Seward – Anne Seward, the Romantic poet, often known as 'The Swan of Lichfield' – at the inn they stayed at on one of their visits to Lichfield. Letters to Lucy from Dr Johnson in 1782 and 1783 request that his thanks and compliments be passed on to Mr Pearson 'and all that have shewn attention to me'. In late 1783, when Dr Johnson was ailing – he would die the following year – he closed another letter to Lucy with the words: 'Pray for me, and write to me, or let Mr Pearson write for you.' It is clear from the correspondence that she was not well either at the time and that John had become an important and trusted companion.[9] Insights into John's character appear in Boswell's private papers – 'a modest, well-behaved young man, much esteemed by Mrs Porter' and in a book entitled *Dr Johnson's Lichfield* by Mary Alden Hopkins:

> She spoke her mind did Lucy. She said in Johnson's presence to her friend Rev John Batteridge Pearson, perpetual curate of St Michael's: 'Why, Mr Pearson, you are just like Dr J, I think; I do not mean that you are a man of the greatest capacity in all the world, like Dr J, but you contradict one every word one speaks, just like him.' She evidently liked that type of man, for she left her fortune to the same Rev Pearson.[10]

After Lucy's death, John commissioned a tablet to her in St Chad's Church, Lichfield 'in gratitude for her liberal acts of friendship conferred on him'.

George is our primary concern here, and we know that he never met Dr Johnson because he wasn't born until seven years after his death. However, he must have been aware of the family connection with him. Amongst the more personal possessions that John inherited from Lucy were Dr Johnson's walking stick, his writing desk and a copy of his famous dictionary. This last item, astonishingly, was destroyed when a housekeeper mistook it for a book of no value and tore out leaves to fuel a fire. As George's mother survived his father by almost half a century, many of these pieces would have remained in the family for some considerable time.[11] A publication of 1848 entitled *A Catalogue of Engraved Portraits of Nobility, Gentry, Clergymen and Others* by John Meridew states, 'There is a portrait of Mrs Elizabeth Johnson [his wife] in Dr Johnson's house in London bearing the following words beneath it: "Engraved from an Original Picture, in the possession of Mrs Pearson, Lichfield".'

Dr Johnson had other links to Chester and our book club people. For many years a close friend and confidante was Mrs Thrale, wife and later widow of Henry Thrale, the successful Streatham brewer, to whom he was also strongly attached. We saw in Chapter Five how Dr Johnson had visited Combermere Abbey with the Thrales in 1774. This location featured in their travels because Mrs Thrale was related to the Cotton family on her mother's side. Her grandfather was Sir Thomas Cotton, 2nd Baronet Combermere, and her maiden name was Hester Lynch Salusbury, her mother having married the celebrated diarist Sir John Salusbury. An earlier Sir John Salusbury, of Lleweni, was thought to have been an acquaintance of William Shakespeare and one of the subjects of his allegorical poem *The Phoenix and the Turtle*.[12] Sir Thomas Cotton, 2nd Baronet, was also the great-grandfather of Catherine Humberston. Within Mrs Thrale's social circle, and in regular correspondence with her in the 1780s, were Daniel and Samuel Lysons, who later worked so closely with William and Dorothea Nicholls.

Dr Johnson accompanied Mr and Mrs Thrale as they travelled north to claim an inheritance that she had come into. That expedition included a visit to Chester, which Dr Johnson documented in *A Diary of a Journey into North Wales* in 1774:

In the afternoon, we came to West-Chester; (my father went to the fair when I had the small-pox). We walked around the walls, which are complete, and contain one mile and three-quarters, one hundred and one yards; within them are many gardens; they are very high and one may walk very commodiously side-by-side; on the inside is a rail; there are towers from space to space, not very frequent and, I think, not all complete.

We staid at Chester and saw the Cathedral, which is not of the first rank, and the castle (in one of the rooms the assizes are held); and the refectory of the old Abbey, of which part is a grammar school. The master seemed glad to see me. The cloister is very solemn; over it are chambers in which the singing men live.

In one part of the street was a subterranean arch, very strongly built; in another what they called, I believe rightly, a Roman Hypocaust ... Chester has many curiosities.[13]

His fastidiousness in counting his paces round the walls caused some annoyance on Mrs Thrale's part. It was going dark, and it was past her daughter's bedtime: she apprehended some accident to her, and – if he wasn't careful – to him![14]

Dr Johnson's comment on the cathedral seems harsh, but perhaps it suffered to his mind by comparison with Lichfield. Had he visited a century later, when the great Victorian restoration was well-advanced, he may have taken a different view. The school was the King's School, which was then located within the cathedral.

When Boswell visited Chester alone in 1779, he wrote effusively to Johnson:

I was quite enchanted at Chester, so that I could with difficulty quit it. But the enchantment was the reverse of that of Circé [a sorceress in Homer's *Odyssey*]; for so far was there from being anything sensual in it, that I was all *mind*. I do not mean all reason only; for my fancy was kept finely in play. And why not? If you please, I will send you a copy, or an abridgement of my Chester journal, which is truly a log-book of felicity.[15]

Unfortunately, this journal, which would surely do more great credit to the city, appears to have been lost. The letter adds that Dr Johnson's regret at not having spent more time in Chester himself had been conveyed to the bishop, who had offered to host him on a future occasion. Perhaps because of ill-health, this visit never came about.

There is a centuries-old affinity between Chester and Lichfield, which makes a visitor from one city to the other feel at ease there. This must have been the case with Dr Johnson and, a little later, George Pearson. Both are ancient cathedral cities of a comparable size and with historical ties. Werburgh, patron saint of Chester, was born in Staffordshire in the mid-17th century. Her father was Wulfhere, King of Mercia, which encompassed both Chester and Lichfield in its huge extent. One of the people under whom she trained to be a nun was St Chad, later Bishop of Lichfield. She was involved in convent reform and became abbess of Ely. She died in 700 and was buried at Hanbury in Stafford.

Her reputation as a miracle-worker led to the creation of a shrine, which was relocated to within the walled city of Chester when threatened by Viking incursions in the 9th century. This has retained its status as a place of veneration, though important artefacts were damaged or destroyed at the time of the Dissolution. A similar site was established at Lichfield for St Chad, and a pilgrimage route known as the 'Two Saints Way' developed between the two cities. This was especially popular in medieval times, when pilgrims, bearing small wooden crosses as an aid to meditation, traversed it.[16] In *Old Chester*, Crickmore describes a carving in the chapel at Eaton Hall of 'St Chad with the body of the blessed St Werburgh for burial in the Abbey at Chester'. Despite the anachronism, this is further evidence of the linkage between the two saints and their adoptive cities.

Chester also once formed part of the bishopric of Lichfield, with St John's being regarded as one of the three cathedrals of the diocese in pre-Reformation times. Peter,

Bishop of Lichfield from 1067 to 1086, based himself in Chester before his successors reverted to Coventry, which was traditionally the principal seat in the diocese.[17]

With some sense of this connection and having been settled in Chester for some time, George's next move may come as something of a surprise. In 1825, before his marriage to Catherine, but presumably with her full knowledge and consent, he accepted the offer of a rectorship at Castle Camps, a small rural parish in Cambridgeshire. As an adjunct to this, he became Christian Advocate for the University of Cambridge, his old alma mater, and would later be appointed a magistrate for the county.

Having moved into the ample rectory, looking across rolling fields to the isolated church in the distance, George and Catherine started a family. Over the next twenty-two years, they had twelve children: seven boys and five girls. The first, George Falconer Pearson, who would become an army colonel in Madras, was an exception in that he was born at The Friars, Chester, the remainder being born at Castle Camps. Another son, Charles, became college principal at Agra in India, after first attending and then teaching at Charterhouse. The third-born was christened John Batteridge Pearson, after his grandfather. He and another son, Edward Lynch Pearson, entered the ministry like their father, in Edward's case succeeding him at Castle Camps. The two other sons, Philip Pennant and Thomas Hall, also bore ancestral names.

Eight of the children lived well into the 20th century, but four died young, beginning with Henrietta in early infancy in 1848 and Thomas Hall at the age of 11 in 1853. The following year, James Falconer Pearson, reportedly a distinguished scholar at Charterhouse, drowned at Llandudno after hiring a bathing machine in relatively benign conditions.[18] Further tragedy would follow. In 1859, George's wife, Catherine, died at Castle Camps. On 13th May 1860, George was making his way back from London when he was fatally seized with apoplexy near Saffron Waldon. When the news reached home later in the day, his daughter Anne – described in the press as 'an invalid' – ruptured a blood vessel and also died. George was 68 years old and Anne a mere 21.[19]

Obituary writers were rueful at his passing but positive about his accomplishments. The *Gentleman's Magazine* described him as having been possessed of 'high classical and theological attainments'. Elsewhere, his profession was simply cited as 'orator'. Portraits that adorned the walls at the rectory were passed on to sons George and Philip. One, which was full length, was of Captain Jervis Henry Porter RN, Dr Johnson's stepson. Another was of Lucy Porter as a child and a third, the portrait of Mrs Johnson. These had come down to George through his father and mother, having originated with Dr Johnson and Lucy Porter. Legacies don't come much rarer than that.

When probate was granted to sons John Batteridge and Philip Pennant in June 1860, George's estate – which may have excluded or undervalued the paintings – came in at £25,000. For a while, the portraits of Mrs Johnson and Lucy Porter hung at Nantlys Hall near St Asaph, which was inherited by Philip Pennant Pearson from the Pennant family when its direct line expired. In recognition of this legacy, he changed his name to Philip Pennant Pennant in 1860. He soon became High Sheriff and Chairman of the Quarter Sessions in Flintshire, marrying the daughter of the Reverend Edward Bankes of Soughton Hall in 1862. Philip's sister, Adelaide Sophia, became the second wife of John Scott Bankes of Soughton Hall in 1883. They would have been well acquainted with surviving relatives in nearby Chester, most notably the Humberstons.[20]

One of George's siblings and her family should not escape comment here. His sister, Mary – ten years his junior – married Edward Thornewill, the owner of an iron foundry in Staffordshire, in 1829. They had a son, also called Edward, who became a successful Liverpool-based corn merchant and racehorse owner. In 1887, his horse, Gamecock, triumphed at the Grand National.[21] His wife, Anna, was the daughter of Roberston Gladstone who, in turn, was the brother of William and son of John Gladstone. Whilst this does not reflect a familial relationship between George Pearson and Anne Glynne, whose niece married William Gladstone, this is further evidence of peripheral connections across broad social networks.

A final footnote on George Pearson and his book club reference: a deeper analysis of his family tree turns up the surname 'Bowdler'. His great-grandfather, Reverend Samuel Pearson, married an Ann Bowdler in the late 17th century. She lived and died in Much Wenlock in Shropshire, a short distance from Hope Bowdler, which is where the family of Thomas Bowdler, the shameless expurgator of Shakespeare, originated. There is a strong possibility that they were related and that the same Bowdler blood ran in George Pearson's veins, albeit strained through several generations.

Thomas Bowdler had an elder brother, John, who was of a similarly prudish cast of mind. He wrote prolifically in favour of church reform, railing against the immorality and irreligion of the nation and petitioning Parliament to abolish lotteries.[22] In 1818, he was involved in the foundation of the Society for Promoting the Enlargement and Building of Churches and Chapels, alongside the Bishops of Chester and Lichfield. He may have been less impressed with another fellow founding member, the unfortunately named MP, Mr E P Bastard.[23]

Chapter Eighteen

September

In September, the warm summer weather gently took on a more autumnal feel. Recent light rain and above average temperatures had led to bumper crops of foodstuffs such as mushrooms. This pattern was not uniform throughout the country, however. In Exeter, where people were accustomed to a more congenial climate, snowfall was recorded. Swimmers still disported in the waterways in and around Chester, which resulted in further drownings in the canal, the river and the estuary. This was another stimulant to the Royal Humane Society.

Other organisations were active in the city at this time. There was a Friendly Society meeting and procession, concluding at St Peter's Church, where Reverend Thomas Armitstead delivered the sermon. The lodges were out in force, including marches and annual celebrations on the part of the Odd Fellows, Brothers of the Prince of Wales, and Wellington Lodge at various hostelries around the city. There were auxiliary meetings of the Missionary Society at Queen Street Chapel and the Society for Promoting Christianity amongst the Jews at the Town Hall, which was chaired by Earl Grosvenor and profusely attended.[1]

The character of the city and surrounding area was continuing to change in small but meaningful ways. Further enclosure was taking place – for example at Northop, just over the Welsh border – and moves were afoot to create a new water works and public baths in Chester. A site had been identified at Barrel Well, by the river at Boughton, and a company set up in which shares were selling fast. One of the aims was to supply spring water to the town houses in the city centre, to the benefit of our book club members who lived in the likes of King Street, Stanley Place and Nicholas Street.

The castle and armoury were satisfactorily inspected, and the city gaol had been up-graded to comply with legislation. When Prince Hermann Pückler-Muskau visited the cas-tle and its cells in January 1827, he was mightily impressed:

The whole arrangement of it seemed to me most humane and perfect ... The cells are separate and radiate from a centre; the little piece of ground in front of each is a garden for the use of the prisoner, in which he is permitted to walk ... In each divi-sion of the building behind the cells is a large common room, with a fire in which prisoners work ... The view from the upper terrace – over the gardens, the prison and a noble country, with the river winding below, just behind the cells; on the side, the roofs and towers of the city in picturesque confusion; and in the distance the mountains of Wales – is magnificent, and *à toute prendre*, our country counsellors of justice [in Saxony] are seldom lodged so well as the rogues and thieves here.[2]

Perhaps the quality of the accommodation diminished its value as a deterrent to crime, though extra-custodial punishment could be severe, as we have seen and will see again.

Whatever fate awaited the perpetrators, crime still stalked the streets of Chester. A fire which destroyed the Foregate Street premises of Messrs Parry and Truss, coachmakers, was strongly suspected to be the work of an arsonist. Witnesses who noticed lights in the building in the small hours of the morning, long after work had ceased for the day, raised the alarm. The low state of the river prevented an effective response: at 4.30am the roof fell in, and at 5am little more than a pile of ashes remained. The watchman, Hugh Wil-liams, had been discharged after being found asleep on duty the previous night by George Burgess, his boss, meaning the area was unpatrolled.

A great number of carriages had been destroyed, though a brewery and timber yard either side were unaffected. The *Chronicle* described the spectacle as 'at one time strikingly grand, the burning embers ascending to a great altitude, and illuminating the tops of the loftiest buildings in the city, till their glare was obscured by the golden beams of the rising sun'.[3] The proprietors are unlikely to have dwelt on this prospect, though they had taken care to insure their business after a similar experience the previous year. Within a week they had set up in alternative premises and were soliciting further custom in the pages of the press.

Mr Burgess was soon in action again, arresting house burglars in Upton and Bretton and seizing a haul of lead in Chester. It seems he had a small force of constables working under him, but they weren't pulling their weight and were criticised by magistrates for their indolence. Drunk and disorderly behaviour in the city centre was a problem, particularly on the part of Irish immigrants, who were frequently referred to in official reporting as 'Emerald Islanders', 'Patlanders', or simply 'Pat'. Expulsions or committals were common in such cases.

Petty crime was often driven by need. Priscilla Nicholson was convicted of begging and playing a tambourine and Mary Oldfield of stealing a tin of treacle from a grocer's shop in Northgate Street, both of whom pleaded poverty. At the other end of the social spectrum, an oyster house had just opened in Castle Street selling the 'choicest flavored London oysters' and there was a new tea warehouse on the corner of Bridge Street and Pepper Street offering 'the finest East India teas'. Tea could only be sold at a regular shop or warehouse, and stiff penalties were issued to anyone caught 'tea-hawking'.

Other thefts during the month included gold and silverware from the Feathers Hotel, which was traced back to a night porter, and wheels from the cart of a plasterer working on new houses in Brook Street. On the Wrexham road, John Casey, a pig dealer, was set upon at 11pm by three highwaymen, who took money and most of his clothing before binding him to a nearby gate. Rewards were offered in these last two cases, but expectations of redress were low.

Crimes against the person were on the agenda too. A grand jury had considered the case of William Parkinson in absentia and decided that the charge, if and when it could be brought, would be one of manslaughter rather than of murder. Repeated appeals for his arrest continued. Assaults upon children of the most heinous kind were tried, including one case in which a nine-year-old girl was cross-examined in the witness box. When a guilty verdict was arrived at, a sentence of three years imprisonment was passed. Meanwhile, a man who stole a cow was sentenced to death.[4]

Felons who were convicted but spared capital punishment occasionally profited from their crimes. Thomas Lyon, who had been transported to Australia in 1816 for the theft of geese, returned to Chester in September 1824 to collect his wife and family. He had been given a large grant of land in New South Wales and was keen to develop it. It was noted that there had never been a single case in that part of the world of smallpox, measles, whooping cough or scarlet fever, all of which were frequently fatal in Britain.

Horses could be problematic, even when they were not the object of criminality. Mrs Hancock of Queen Street was knocked down by a horse and cart in Northgate Street and had her leg broken. A pedlar returning from market at Liverpool was killed when his cart overturned and landed on top of him, though it didn't help that he was drunk and his horse was blind. In a similar, though inconsequential case, a man was found asleep on his cart in Eaton Road, being led by a blind horse.[5]

There was people news that would have been of interest to our book club members, as at least some of the individuals concerned would have been personally known to them. Monsieur Doré had announced his retirement as leader of Chester Choral Society, ceding his role to Mr W Venables, who ran a music academy at 53 Watergate Street – across the road from Mrs Mainwaring's house. Opposite the Massie townhouse, a Mr Pickering was offering landscape drawing lessons at 2 Stanley Place. Perhaps some of the Massie children, talented artists as they were, supported this endeavour. Thomas Lowe was granted the freedom of the city for services to silver, and Charles Kynaston Mainwaring celebrated his coming of age at Oteley, under the proud oversight of his mother. Cestrian, William McGeoch, had less cause for rejoicing as he publicly disowned and disclaimed all liability for his wife on account of her improper conduct with Mr Black, the cathedral organist.

Elsewhere in the country, Mr Sadler continued his busy schedule of ascents, most recently enthralling crowds at Wigan. The event at Hull the previous month was reported to have been attended by an estimated 150,000 people, despite the population of the city being less than a third of that figure.[6] Another journey that excited much publicity, but that was shrouded in grief, was about to begin – the bodies of the King and Queen of the Sandwich Islands were being repatriated for burial. As that expedition departed, Sir Stamford Raffles arrived, alive and with what remained of his possessions and his entourage in tow.

Across the Channel in France, the death was announced of King Louis XVIII. This was treated lightly in the British press, with the *Chronicle's* comment that it had no effect on the financial markets not atypical.[7] In France itself, seven months of mourning was declared. Trouble-spots near and far continued to command press attention. The Greeks had the upper hand in ferocious fighting with the Turks, but there was less to report in Ireland and the West Indies. In Jamaica, 23 enslaved people had been convicted of conspiracy, 12 of whom were condemned to hang, which served as a deterrent to further agitation and revolt. The main news from the subcontinent was that the East India Company had turned in a profit of £2 million on a £22 million turnover the previous year – not bad for an old-established institution whose star was on the wane.[8]

Someone else with an eye for a profit was an enterprising cooper in London who had bought Lord Byron's bathtub, painted the late-lamented poet's name on the side and put it on display to an admiring multitude. Back in Chester, at the end of the month, a significant loss was reported, though not of a financial nature. George Burgess, Chief of Police, physically scarred and suffering the weight of responsibility and insubordination, had resigned. There was much regret and wringing of hands at the news, but his mind was made up. This policeman's lot was not a happy one.

Hester Lee Townshend and Richard
Massie marriage oath

Stanley Place, Chester – Massie, Potts, Townshend and
Venables connections

Hugh Hamon Massie (1854-1938), nephew of
Mrs Massie

Representation of Mr Sadler's historic first crossing of
the Irish Sea in 1817

Chorlton Hall, site of home of William and Dorothea Nicholls (remodelled 1846/7)

Meriel Leicester (1705-1742), Mrs Nicholl's grandmother

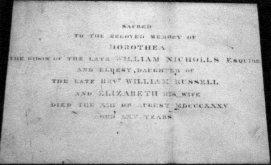

John Byrne of Timogue (1707-1742), Mrs Nicholls' grandfather

Mrs Nicholls' memorial, Chester Cathedral

Paul Panton (1737-1797), father of the Panton sisters

Plas Gwyn, Anglesey, childhood home
of the Panton sisters

Panton sisters' memorial, Chester Cathedral

Reverend George Pearson

Potts family memorial, Chester Cathedral

Eliza Potts by William Owen Harling 1847. *Reproduced with the kind permission of the Grosvenor Museum, Chester.*

A further Potts family memorial in Chester Cathedral

Watergate House, home of Henry Potts

Woodhill, Venables' family home

Roots and Venables car. Credit *Grace's Guide to British Industrial History*

King's Buildings, King Street – connected with the Mainwaring, Nicholls and Potts families

Newgate Prison on the Morning of the Execution of Henry Fauntleroy by W Thomson

Early representation of the Grosvenor Bridge, Chester

William Foxley Norris, on King George VI's immediate left, whilst officiating at his coronation. Credit Getty Images.

King Street, looking up from King's Buildings

Annotated extract from John Wood's *Plan of the City of Chester*, 1835

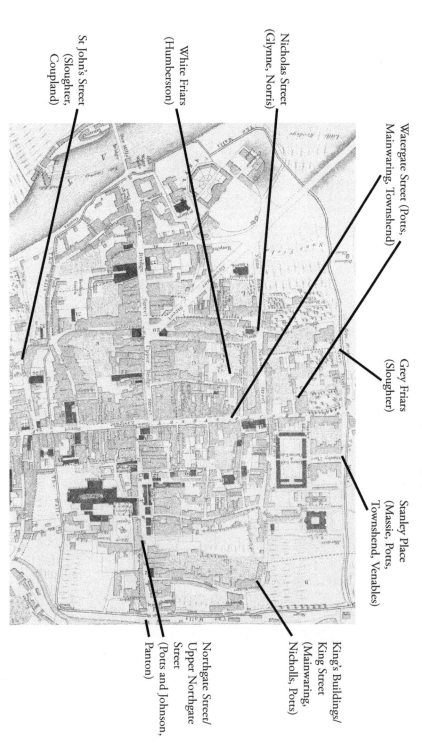

St John's Street
(Sloughter,
Coupland)

White Friars
(Humberston)

Nicholas Street
(Glynne, Norris)

Watergate Street (Potts,
Mainwaring, Townshend)

Grey Friars
(Sloughter)

Stanley Place
(Massie, Potts,
Townshend, Venables)

King's Buildings/
King Street
(Mainwaring,
Nicholls, Potts)

Northgate Street/
Upper Northgate
Street
(Potts and Johnson,
Panton)

Chapter Nineteen

Mrs Potts
Lot 10

The Comforts of Human Life, a fine folio edition, particularly well bound, and in excellent preservation

In 1806 a book was published entitled *The Miseries of Human Life; or the Groans of Timothy Testy and Samuel Sensitive, with a few supplementary sighs from Mrs Testy* by James Beresford. In twelve dialogues, these allegorical figures take a whimsical jaunt around 'the petty outrages, minor humiliations, and petty discomforts that make up everyday human existence'. It sold so well that a year later a follow-up – or counterpoint – came out: *The Comforts of Human Life; or Smiles and Laughter of Charles Chearful and Martin Merryfellow*. Testy and Sensitive were once more amongst the *dramatis personae*, but this time their philosophy was under challenge. The fact that *Comforts* rather than *Miseries* was selected for Mrs Potts suggests that she was more inclined to see the rose amongst the thorns than the thorn amongst the roses. She was also no stranger to some of the finer material comforts of the day, as we shall see.

The Potts family was well-known and became well-established in the legal profession in Chester over many years and several generations. It was another large family with lots of overlapping names, making identification difficult in some cases. Regarding our book club member, there are two potential candidates, one of whom soon comes to the fore. In 1824, there was a Mrs Anne Potts living at Watergate House, near the Water Gate, and a Mrs Lydia Potts at King's Buildings in King Street. Anne was the wife of the prominent Chester solicitor and Clerk of the Peace, Henry Potts, and Lydia was the second wife and now widow of Charles Potts, Henry's father. Henry himself was the product of Charles' first marriage to a lady by the name of Anne Kay, who had died in 1796.

Lydia was born in 1761, whereas Anne – wife of Henry – was born in 1785. In the year of the book club meeting, they were therefore 63 and 39 respectively. To suggest that a lady in her thirties is in a state of 'excellent preservation' may be deemed insulting, but to a lady in her sixties, it is more likely to be taken as a compliment. On top of that, Anne had eight children in her household, the youngest of whom was in early infancy, so her opportunities to dwell upon 'the comforts of human life' were more limited. It could have been meant ironically, of course, but Dr Norris had already taken that line overtly with Mrs Massie and was unlikely to deploy it again. Finally, Lydia's presence at King's Buildings, where Mrs Mainwaring and Mrs Nicholls also had a base, links her directly with other members of the group. It is not simply that these ladies got on with each other, but that they aged and socialised together in nourishing and mutually supportive ways.

Lydia's family origins are obscure. On 19th June 1798, the *Chester Courant* reported a marriage between Charles Potts and 'Mrs Kennedy of Manchester' at St Oswald's, Chester. We know that this was her second marriage because Charles' will, drafted some years later and in which Lydia is a beneficiary, attaches conditions to her legacy in the event of her marrying for a third time. There is little available information relating to widowed ladies with the surname Kennedy in Manchester at this time. There is, however, a copy of a licence granted to a Lydia Owen and Gilbert Kennedy 'of Manchester' upon their marriage in Frodsham, Cheshire in 1791.[1] This is corroborated by an entry in the *Leeds Intelligencer*, which adds that Miss Owen – no relation to the Owens of Glansevern – was the daughter of the late Reverend Humphry Owen of Manchester.[2] Gilbert, who was involved in the cotton trade in the city, died in 1795, leaving Lydia free to remarry. Further investigation reveals that a Lydia Owen had been baptised at St Anne's Church in Manchester on 23rd December 1761, which reconciles perfectly with Lydia Potts' recorded age at the time of her death in Chester many years later.

The Potts family had strong connections with the Manchester area. Henry Potts, who was acquainted with George Ormerod and supplied material for his *History*, advised him that they were descended from Roger Pott of Taxal, near Stockport. Roger's three times great-grandson, Edmund Pott, is mentioned in William Dugdale's *Visitation* of 1663 to 1664, and the family possessed land in the township until the 18th century.[3] By this time, however, their main base was further west, at Ollerton, near Knutsford. The Lysons brothers in *Magna Britannia* place their origins emphatically in the Macclesfield Hundred, stating that 'Charles Potts esq. is a representative of the Potts of Pott'.[4] This most likely refers to Pott Shrigley, not far from Taxal.

Charles' first wife was from Manchester, as was the other Anne, Henry's wife. Both marriages took place in the Collegiate Church in Manchester, in 1771 and 1805 respectively. Anne – Mrs Charles Potts – was the daughter of John Kay, a Manchester-based attorney. Anne – Mrs Henry Potts – was from the Taylor family of Moston, Manchester, long-established mill-owners and textile manufacturers, who made a considerable fortune when they transitioned their main line of business from thread-making to cotton fabrics. Much of this success was dependent on raw materials sourced through the transatlantic slave trade.[5] They were able to develop Moston Hall and acquire Eccleston Hall near St Helens, which they rebuilt sumptuously in the early 19th century.

Anne's half-brother, Colonel Samuel Taylor, was a prominent Protestant loyalist and freemason. He became the first Grand Master of the Grand Lodge of England in 1808, which met in Manchester until its move to London in 1821.[6] This family is not to be confused with the Taylors of Lymm, who were discussed in Chapter Nine. Anne Taylor's three times great-grandfather had a daughter called Elizabeth, who married Robert Kay – Anne Kay's great-uncle. Elizabeth and Robert had a son called Richard Kay, who was an eminent doctor and diarist. His diary contains a genealogy of the Taylors of Moston, which enables us to see the connection between the families into which Charles Potts and his son Henry married. The content is very much centred in and around Manchester.[7]

The man Lydia married in 1798 was one of several fathers and sons called Charles Potts. We will refer to him as 'Charles senior', once we have dealt with Lydia's father-in-law, who is important in our story, not least because he practised law in Chester and enjoyed considerable wealth, upon which future generations would build. This Charles Potts was admitted as an attorney in Chester in 1729, though it seems he continued to live at Ollerton, as his children were born there in the middle years of the century.[8] When he died in 1773, he left land and property in Cheshire, Derbyshire, Leicestershire, Northamptonshire, Warwickshire, Northumberland, Kent and London. The Cheshire property included a silk mill at Nether Knutsford, and in London there was a fashionable town house in Water Lane, off Fleet Street, which was inherited from a wealthy uncle by the name of Charles Yarwood. Charles Potts' assets in the Midlands probably accrued from his marriage in 1741 to Eliza Rogerson, who came from that part of the country. Amongst numerous monetary bequests in his will, the sum of 20 guineas was left to 'my worthy friend George Lowe of Christleton', near Chester: the likelihood is that this was the renowned silversmith, of whom mention has already been made.[9]

The main heir and beneficiary was our Charles senior, who could therefore have lived the life of a carefree landed gentleman, but too great a spirit of enterprise and civic duty ran in the ancestral blood. Like his father, he became a solicitor in Chester, but he chose to settle in the city. At the time of his first marriage in 1771, he is recorded as being of 'St Olave's' parish, on the south side, towards the river. Henry, the eldest child, was born in 1777, followed by Charles in 1779, Sarah in 1781 and Anne in 1783. Sadly, Charles died at the age of 19 months, so the final child, born in 1789, was also christened Charles.

By the turn of the 1790s, Charles senior's professional reputation had brought in some important commissions. He was Clerk to Chester Castle, in which capacity he secured an Act of Parliament for a major rebuilding programme, necessitated by serious dilapidation.[10] Thomas Harrison, then of Lancaster, was appointed architect, creating and implementing an ambitious scheme of work in the Gothic Revival style which spanned over a quarter of a century, resulting in much of what can be seen at the castle in the modern day.[11] This also spawned a long and fruitful partnership between Harrison and the Potts dynasty, led first by Charles senior, and then Henry.

By now, Charles senior had entered into partnership with a solicitor from Shropshire by the name of Stephen Leeke. Their business premises were listed in the *Cheshire Directory* of 1792 as being at 'Higher Northgate Street'. They and their practice were heavily involved in enabling the construction of the Ellesmere Canal, which linked the pre-existing but commercially challenged canal network in the region to the River Mersey at what would become Ellesmere Port. This aspect of the project, completed in 1795, was a success in absolute terms but it also accelerated the demise of Chester as port, as ocean-going traffic could now by-pass it completely.[12] Numerous notices appeared in the press in 1794 and 1795 summoning shareholders to meetings and making cash calls upon them. In one case, it was stated that 'the Committee for conducting the business of the Ellesmere Canal Company have authorized no other parliamentary notices, except those which are signed by the names of Messrs. Potts and Leeke, solicitors to the said company'. It was signed, 'By order of the sub-committee, THOMAS TELFORD, General Agent to the Company.'[13] They operated from the canal basin in Chester in a building which still stands, alongside the factually named 'Telford's Warehouse' public house.

Charles senior and Thomas Telford also collaborated on the construction of the Pontsycyllte Aqueduct, which straddles the upper Dee valley so imperiously near Llangollen. The aqueduct and canal in this area constitute a World Heritage Site. The original patrons of the canal, including prominent MPs and landowners, later acknowledged the services of Messrs Potts and Leeke in preparing materials for the Acts of Parliament and carrying them through both Houses. The total value of this business, which spanned the period 1791 to 1805, was reported at £9,000 – well over half a million pounds in today's terms.[14]

Whilst Charles senior was most fully immersed in his work, which was groundbreaking in every sense of the word, another family tragedy was looming. In June 1796, his wife, Anne, died at the age of 52. It is reasonable to suppose that he felt regret, perhaps even guilt, at not having spent more time with her in her final years. The business took on fewer grand commissions after that, until Henry was ready to reinvigorate it once he had gained his spurs.

When Charles senior married Lydia, two years into his widowhood and three years into hers, the older Potts children – Henry and Sarah – had reached early adulthood, but the other two were of an impressionable age: Anne was 14 years old and Charles junior had just turned nine. Lydia would have done her best to fill the void left by the loss of their mother and contribute positively to the remainder of their upbringing.

Towards the close of the century, amidst his routine professional duties, Charles senior faced a new and perhaps unforeseen responsibility: mobilisation of the Cheshire Militia. Renewed hostilities with France and the Irish Rebellion of 1798 led to parliamentary legislation aimed at shoring up homeland security and guarding against foreign invasion. Acting on behalf of the deputy lieutenants, he posted notices in the press requiring eligible men to convene at Chester Castle to receive 'clothing, arms, accoutrements and billets', adding that anyone who failed to comply would 'be deemed deserters, and punished as such'.[15]

All of this needed to be paid for. A local fundraising committee was set up, under the auspices of the Bank of England, meeting daily at the Pentice – a wooden structure then attached to the south wall of St Peter's Church – to receive contributions. Charles senior and William Nicholls came in with £100 each. Other members of the Nicholls family, including Dorothea, subscribed several pounds, and Mainwarings, Massies and Pantons played their part too. There was £10 from Mrs Sloughter's household, including £3 from 16-year-old Anne and £2 from their servants. Over £50 came from collections at three Chester schools, where the children were turning out their pockets for king and country.[16] The state of alert would remain, to a greater or lesser extent, until the defeat of Napoleon at Waterloo in 1815.

By September 1803, Henry, caught up in the fervour towards the defence of the realm, had joined the Western Cheshire Yeomanry. In October 1805, less than two months after his marriage, he was on the march. *The Cheshire Sheaf,* which identifies Henry amongst the serving officers, picks up the story:

On 21ˢᵗ October 1805 the three quarter troop of the Western Cheshire Cavalry, under Colonel Dod assembled at Abbey Court, Chester and proceeded on a march to
Shrewsbury for 14 days duty ... The whole corps halted at Hampton Heath near
Malpas where they were regaled of with an abundance of cheese and ale and three
standards were presented by Miss Dod, daughter of the commanding officer ... She
expressed herself in the most animating, patriotic and loyal strains. 'Gentlemen, you
have numberless motives for your manly exertions; your country, your King, your
matchless constitution, would sufficiently animate your breasts, but you have more
than these – the aged and infirm, your wives and children, and all the tender objects
of your affections call powerfully upon you for protection against violence and outrage from the merciless tyrants of France ...'[17]

Whilst Henry was so occupied, his father was maintaining the business of the legal
practice in Chester. Some significant enclosure bills had been secured and were being
implemented, including at Saltney Marsh and St Mary's on the Hill, and on family-owned
land in and around Ollerton. Charles senior's younger brother, Josiah, was involved as an
unofficial land agent and appears to have had some sympathy with the tenantry who were
being displaced. However, the power dynamic within the firm and within the family was
such that he was unable to influence proceedings in their favour.[18]

In 1806, Henry and Anne's first child was born. Another Charles, he suffered the same
fate as the first Charles of the previous generation – dying in early infancy – in 1809. There
was also a Mary Anne Potts, born in 1807, who died in the same year as Charles. The first
child to survive – Eliza – born in 1809, would become a distinguished, not to say pioneering, botanist; her achievements hugely embellished by the constraints that had to be over-
come by women in many spheres of life, including education and science.

The Grosvenor Museum in Chester has done a great deal to preserve Eliza's output
and promote her legacy. The Potts Herbarium is stored there, some of which is on public
display, alongside a fine portrait of her painted by William Harling Owen in 1847. It shows

her in pensive mood amidst an arcadian setting with a sprig of herb held aloft in her left hand. In the background appears to be Moel Famau, the highest point on the Clwydian Range. This area, to which the Potts family had a strong attachment, is where Eliza collected many notable and previously undiscovered botanical specimens. She was also active in Cheshire and on the Wirral Peninsula, contributing to important bodies of work and being recognised by other leading botanists of the day. She died in Chester unmarried in 1873, leaving, amongst other gifts, a lectern to Chester Cathedral.[19]

When the Reverend Henry Poole ventured north in the summer of 1809, alongside the social engagements with the Cottons, Gladstones and Humberstons recorded in his diary, as detailed in Chapter Five, is an entry that reads: 'Saw Mr Potts on subject of sewers at Stanlow Cop', near Ellesmere Port. His contact is most likely to have been Charles senior rather than Henry. This provides some idea of the minutiae in which they were involved around the canal system which they had been instrumental in creating.

Henry Taylor Potts was the next child to be born, in 1811. He would make his mark with the most exceptional achievement: in 1837, he won what is regarded as the first ever Grand National horserace, as an amateur jockey. He did this as a late stand-in, probably for Captain Martin Becher – after whom Becher's Brook at Aintree Racecourse is named – on The Duke, which was owned by a close friend, Mr Sirdefield of Great Crosby. The Duke's hoof was passed down through the eldest male in subsequent generations of the Potts family as a memento. Henry Taylor had not disclosed his participation to his parents, both of whom were still alive at the time, perhaps because it was then, as it still is, a precarious event, especially for an ill-prepared amateur.[20]

These circumstances make his victory all the more remarkable. He is recorded as having ridden his own horse, The Countess, in the same event the following year, but his undoubted prowess in this field appears not to have led to a career in it. He remained an avid hunter with the Cheshire Hounds, which he did from his Watergate Street base, keeping livestock out at Beeston. In 1844, he married Cecilia Anne Martin, daughter of a major in the British Army and niece of Sir William Grant, Master of the Rolls. Henry

Taylor held military commissions himself, including as a captain in the Royal Cheshire Militia and major in the Chester Rifle Volunteers. He was High Sheriff of Flintshire in 1852 and of Denbighshire in 1877. In later life, he was also a JP for Denbighshire. Both he and his wife died in Chester, in 1884 and 1906 respectively.

The next four Potts children – Sarah, born 1812; Arthur, born 1814; Charles William, born 1816; and Harriet, born 1817 – all survived until the later years of the century. Sarah spent her life in Chester, marrying Richard Barker, another solicitor based in the city. She died in 1881, after four years of widowhood. Harriet moved away following her marriage to Manchester-born merchant, Henry Garnett, who for a time had rented Bache Hall, on the north-east fringe of Chester. It will be recalled that this was later the home of Philip Stapleton Humberston and his wife, Elizabeth. Initially Harriet and Henry lived in Hartford, near Northwich, before moving to Wyreside, Lancaster, where Henry had family property and where he became a JP and Deputy Lieutenant of the county. Harriet died there in 1884, Henry living on another 13 years.

Arthur, who, in his bachelor days, lived at Sandy Lane, Boughton, was an engineer. With financial support from his father, he bought into the Viaduct Foundry at Newton-in-Makerfield in 1844. Operating in partnership with John Jones, it became known as Jones and Potts. Much of their business was with local collieries, including the construction of locomotives. It was said that Stephenson's *Rocket* was serviced and watered at the premises and that Arthur, at the time of his apprenticeship, was personally known to Robert Stephenson. By the early 1850s, the business was in decline, but there was demand for the premises. In 1853, they were leased to the burgeoning London and North Western Railway Company and sold outright seven years later for £15,000. The director who led negotiations on behalf of the railway company was none other than Sir Hardman Earle, son of Thomas Earle of Spekelands. The settlement for employees built nearby became known as Earlestown.[21]

Arthur's wealth was amplified by his marriage to Elizabeth Wardell, daughter of Chester banker, William Wardell. William was in partnership with members of the Dixon family, who took on the business entirely after William's death in 1864. Dixons & Co was acquired by Parr's Banking Company in 1878, and this in turn was subsumed into what later became the NatWest Group.[22] So it is that the premises of Dixons and Wardell on the west corner of Eastgate Street and St Werburgh Street, dating from the early 19th century, are now occupied by a branch of the NatWest Banking Group.

In the late 1850s, Arthur bought Hoole Hall, erstwhile home of John and Thomas Baldwin. Both he and Elizabeth were keen gardeners and horticulturalists, cultivating exotic plants and staging floral displays in the grounds. When Arthur died in 1884, he left an estate valued at approaching £90,000. Both he and Elizabeth, who lived on until 1911, are buried and remembered alongside her father at Overleigh Cemetery, Chester. Their names also feature in a stained-glass window in the south transept of Chester Cathedral.

Charles William followed in the family footsteps, practising law in Chester and becoming Clerk of the Peace for Cheshire in 1860, after a spell as Deputy and County Treasurer. He was also a senior churchwarden at St Mary's on the Hill, where he would have been closely acquainted with William Massie. Indeed, in January 1856, he chaired an influential meeting in the parochial schoolroom which raised generous subscriptions towards memorials to the late rector in his churches at St Mary's, Saltney and Upton. Charles William lived for many years at Heron Bridge, south-west of the city, mostly as a widower. His wife, Laura, died in 1864 at the age of 39, leaving him with three small children. All five are buried and commemorated together, also at Overleigh. Charles William was 74 when he passed away in 1890.

In November 1817, three months after the birth of his granddaughter Harriet, Charles senior died, leaving Lydia a widow for the second time. This death occurred at Glan-y-Afon, a large country estate that he had acquired near Mold and upon which, in about 1810, he had commissioned Thomas Harrison to build a villa. Soon afterwards, Harrison designed the Jubilee Tower on Moel Famau, at the foot of which Glan-y-Afon stands. Though George III's Golden Jubilee fell in 1810, and that is the year in which the foundation stone was laid, the full design and construction were delayed, resulting in a modified tower being completed in 1817. Glan-y-Afon survives into the present day and is Grade II listed.[23] It was in this area that Eliza would later conduct much of her botanical work.

Charles senior's will vested in Lydia considerable home comforts, though his bequests to her were not unconstrained. They included life interests in property at Crick in Northamptonshire and Hill Morton in Warwickshire, as well as in a house at St Martin's in the Fields, Chester, which, though unspecified, is likely to have been in King's Buildings. She was also granted plate up to a hundred ounces 'as she shall choose with liberty for her to alter the fashion thereof not diminishing the weight except by reasonable wear'. This is prescriptive, not to say parsimonious. Perhaps it is no coincidence that one of the trustees was Richard Richardson, one of a long line of noted Chester silversmiths, who would have been as well placed as anyone to police this requirement.

Also granted to Lydia were clothes, jewellery and liquors, as well as 'use of linen, household goods, china and books not exceeding £400 upon a fair appraisement'. To this was added a clause that she should sign an inventory of her chosen goods as soon as possible after his death and be prepared to relinquish them in the event of a third marriage. Whilst this may smack of some mistrust, perhaps it can be put down merely to the innate circumspection of a legal mind.

Charles senior's eldest son, Henry, did well out of the will, inheriting several properties in North Wales, including Glan-y-Afon, along with £2,000 and 'horses, carts, carriages, cows etc about my stables, cow houses, hay sheds in or near Chester'. This was on top of property he had been gifted in Ollerton and Knutsford at the time of his marriage to Anne Taylor. Charles junior was also handsomely endowed, picking up parts of the estate elsewhere in North Wales, Chester and London. He was empowered, in conjunction with the trustees – the second of whom was Thomas Wedge, agriculturalist and land agent – to dispose of the property in Crick to which Lydia had been granted rights, subject to her being compensated for any disturbance. The Chester property left to Charles junior was partly in Hoole but mostly in the city centre. There was 'a dwellinghouse on the west side of Northgate Street, now or late in my own occupation, and other rented houses on the west side of the same street and house, garden and field at Windmill Lane'. To this was added the stipulation that 'housekeeping shall be continued in my present dwellinghouse in Chester under the direction of my wife for six months from my decease from my estate', which suggests they were living apart, albeit not far from each other.

Stock in the River Dee Navigation – an enterprise set up to recover and preserve the waterway – went to Charles senior's brother, Josiah. Cash sums were granted to sundry relatives, friends and business associates, most substantially to daughters Anne and Sarah to secure them some independence before and potentially within marriage. One year's wages would go to each servant who had served for at least a year at the time of the testator's death, apart from Thomas Smith, whose exclusion is unexplained. As if to drive it home, the same Thomas Smith was required to witness two later codicils, neither of which brought him into scope as a beneficiary. The interest on a £100 lodgement was set aside for poor people in the borough of Macclesfield, to perpetuate support provided to them by Charles senior's father and maintain a long-standing connection with that community. Henry, Charles junior and Stephen Leeke – all now running the firm – were required to direct the trustees in the execution of the will 'so at to make it as little troublesome to them as may be'. As lawyers and beneficiaries, they surely obliged.[24]

Through this period, Leeke and Potts – in the plural – are repeatedly referred to in trade directories as attorneys, based in Northgate Street. The business premises were prominently located to the rear of the Exchange, on a site now occupied by Storyhouse.

In June 1819, Stephen Leeke died, at the age of 64, prompting his brothers to place a tablet in his honour on the north wall of the chancel in Chester Cathedral, close to the Panton sisters' memorial. His will includes £20 legacies to several members of the Potts family, who are described as 'my friends'. First mentioned is 'Mrs Potts of Chester –

widow of my late friend Mr Potts'. There is a separate reference to 'Mrs Henry Potts', which serves as further corroboration that our Mrs Potts was Lydia rather than Anne.

Eliza is noted in the will as Stephen Leeke's goddaughter. He had worked so closely and successfully with Charles senior that he had almost become part of the family. Charitable donations are made to the infirmaries at Shrewsbury and Chester, to the Blue Coat School and to the Benevolent Institution at Chester 'for delivering poor married lying-in women at their own habitations'. Henry Potts is charged with the distribution of clothes and blankets to the poor and with assisting in the recovery of Stephen's personal estate on behalf of his beneficiaries, for which he would 'be paid in the most liberal and handsome manner that may be for his rare trouble and attendances'. Henry was clearly a man of great competence and integrity, held in the highest regard by those around him.

The will includes further gifts of £20 each to Roger Barnston and his sister, Mrs Letitia Barnston, with whom Stephen must also have been on intimate terms. The Barnstons are an old-established Cheshire family, most closely connected with Churton and Farndon. For many years they owned and occupied Forest House in Love Street, Chester. It was at this residence that they received the Duke of Wellington whilst he was in the city, but he may not have been the first eminent visitor to cross the threshold. When James Boswell came to Chester in 1779, he included in one his letters to Dr Johnson the words: 'I told a very pleasing young lady, niece to one of the Prebendaries, at whose house I saw her, "I have come to Chester, Madam, I know not how; and far less can I tell how I am to get away from it".' A footnote identifies the young lady as 'Miss Letitia Barnston', who, forty years later and still unmarried, would appear in Stephen Leeke's will.[25]

His loss created a vacancy in the firm, which was filled in due course by George Johnson of book club fame. There was always an appetite to have an unrelated party involved, presumably to keep on top of a challenging workload and in the interests of good governance.

A month after Stephen's death, Henry and Anne Potts were blessed with another son, whom they named Frederick. He too entered the legal profession and the family firm. He was a keen oarsman as a young man and a life member of the Royal Chester Rowing Club. In 1862, he witnessed the complete destruction of the Exchange by fire, which, apart from being a dreadful occurrence in itself, must have been a threat to the Potts' business premises a few paces away.

For a while, Frederick lived in the south-east of England with his London-born wife, Jane, and their son, Frederick Arthur. In later life, he was a director of the Chester United Gas Company and the Isle of Man Mining Company. He died at his home at Horsley Hall in Gresford in 1898 and is buried close to other family graves in Overleigh Cemetery, alongside his wife, who survived him by 24 years. An obituary in the *Chester Courant* commended his 'genial disposition' which 'made him popular with all classes'.[26]

In 1820, Henry Potts built himself a new house, or rather Thomas Harrison did it for him. This was around the same time that Harrison built his own house, St Martin's Lodge, at the end of Nicholas Street, near the structures he designed at Chester Castle. Henry's house was not far away, at the south-west extremity of Watergate Street, overlooking the city walls and the racecourse.

St Martin's Lodge is now a pub, named 'The Architect' in Harrison's honour. Henry's property – known as Watergate House – is also in commercial use. It is a robust Georgian building of brick and stone on three floors, with a grand colonnaded entrance, raised and facing out obliquely onto Watergate Street. At the rear, large windows would have faced down across the garden to the racecourse and, on a clear day, would have afforded a view of Moel Famau, rising above Henry's country estate at Glan-y-Afon. Hemingway described the view as 'exquisitely delightful'.

Perhaps controversially, to create the space for the development, Henry pulled down what has been described as a 'picturesque timber mansion of the orthodox black and white type, so characteristic of Cheshire'. In the 17th century this had been a residence of the Grosvenors and was afterwards owned by the Brooke family of Norton Priory, until Henry purchased and demolished it. At one time it was occupied by Dr William Currie, physician at the nearby infirmary. It had been known as the Black Hall, having been sited on land owned by the Black Friars in pre-Reformation times.[27] The street now called Nicholas Street Mews was once known as Brooke Street – essentially a service road for the property. The location is a short walk from where Mrs Sloughter, Mrs Glynne, Mrs Mainwaring, the Panton sisters, the Humberstons and the Massies are all known to have lived. Lydia Potts and Dorothea Nicholls on King Street would have been near neighbours too.

The next of Henry and Anne Potts' children, Anne Mary Potts, was born at Watergate House in August 1822. We saw how her brother Arthur married Elizabeth Wardell, daughter of banker, William Wardell; Anne Mary Potts married one of his business partners, Thomas Dixon, whose father of the same name had established the bank in 1817 and was still a partner in it himself. Thomas's grandfather – yet another Thomas Dixon – had derived some wealth from a timber yard and shipyard that he set up at the Port of Chester in the late 18th century. This was after he retired from the navy and, ignobly, from transporting enslaved people across the Atlantic on behalf of the notorious Liverpool-based slave trader and anti-abolitionist, James Penny. The Dixon family seat was at Littleton, just to the east of Chester, where they used their money to good effect, for example by building alms houses and endowing the church at nearby Christleton.[28]

Anne Mary and Thomas were married at Holy Trinity in 1843, and soon afterwards they started a family together. Thomas died in 1859, in his early 40s, meaning that Anne Mary would live most of her life in widowhood, until her own death in 1905. She never strayed far from the place of her birth, settling with her daughter, Phyllis, at 14 Stanley Place – now part of the Queen's School – after the loss of her husband. She left an estate valued at £24,000, or £1.9 million in today's terms.[29] An 'Old Soldier', whose reminiscences appeared in *The Cheshire Sheaf* in the early 20th century, feared that he 'must have been a very proud boy [around the year 1840] for legend says that I only took my hat off to the Bishop and Miss Anne Potts, a dear, kind soul who showed us much hospitality'.[30]

Hemingway's reference to the great storm of December 1822, as mentioned in Chapter Thirteen, identifies Mrs Potts' chimney as a casualty, alongside Mrs Nicholls'. This strongly suggests that Lydia and Dorothea were near neighbours in King Street at that time. The roof of King's Buildings, elevated above contiguous properties, would certainly have been vulnerable in extreme weather.

In 1823, J H Hanshall's *The History of the County Palatine of Chester* was published. We recall from Chapter Twelve that he was editor of the *Chronicle* and, in due course, would be appointed secretary to the organising committee for Mr Sadler's visit. His book makes explicit reference to the Potts family and some of their property in Chester in 1823. There was a large brick structure, known as The Judge's Lodgings, which opened out on to what was then Market Square. It belonged to the Potts' legal practice from the late 18th century and was the home of Stephen Leeke up to his death in 1819. A house immediately to the north, on the site of what had previously been the Hope and Anchor inn, is described as 'Messrs Potts and Johnson's'. A later chronicler talks of this building as having been four houses south of the junction between King Street and Northgate Street, brick built in the 18th century and having a beautiful overhanging cornice. It was demolished towards the end of the first half of the 20th century.[31]

The year 1824 brought mixed fortunes for the family. Sarah Potts – the eldest daughter of Charles senior and his first wife, Anne – died in her early 40s in Leamington Spa. Her siblings, Henry, Charles junior and Anne, would have been deeply affected by this, as would Lydia, her stepmother. Charles junior was involved in something of a wrangle on behalf of St Oswald's Church after a mandate was received from the bishop requiring urgent repairs to be made. Though part of the cathedral building, it was withheld from the dean and chapter and not fully incorporated until 1967. This singular arrangement gave rise to questions around liability for upkeep and often delayed or frustrated essential maintenance work.

By this time, Henry was fully established in his role as Clerk of the Peace for the county. As such, he was responsible for much of its infrastructure, including toll roads and bridges, and continued his father's work in overseeing the operations of the Ellesmere and Chester canals. In his private practice, he was directly involved in the alleged case of horse-stealing by David Jones – mentioned in Chapter Fourteen – which was heard by a full bench of magistrates at the offices of Potts and Johnson. Jones had been arrested by George Burgess and held in Chester Castle pending trial. The process was thorough, involving several witnesses on both sides and the horse in question as Exhibit Number One, penned in an adjacent yard and subject to inspection as a core part of the trial. It was proved to be some years younger than the one that had disappeared, which resulted not only in Jones's discharge but in his avoidance of the drop, or transportation for life at best. Perhaps this was typical of the diligence exercised by the firm and the justice that could be achieved by it.[32]

As such a pillar of the community, it is little wonder that Henry was called upon to join the organising committee for Mr Sadler's ascent from Chester Castle in June 1824. It is conceivable, but by no means certain, that he was to accompany the aeronaut on his flight until that aspect of the plan came unstuck in the calamitous lead up to it. It is possible too that he was one of the committee members who felt the sharp end of Mr Sadler's tongue as he railed against what he saw as defective preparations. The fact that these concerns were sufficiently addressed to enable the flight to proceed, when at one point the odds were stacked against it, reflects some credit upon Henry and his colleagues.

At the pivotal public meeting about the merits of a new bridge over the Dee in August 1824, Henry's considerable powers of persuasion were on full display. With a lawyer's finesse, he directly challenged and undermined the arguments of the nimbies and the naysayers, particularly on the feasibility of developing the old Dee Bridge for the same purpose. So compelling were his arguments, that the principal reactionaries withdrew their objections and quietly pledged their active support for the scheme. Though a Chester man born and bred, he was not slow to point out 'the curiosities in which the city abounded, and which were so much the theme of admiration by travellers'. The new bridge would be another 'splendid work of art', with aesthetic appeal and practical value in helping to preserve Chester as a major transport hub between Great Britain and Ireland. There were other bold, undaunted people in the room who delivered immeasurable benefit to posterity by defending the scheme and then ensuring its implementation.[33] Soon, Henry would be involved in the mechanics of seeking parliamentary approval, just as his father had done on other major civil engineering projects before him.

In the autumn of 1824, after the main season had subsided, the Potts family took a break in Parkgate. Amongst the party were Lydia; Henry and his wife, Anne; Charles junior and his wife, Emma; and 'Miss Potts' – presumably Eliza. George Johnson was listed too.[34] Henry would certainly have welcomed the opportunity to relax and unwind in the wake of recent professional exertions. Not long after his return, he was driving forward another proposal amongst the city magistrates and with the Quarter Sessions of the Peace – the foundation of a 'Lunatic Asylum' or 'House for the Reception of Lunatics'.[35] As we know from the case of Charles Massie, this was realised in Chester in 1829, though he was accommodated elsewhere.

As our book club year drew to a close, Henry subscribed, alongside the Panton sisters, towards the welfare of James Forshaw and his family, who suffered so extremely as a result of the election riots. Perhaps he was aware that he could just as easily have been a victim, looking out from his office behind the Exchange as the disorder took hold.

In 1825, the last of Henry and Anne's children – Emma Susan – was born. She was baptised at Holy Trinity and was married there 22 years later, to Liverpool-based cotton broker John Molyneux. Tragically, she died at their home in Toxteth Park, Liverpool, two years into the marriage, on the same day she gave birth to their second child, the first – Fanny – having passed away in early infancy not long before. Christened Emma after the mother she never knew, this child lived and prospered into her late 80s.

When Henry signed off the accounts as County Treasurer in 1825, almost a quarter of expenses totalling £31,131 were attributable to the gaol, houses of correction and the conveyance of convicts to the hulks for transportation. In 1829, he was directly involved in a high-profile transportation case. Several convicts travelling from Chester, bound for the hulks at Chatham, overpowered a coach driver and guard in the dead of night in the

Coventry area and escaped. Five were still at large when Henry wrote to the commission-ers with details of their names and descriptions, requesting that a hue and cry be raised by Special High Constables in areas which 'it is considered would materially furnish the ends of justice'. The odds were heavily stacked against the absconders, some of whom still wore irons, and they were soon apprehended. The letter, held at the National Archives, shows Henry's handwriting to have been elegant and clear – a necessary requirement for some-one involved in such important business.[36]

Various publications through the late 1820s and early 1830s show Potts and Johnson to have had a constant presence on Northgate Street and Lydia to have been settled in her home in King's Buildings. Indeed, she was identified as 'Mrs Potts of King's Buildings' to differentiate her from Henry's wife in a list of attendees at a Royal Hotel ball in January 1829. Others present included several Mainwarings, Humberstons, Pantons and Massies, as well as George Johnson and Mad Jack Mytton.

When Hemingway's *The History of the City of Chester* came out in 1831, it noted Henry's role as one of 12 trustees at Chester General Infirmary, alongside the Reverend Richard Massie. It added that the gentlemen's committee would 'elect 12 ladies from the list of subscribers, or wives of gentlemen being subscribers, as a committee of ladies'. Regretta-bly, no ladies' names are detailed, but there is a good chance that names familiar to us would have been on the list. Also in 1831, we see something of Henry's political leanings, as he lent his support to Cheshire MPs in backing Lord John Russell's Reform Bill. This was a divisive issue: there was vehement opposition elsewhere, particularly in the east of the county.[37]

On 16th August 1832, *Gore's Liverpool General Advertiser* carried a death notice: 'On Tuesday, the 7th instant, at her house, in King's-buildings, Chester, Lydia, relict of Charles Potts, Esq. of that place.' The same column, by coincidence, recorded the passing of Thomas Gladstone, nephew of John, in Demerara whilst on family business there. Lydia was 70 years old. A month later, Messrs Potts and Johnson were advertising for immediate let 'an excellent family house in King's Buildings, Chester, lately in the occupation of Mrs Potts, deceased'.[38] The particulars included large dining, breakfast and drawing rooms; five 'best' bedrooms; servants' rooms and attics; an excellent kitchen; a butler's pantry; and a good garden. The property had been put up for auction, subject to her tenancy for life, in March of the previous year, suggesting she was then in terminal decline. She is prominently commemorated, amid several other members of the Potts family, on the south wall of the nave in Chester Cathedral.

Another property transaction, dated 12th September 1835, binds two of our book club families together more closely still. Philippa Richards had just inherited the house on Nicholas Street that belonged to her recently deceased sister, Dorothea Nicholls, as detailed in Chapter Thirteen. The solicitor to whom it was conveyed in trust was none other than Henry Taylor Potts, the consideration being the nominal sum of ten shillings, with the opportunity for Philippa to lease it back. Her dispossessed husband, William Richards, appears to have sanctioned the arrangement.

Indeed, his will of 1837 vests in Philippa, amongst other things, 'any interest I may have in her late sister's property'. Frederick Potts is noted as Philippa and William's godson and, as such, is left £50. Witnesses include Charles William Potts and George Johnson. When Philippa died in 1851, she left her property in Nicholas Street, along with stables and a coach house in the mews, to 'my young friends Charles William Potts and his brother Frederick Potts in the said city'. The legal instrument appears to have been effective because William Richards had surviving relatives, none of whom had a claim on Nicholas Street. Charles William and Frederick Potts were also residual legatees on Philippa's handsome estate, as well as executors and provers of her will. Their sisters Eliza and Harriet were remembered in it too.

The year 1844 was significant for the Potts family. Henry Taylor married and Charles junior, now in his mid-50s, was elected Mayor of Chester, in which capacity he attended a grand banquet to mark the laying of the foundation stone at Birkenhead docks. When Henry Taylor and his new wife, Cecilia, attended the Mold Ball in February 1844 they were listed as being 'of Glan-y-Afon', suggesting that was their first marital home. Other family members were at the function too, including Henry and Anne, though they were described as 'of Chester'. By this time, they were long settled at Watergate House and their children had flown the family nest. According to the 1841 census, they also had seven servants living under their roof.

The equilibrium would be cruelly shattered in 1845 with the death of Henry, on 10th November, at the age of 68. Like his father before him, he passed away at Glan-y-Afon, amid the idyllic country landscape that he had come to know and love so well. A week later, he was interred at Chester Cathedral, where there is a now-faded memorial stone on the floor towards the north wall of the nave and a more conspicuous tablet to various members of the Potts family, Henry included, on the south wall. The funeral procession began in Flintshire, in the company of Henry's tenantry there, and was met at Hough Green, Chester by many of his friends and associates in the city. These included George Johnson and Dr Thackeray. The service, read by the Dean of Chester, made a deep impression on the large congregation and was a fitting tribute to a popular public servant.[39]

Henry's will – proved by his brother, Charles junior, in March 1846 – is lengthy and complex. There is a huge amount of property in play, principally in Chester, London and north Wales, as in his father's will before him. There is still land at Ollerton and in Northamptonshire and Warwickshire, where usage rights conferred upon Charles senior's trustees, Richard Richardson and Thomas Wedge, are retained. The Chester property includes the buildings in Watergate Street and Northgate Street, and others in Brook Street, Saltney and Hoole. 'My garden ground near the church in the new town in Chester' and 'my two offices in Boot Lane' are mentioned too. The town house off Fleet Street in London, left to him by his father, appears to have been added to by Henry, who now has 'several dwelling houses in George Court' nearby. There is further land in east Cheshire and Staffordshire which he acquired in his own name.

The main beneficiaries are widow, Anne, and eldest son, Henry Taylor Potts, though the other children are by no means overlooked. Anne took possession of Watergate House and Henry Taylor of Glan-y-Afon and other properties in the area. Previously, there had been a dispute between the Potts family and Thomas Wedge over the rights accorded to him in north Wales in the will of Charles senior. The case was tried at the County Sessions at Ruthin and at the Chancery Court in London, but it must have been settled to the satisfaction of both parties because Henry continued to transact with Thomas Wedge, who is also noted as a legatee.

Another throwback in the will is a reference to an indenture of 1805 in which £4,000 was conveyed from the Taylor family to the Potts family on Henry's marriage to Anne. One of the trustees charged with investing it, for the benefit of them and any children they may have, was Hugh Robert Hughes, whose daughters married into the Humberston and Massie families, as we have seen. The fact that it is mentioned in Henry's will suggests that the arrangement was still in place at the time of his death 40 years on.

Later, but in a similar vein, there was a transfer of land when Henry Taylor Potts married Cecilia Anne Martin in 1844. Because of charges upon the land there were various signatories to the indenture, including Philip Humberston and Thomas Dixon; another indenture was signed by William Peploe Hamilton and George Johnson. This shows how deeply inter-connected these families were, on a business as well as a personal level.

Sums totalling £8,000 are left to daughters Eliza and Emma Susan, and £9,000 to each of the sons, except Henry Taylor, who is granted only £500 in view of his inheritance of other property within the will. Arthur's share is discounted by £7,000, representing the amount that Henry had invested in the Viaduct Foundry to help him buy into the business. A further debt of £1,000 due by Arthur to his father is cancelled. Anne Mary fares less well than her siblings, presumably because she was married and well provided for in that relationship.

Other entries reveal something of Henry's personal interests and proclivities. His telescope and microscope are granted to his brother, Charles junior. It is easy to imagine that telescope in the large bay window at the rear of Watergate House, trained on the variegated Welsh hills in the distance and, on a clear night, on the gaping cosmos above. The microscope may have shed new light on old artefacts or, in the hands of Eliza, the latest botanical specimen she had unearthed. 'Coins, medals, portfolios of prints, engravings and curiosities' go to Charles William and Frederick, forming the nucleus of a collection that Frederick would later build upon.

Amongst their other attributes, the Potts family were keen environmentalists. Charles senior had led the way by planting a wood near Nerquis in Flintshire, and Henry had followed suit at Llanferres, near his Glan-y-Afon estate. These were named Coed Charles and Coed Frederick respectively. Another plantation at Llanferres was created by Dr Thackeray, the eminent surgeon, who, the will reveals, was Arthur's godfather – hence it was named Coed Arthur. These plantations are bequeathed according to their eponyms, with Coed Charles going to Charles William. Dr Thackeray was particularly adept in this line, twice winning the 30 Guinea Gold Medal for planting trees from the Society of Arts. Such feats of afforestation, when woodland was far more abundant than it is today, were truly ahead of their time.[40]

When Henry passed away, he was still Treasurer of the County of Chester. The *Liverpool Mail* stated, not entirely facetiously, that the office had been 'hereditary' in the Potts family for 120 years. There is no suggestion of unworthiness through nepotism. Henry had also been Clerk of the Peace, a role that George Johnson then assumed. The legal practice had moved on – a new partner, William Henry Brown, was in place and he would take it forward with the next generation of the Potts menfolk.

We have seen before – with the Massies and the Blomfields, for example – how families closed ranks in response to bereavement, providing each other with emotional and practical support. In 1851, living at Watergate Street with the now widowed Anne Potts were John Molyneux, her son-in-law and widower, and her one-year-old granddaughter, Emma. In the same census, an unmarried lady of 67 named Anne Potts is listed at King's Buildings as 'landed proprietor' with five servants, including a butler. This would have been Henry's younger sister, who must have taken up residence at the property that her stepmother, Lydia, had occupied until her death almost three decades earlier. This Anne was also a contributor in 1846 towards a repair fund for the Jubilee Tower on Moel Famau, which had suffered a collapse.[41] She would have remembered its construction and may even have observed some of the dealings that her father had with Thomas Harrison concerning it. Unfortunately, the repair never took place, so we continue to see the tower in its much-diminished state into the present day.

By 1871, Mrs Anne Potts – Henry's widow – was still at Watergate House, now in the company of daughter Eliza and their staff. She died soon after the census was taken, at the age of 86, in June of that year. She shares a grave at Overleigh Cemetery with Eliza, son Henry Taylor and his wife, Cecilia. Probate, which valued her estate at £50,000, was granted to Frederick, her sole executor.

There is a certain randomness to the collection of names on the two Potts memorial tablets on the south wall of the nave at Chester Cathedral. The first reads:

> Near this place lie the remains of Charles Potts of this city esq who departed this life 17th November 1817 aged 73 years. Also Anne his first wife who departed this life 14th June 1796 aged 52 years. And Charles their son who died 17th March 1781 aged 1 year and 7 months. Also of Charles son of Henry Potts of this city and Anne his wife who died 28th February 1809 aged 2 years and 8 months. And of Mary Anne their daughter who died 9th March 1809 aged 1 year and 9 months.

There is something deeply moving about the inclusion of children taken at a tender age, especially when close relatives who died in their maturity are omitted. The second memorial is not insensible to this fact either:

> Near this place lie interred the remains of Henry Potts of this city esq who died at Glan r Avon near Mold on November 10th 1845 aged 68 years. And also the remains of Sarah, eldest daughter of Charles Potts esquire and sister of the above named Henry Potts 27th day of April 1824 aged 43 years. And also Lydia the second wife of the above named Charles Potts who died on the 7th Day of August 1832 aged 70 years. In beloved memory of second lieutenant Charles Potts, Cheshire Regiment

who died in action in France from wounds received at Messines on 11th June 1917 aged 19 years, eldest son of Hubert and Rosa Potts of this city, and great-grandson of the above named Henry Potts. Henry Potts 1901 - 1981 and Prudence his wife 1901 - 1999.

Though not excessive in its content, this memorial spans five generations of the family, with Lydia as the earliest. Hubert was the son of Charles William Potts and father not just of the Charles who died in the trenches of the First World War but also of the last-mentioned Henry. We know that there are many other worthy members of the family who are not commemorated so overtly and in such a magnificent setting. It is important to remember them too.

Finally, as the history of Chester is a foremost concern, we should not overlook the role that members of the Potts dynasty have played in preserving it. William Nicholls' correspondence refers to 'Mr Potts' Old Book of Signatories', which was useful in clarifying bygone ownership of manors near Chester. Charles senior was alive at that time, so the reference was most probably to him. The Lysons brothers in *Magna Britannia* disclosed Henry to have been the possessor of a fragment of 2nd century slate on which was cut the figure of a retiarius – a gladiator who fought with a trident and net – which had been discovered during digging in the Chester marketplace in 1738.[42] This is now housed is Saffron Waldon Museum in Essex, with a copy held at the Grosvenor Museum, Chester. Henry was a subscriber as well as a contributor to Ormerod's *History*.

In 1839, the British Geological Society discussed a slab of sandstone 'at the house of Henry Potts, Esq., of Chester' which contained an impression of the feet of a prehistoric animal known as *Chirotherium Hercules*. This was essentially a dinosaur, although that term was not coined until 1842. The slab was reported to have borne traces of three hind and two fore feet, though subsequent research has shown it to have been a four-legged creature.[43]

After Henry died, Frederick continued the family tradition of collecting antiquarian objects and curiosities. The Duke's hoof would not have been out of place in the collection. This was a family, after all, who didn't merely absorb history: they created it.

Chapter Twenty

October

October was a maelstrom of a month in Chester, to some extent literally on account of the weather. It began with hailstones, powerful enough to damage thatch roofs, and snow was visible on the Welsh hills. Strong frosts and gales soon developed, endangering shipping, though no loss of life was reported at sea. Inland, however, a thousand measures of wheat belonging to Messrs T & A Frost perished when the vessel containing them sank, and, worse still, a 13-year-old boy was struck and killed by a falling branch.

The tempest played out figuratively in the form of civic elections for mayor and sheriff. Some of the detail, which includes implicating Philip Humberston in alleged malpractice, is captured in Chapter Five. In the lead up to voting, two bands paraded up and down the main streets of the city: the Royal Cheshire Militia Band for Mr Whittakers as sheriff and the Corporation Band for Mr Shearing. According to the *Chronicle*, the militia band was accompanied by 'an intense mob', vastly outnumbering the 50 or so followers of the Corporation band.

Confrontation soon ensued: the Corporation colours were seized and members of the band were assaulted and forced to flee. An inflammatory gathering behind the Exchange also erupted into violence. One target was the nearby Saracen's Head inn, run by Mrs Leet, where the windows were almost entirely smashed. The announcement of the poll result, in which Mr Shearing triumphed, added further fuel to the fire. Now the Exchange itself came under attack: missiles were thrown, magistrates were physically ejected, priceless artwork was damaged and more than a hundred large panes of glass were broken. Aggression and fear were the triggers for deafening cries, which only subsided after more than an hour of anarchy.

The mob then moved, locking arms six to eight people deep, round the Exchange and in the direction of the Lower Bridge Street shop premises belonging to Mr Shearing. The militia band again led the way. Perhaps this gave the ringleaders time to reflect, because, on arrival, they dissuaded their followers from further destruction.

When the miscreants dispersed into the night, Chester was described as having the appearance of 'a place in possession of conquering army rather than a respectable city whose streets were trod only by its own inhabitants'.[1] For some of the offenders, there would be legal ramifications. There was a strong feeling that Whittakers, a man of means, had assembled a mercenary cabal who would stop at nothing in their attempts to fight his corner.

Sporadic acts of violence, unrelated to the election, continued to occur. There was an assault on Bridge Street Row upon a Mr Errington, whose physical reaction to his assailants at the time was deemed sufficient by the bench to represent justice. Mr Burgess was still active in the police, perhaps in a reduced capacity or serving his notice. His fortunes had not improved, however, as he was hit by a brick, rendering him quite helpless, as he escorted a man to gaol.

George Harrison, in one of his first acts as mayor, took steps to bolster police resources and appoint an experienced head with a competent salary and adequate assistance. He also directed that strict notices be issued to counter 'the assembling of loose and disorderly persons in the streets and on the Rows, especially on the evening of the Lord's Day and during divine service'. Shops were to be closed and any form of commercial cart or waggon prohibited from passing through the city on a Sunday.[2]

Thefts that were tried included those perpetrated by Mary Hewitt, at a draper's shop, and George Taylor, who stole watch chains and two waistcoats. Both were transported for seven years. Meanwhile, a man named Hughes, who had been the night porter when gold and silver disappeared from The Feathers Hotel, as reported in Chapter Eighteen, was found not guilty and acquitted. A Mr Twiss was fined £7 for taking passengers in his cart and, in Liverpool, no less a personage than the Earl of Derby was penalised for not having his name and address painted on his mode of transport – an offence against which informers and prosecutors were being appointed around the country. This shows how tightly regulated such conveyances were; there was a strong will to protect legitimate commercial interests and trace transgressors on the highway.

Even places of worship were not untainted by disorder. Shameful scenes were reported in St John's Vestry as the inquiry progressed into the arrears accumulated under Mr Pritchard. A meeting had been ordered by the board of the House of Industry, concerned about their funding shortfall. The atmosphere was not helped by the peremptory exclusion of women, who were made to stand outside in the rain; a decision defended with the limp assertion that they were not ley-payers and that 'ladies are admitted to no deliberative assembly in the kingdom'.

Despite the bishop having said that any more offending at such meetings would lead to proceedings in the Spiritual Court, matters quickly descended into chaos. Some attendees were accused of seeking to prevent and avoid collection. Pritchard responded to one disruptive presence – a Mr Corlett – by saying he had a notice of bastardy for him, which prompted vociferous calls for him to be turned out. A vote on Pritchard's remaining in office was attempted but the clamour became so great that the presiding vicar, the Reverend William Richardson, left the chair and the meeting was dissolved, nothing having been achieved.[3]

The Chester Auxiliary Bible Society, whose mission was to help spread peace and enlightenment around the globe, was no stranger to fractious meetings either. Long speeches at one of these, extolling the extent to which Christian texts had been translated and disseminated, kept people in their seats for almost four hours, giving rise to a slow hand clap. The news, for example, that every family in Iceland had a copy of the bible in their own language did little to mollify them.

The Society for Promoting Christian Knowledge was a similar body, but with a greater focus on improving literacy and religious observance on a general level, including closer to home. In Chester, it was strongly endorsed by the bishop and the mayor and, as we have seen, supported by parties connected with our book club. The October meeting highlighted a recent grant of £5,000 for the establishment of a college for Christian preachers in Calcutta and missionary schools in India, under the aegis of 'that learned and excellent prelate, Dr Heber'. In Chester, a new parochial lending library specifically for 'the poor' had come into being, and others were encouraged around the region.[4]

The Royal Hotel hosted another substantial meeting to mark the fourth anniversary of the Northern Whig Club, which encompassed nine counties. Sir Thomas Stanley was in the chair. The main topic of conversation was electoral reform, including shorter parliamentary terms, more balanced representation and improved voting systems. This last point would have resonated strongly in Chester, where elections were routinely accompanied by violence and corruption. Lodge anniversaries were also celebrated, including a procession which culminated at the home of 'Brother Jepson' on Foregate Street, where many loyal toasts were proposed and a fine dinner served.

Business and commerce in the city met with fluctuating fortunes. The great Michaelmas Fair was sparsely attended. The cattle market was a big draw but the quality of stock at the horse fair was eroded by crossbreeds. Some manufacturers who customarily displayed their wares stayed away, which, though detrimental to the event itself, was a sign that their businesses were flourishing and needed their full attention. The Tea and Coffee Warehouse in Shoemakers' Row, close to the Exchange, advertised superior stock acquired at a recent East India Company sale, and a former employee had set up a new grocery warehouse for the wholesale and retail market on Northgate Street. Merchandise from France was in fashion and Kendall & Son – purveyors of fancy goods, toys and perfumes, based in Union Hall – had created a French Depot in response to the demand. There was also a Mr Marinus from Vienna advertising his services as a chiropodist, with a sideline in dentistry.

The great infrastructure projects that have been mentioned remained to the fore, and in some cases, were gathering momentum. A parliamentary application was underway for the construction of the new bridge and its environs, including the relocation of St Bridget's to a site nearer the castle. An anonymous but well-founded letter addressed to 'The Rt Hon Earl Grosvenor and Gentlemen of Chester' and published in the press, advocated a bridge made of white stone rather than iron, 'which would endure for ages to come and bear the heaviest burdens'. It would be 'the admiration of every beholder', unparalleled in

Europe, and would cost no more than an iron bridge. The letter was either influential or prophetic, because the plans were changed, and a magnificent stone bridge ultimately emerged.[5]

An application to Parliament was also required for the new Water Works Company to overturn an exclusive and perpetual right granted by Chester Corporation in 1692 to John Hadley of Worcester and John Hopkins of Birmingham, and their representatives, to supply water to the city. A transport initiative – more relevant to Chester in 1824 than may be supposed – was the proposed railway line from Liverpool to Birmingham, for which a survey had been undertaken. This involved a route cutting through the suburbs of Hoole, Newton and Upton and connecting with new wharves to be built at Birkenhead. Here too plans subsequently changed and the line than eventually transpired ran considerably further east. On the roads, a meeting of the commissioners of police ordered that part of Northgate Street be macadamised, as a potential precursor to its adoption on all the main streets.

Business at the Exchange included the admission of new freemen, not by accident timed to coincide with the civic election. One of these admissions was Bishop Blomfield. This briefly interrupted his busy schedule, which included the ordination of priests and deacons, and the confirmation of 2,800 children in a single calendar month.

Despite upheaval on the streets of Chester, benign and genteel activities were not completely displaced. The Chester Choral Society was preparing for its next quarterly performance in the splendidly lit Gothic Room in the cathedral and no less an actor than William Charles McCready was appearing at the theatre. He was amongst the greatest classical performers of the day, and more reliable than Kean, who was increasingly inclined to drink.[6] There was a teaser in the press early in the month for another major event: the return of Mr Sadler. The Saturday of the next race week was mooted for another ascent above the city, for which there was already a growing sense of anticipation.

Some reports from beyond Chester in the local press may well have struck a chord with the reader. There was a new steam packet – the St David's – in operation along the north

Wales coast, where the Conway Bridge project was now well-advanced, unfortunately at the expense of three deceased workers. Poor construction standards claimed 19 lives in Salford – 16 women and three children – and many more were injured, when part of a factory collapsed. Public health was a concern too: there was an outbreak of typhus in Stockport and, in Worcester, there was talk of denying relief to paupers with dogs – often important companions – as a defence against rabies.

Some particularly hideous crimes were in the news, including the purloining of children from the streets of Pimlico by two well-dressed women. In Liverpool, resurrection men were again at work, at great risk to themselves if caught. As we have seen, even minor crime occasioned the severest punishment. In the House of Correction at Lewes, it was reported that prisoners were required to work the treadmill at 6,600 feet of ascent each day – one and a half times the height of Ben Nevis. Two convict ships left British shores with 150 women on board, bound for New South Wales, which was trumpeted as 'glorious news for the males!'.

Back in Liverpool, a prize fight for 50 guineas took place, once more involving Boscow, the butcher, this time against Magee, a labourer. When Boscow triumphed for a second time, he was escorted through the streets of the city in a chaise by what the *Chronicle* termed 'a rabble'. The fight itself was described as 'disgusting and brutal' and part of an emerging trend 'amongst a certain class in Liverpool'. The combatants were contrasted, snobbishly, with 'the heroes of the fist' hitherto 'only patronised and encouraged in the metropolis', though they weren't denied column inches. Praise was reserved for another event taking place nearby: the presentation of 28 pieces of plate valued at £1,400 to John Gladstone by the merchants of Liverpool. 'Well does he deserve it,' went the cry.[7]

Throughout the country, more great schemes in transport and engineering were emerging. One example was the proposed railway line from Edinburgh to London, with an estimated 99,000 tons of iron required for the track alone. In road travel, a company was looking to raise £200,000 to apply a gas engine to a wheeled carriage with the object of driving it from York to London at an average speed of ten miles per hour.

Ocean going transport was in the news too. Any Cestrian with a taste for port would have would have been pleased to hear that streamlined ships from Porto were arriving in the city after seven days sail, compared with ten previously, their merchandise bound for the wine vaults of Messrs Hassal and Foulkes on Bridge Street. It was revealed that approximately seven hundred British vessels were arriving in St Petersburg annually, indicating that trade in that region of the Baltic was buoyant, despite political unease with Russia. Journeys in northern latitudes, often into uncharted territory, were hazardous. There was concern for a fleet of whalers that had ventured up the Davies Straits, between Greenland and Baffin Island, which was expected back in Britain but had failed to return. This did not discourage exploration in the area. In the eastern Mediterranean, almost a hundred Turkish ships had been destroyed, tilting the conflict in favour of Greece. There were also rumours of the seizure of British shipping by the Greeks, generating unforeseen tensions.

A few other piecemeal items may have provoked a reaction from the reader, including more displays of eccentricity. A Mr Skipper walked 1,200 miles in 21 successive days at Exeter, but Mr Jenkinson, reputedly the fastest walker in the kingdom, failed to cover 17 miles in three hours, frustrated, it would seem, by the weather. When a solicitor from Soho, by the name of Tetham, was called away to Wales, his servants consumed two hundred pounds' worth of his wine collection, resulting in criminal charges for the chief cellarman. An account from Munich claimed that a carriage was going about drawn by two wolves, muzzled for the purpose. That, of course, was the home city of Professor Gruithuisen, whose assertion that there was civilised life on the moon continued to arouse interest. One correspondent in the Chester press enquired waggishly whether the roads he had observed through his highly magnifying telescope were macadamised or not. A commentator from north of the border scoffed at the notion of a sentient lunar presence because nothing had been ordered from Glasgow, which was then enjoying an export boom.[8]

Any mirth engendered by these snippets would have been annihilated by another piece of news: Mr Sadler had been involved in an accident. He had ascended from Bolton in the company of a gentleman and, whilst performing a routine descent near Burnley, his grapples had missed their hold and the balloon had been propelled into the air again. The car struck a chimney at Church – midway between Blackburn and Accrington – and, after a desperate attempt to cling on, Mr Sadler fell from it at height, sustaining a fractured skull and much bruising. His companion carried on to Whalley, where he was pitched from the car, also severely injured. Mr Sadler was taken to a nearby inn, where the landlord quickly summoned a surgeon.

Later that day, a Captain Fregen of HM Revenue Cruiser *Lapwing*, whilst negotiating a storm off Flamborough Head on the Yorkshire coast, noticed a balloon disappearing into what was then known as 'the German Ocean' and, assuming it had occupants, gave frantic chase. Ignorant of the facts, he reported his exertions to have been ineffectual. In the meantime, Mr Sadler was being operated upon, during which he spoke once, before passing away at 8am the following morning. He was a mere 28 years old and had undertaken 31 ascents, 16 of which were with the balloon he had deployed in Chester four months earlier. There were other such aeronauts but he was distinguished by his daring intrepidity and ballooning pedigree: he was the son of the first Englishman to fly, in Oxford in 1784.

On receiving the dreadful news, his disconsolate widow – in the advanced stages of pregnancy with their second child – travelled from Liverpool for the coroner's inquest. He was buried at Christ Church in that city within a week, where four thousand people attended his funeral, despite a request for privacy. Subscriptions in support of his family were begun in places where he had enthralled and amazed his onlookers. They were genuinely needy because he had recently invested heavily in an establishment on Hanover Street, Liverpool, providing warm water baths, which promised much but, as yet, had delivered little.

The disruption experienced at his only Chester appearance – now destined never to be repeated – seems to have acted as a disincentive to donate. When other towns and cities had raised many hundreds of pounds, Chester had mustered only six. After the *Chronicle* highlighted the paucity of this response, consciences were pricked and the value of the pot rose to £250. Like his father before him, who had been a humble pastry chef in the family business, he achieved little lasting recognition compared with the scale of his impact and achievements.[9] There is a Sadler Street close to where he died, which is short, nondescript and occupied by a few small industrial units. Perhaps this is all the reverence he would have wanted.

Chapter Twenty-One

The Misses Townshend
Lot 11

Illustrations of Country History, 2 vols., embellished with two fine portraits; hand-somely bound in blue Morocco. Very choice copies.

So inter-connected were the families at The Chester Book Club, 1824 that we start to circle back in our observations on the membership. As can be inferred from what has been covered so far, the Townshend family was extensive, with strong concentrations in north Wales, east Cheshire and the city of Chester. To identify the two Misses Townshend coupled together here by Dr Norris, we must focus on the last of these places. However, even with this filter, the process is by no means straightforward.

We have seen how Susanna Mainwaring, née Townshend, had sisters called Frances Anne and Frances Sarah, both spinsters, who also lived in Watergate Street. There was also a clutch of 'Misses Townshend' who lived in Stanley Place: Sidney, Barbara, Arabella and Frances. These were the younger sisters of Hester Lee Townshend, who married the Reverend Richard Massie and lived elsewhere on the same street. The Misses Townshend of Watergate Street were cousins of the Misses Townshend of Stanley Place, their fathers respectively being John Townshend of Trevalyn and his younger brother, Edward Townshend of Wincham.

Barbara died in 1816, which means that by 1824 there were three Misses Townshend at Stanley Place. Frances Sarah was born in 1766 and Frances Anne in 1768, whereas their cousins arrived between 1779 and 1789. Their ages compared to the ages of other book club members – the oldest of whom was Anne Glynne, born in 1749 – and the fact that there were two of them rather than three, makes them the likeliest candidates. We are also reminded of the convention that the eldest 'misses' were referred to without an initial, and that is how they are presented here.

The book, which appears to be fictitious, the portraits and the binding render little in the way of additional clues. It is not clear whether 'country' points to natural history or national history, but either would fit the bill. Indeed, when we scratch a little beneath the surface, we find that the Townshends are another family who made a mark on a global scale. We have seen this already with the sisters' nephew, George Townshend, in New South Wales, and we see it elsewhere as we probe their genealogy.

Sir Robert Townshend, who was active in the Civil War and at the time of the Restoration, was the son of a London-based merchant by the name of William Agborough. William died young and Robert later took the surname 'Townshend' from his stepfather. Robert married firstly Anne Spencer, the granddaughter of Henry Wriothesley, patron of William Shakespeare, and, secondly, Mary Askew, through whom he acquired Hem House at Trevalyn.[1] This is how the family first established a foothold in this area, just over the Welsh border from Chester.

At its head in the 18th and 19th centuries was a succession of John Townshends, including the sisters' father – an officer in the second regiment of the Dragoon Guards – and their brother, John Stanislaus Townshend. Frances Sarah, Frances Anne and Susanna all moved to Chester. Perhaps the ties to their ancestral home were loosened when their parents died – first John in 1778 and then their mother, Anne, in 1780.

From their early years, the Townshend siblings would have had a strong connection with the theatre. Hemingway, referring to the site opposite Shoemaker's Row, at the bottom of Northgate Street, tells us:

The Chester theatre was erected by a company of proprietors in 1773 on the site of St Nicholas' Chapel ... In 1777 the mayor thought fit to issue an edict against the further continuance of dramatic performances, probably thinking them more demoralising than the annual bull bait ... In this emergency the proprietors appealed to the Crown and obtained a patent dated 16th May 1777 in the name of J Townshend esq constituting their theatre as a theatre royal.[2]

The patent was signed by the Lord Chamberlain on behalf of King George III. Despite John's death not long afterwards, it remained in the family and became the property of John Stanislaus, as confirmed in a renewal document of 1798. He retained this right for the remainder of his life, transferring it to his eldest son in his will.

In this capacity, the Townshends would have rubbed shoulders with some of the foremost performers of the time, and indeed of all time. The great tragedian, George Cooke, appearing as Hamlet, made only his second appearance on stage at the Theatre Royal, Chester, in 1784, and would return many times thereafter. Edmund Kean played Richard III in 1815, and brother and sister, Charles Kemble and Sarah Siddons, trod the boards there too. Mrs Jordan, a regular visitor, sailed to her native Ireland from Parkgate and may well have favoured Chester as a venue above other places for that reason. A great friend of the poor, she once paid for the release of a washerwoman in the city who had been imprisoned for debt.

By all accounts, the theatre had declined by 1824, and it was still subject to legal constraint and puritanical derision, probably not helped by its proximity to the cathedral and the Exchange. Perhaps seared into the sisters' infant minds was an appalling tragedy that occurred in a performance space on Watergate Street Row in 1772, when 23 people were killed and many more wounded at a puppet show by the explosion of gunpowder stored beneath.[3]

A significant marriage in the ancestral line involved their grandfather, John Townshend, and Frances Lee of Darnhall Hall, near Northwich. From this point on, the Christian name 'Lee' appears in the Townshend family on both the male and female side, including in the case of Hester Lee Massie, née Townshend, of course. These families were close and grew closer still. The men in Frances's family were often of a military bent, including her brother, John Lee, who became a major general in the British Army. In 1720, he married Isabella, daughter of Sir Henry Bunbury, 3rd Baronet of Bunbury and Stanney, to the north-east of Chester. Their daughter, Sidney Lee, chose to live in the heart of the city, between Foregate Street and Forest Street.

Sidney's will, drafted not long before she died in 1788, includes some quite specific legacies, net of which all her fortune is left to her 'cousins german', Frances and Susanna Townshend to 'share and share alike'. It is not clear which Frances she is referring to here – she may even have left it open to allow them both a claim on her estate. The value of her assets is uncertain too, but considerable wealth can be inferred from other items in her will. Some of her possessions and connections were remarkable, to say the least.

There is a 'picture of his late majesty of Poland', left to Harriet Bowdler, daughter of Thomas Bowdler of Bath. The subject of the picture is likely to have been King Stanislaus I, whose reign ended in 1738, through abdication, though he lived on until 1766. Harriet Bowdler was in fact the young Henrietta Maria Bowdler, who would become a renowned religious author and poet. She was the sister of the Thomas Bowdler mentioned in Chapter Seventeen. Research has shown that she had more of a hand in the first edition of the Bowdler Shakespeare than her brother but was shamefully denied credit for almost two centuries because a woman was not thought equal to the task or suited to poring over salacious aspects of the text. There was a blood relationship between Sidney Lee and Henrietta Bowdler, as they stem from different branches of the Cotton family, but this goes back several generations and is probably too tenuous to explain the gift in the will. They must have become known to each other socially, perhaps when Sidney visited the fashionable city of Bath. Why she chose to leave the picture to her, with the added complication of conveyance, we may never know.[4]

Another curiosity in Sidney Lee's will is the gift to a third 'cousin german', Henry Bunbury, of £2,500 – a princely sum – and 'the large picture in oil colours supposed to be the produce of Paul Ruben's pencil that now ornaments the chimney piece of my eating room'. The mere thought of such a priceless artefact hanging casually above a Chester fireplace is astonishing in itself.

Henry Bunbury was a colonel but better known as caricaturist, in the vein of Gillray and Rowlandson, and of a similar calibre. His work, which was exhibited at the Royal Academy, included contributions to Boydell's Shakespeare. His son, also called Henry, became 7th Baronet of Bunbury and Stanney, albeit his home was at Barton Hall in Suffolk. Much of this Henry's early life was spent in continental Europe, fighting the French with distinction and ultimately reaching the rank of lieutenant general. He documented his martial experiences in works such as *Narratives of Some Passages in the Great War with France*, gaining a reputation as a highly accomplished soldier-historian. His most notable individual act, however, came in 1815 when, in aftermath of the Battle of Waterloo, he informed Napoleon of his sentence of deportation to St Helena.[5]

Challenging though it was, Sidney's brother – Charles Henry Lee – achieved the greatest measure of military fame in the family. Born at Darnhall and baptised at St Martin's Church in Chester in 1732, he entered the army as soon as his education was complete, initially seeing action in Ireland and then in the Seven Years' War in North America, fighting amongst the colonists, the French and the indigenous population. During a lull in hostilities, he so befriended and integrated into a tribe of Mohawks that he was given the name *Ounewaterika*, or 'Boiling Water' – perhaps reflective of his temperament – and married the daughter of a chief. He soon reverted to type, however, moving north to support the British conquest of Canada, followed by a campaign on the Iberian Peninsula.

When his regiment was disbanded two years later, Charles travelled to Poland, becoming aide de camp to King Stanislaus II and being appointed a major general in the Polish-Lithuanian Army. He fought against Russian imperialism in the region and was invalided back to Britain in 1770 after losing two fingers in a duel. After a couple of unsuccessful attempts to rejoin the British Army – impeded by an earlier complaint to George III in person about a lack of promotion – he moved to Virginia, where he purchased a large estate. He developed sympathy for the patriot cause and offered his services to the Continental Congress in Philadelphia at the outbreak of the American Revolution in 1775. As a vastly experienced military man with an intimate knowledge of the enemy, he expected to be appointed as commander-in-chief, but was passed over in favour of George Washington, on account, it seems, of his brusque communication style and slovenly appearance. Acting as Washington's second-in-command, he was at the forefront of operations when Boston was besieged and when New York was defended. As a result, the settlement at Fort Lee in New Jersey was named after him.

Under military pressure, the relationship with Washington became strained and Lee wrote to Congress complaining about him. He was then captured by a British patrol whilst acting indiscreetly in a tavern and held as a deserter from the British Army. In response, he used his inside knowledge to produce a plan for the defeat of the American forces, an act of treason which was not made public until 1857. Perhaps comforted by this action, his captors allowed him to be included in a prisoner swap. Back in a position of authority, he erred tactically during the Battle of Monmouth Court House, but the situation was recovered by Washington and his troops. Still at odds with his superior and with his reputation impugned, Lee wrote more insubordinate letters to Congress and requested his own court martial to clear his name. He was found guilty of disobeying orders in the face of the enemy and disrespecting his commander-in-chief. He was dismissed from Continental Army 1780 and died in Philadelphia in 1782.[6]

This is quite a story in itself, but it also sheds light on questions raised earlier in this book. Charles Lee broke his Polish service at least once to return to England. He would have related his experiences at the court of Stanislaus II and brought back gifts for his nearest and dearest. Stanislaus I, who ruled Poland in the early 18th century, visited England and kept in touch with Englishmen he met on his or their travels. It is possible that a Lee or Townshend was amongst this cohort. Stanislaus I seems to have had a positive, even mystical allure amongst the English, creating an enduring image to which the words 'wise', 'gracious' and 'enlightened' were attached.[7]

Now we better understand why the sisters' brother, John, possessed the middle name 'Stanislaus' and why their benefactor, Sidney Lee, had a picture of a Polish monarch. We remember, too, the Polish references made in Chapters Nine and Ten: Maria Sobieski Massie being Hester Lee Townshend's aunt by marriage, and Polish aristocracy staying at the Albion Hotel in May 1824. Finally on this note, there is a circular disc embedded in Music Hall Passage in Chester, alongside what was the Theatre Royal, as part of the Millennium Trail. It carries a representation of 'Sig. Stanislaus', a Polish performer who appeared at the theatre in 1842, specialising in contortion and feats with fire and improbably heavy weights.[8] Though this is well after John Stanislaus Townshend's death and the overlapping names be coincidental, it is possible that the origins of the appearance lie in the family's old-established links with Poland.

The *Chester Directories* of the 1790s show a sprinkling of Townshends, from both the Trevalyn and Wincham sides of the family, living in the city. There is a particular concentration in Stanley Place, with other fashionable addresses in Foregate Street and Abbey Square. When Susanna married Charles Mainwaring at Holy Trinity in 1800, her cousin Sidney of Stanley Place was a witness. In 1801, another cousin, Edward Venables Townshend, married Cornelia Anne Dupre, the daughter of the Governor of Madras, in Hanover Square London. This was also the year in which they lost an uncle, George Salisbury Townshend. He shares a plaque at Chester Cathedral with his wife, Frances, who predeceased him by a quarter of a century.

Edward Venables Townshend was one of the better-known members of the family in and around Chester. He lived at Wincham Hall, whilst his sisters mostly lived in Chester. In 1806, he was President of the Tarporley Hunt, whose membership included Sirs Peter Warburton, Harry Mainwaring and Stephen Glynne. This was one of many official posts he held in Cheshire-based institutions. He was particularly active in the year 1818, being sworn in as Deputy Provincial Grandmaster in the Grand Lodge in a ceremony at Chester Castle and doing important business as one of the proprietors of Chester Races. This group of individuals, which also included Henry Potts, committed to giving a hundred guineas towards a gold cup to be competed for each May. This was the forerunner to a race established in 1824, which later became and still is the prestigious Chester Cup. A new grandstand was opened at the Roodee in 1818, enhancing both the viewing experience and gate receipts.[9]

Edward was ever-present at the Chester Race Ball at the Royal Hotel each May, including one which developed into a fracas in 1825, reports of which found their way into the national press. Two Irishmen by the names of Fitzgerald and Rawlins, the former having aristocratic pretensions and the latter being a barrister at the Irish bar, disrupted the dancing and picked arguments in the card room. When a steward tried to intervene, Fitzgerald challenged him to a duel. They were eventually hustled out but remained in Chester for some days, raising a scurrilous pamphlet and challenging sundry other parties to a duel, including the Earl of Wilton. They even brought over their seconds to fight on their behalf but could find no takers. The pen then being their only weapon, they spilt their ink to no avail.[10]

Edward was engaged in politics at this time too, standing as an independent candidate alongside the Tory, Sir John Egerton, when the two Chester parliamentary seats were contested in 1818. They opposed the Whig faction of Lord Belgrave and his cousin and sitting MP, General Thomas Grosvenor. Hemingway described Edward as an 'old useful candidate and excellent country gentleman'.[11] This praise was rooted in widespread dissatisfaction with the Grosvenors, who, it was felt, were becoming complacent in their duty to represent the city and were apt to gerrymander the election process. Examples included the questionable appointment of pliant freemen and the registering of votes from parties who lived outside the constituency.

Predictably enough, the atmosphere around the election of 1818 was febrile. At one point, when opposing parties met by chance on the narrow Dee Bridge, an unseemly clash took place and General Grosvenor was tipped into the river. Surviving this experience – which was by no means a given – he made light of it, and thereby helped to restore order. It has been said that this occurrence highlighted the need for a new bridge. When the election result turned out in favour of the Grosvenors – the official voting tally was Belgrave 771, Grosvenor 698, Egerton 680 and Townshend 604 – Egerton petitioned the House of Commons, unsuccessfully, alleging improper conduct. A similar outcome arose in the election of 1826, when the losing candidates were Edward once more and Sir Philip Grey Egerton, his brother John having died the previous year.[12]

Edward was pitched into a political cauldron yet again five years later, this time lending his support to the Great Reform Bill and bemoaning its turbulent and uncertain passage towards the statute book. After its first defeat in March 1831, Edward joined a committee of what was essentially a pressure group to keep it alive, at one point assembling every day in the Royal Hotel, Chester. On 9th May, he chaired a high-profile meeting in North-wich challenging reactionary landed interests and ensuring Cheshire's representation in Parliament was on the side of reform. The *Courant* described it as 'the most important loco-political meeting that ever took place in the county'.[13]

When a revised bill received the assent of the Commons but was defeated in the Lords in October, civil disobedience broke out around the country. At a hastily convened meeting, again in Northwich, Edward seconded a resolution proposed by Sir John Stanley for presentation to the king that 'the freeholders of Cheshire had witnessed with the deepest sorrow the rejection of the Reform Bill and that their attachment to the principle of the bill was unaltered and unalterable'. The meeting was chaired by Philip Humberston in his capacity as Under-Sheriff to the county. Eventually, such lobbying bore fruit and the bill in its final form was adopted in June 1832.

Edward's family would have observed his involvement in social and political affairs with pride and occasional disappointment, according to his fortunes. They also had to deal with some significant bereavements in these years. His father, another Edward, died in 1811, followed by his sister Barbara Anne at Stanley Place in 1816. She must have known she had a terminal condition because the residual legatee in her will – proved by her brother-in-law, the Reverend Richard Massie – was her mother, who outlived her by nine years. Then came the losses of Edward's cousins – our book club members, Frances Sarah Townshend in 1828, Susanna Mainwaring in 1829 and Frances Anne Townshend in 1832. As Susanna's will was drafted in 1826, Frances Sarah was included in it, with £200 each earmarked for her and Frances Anne.

The main beneficiaries in Frances Anne's will are Dorothea, widow of John Stanislaus Townshend, their children and the children of Susanna Mainwaring. Nieces Anne and

Susanna Townshend are left the house on Watergate Street. The sum of £1,800, along with unspecified books, goes to Henry Townshend and similar amounts to sundry other nephews and nieces. The £1,000 left to George Townshend, who by that time was out in the Hunter Valley, may have helped to finance his Australian adventure. John Townshend, the eldest nephew, is another significant beneficiary and the prover of the will. Some items left to John are specified quite precisely, including Chelsea and Dresden china and 'the two dancing figures he brought me from abroad'. Emerald and diamond earrings, brought from Paris by Charles Mainwaring, go to his sister, Susan.

Frances Anne's sister, Susanna, also travelled overseas and returned with valuable gifts which are detailed in the will, including diamond and gold bracelets. There are precious stones aplenty and albums, drawings and prints, all of which are retained within the close family. Particularly striking, and an indication of the wealth and benevolence in play, is an invested sum of £1,000 – upwards of £60,000 in today's terms – granted to pensioners who already derived weekly benefit from the interest upon it. She refers a couple of times to 'my poor sister Fanny', intimating the strength of their relationship and the impact of her loss. Amongst the witnesses are George Becher Blomfield – Rector of Tattenhall, and son-in-law of Hester Lee Massie – and Robert Yarker – Minister of St Olave's and son-in-law of Catherine Humberston.[14]

Not long after Frances Anne died, a property was put up for sale in Stanley Street, which was 'late the residence of the late Miss Townshend'. Stanley Street runs across the top of Stanley Place, where some of her closest surviving relatives lived and which was the location for the auction of her remaining household goods six months later. It seems the sisters had both this and their property in Watergate Street at their disposal: both fashionable addresses, providing a further insight into their financial status.[15]

Nephew Henry Townshend, mentioned in the will, entered the army, ultimately becoming a colonel in the 24th Regiment, which had distinguished itself in the defeat of the French in Egypt in 1801, taking possession of the Rosetta Stone in the process. Almost 80 years later, the same regiment was all but wiped out at the Battle of Rorke's Drift in the Anglo-Zulu War. Henry was in command when its stock was high and was immortalised in ballad when he paraded his troops on Glasgow Green in 1843. Here is a brief extract:

The honourable COLONEL TOWNSHEND on a warlike steed,

In front of his fine Regiment on that day did proceed;

Appearing like to Blucher on the plains of Waterloo,

As he rode before his gallant corps to the Glasgow Grand Review ...

They did defeat the French that were commanded by Menou;

The Sphinx that day they did display at Glasgow Grand Review.[16]

The author, perhaps for good reason, chose to remain anonymous.

Henry died at Trevalyn in 1882 and is buried in the churchyard at St Mary's, Rossett, not far from his brother, John, who had passed away two decades earlier. There are more family graves, tablets and memorial windows at the older-established All Saints Church in nearby Gresford. There is also a brass lectern in memory of Frances Anne. Intermingled amongst the graves are several Townshend servants from down the generations and any number of Boydells.

There are other Townshend memorials in Chester. For example, when Arabella died in 1852, she stated in her will: 'If I die in Chester [which she did], I beg my body may be deposited by the remains of my dearest father [Edward] and brother [Edward Venables] and my sister Barbara Anne Townshend in Trinity Chapel'. This will was proved by Edward Venables' son, Lee Porcher Townshend, whose daughter Mary Charlotte has a tablet dedicated to her in the north aisle of Chester Cathedral. She died in 1891 whilst on missionary work in Zanzibar. This was a cause that the Townshend family had long held dear. Frances Anne, for one, had been a generous subscriber to the Society for the Propagation of the Gospel in Foreign Parts.[17] Hemingway tells us that there is a memorial to the sisters' uncle, Thomas Townshend, in St Olave's Church, Chester, but that is no longer accessible to view.

The Townshend sisters demonstrate perhaps more than any of our other book lovers in 1824 just how deeply intertwined the lives of some of the members really were. Another sister and a cousin were in the book club, as we have seen, but the tendrils spread much wider than that. The Thomas just mentioned married into the Mainwaring family of Bromborough; Charlotte Hester Townshend, the daughter of Edward Venables, married her cousin, Admiral Thomas Leche Massie; and, of course, there is Townshend Mainwaring, second son of the book club member, whose widow laid the foundation stone at St Mary's Church, Rossett, where later generations of the Townshend family came to rest.

For the first three decades of the 19th century, almost all the families represented at the book club were at the best balls and concerts that Chester had to offer and joined forces to dispense what philanthropy they could, where and when it was most needed. Least visible was Anne Coupland, because circumstances dictated that she spend time elsewhere, but she was still not completely detached. When she and Elizabeth Sloughter exchanged news about Princess Victoria's visit to Chester in 1832, the recent death of Frances Anne Townshend was lamented. As we saw in Chapter Ten, there is also an intriguing possibility that one of the sisters met the king, in the company of Anne Coupland's kinswoman, Lady Warburton, but the lack of precision in reporting means that we may never know for sure.

Chapter Twenty-Two

November

At the start of November 1824, Chester was licking its post-election wounds. Grievances ran deep, especially amongst establishment figures who felt their authority was being subverted. In some instances, retribution was swiftly sought. The case of the *King v Faulkner* – an attorney's clerk – *and Others* called on the defendants to 'show cause why rule could not be moved against them for riotous conduct at the recent election'. None of them were freemen, and they were therefore unable to vote, but they had sought to influence the outcome nonetheless, by fair means or foul. They were bound over for trial at the Spring Assizes. Allegations that the dean and chapter, through the offices of their 'agent', Philip Humberston, had exerted undue pressure in favour of the defeated party were repeated but could not be proved.

There was a legal challenge to the victors too, citing breach of process. A clause in the city's charter was examined: it required the sitting mayor to be supported by a majority of aldermen, yet only seven out of 24 had been present when votes were cast. This objection was not sustained, and he remained in post. The *Courant*, which had thrown its weight behind the defeated candidate, railed against what it called the 'defiance of British feeling' by propping up feudalism rather than embracing greater democracy. It pointed to the fact that, amongst a population of 24,000, a mere 1,500 freemen were entitled to vote. Whilst it condemned 'the great commotion', it also anticipated 'some amusing anecdotes'. There was an optimism that protest would lead to electoral change, which was validated within the decade.[1]

Civilised gatherings began to reclaim the streets of Chester. A procession took place to the cathedral to mark the mayoral inauguration, at which the mayor, sheriff and aldermen were accompanied by a band, the children of the Blue Coat School, and various officials, including the sword and mace bearers. The bishop preached a conciliatory sermon, bemoaning the 'bitterness of party feeling' which had 'blighted the prosperity of Chester' and advocating the application of Christian principles.[2]

Any disorder that now prevailed was of a more routine, apolitical nature. Concerns remained about 'frightful scenes of juvenile and matured depravity' on the streets and Rows, and repeated appeals were made for parents and masters to take their charges in hand. The walls, and Eastgate in particular, were 'the principal haunts of these orgies of sin'. The police, perhaps chastened by what had happened to George Burgess, were seldom on patrol.

A furious public row took place between a Mrs Anne Prescot and Mrs Mary Hill, which appears to have re-erupted in court. The former accused the latter of a dalliance 'at the 'Change with a gentleman', the outcome of which was that Mr Hill was bound over for 'his rib' to keep the peace for 12 months. Press reports of the time were capable of the utmost condescension. Two drunken and voluble Irishmen who were forcibly removed from Foregate Street to the House of Industry were described as 'Paddies' and 'Emerald Islanders', as if that were their defining characteristic. Publicans continued to be fined for serving alcohol during the hours of divine service.[3]

One victim of a nuisance offence was Monsieur Louis Doré, the musician and impresario, whose door at 43 Watergate Street was rapped upon at an unseasonal hour by two young men. On this occasion, a watchman was on hand and the fines meted out went in part to him and in part to the lying-in charity. Petty though it was, this would have been an unwelcome intrusion into the life of Monsieur Doré, who was busy fitting up a new assembly room at 53 Watergate Street, for pleasure and instruction. An opening date was set for the evening of 13th December, when the examination of pupils would take place, followed by a ball for them and their parents.

The entertainment scene in the city in general was gathering pace as the winter season approached. The first subscription assembly took place at the Royal Hotel on 11th November and there was a sell-out concert for ladies only, featuring the famous Italian operatic duo, Madame and Signor de Begnis. Care was again taken to manage the flow of traffic, with carriages required to set down in Eastgate Street and pick up at The Cross. A performance by the Choral Society Band, led by Mr George Eyton, was also well attended. A celebratory dinner was hosted by the new mayor in the Exchange, with over 100 members of the nobility and gentry on the guest list.

The retail apparatus of the city was gearing up for the season too. William and Henry Brown had just returned from London with 'new and fashionable articles', as had several milliners. Whilst their businesses were prospering, others were in decline. Mr Broster, the bookseller, had put his entire stock up for auction – our book club members may have enjoyed some pickings but would have been disappointed at this turn of events.

At the Royal Hotel, busy as it was, Mr Willoughby was also selling off stock, as a prelude to his retirement as proprietor. There appears to have been some financial imperative, as the operation was struggling to cover its costs.

Various forms of transport continued to make the news. There was some optimism that the shipbuilding trade in Chester would revive, with two large brigs and a steamboat commissioned. Timber was cheaper than in Liverpool and there was a ready supply of skilled labour. A new steam packet – the Lady Stanley – was running between Eastham Ferry and Liverpool, connecting with coaches from Chester. The total journey time was two-and-a-half hours and there were three sailings a day.

Already there were signs of the impending pre-eminence of the railways as a mode of transport. Mr Lea, a broker on Watergate Street, was offering to convert existing shares in canal companies to shares in emergent railway companies.[4] An application to Parliament was being prepared for the Liverpool to Birmingham line, with Upton, Newton and Hoole still part of the proposed route.

A project already underway was the creation of the new water works in Chester; the feculent waters of the River Dee had long been regarded as unfit for domestic use and a persistent health hazard. Two-thirds of the £12,000 capital required had been subscribed and a deal had been done with Colonel Hicks for the purchase of his premises at Barrel Well Hill.

There was some hope that the treatment of the sick would improve as plans for extending the infirmary were now well advanced, bolstered by a £50 donation from Wilbraham Egerton. One of the physicians at the infirmary – Mr Pigot – was pressing magistrates to improve the old asylum at Chester to prevent paupers from having to be sent to neighbouring counties for treatment. A new asylum was opened five years later, as we have seen.

Two tragedies that touched Chester this month were the deaths, separately, of Edward Thomas and Mary Anne Brown. Edward was killed horrifically whilst attempting to repair a corn dealer's damaged water wheel. Mary Anne, aged 11 and the daughter of a deceased army captain, had been born in Whitchurch but died in Chester. The cause went unreported. Her mother, who was inconsolable, accompanied her funeral procession through the city in a carriage drawn by four grey horses and attended by servants and officials – on foot and on horseback – including two mutes to add to the solemnity of the occasion. The hearse, with the coffin draped in gold and velvet, and a second mourning coach were drawn in the same manner. Observers unacquainted with the family, pausing briefly on a raw November day, would have sensed the well of grief and noted the slightness of the coffin.[5]

On some days, and in some parts of the region, the weather was particularly inclement. There were gales at the start of the month, resulting in shipwrecks and loss of life off the north Wales coast. In Liverpool, the temperature dipped far below zero, which some felt presaged an earthquake that never materialised. Floods in Derbyshire and Lincolnshire killed many sheep and threatened the livelihoods of farmers to whom they belonged.

One ship that made it into port, albeit precariously, was the *Columbus*, a huge timber-laden vessel arriving at Gravesend from Canada. Vast crowds lined the south coast and the Thames estuary to greet its arrival. It was taking on water, however, and 70 salvage men were sent to pump it out. Once the cargo was safely disembarked, the ship had to be dismantled.

Meanwhile, more and more vessels continued to dock at Liverpool. An application had been made to Parliament for a significant expansion in the port, including improved regulation and an optical telegraph connection to Hoylake or Holyhead. On land, there was incipient resistance to the proposed railway route to Birmingham, with several landowners registering their objection. Still in Liverpool, the resurrection men who had been active the previous month had been arrested, tried and sentenced to 18 months imprisonment.

At work underground in a less nefarious capacity were the excavators of a recently discovered cave system in Somerset – the Banwell Bone Caves, which contained extensive pre-historic animal remains. The land was owned by George Henry Law, Bishop of Bath and Wells, lately of Chester. He understood the importance of the site, developing it as a tourist attraction and even retiring there himself in later years. His firm belief was that the bones were the remains of animals which had perished in Noah's flood, with its powerful didactic message to the ungodly. In fact, they were between 50,000 and 80,000 years old.[6]

For a while there had been simmering interest in a forgery trial at the Old Bailey in which disgraced city banker, Henry Fauntleroy, admitted misappropriating funds held in trust by his firm. It was rumoured that he had squandered the money on a debauched lifestyle, but it is more likely that he was trying to keep the firm afloat by plugging an increasingly ominous hole in the accounts. Now, a guilty verdict had been passed and, forgery still being a capital offence, a date for execution had been set. For those who had followed the case from the start – of whom there were many up and down the land – this final act in the drama was a source of much anticipation.[7]

Compared with previous months, there was less reporting of conflict beyond mainland Britain, indicating some abatement. Though far from settled, Ireland was described as 'less disturbed by the day' and William III's November birthday – a perennial flashpoint – had passed without major incident. In Greece, the struggle for independence had been aided by the defeat of the combined Turkish and Egyptian fleets, and the French had partially withdrawn from Spain. Other than hints of an insurrection in Trinidad, there were no significant new outbreaks of revolt in the British colonies, despite strong underlying tensions.

Curiosities and novelties that may have aroused interest include the arrival of the striped offspring of a lion and tigress at Windsor and the discovery of three sunspots, which were reported as having just appeared on the surface of the sun, rather than having been observed for the first time. The sun, it was stated, was previously universally bright.

Mr Lipscombe, an equestrian, rode 90 miles on eight horses on the route from London to Bath in a little under five hours, pocketing a five hundred sovereign stake in the process. The King of Prussia married an Austrian countess with his left hand – a practice used with a spouse of inferior rank. Great sensory feats were in the news too. A boy in Sheffield, blind since birth, was said to be able to differentiate between colours by touch alone. A man called Curtis had produced a treatise on physiology and diseases of the ear, as well as an improved hearing trumpet. These were accompanied by a claim that 60 people had already been cured of hearing loss, which may have appealed to members of our book club whose faculties were on the wane.[8]

Chapter Twenty-Three

Miss Venables
Lot 12

The Balance of Comfort, a new edition, interspersed with original poetry, a handsome copy in high preservation, embellished with an expressive title page.

The Balance of Comfort was a real work, published in three volumes in 1818, by the popular and prolific author, Mrs Ross. Its full title was *The Balance of Comfort; or the Old Maid and Married Woman* but Dr Norris, aware that offence may be taken, prudently resisted using this. It is a book about social relationships amongst families and between the sexes, moralistic but not excessively religious in tone, advocating tolerance and good humour as the route to contentment. It is interspersed with poetry from literary and classical sources, and therefore not original. It may be that Miss Venables wrote poetry herself and that this is glanced at here. We see again the familiar trope 'a handsome copy in high preservation', as a means of acknowledging seniority of years and how well the subject was ageing. In modern parlance, Dr Norris may be termed a 'sweet talker'. The highlighting of the title page suggests it must have held some special significance. Lines from William Cowper's poem, *Mutual Forbearance*, feature on it, culminating like this:

> The kindest and the happiest pair
> Will find occasion to forbear;
> And something, every day they live,
> To pity, and perhaps forgive.

'Venables' was and is a far from unusual name in Cheshire and care needs to be exercised in making familial connections.

In the wake of the Dissolution, a Thomas Venables was one of the commissioners of the Crown who laid bare consecrated buildings, appropriating goods or donating them to the local clergy or the poor. His descent is unclear.[1]

We met Edward Venables Townshend in Chapter Twenty-One. His middle name derives from his two times great-grandmother, Frances Venables, who was the daughter of Robert Venables, a renowned soldier under Oliver Cromwell. He fought at the Battle of Rowton Heath in 1645 and led the invasion of Jamaica during the Protectorate, alongside William Penn, as we saw in Chapter Five. Robert was appointed Governor of Chester, but this was undone at the Restoration. Discredited but safe, he bought the estate at Wincham, to which he retired and where he died in 1687.[2] This means, of course, that not only was Edward Venables Townshend directly descended from this notable historical figure, but so too were our book club members, Mrs Massie, Mrs Mainwaring and the Misses Townshend.

Hemingway talks of a 'Mr G Venables' – apparently unrelated – who was a surgeon at Chester Infirmary in the late 18th century and of 'the present master' of the Blue Coat School, Samuel Venables, whom he describes as having 'for a long course of years obtained the uniform approbation of the Board and Public'.[3] Samuel's tenure in this role lasted for over 40 years from the turn of the 19th century. He died in 1848, at the age of 77, and is commemorated with a fine monument in Overleigh Cemetery, Chester, erected by former pupils, who commend their learning under him as 'the source of their happiness in life'. Fenwick also identifies him as the author of 'Local Rhymes' and relates a curious incident in which his son, John, sent him a letter from London to his home in Crane Street, Chester with a rhyming address. We might consider Dr Norris's inclusion of 'original poetry' in Lot 12 and wonder whether there is any correlation with this versifying Venables.

In fact, the Miss Venables in whom we are interested springs from a different line entirely, both from Samuel – who was born in Dodleston, south-west of Chester – and from the book club members just mentioned. They, like most of their local friends and contemporaries, would all have known of Samuel. He would have been especially familiar to the Panton sisters, who lived directly opposite his school.

First, we need to differentiate between two siblings. Elizabeth and Mary Hannah Venables came originally from Shropshire, and their residence in 1824 was in Stanley Place, which provides an immediate link to our book club. Elizabeth was born in 1775 and Mary in 1784, both in Oswestry, to Lazarus and Elizabeth Venables, née Jones. As the elder sister, closer in age to other members, Elizabeth emerges as the likeliest candidate.

Lazarus Venables was, at one time, a tax inspector in Oswestry, where his father, Joseph, was a church minister.[4] There was a Cheshire connection through her paternal grandmother, yet another Elizabeth Venables, who referred to land owned in Rostherne, near Altrincham, in her will of 1765. Perhaps the most noteworthy ancestor was the sisters' great-uncle on their mother's side, Valentine Jones. A career soldier in the British Army, he fought with distinction in many campaigns, eventually reaching the rank of colonel during a 14-year spell in North America. He played an important role in maintaining peace and order in Quebec before being transferred to Boston in 1774, where unrest against British rule was fermenting. He and his troops were inevitably drawn into the American Revolutionary War. As commander of forces in the city of New York in early 1778, he may well have encountered General Charles Lee on the opposite side. Ill health overtook him, however, and later that year he was forced to return to England, where he sought respite in Bath. In the event, his condition continued to deteriorate and he died in Llanidloes, Montgomeryshire, in November 1778.[5]

Elizabeth and Mary spent their formative years at the family home at Woodhill, near Oswestry. This property still stands as Woodhill Park, an impressive privately-owned Georgian house set in extensive grounds. In the 20th century, it belonged to Lord Harlech, British ambassador to the USA and a great friend of President Kennedy. Jackie and Robert

Kennedy both stayed there. A great-great-grandson of Susanna Mainwaring – Mark Kynaston Mainwaring – married Auriol Howes of Woodhill in 1942.

It is clear from Lazarus's will, proved by his widow shortly after his death in January 1813, that the family were of ample means. When they married in 1771, there was land on both sides, becoming entirely the property of Lazarus, in return for which he paid an annuity to his wife and developed what he had received from her. In 1800, he upgraded Woodhill from a farmhouse to a fine country residence.[6] He acquired other land, at Llanllugan in Powys, which he left to his wife, and at Rod Meadow in Oswestry, which he left to his daughters, Elizabeth and Mary.

Although their mother and brothers were the main legatees, the sisters were bequeathed £1,500 each, due upon their mother's death or remarriage.[7] When she died in 1820 therefore, the sisters, already comfortably off, were further enriched. Not only did they receive the money from their father, but they also inherited more money and possessions from their mother. Precisely when they moved into their fashionable town house in Chester is uncertain, but there was no financial barrier to them doing so. There is evidence of a connection with the city before their mother's death because, when she drafted her will in 1817, it was witnessed in the presence of 'Henry Potts of Chester'.

On top of such contacts, an attraction of the location may have been the fact that their eldest brother, Lazarus Jones Venables, was professionally established in Liverpool, where he was a leading barrister. He had married into a Liverpool family, by the name of Jolly, in 1805. A Chester base afforded the sisters relatively straightforward access to both there and Oswestry. By this time, Woodhill belonged to Lazarus Jones, and he was busy developing it still further. This included creating formally laid out grounds, which were well-wooded but easily traversed by path.

Cheshire directories of the 1820s list 'Miss Venables' at Stanley Place. The number is omitted, as is any mention of her sister. That is not to suggest that Mary wasn't living there – it merely recognises Elizabeth as head of the household. One of the revellers at Mrs Mainwaring's masquerade in January 1823 was a 'Miss Venables: a complete witch with her black cat on her shoulder'. Though not conclusive, this is also likely to have been Elizabeth.[8]

There are comparatively few references to the sisters during their time in Chester, even though it spanned several decades. This probably reflects low-key lives and the fact that they enjoyed regular and extensive periods elsewhere. Even after their brother inherited Woodhill upon their father's death, they would still have regarded it as their family home. They may even have worshipped at Oswestry, a practice that would have been instilled in them when their uncle, the Reverend Joseph Venables, preached there, following in his father's footsteps. The Reverend Joseph died in 1810. A plaque in his honour at St Oswald's Church, Oswestry, talks of 'his piety, benevolence and general conduct as a man' and specifically that 'To his relations, his affections and kindness were unbounded'.

There was a common strain of deep religious conviction running through this branch of the family. Three of Elizabeth and Mary's four brothers – Joseph, Richard and George – entered the ministry, the most distinguished of whom was Richard, who held the post of Archdeacon of Carmarthen between 1832 and his death in 1858.

Joseph's son, Rowland Jones Venables, was born in Chester in 1813, though he seems to have spent most of his life in London and Shropshire. He was a director of the Great Western Railway. A schoolroom and lychgate in his memory were erected at Sellatyn, near Oswestry, after he passed away in 1868.[9]

Three of the sisters' other nephews – all sons of Lazarus Jones Venables – also merit mention. John, born in 1810, followed his father into the law but was unable to fulfil his promise because he died, aged 24, of unknown causes, in his chambers at the Inner Temple, London.

Edward, five years younger, also met with an untimely death, in his case in 1858. He is described in the *Dictionary of National Biography* as 'one of the heroes of the Indian mutiny'. Having gone out to India as a young man as an indigo planter, he settled near Azimghur in the North-West Provinces. When the uprising began in 1857, he immediately took arms and led a troop of cavalry with great distinction, despite his being a volunteer. After a number of intrepid ventures and military successes, his health suffered and he resolved to return to England. By this time, his father had died and he had inherited Woodhill. However, the Governor General, Lord Canning, who valued him highly, persuaded him to stay in post. He was mortally wounded in combat not long afterwards, in the spring of 1858.[10] A memorial window dedicated to him in St Oswald's Church, Oswestry includes the following encomium:

The outbreak of the Indian Rebellion in 1857 called him from the peaceful avocations of private life to take up arms in defence of his country. Undaunted by difficulty, gallant in fight and fertile in resource both as a soldier and civilian, he zealously devoted to the state the short remainder of his patriotic life, receiving the thanks of the Governor General in Council and honoured in death by the tribute of a public memorial in Calcutta.

When news of Edward's fate reached Britain, some of the many obituaries touched on the fact that his brother was a minor canon at Chester Cathedral. This was the Reverend Henry Venables. Born in 1823, he was educated at Rugby School and Jesus College, Cambridge, before being ordained deacon at Chester in 1846 and priest in 1848. Through the late 1840s and early 1850s, he held curacies in Lancashire and Gloucester, followed by his appointment as minor canon and precentor of Chester in 1857. As his brother Edward died childless, he inherited the family estates in 1858. He married Jesse Maria Fisher in Kent in the same year, and they had four children – Agnes, Edith, Cuthbert and Mary, all born in Chester between 1859 and 1865. Census records show them living at 5 Abbey Court. The family later lived in Leamington Spa, Reading and, finally, Oxford, where Henry died in 1889.

Whilst Henry's widow and daughters appear, for the most part, to have stayed in Oxford, his son, Cuthbert, was more peripatetic. After attending Charterhouse and Pembroke College, Cambridge, he became a mechanical engineer in the mid-1880s. In the 1891 census, he is listed as a marine engine draughtsman in Barrow-in-Furness. The most significant entry, however, is in the 1901 census, in which Cuthbert appears as a 'motor vehicles mechanical engineer', lodging in Lambeth.[11]

In 1892, he joined forces with James Root, with whom he formed the company Roots and Venables, developing motorised road vehicles. After experimenting with tricycles powered by heavy oil, they soon moved on to petrol-driven motor cars. A poster headed 'The History of Modern Transport' carries a picture of a three-wheeled two-seater and the words: 'The first petrol-engined automobile made in England was this Roots and Venables car. In 1896, the inventor, J D Roots, was fined for driving the car without a man walking before it carrying a red flag.' A report from 22nd May 1896 states:

Yesterday a motor-car passed southwards through Redhill, creating no small excitement in its passage through the town. It was the Roots petro-car ... All who saw it must have been struck with the perfect ease with which it was propelled and guided on its way.

The following year it became the Roots Oil Motor and Motor Car Co, in which Cuthbert was one of five directors. It was sold in 1902 to Armstrong Whitworth, a major British manufacturing company of the early 20th century.

This rousing story does not have a happy ending, however. Cuthbert's obvious entrepreneurial and engineering skills were not allied with financial acumen. In 1911, he was declared bankrupt, having lost money in business and having speculated in residential property, borrowing at high rates of interest in a falling market.[12] He is even reported to have given £2,000 to 'a man who declared that he could chemically improve emeralds'.[13]

He moved from London to Oxford, where he appears in the 1939 Register in a shared cottage attached to his sister Mary's house in Cumnor Hill. When he died three years later at the age of 79, his effects were valued at £327. His sister Agnes had died in 1919 and Edith in 1938. Edith left an estate worth £19,000 and Mary, when she passed away in 1950, £26,000. Cuthbert was very much the poor relation.

A leaded window placed in the south aisle of the cloisters at Chester Cathedral bears the inscription: 'This window is given in memory of the Reverend Henry Venables MA 1823-1889 and of Jessie Maria his wife 1823-1901 by their children, Cuthbert, Edith and Mary 1824.' Edith and Mary must have picked up the lion's share of the cost. Nonetheless, this gesture represents not just the siblings' devotion to their parents, but also to the city of their birth, where they must have retained contacts throughout their lives.

Though this is important family history, we are a century beyond the era of our book club and, inevitably, Elizabeth and Mary didn't live to see it. At either end of the year 1846, two brief death notices appeared in the press:

On 1ˢᵗ inst. [February] At her house in Stanley Place, Chester, in the 71ˢᵗ year of her age, Elizabeth Venables, eldest dau of the late L Venables of Woodhill, near Oswestry.[14]
On the 3rd inst. [October] In the 62ⁿᵈ year of her age Miss Mary Hannah Venables of Stanley Place, daughter of the late L Venables esq of Woodhill, Shropshire.[15]

In due course, like members of the Humberston family, they were commemorated on a tablet in St Bridget's, recorded in church registers but now obliterated by development:

Sacred to the memory of Elizabeth Venables, late of Stanley Place in this city and oldest daughter of the late L Venables esq of Woodhill near Oswestry, Shropshire. Born 7ᵗʰ September 1775 died February 1ˢᵗ 1846. Also in memory Mary Hannah Venables her only sister, born November 30th 1784, died October 3ʳᵈ 1846. The remains of both are laid beneath this stone.

Chapter Twenty-Four

December

By the start of December, winter had truly set in, and the weather was harsh and unforgiving. There were sharp frosts and snow, delaying cross-country mail coaches. Gales and occasional thaws resulted in flooding, including at the Earl's Eye in Chester and upstream at Farndon, Bangor and Overton, where much livestock perished. Offshore there was widespread loss of life, and damage to coastal settlements and shipping on such a scale that Lloyds of London suffered severely.

Chester was also still in the grip of a post-election chill. Accusations were levelled by both sides and litigation swiftly followed. Magistrates made an order for financial compensation to be paid by the parish of St Oswald's to the Saracen's Head inn and to the Corporation in respect of the Exchange, these premises having felt the full force of the rioting. On the other part, the case of the *King v George Harrison esq*, Mayor of Chester, for breach of the election process proceeded to a preliminary hearing before the Lord Chief Justice. Had the matter not been so serious, there might have been a comic element to how it unfolded. The case was based on a clause in the ancient city charter, granted by Henry VII but derived from the Norman Earls, which had been written in abbreviated Latin and questionably translated into English. When the mayor's defence counsel produced and began to read from what he asserted was an accurate version of the document, the Lord Chief Justice quickly intervened, pronouncing that enough had been disclosed already to proceed to trial. This took place at the Shrewsbury Assizes, where the jury found in favour of the Crown. However, an appeal was permitted, making the case somewhat academic because Mr Harrison completed his term of office before it was heard.[1]

Riot victim, James Forshaw, had by now become a focal point for pacifist sentiment. Those still intent on challenging the status quo were putting money by for further action.

In the words of the *Chronicle*: 'We have heard that some deductions are being made from the wages of workmen by the Annual Row Mongers to fund hostilities against the body corporate and peace of the city.'[2]

Another high-profile legal battle commenced which some felt was politically motivated, because the defendant was Earl Grosvenor and the prosecutor acting on behalf of the plaintiff – Mr Willoughby of the Royal Hotel – was opposed to the ruling elite in Chester. This case sheds further light on Mr Willoughby's decision to 'retire' and sell up. He had relocated from London in 1819 and, after what he felt was adequate due diligence, decided to take on the tenancy of the hotel, which was owned by Earl Grosvenor. The business failed to fulfil its promise and Mr Willoughby struggled to pay his rent and instalments towards the purchase of contents. Whilst the Earl, through his agent, attempted to recover arrears, at times with recourse to the law, Mr Willoughby began to argue that the business had been misrepresented at the time he entered into it.

Matters came to a head in March 1824, when he was served with notice to quit. With a promising season in the offing, he managed to stall, but still could not fully meet his obligations. By December, Earl Grosvenor had secured an injunction to prevent Mr Willoughby from selling the contents, the value of which would fall short of his liability. Mr Willoughby, in turn, sought to have this lifted. The decision taken in Chancery was that he could continue with the sale or use the items as part of a going concern in return for payment of a set sum by way of damages, plus costs. This was another case that would not have come cheap, and, in this respect, Mr Willoughby had not helped himself. His sworn affidavit ran to 230 pages, which one wag compared to the plan for the Liverpool to Birmingham railroad, itself 33 feet long.[3]

More run-of-the-mill cases of a criminal nature were heard by the magistrates of Chester. Thomas Williams, a carter, had breached the peace and threatened to shoot a watchman in the small hours of Sunday morning. A similar offence had been committed by Richard Boulton, but he had 20 or 30 accomplices and so was dealt with more severely.

Christmas and, for some, the temptation to over-imbibe, may have fuelled transgression. Philip Dillon, a nail maker, fined for being drunk in St John Street on Christmas Eve, had also stripped off and challenged officers to a fight. The aptly named Peter Clubbe had committed such a serious assault upon a constable in Watergate Street on Christmas morning that the victim had been unable to give evidence at trial. Daniel Charles and Roger Byron disputed so abrasively over dinner in Cuppin Street that they spilled out onto the pavement and were fined for the fracas that they caused. Of all the crimes against the person that were being reported, one stood out markedly as being unwhipped of justice: William Parkinson, the alleged killer from Dunham-on-the-Hill, was still at large.

Despite inhospitable conditions, begging remained rife in Chester, particularly amongst Irish immigrants. Two were sentenced to three months' imprisonment and three floggings if they refused to quit the city. In another case, three Irishmen who were lodging in a small house where there were six to a bed, were accused of dealing in soap without paying the taxes due on it. One was found guilty and sentenced to two months' hard labour in default of a £20 fine, which he couldn't afford.

The conviction of women, for sundry offences, was prominent in the news at this time. A scam that had become commonplace involved women falsely claiming that their husbands were servicemen who had been sent overseas, entitling them to parish relief. Prostitution was in the frame too. Charlotte Lathbury was another recipient of two months' hard labour, in her case for 'being found in the street at an untimely hour of the night'.

An alternative to streetwalking was offered by Suddrick's, a notorious brothel in Linenhall Street. In one incident, six boisterous men were followed down Watergate Street to this establishment, where they were soon arrested and taken to the House of Correction by a posse of watchmen. Also arrested were 11 women and two more men, who were described as 'bullies to the brothel'. Tried before the mayor, the bullies were reprimanded, the clients fined £10 each and the women sentenced to seven days in prison on a bread and water diet. The whole operation was roundly condemned and separate proceedings initiated against Mary Weaver, the proprietor.[4]

Meanwhile, a Mrs Orme was taking steps to rid herself of male company, specifically her husband. When she petitioned the Consistory Court to intercede, because, in her words, they were not living 'like man and wife', she met with a rebuttal, the court declaring that it had no such power where the parties were living under the same roof. Conversely, one young lady – Miss Beddoes of Much Wenlock in Shropshire – was eager to marry. Before daybreak on Tuesday 14th December, she arrived in Chester in a chaise and four in the company of Captain Gore. They stopped briefly to have their horses reshod before resuming their journey to enlist the services of another blacksmith, though for a different purpose, in Gretna Green. Two to three hours later, a more numerous party of her close acquaintance passed through in hot pursuit. The race was lost, however, and the deed was done.

Some hope that law and order might improve came in the shape of Mr Dawson, who was appointed to the position of Chief of Police, as vacated by George Burgess. He was given an office in the Fish Market. One of his first duties was to take to task four constables who had failed to report for duty on a Sunday and to bring forward the start of their regular Sunday shift by one hour to 5pm. Two persistent crimes he set out to address were salmon poaching in the Dee and wanton damage to the city walls. There were also the general issues of congestion and unsightliness around the city. Regulations were reinforced relating to the loading and unloading of vehicles and the presence of tradesmen's stalls in the street. Filth, not least of equine origin, was a common topic of complaint, particular hotspots being the junction of Newgate Street and Eastgate Street and the whole length of Bridge Street. A more rigorous sweeping regime was recommended, and additional contractors were sought.[5]

None of this helped to alleviate pressure on the parish purse, so other measures were adopted to this end. One recent byelaw required that all illegitimate children over the age of four be admitted to the House of Industry. Concerns were raised that the measure was inhumane and led to the enervation and enslavement of the child. At a meeting of guardians of the poor and the governor, a sample of healthy-looking children was paraded and the matter was put to the vote. A proposal that each case should be treated on its own merits was dismissed as unworkable and the byelaw was confirmed by 30 votes to 23.

Of course, shortfalls in ley payments from parishioners compounded the problem. There were calls for investigations such as the one at St John's to be undertaken in other parishes. Even the clock had stopped at St John's, though those who lived within earshot of its chime saw this as a blessing rather than a curse. The Chester Benevolent Society, also active in supporting the needy, claimed to have relieved 120 cases of extreme poverty in the preceding 12 months. Bishop Blomfield again preached in aid of the Blue Coat School, and ordained more priests and deacons, one of whom was his brother, George. He installed a new vicar at Tarvin, south-east of Chester, though this was on behalf of the Bishop of Lichfield and Coventry, within whose diocese the parish still anachronistically resided. Christmas Day was solemnly observed in all the city churches, if not always outside them, and all shops were commended for remaining shut. Eminent local families such as the Grosvenors and the Barnstons again distributed food and clothing amongst the poor.

The festive season and inclement weather appear not to have unduly impeded the business of the city. A new steam vessel was commissioned to work the coastal route from Chester to London, with a greater speed and payload than any of its predecessors. Though four days for the end-to-end journey does not sound objectively impressive, comparison was made with a hundred ton shipment of cheese which had left Chester in October bound for London and had still not progressed beyond Liverpool. The medium to long-term benefits of rail transport were recognised and Chester businessmen backed infrastructure developments wholeheartedly.

Plans for the new bridge over the Dee were moving forward nicely too. Henry Potts, as Clerk of the Peace, announced that the committee had been authorised to approach Parliament for permission to appropriate a sum not exceeding £1,200 from the public rate and that the matter would be a standing item on the agenda at the General Quarter Sessions. Meanwhile, and not unrelated, the land agent at Eaton had started to construct what was described as 'a beautiful new line of road branching from the present road below Eccleston Hill to the Holyhead road, where a lodge will be built'. It went on to add that 'in event of the new bridge being built the lodge and road will form striking objects to the north side of the river'.[6] Further upstream, the site earmarked for the water works was being secured, now that the capital was almost fully subscribed and the draft Act of Parliament forwarded to London.

Anyone hardy enough to venture out socially had options at their disposal. The second Winter Concert was performed by Mrs Eliza Salmon, doyen of the Royal Opera House, who was described as an 'exquisite English warbler'.[7] She would not be engaged for another season because, early in 1825, her voice collapsed and, with it, her career. She died in destitution a quarter of a century later.

At the King's School, the Choral Society were performing the Messiah. This piece has a unique and somewhat ignominious connection with Chester. When George Frideric Handel was holed up at the Golden Falcon inn on Northgate St awaiting safe passage to Ireland in 1741, he enlisted some local choristers to rehearse his new work. They failed miserably in their execution of it and incurred his wrath. However, this experience appeared to be no deterrent to future performances of the Messiah in the city and may even have elevated it in terms of a challenge.[8]

There was reference in the pages of the press to leisure trips to Beeston Castle by canal – a popular excursion, first offered ten years earlier – but interested parties may have wished to wait until the spring before participating.

If any evidence were needed of the forthcoming supremacy of railways over canals for commercial purposes, it came in the form of share prices. For example, by the end of 1824, shares in the Liverpool to Manchester rail road, as it was then called, were fully subscribed and trading at a £40 premium. New schemes were emerging of even greater scale and ambition. The London Northern Rail Road Company launched a prospectus to raise £2.5 million to connect London, Birmingham, Derby, Nottingham, Hull and Manchester by rail. One small rail enterprise that catches our attention is the plan to link Treuddin in north Wales to nearby Flint, because Henry Potts was one of the landowners opposing it. The intended line would run directly through his land at Glan-y-Afon. Progressive as he was, he was not above a spot of nimbyism himself.

Canal shares were depressed accordingly, and some of our book club members would have suffered as a result. Such investments were disproportionately popular in the community because Chester was a hub on the canal network and the Potts family, amongst others, promoted them. One firm that would benefit enormously from the railway boom was Chester bankers, Dixons and Wardell – two families into which Potts children married – and its later incarnations. It financed the ventures of the great railway builder and Cestrian, Thomas Brassey, all around the world.

One banker whose fortunes were very different was Henry Fauntleroy, executed for fraud in 1824. Graphic accounts of this event appeared in national and provincial newspapers in early December: it occupied several columns in the Chester press. It was presided over by the Reverend Horace Salisbury Cotton of Newgate Prison, with whom we became acquainted in Chapter Five. Over a hundred thousand people travelled to the area around Newgate and the Old Bailey to witness the spectacle and indulge whatever grief they felt. They started arriving from midnight, despite the bitter cold, and, by 4.30am, those who had bought tickets in nearby dwelling houses were in position at the windows. Many mounted roofs, in defiance of the obvious dangers. It was a complete cross-section of society, male and female, all dressed in black. Barriers were erected and hundreds of extra policemen were brought in to keep order, which they barely did.

Shortly before 8am, inside the prison, the Reverend Cotton read the funeral service in stentorian tones. He then led the prisoner, also neatly attired in black and now pinioned, out onto the scaffold, in full public view. After a short prayer, the executioner removed Fauntleroy's carefully tied neckerchief, drew a cap over his face and adjusted the rope around his neck. Moments later, the platform dropped and life was extinguished in a single convulsive movement, to many audible gasps.

His body was left to hang for one hour and one minute, before being cut down and prepared for delivery to his family and friends. The swell and press of the crowd led to minor injuries, but no other fatalities occurred.[9] By the end of the month, however, Fauntleroy's mother was dead, reportedly of a broken heart. Also, 'a fine 14-year-old boy' by the name of Anthony Rawlings had hanged himself: he had been heard to say that 'he should like to try whether Mr Fauntleroy suffered much'.[10]

The Scottish capital was in the news too, on account of an appalling tragedy. The Great Fire of Edinburgh, which lasted five days, caused an estimated £200,000 worth of damage and rendered three hundred families homeless. New houses would be required there, as they were in London, which was expanding rapidly, more so than the general population.[11] Indeed, 25,000 homes were already under construction.

In Ireland, the population was growing unsustainably, and discontent was manifesting itself in new and destabilising ways. Such was the alarm that the cabinet debated the matter for ten consecutive days. The political activist, barrister and, later, MP, Daniel O'Connell, championed the Irish Catholic cause. He was arrested for sedition after suggesting to the Catholic Association that Ireland may have to 'rise like the Greeks or Bolivar in South America to have its rights restored'. If anything, the arrest galvanised the root and branch still further, not just in Ireland but in England too. Chester was not impervious to the ferment across the sea. As the military force increased, troops passed through the city and the port in ever greater numbers. Major Warburton, the police commander in Connaught, took refuge in a rented house in Stanley Place. Landed families of English origin retreated in similar ways.

Looking east across the sea, there were incipient signs of rapprochement with France. French troops bound for Martinique were forced by the gales to dock at Dover and share barracks with British troops. The fact that this passed off without friction was viewed in a positive light. In parallel, the Duke of Wellington, Napoleon's nemesis at Waterloo, was invited to the coronation of the new French king.

George IV, meanwhile, was confined to London with an attack of gout, which affected his plans to travel to Brighton for the festive season. He ascribed this to a lack of opportunity at Carlton House for his accustomed exercise due to the apartments and grounds being too confined. It is no coincidence that this property was demolished two years later and preparations made to create a palace from the far more modest pre-existing Buckingham House. One aristocrat who was ready for Christmas was the Duke of Devonshire, whose Chatsworth House was fitted up magnificently for the occasion. Open to the public, it was described as the finest attraction of its kind in Europe.[12]

Also in full swing was the Eisteddfod at Llangollen, where the esteemed 'Ladies' of that place were guests of honour. Not far away a fox was being cornered and killed at Chirk Castle Park by the Shropshire Hounds, who had chased their quarry for three hours to that end. Such was the level of exhaustion amongst the horses that three died and many others suffered. Mad Jack Mytton led the chase. Fearless and eccentric, he was even known to ride naked through snowdrifts and rivers in full spate. One week after the Chirk excursion, Mytton's huge stock of horses and hounds was up for auction. An inveterate spendthrift, he had squandered his ample inheritance and was on the road to ruin.

Another brutal event that hit the news was the prize fight in Surrey between Jem Burn and Ned O'Neale, which lasted 55 punishing rounds over one-and-three-quarter hours. O'Neale emerged victorious, scooping the £100 purse. Burn, beaten in every sense of the word, was his uncle. The dog Billy was also in action again, in what passed for some as entertainment. On this occasion, he killed a hundred rats in 12 minutes flat. By way of a sideshow, a bull terrier put paid to a bulldog and a badger.

In industry, the forces that would fan the flames of Victorian prosperity were already apparent. An account of the process to convert pig iron to plate at the Staffordshire Iron Works stated that 'Etna and Vesuvius, with their roaring fires and flowing lava, are present to the imagination, and the story of Vulcan and his Cyclops, forging thunder and lightning, appears no longer a fiction'. Precision manufacturing reinforced the drive to standardise weights and measures. An Act of Parliament was passed that introduced complete uniformity based on the imperial system. This remained in place until the metric system began to gain the upper hand from 1965 onwards.[13]

A buoyant economy at home continued to fund British exploits – for good or ill – abroad. Military action against the Ashantee in West Africa was showing signs of success, though substantial casualties were being incurred on both sides. Growing conflict in India and Burma necessitated the presence of more troops, though the use of more advanced weaponry was proving effective too. Lord Combermere, of whom we have heard much, was being touted as the next Commander-in-Chief in India, a prediction which answered the following year. Spain was still under the cosh from France, though it was able to send a flotilla of two thousand men on a colonising mission to South America. Refugees continued to flee the country in their droves, many bound for England. There was resentment that generous subscriptions enabled them to receive five shillings a week, in excess of the relief granted to some poor native families.

Another popular subscription, especially amongst those wished to expiate their feelings on slavery, was in favour of the widow of Missionary Smith, which was now well into four figures. Religion was still seen as the way forward for the benighted colonies in the West Indies, and, with that in mind, two more bishops and four more clergymen were bound there. In the Vatican, the Pope was stirring against the propagation of the Anglican faith through bible societies and missionary work. A papal bull had been drafted and would soon be released inviting all the faithful to visit Rome for 'the most plenary and complete indulgence, remission, and pardon of all their sins', adding that anyone opposing this injunction 'will incur the indignation of omnipotent God'.[14]

In London, routes towards the enfranchisement of enslaved people were being explored, albeit not in a very practical way. The Lord Mayor was granted the power to manumit them by assigning them to someone coming to or living in Britain in return for the sum of seven pounds. Of course, that someone could not be the enslaved person. Even if the fee were affordable, there was no guarantee against further enslavement and other human rights abuses.

Although there was no open conflict with Russia, it still maintained a brooding, sinister presence. Jacob Perkins, an American who had settled in England, had developed a steam gun that was deemed to be 20 times more effective than any other artillery then available, and a game-changer in the context of international warfare. A review in the *Mechanics' Magazine* asserted that its destructive capabilities were such that it would produce a universal peace, adding this by way of a caveat:

> We have heard that the Emperor of Russia … has sent an agent here to procure a supply of Perkins's Steam Guns, which that gentleman's patriotism will not allow him to offer. We almost fear, however, that our description will enable the Autocrat to get cannons made upon this principle. If Alexander really has such an intention, let us hope that he will apply them to a good cause, and so secure the approbation of posterity.

Amongst the more whimsical and diversionary entries in the Chester press was a feat of pedestrianism by Mr McMullan of Hull, who walked 16.5 miles in three hours, one-third backwards. Mr Moore asserted in his almanac for 1825 that the year would be 'disagreeable to young ladies but highly palatable to old maids'. Perhaps some of the benefit would come from the use of new cosmetic products entering the market, one of which was Rowland's Kalydor. Patronised by royalty and recommended by physicians, it promised to remove all skin blemishes, provide protection against the sun, soothe nursing mothers and their infants, and double as an aftershave for men. There was also another a new cure for deafness that involved 'washing the ears in the liquor in which poppy seeds have been boiled'. Anyone thoroughly dissatisfied with their lot might have wished to repair to Brighton to join the Society for the Encouragement of Vice. Newly formed, it already boasted 40 members.[15]

Chapter Twenty-Five

Dr Norris

So, what of Dr Norris, the orchestrator of all of this? We are well acquainted with his conceit, and with the gentle humour and deference that pervades it, but what can we determine of the man himself?

The name 'Norris' – or its earlier variants 'Norres' and 'Noreis' – has connections with Chester going back many centuries. Sir Henry Norres of Speke married the daughter of Roger Erneys of Chester at the start of 15th century, thereby acquiring property at St Mary's on the Hill and in Bridge Street, or Brugge Street as it was then called. In the Elizabethan era, Sir William Norris leased Blacon Hall, near Chester, from the Earl of Oxford, before it was sold on to Sir Christopher Hatton, the Chancellor.[1] There were also notable branches of the Norris family to the east of Warrington and at Blackrod, near Bolton. In 1850, George Ormerod presented a paper to the Historic Society of Lancashire and Cheshire, explaining the difficulty of connecting these families, given their complexity and errors in previously documented genealogies.

If Dr Norris belongs to any of them, it is most likely to be the Norrises of Blackrod. Though Thomas – his Christian name – was born in Hull in 1789, his father, William, was from Bolton. Thomas married Eliza Pilkington, a native of that town, in her local parish church in 1820. By that time, he was qualified and established as a doctor, like his father before him. He had trained at Edinburgh – one of a handful of elite institutions able to issue medical degrees – and set up his practice in Liverpool.[2] On March 10th 1822, Thomas and Eliza's first child, Eliza Jane, was born in Chester and baptised four months later at St Mary's Church, Ratcliffe, near Bolton, by the Rector there, Thomas Foxley, who was also Thomas Norris's uncle.

The following year, a son – John Pilkington Norris – was born. It is a sign that the family was becoming increasingly settled in Chester that he was baptised at Holy Trinity in the city. In 1825, a third and final child – William Foxley Norris – arrived, being baptised in the same church as his brother. Holy Trinity Parish Registers describe the father in both cases as a 'Doctor of Medicine'. He was also entered in the Index of Physicians and Surgeons as 'Thomas Norris MD, Chester'.[3]

In the year of our book club, he was engaged in critically important work in the field of infection prevention and control. Not three decades earlier, Edward Jenner had developed the world's first ever vaccine in the form of a cowpox antidote to smallpox, a disease which was responsible for the deaths of an estimated ten per cent of the global population. In towns and cities, depending partly on sanitary conditions, this figure could rise to as much as 20 per cent.

Chester had an enviable reputation in this area, mainly because of the pioneering work done at the infirmary under Dr John Haygarth in the last three decades of the 18th century to prevent the outbreak and spread of fever. Thomas Norris's interest in it may have attracted him to the city. By 1824, there was confidence in Jenner's findings, including on the part of the Royal College of Physicians, who had supported his work, but it was not until 1840 and the passing of the Vaccination Act that the medical establishment signalled its approval for the cowpox solution en masse. As Jenner had died in 1823, it was left to others to continue to put the case in its favour.

Thomas based his treatment and recommendations to his peers in the profession on forensic studies of large samples of patients. One letter he wrote to the *Chester Chronicle* in October 1824 talks of his having reviewed and analysed almost 1,200 cases related to smallpox amongst children and found that those with the clearest evidence of effective vaccination with cowpox had the highest immunity to the disease.[4]

He was also deeply concerned about conditions at the infirmary, which were not conducive to the restoration of health or the avoidance of infection from within the building. In another letter of the following month, in which improvement plans were discussed, he stated:

It is manifest to even an occasional visitor that the construction of the Infirmary is faulty – that the area is a well of stagnant air, the ventilation imperfect, and the size of the wards out all useful proportion to the number of patients, that the baths and other comforts dependent on an abundance of water are wanted and that the shop department and other offices need much alteration and improvement ... With respect to the classification and separation of patients, and all matters of internal economy, there is enough to engage the serious attention of the friends of the sick poor.

The subtext of the full letter is that improvement plans should be directed towards patient care, regardless of status or means, rather than the embellishment of the building, for which some influential stakeholders were lobbying. Passionate about his argument and unashamed of being identified with it, he closed the letter thus:

When I sat down to this paper, it was not my intention to send it forth with my proper signature – but my respect for the ability and industry which have already been displayed by the Committee and my general dislike of anonymous communications on serious matters induce me to acknowledge myself.
Yours,
Thomas Norris,
Nicholas-street, Nov. 3rd.[5]

It was common practice for correspondents in those days to vent their spleen from beneath a cloak of anonymity, but Thomas was cut from a different cloth. His approach, founded on strong personal integrity and professional credibility, was bold and energetic. Influential as he was, he is not regarded amongst the first rank of medical men who practised at the infirmary in Chester – that accolade justly goes to men such as Haygarth and Thackeray. However, he wasn't seeking the approbation of posterity; his sole focus was the welfare of the patients in his care.

Despite the importance and gravity of his work in and around 1824, Thomas was still able season it with a little amusement. We are well acquainted with his role at the book club and we have seen how he attended Mrs Mainwaring's masquerade as Sir Thomas Testy, a character from *The Comforts of Human Life*, the book he recommended for Mrs Potts. Local press reports were complimentary about the way in which he carried this character off, suggesting he had some theatrical zeal and social flair.

We know from the published correspondence that the Norrises lived in one of the upmarket late 18th century town houses built by Joseph Turner on Nicholas Street. Popular with doctors, they were long referred to as 'pill-box promenade'. The Norrises were cheek-by-jowl with Anne Glynne, Elizabeth Sloughter and the Humberstons, as well as being a short distance from their mutual friends in Stanley Place and King Street. They maintained their family connections in Bolton too. Thomas's sister, Sophia, was described as 'of this parish' when she married in Radcliffe in 1826. Nor had they been forgotten in Hull either. When Thomas's mother died near Bury in 1832, she was referred to in the *Hull Packet* newspaper as 'the relict of the late William Norris Esq MD of this place'.[6]

By 1841, the Norrises had left Chester and taken a house in Rugby, where John and William were being educated. The boys would have come under the tutelage of Thomas Arnold and George Cotton and studied alongside Henry Venables. Also at the school, completing his secondary education, was Matthew Arnold, the headmaster's son, who would go on to become one of the best-known English poets of all time. By now, Thomas was in his early 50s and, having completed his life's work, was investing in his children. The census shows him to have been of 'independent means'.

By the late 1840s, John and William had graduated from Oxbridge and were beginning to forge their own careers. John had become an inspector of schools in the Home Counties and would later enter the ministry. William took holy orders at the first opportunity, starting out as a curate at various locations in and around London. Both brothers were the authors of esteemed religious works, which would have been career-enhancing for them.[7] William's *Lays of the Early English Church* is still available today.

Thomas and Eliza, it seems, continued to follow their children south because, in the censuses of 1851 and 1861, they are shown as living in Weybridge, Surrey. In both cases, Thomas describes himself as a Doctor of Medicine from Edinburgh University, not practising. They have a cook, housemaid and footman living with them and, though Eliza Jane is with friends in Northampton in 1851, she is back living with them in 1861 as a 39-year-old unmarried lady.

Two years later, on 29th July 1863, Thomas passed away quietly at Weybridge at the age of 73, after enjoying a long period of retirement. He appointed his widow sole executrix over his estate, valued at £6,000. Eliza lived on for another six years, conveying the estate, unchanged in value, to her children. John is the only one mentioned in probate records, where he is described as 'The Reverend John Pilkington Norris of the Abbey House in the City of Bristol, Clerk Canon of Bristol Cathedral … one of the executors'.

The fact is, both sons' careers were on a strong upward trajectory within the Anglican Church. Some time later, on 29th December 1891, a notice appeared in the *Morning Post*:

The Queen has been pleased to approve the appointment of the Ven. John Pilkington Norris, DD, Archdeacon of Bristol, to be Dean of Chichester. The new dean was educated at Trinity College, Cambridge, and graduated BA in 1846, having obtained first class in the Classical Tripos. He became MA in 1849, and DD in 1881. He took Deacon's orders in 1849 and was ordained priest in 1850. From 1877 to 1882 he was vicar of St Mary's Redcliffe, Bristol, and became Archdeacon of Bristol in 1881. Dr Norris is the author of several learned theological works.

Tragically, on the evening of his ordination at Chichester, he died of a bronchial condition. The obituaries, warm and generous, began the following day. In some cases, they also covered the achievements of his four sons, which was some measure of his own success in life. The first, Stephen Leslie, was a captain in the Royal Engineers; next was Edward

John, a vicar in Reading; third came Hugh Littleton, a painter; and, finally, Francis Lush-ington, a missionary in north China.[8] John is buried and commemorated in Bristol Cathedral, which he had a hand in developing during his tenure there.

The Reverend William Foxley Norris, Thomas's second son, born in Chester like his siblings, lived on until 1906. He had been Vicar of Buckingham from 1862 to 1879, when he was presented by the Bishop of Oxford to the vicarage of Witney, a benefice he retained until 1904. Here he worked with Sir Giles Gilbert Scott on the reconstruction of the church. He lived out his last couple of years in Lechlade, a small market town on the edge of the Cotswolds.

He had a son, also called William Foxley Norris, who became an even more prominent churchman. He was born in 1859, and so was known for a few short years to his grandfather Thomas. Rising through the ecclesiastical ranks, he became Dean of York in 1917, before being appointed to Westminster in 1925. In this capacity, he played a leading role in the coronation of George VI, on May 12th 1937. Though he discharged his duty ably, he was not well at the time. After further deterioration in his condition, he died on 28th September of the same year and was buried in Westminster Abbey.

On top of William's abilities in office, obituaries pointed to his skills as an artist and businessman – not always compatible, but they were in him. Some carried the erroneous line, 'He was born at Speke (Lancashire), and was titular head of the Speke Hall estates, which date from the 14th century.' This had to be retracted when the error was highlighted.[9] By this time, the Norris family of Speke was besmirched by its historical involvement in the transatlantic slave trade, as mentioned in Chapter One.

Following the same direct line from Thomas, we come to Christopher Neil Foxley Norris, his two times great-grandson. A fighter pilot in the Second World War, he was awarded the Distinguished Service Order for his many gallant sorties. His illustrious career continued until 1974, by which time he had been knighted and achieved the rank of air chief marshal. Between 1979 and 1989 he was Chairman of FOREST, the UK pro-smoking lobby group, which may not have met with Thomas's approval had he been around to witness it. He also held the chair of the Leonard Cheshire Foundation from 1982 until his death in 2003.[10] Leonard Cheshire – born in Hoole, Chester in 1917 – had been at Oxford and in the RAF with Christopher and the two remained in contact throughout their lives.

Eliza Jane Norris, though first born, outlived both her brothers. She settled in Weybridge, as we have seen, and made that place her home almost until her dying day. Census records from her later years show her living on her own means, with income from rents and shares. She was alone for the most part, except for a clutch of domestic servants. By 1911 she had been joined by her sister-in-law, Edith Grace Norris, widow of John and 14 years her junior. Now 89, she also had a nurse to attend to the needs and infirmities of age. She died the following year at the property in Lechlade, which remained in the family, distributing her effects amongst her nephews and great-nephews. Comfortably off but denied the education and opportunities that her brothers had enjoyed, she led a quiet, pious life until the end.

Epilogue

In May 1829, an elderly man, lame and partially sighted, was escorted to a police station in east London. Soon he was being interviewed by an officer with a thick northern accent. The man was William Parkinson, formerly of Dunham-on-the-Hill, and the officer, George Burgess, formerly Chief of Chester Police and now serving in Macclesfield. For Parkinson, the game was up; even a bail hearing was beyond his means. There was a neat symmetry to Burgess's involvement at both ends of the case, but, on a practical level, it would also have assisted in the identification process. Obligingly, Parkinson still had at his lodgings the bayonet with which he had dealt the fatal blow five years earlier.[1]

The sorry details of the case were laid out before the Grand Jury at the next Chester Assizes. During the agonising three days before his death, the victim, Joseph Fletcher, had provided a declaration alleging murder from three bayonet stabs. He stated that he had gone to pay his respects to Martha Parkinson, but that her father had objected, which led to a verbal altercation that soon escalated. Martha attended the courtroom in deep mourning attire, suggesting she had some feeling for the deceased.

Parkinson, in his defence, outlined the pressure of his family circumstances. At the time of the incident, his wife was infirm and he had a son, whom he described as 'a poor lunatic', chained up in an adjoining room. He added that he feared for his own life. This resonated with the jury, who returned a guilty verdict but recommended mercy. The charge having already been reduced from murder to manslaughter, he was spared the drop. He was also excused transportation on the grounds of his age, which was given as 80. The sentence pronounced was two years' imprisonment.[2]

Another local man who had been caught up in violence was James Forshaw, the much-publicised victim of rioting at election time in 1824. It seems that fundraising on his behalf initially bore fruit. By 1826, he was advertising his own services as a bookseller on Eastgate Street Row. Specifically, he was seeking copies of Ormerod's *History*.[3] In the 1841 and 1851 censuses he is listed as a bookbinder and bookseller – challenging work for a man with little or no eyesight. He was living humbly, with a dependent family, just off Watergate Street. By the 1860s he was destitute and in the Chester workhouse, where he died, aged 72, during an outbreak of cholera in 1866. He is buried at Overleigh Cemetery.[4]

Other Chester characters that we have come across met with contrasting fortunes. Mercy Tomlinson – the popular and award-winning innkeeper and coach operator at the Feathers Hotel – was nevertheless declared bankrupt in July 1826.[5] Mr Willoughby of the Royal Hotel fared better, despite his costly legal battle with Earl Grosvenor. Perhaps it was this that forced him to postpone his retirement and continue in the business until the early 1840s. A leading light in the masonic movement, he may also have enlisted its support when times were tough. The tenancy was advertised in the *Courant* on 18th May 1841, emphasising the healthy state of trade and high-quality reputation. George Johnson of Eccleston was the agent. Mr Willoughby's will, drafted in 1843 and witnessed by Philip Stapleton Humberston, shows some accumulation of assets, including hotel and ferry interests in Birkenhead. He died in 1850, aged 84, still very much in credit.

On 17th January 1825, Catherine Windham Sadler of Hanover Street, Liverpool was baptised – the daughter of a famous father whom she would never see. She died even younger than he did, aged 18 in 1843. The balloonist's son, John, born in 1823, lived until 1912. He called his eldest son William Windham Sadler in memory of his father. John was a surveyor, and his children worked in insurance and accountancy. The family business was consigned to history.

Some of the major infrastructure projects featured in these pages moved towards completion. The Act for erecting the new bridge over the Dee passed through both houses of Parliament in June 1825.[6] The foundation stone was laid in 1827 and the grand opening took place in 1832, as we have seen. In 1826, ribbons were cut on Thomas Telford's bridges at Conway and the Menai Strait, the latter being the world's first major suspension bridge. All three of these structures are Grade I listed and remain in use today. The proposed route of the Liverpool to Birmingham railway, cutting through Chester, did not materialise. By the time the Grand Junction Railway company formed in the early 1830s, a Liverpool to Manchester line was already in place, so it made sense to run the line further east to link these three major cities. The railways arrived in Chester in 1840, whilst the current station dates from 1848.

The electoral system, so contentious and illiberal, was about to change. By the time the Great Reform Bill was passed in 1832, the freemen of Chester had already had their wings clipped. In 1827 their exclusive right to trade in the city was removed, aligning them with almost every other freeman in the country.[7] By tradition, Chester was reactionary, and radicals received short shrift. Thomas Paine had been burnt in effigy at The Cross in 1793 and Henry Hunt was abused during a private visit in 1823. The *Chester Guardian*, founded in 1817, limped along for five lean years before folding due to lack of interest in its radical agenda.[8] Whilst the 1832 legislation introduced more representative constituencies and broadened the franchise, it fell far short of true democracy. Campaigners such as the Blomfield sisters still had to battle for their rights, and it would be well into the 20th century before women got the vote.

Another piece of legislation from 1832 was the Forgery Abolition of Punishment of Death Act, which would have spared Henry Fauntleroy had been it in place eight years earlier. Other crimes such as horse stealing and robbery were declassified as capital offences in the 1830s. Public hangings were outlawed in 1868, the same year in which the last convict ship sailed to Australia. The use of the treadmill remained in place in British prisons until 1902 and floggings continued until the 1940s.

The Roman Catholic Relief Act of 1829 was a major landmark towards Catholic emancipation, removing barriers to high public office based on faith alone. It had been a long-drawn-out process, however, and resentment in Ireland was already at a high pitch. It also provided no escape route from impoverishment or other forms of oppression. The privations of the 1820s and 1830s led mercilessly on to the Irish Potato Famine of the late 1840s and early 1850s, with its devastating loss of life and mass migration. Home Rule for Ireland was much debated in Parliament in the late 19th and early 20th centuries, William Gladstone being a strong advocate. When its implementation was ultimately impeded by the First World War, insurrection broke out in Ireland. Independence and partition soon followed. Sectarian divisions still exist today, most notably in Ulster.

It would be too much to follow up on every thread of interest overseas, but one or two should not pass without comment.

The bodies of the King and Queen of the Sandwich Islands were repatriated in early 1825, aboard a British vessel. This was taken as an opportunity to extend the work of the Bible Society by ensuring the crew conveyed a powerful message in favour of the spread of Christianity amongst the islanders. By the end of the decade, missionaries were reporting that almost one third of the 150,000 inhabitants had been converted.[9] Before the vessel reached its destination, the journey had claimed another casualty. An official who had travelled to England with the king and queen and who had charge of their bodies, died of smallpox. Though his body was preserved, it was not allowed ashore and was given a respectful burial at sea.[10] There had been a strong awareness of the dangers of imported diseases – borne out of bitter experience – since the arrival of Captain James Cook in 1778. The Russian threat to the islands was not followed through, though their belligerence persisted in other parts of the world. The Hawaiian Islands, as the archipelago soon became known, remained autonomous until annexation by the United States of America in the 1890s.

The Greek War of Independence lasted until 1829, resulting in secession from the Ottoman Empire. Hostilities had opened up in 1827 between the Russians and the Turks, who were unable to sustain war on two fronts. Lord Byron had not died in vain, and Thomas Leche Massie had played his part too.

In India, nationalist sentiment was also gathering pace. Localised rebellions of the 17th and early 18th centuries were dwarfed by large-scale mutiny in 1857 to 1858. We recall how Edward Venables met his end in Chapter Twenty-Three. The mutiny was brutally suppressed and direct control of the country transferred to the British Government from the East India Company, which was now in its final death throes. It was not until after the Second World War that India gained its independence. The office of Bishop of Calcutta, of which we have heard much, still exists today.

Looking west, what else can be said about the slave trade? It was so extensive and so iniquitous that it is impossible to know whether its stain will ever be removed. The Act for the Abolition of Slavery throughout the British Colonies of 1833 was a major milestone, though formerly enslaved people continued to be exploited. They had little in the way of resources and received no financial support, other than subsistence wages for the same back-breaking work. Compensation went to their 'owners', a cynical expedient that was deemed necessary to avoid deadlock. As we have seen, large cash payments were made to families whose biggest challenge for generations had been how to convert plantation riches into other stable assets. Descendants and old-established institutions which had supported the system grapple with how best to respond in the modern day. The origins of much of the racial inequality and activism in our society are not difficult to ascertain.

Finally, we return directly to the Chester Book Club, 1824. We know that it was a friendship group and that members were connected in other ways. Those who survived into the 1830s and 1840s continued to socialise together and pursue common interests; the grand society balls at the Royal Hotel are a good example. Some of the relationships between families go back many centuries. It is therefore no surprise to see that these continued, sometimes intimately, beyond the era of the book club. The marriage between Thomas Leche Massie and Charlotte Hester Townshend in 1844 is a case in point. In 1845, when Dean Anson appealed for funds for 'repainting, restoring and enlarging the Cathedral Church', members of the Glynne, Humberston, Johnson, Massie, Panton, Potts and Townshend families dug deep in support of this great cause.[11] Most of them were represented at the funeral of his successor, Dean Howson, forty years later, by which time the restoration work was almost complete.[12]

We should not lose sight of the fact that the people in whom we are interested were, by and large, near neighbours. It is a short hop from Whitefriars to Nicholas Street and, from there, to Watergate Street, Stanley Place and King Street. This was, and still is, a fashionable part of town and Chester is a compact city. It would have been easy to meet at one of their houses, even when age and infirmity began to limit their mobility. Though much destruction and development has occurred in the meantime, most of these thoroughfares are remarkably well-preserved. Stand at the top of King Street, for instance, and you are looking at Georgian houses either side of a gently sweeping cobbled street. Hear the clatter of hooves and carriages, smell the hops from the adjacent brewery, pick out a figure in their Regency finery – perhaps with a book pressed under their arm – and you are centre-stage in our drama.

Most of our bibliophiles were not from Chester but chose to live in the city all the same. We have talked much about crime, disorder, dirt and disease, yet there was something transcendent that outweighed all of these deterrents. Something more intangible, that has to do with the feel and character of the place. James Boswell experienced it and so did they: an energy and aesthetic appeal, alongside a deep well of impenetrable history, that stirs the senses and awakes the enquiring mind.

There was camaraderie too, perhaps a little contained and exclusive in our case, but no less wholesome for that. Whilst people supported and comforted each other in practical ways, they were also a mutual source of entertainment. With only intermittent public offerings, they made their own fun. Dr Norris at the book club is an understated example, whereas Mrs Mainwaring's masquerades were the high point of the social calendar. Imagine being out of town that day.

They were also conscious that their very privilege came with an obligation to look across society as a whole. When parishes struggled to provide for the needy – which they mostly did – people such as these stepped into the breach, free from snobbery or pretension. We have seen so many examples of great philanthropy, unsolicited and unconditional. When cruelty and conflict command the headlines, it is important to remember that there is an immutable strain of pure altruism that runs through humanity, all of the time.

We don't know whether the book club served a charitable purpose, but there is a real possibility that it did. Perhaps one reason it was such an insubstantial pageant was that members found other outlets for their benevolent instincts. They attended charity balls and church bazaars, and friendly societies were starting to come into their own. Of course, there was movement and mortality too. Mrs Coupland relocated, as did Dr Norris somewhat later. Within five years of the solitary meeting of which we are aware, a third of the membership had passed away. As they parted company, they took with them the satisfaction of knowing that they had bonded over books.

There is one last detail to add. In 1937, a solicitor called Thomas Catt Hughes found a scrap of paper in his home in Lancaster. It contained a note written many years earlier by his father, Thomas Hughes, first editor of *The Cheshire Sheaf*, which was still in production. This gentleman was a subscriber and wrote in to disclose its contents. It was a key to the identities of long-deceased contributors, which had been the topic of recent speculation. 'H', who first publicised the existence of the Chester Book Club, 1824, was revealed to have been Anne Humberston, daughter of Catherine, of Newton Hall, Chester.[13]

Notes

Introduction

1. Wording features as part of *The Cheshire Sheaf* title page

2. *The Cheshire Sheaf*, 1ˢᵗ Series, Vol. 2, p57

3. Strictly speaking, the Regency lasted from 1811 to 1820, when George, Prince of Wales was appointed Prince Regent to discharge royal duties following the relapse of his father, George III, into mental illness. However, most academics, writers and historians take the period to span the years 1789 to 1830, ranging from the French Revolution and the first onset of the king's illness to the death of George IV, and that is how it is treated here.

4. *www.atlasobscura.com*

5. *A Walk Around the Walls and City of Chester*, p82, Broster, J

6. *History of the City of Chester from its Foundation to the Present Time*, Vol. 2, P190, Hemingway, J

7. Listed as 'Booksellers and Stationers', these are: John Broster, The Exchange; C W Leadbeater, Eastgate Street Row; John Parry, Bridge Street Row; Poole and Harding, Eastgate Street Row; John Seacombe, Bridge Street Row; John Tushingham, Eastgate Street Row

Chapter One

1. *www.regencyhistory.net*

2. *Landed Gentry of Great Britain and Ireland*, p1279, Burke, E

3. *The Warburtons of Arley Hall*, p1, Warburton, R

4. *www.mountbarkerwa.com.au*

5. *The Warburtons of Arley Hall*, p62, Warburton, R

6. *www.ddhg.org.uk/hidden-nature/slaughters-rough*

7. *www.chesterwalls.info*

8. *The Cheshire Sheaf*, Series 31, Vol. 3, p71

9. *www.nationalarchives.gov.uk/currency-converter/#currency*

10. *The Cheshire Sheaf*, Series 4, Vol. 11, p28 and Series 3, Vol. 20, p44

11. Cheshire Archives and Local Studies, Ref. ZCHD/6/33

12. National Army Museum

13. National Library of Wales, *Glansevern Estate Records*, Ref. 4614

14. Ormskirk and District Family History Society

15. National Library of Wales, *Glansevern Estate Records*, Refs. 4626-4662

16. ibid., Ref. 4611

17. www.*chesterwalls.info*

18. *Chester Chronicle*, 6th January 1804

19. National Library of Wales, *Glansevern Estate Records*, Ref. 4559

20. *www.slavevoyages.org*

21. *The Slave Streets of Liverpool,* Hearn, D

22. National Museums Liverpool: Maritime Archives and Library: Ref. D/EARLE

23. ibid., Ref. D/EARLE/13/2

24. Ormskirk and District Family History Society

25. National Museums Liverpool: Maritime Archives and Library: Ref. D/EARLE/13/2

26. ibid., Ref. D/EARLE/7/4

27. ibid., Ref. D/EARLE/2/2

28. ibid., Ref. D/EARLE/9/1/8

29. *Gore's Liverpool General Advertiser*, 30th October 1823

30. *Law Chronicle*, 26th July 1832

31. *Liverpool Mercury*, 11th December 1818

32. ibid., Ref. D/EARLE/10/1/7

33. *Magna Britannia*, Vol. 2, Part II, p623, Lysons

34. *A Genealogical and Heraldic History of the Commoners of Great Britain and Ireland,*
Vol. 2, pp380-381, Burke, J

35. *www.historyofparliamentonline.org*

36. National Library of Wales, *Papers of Captain William Owen, RN*

37. *Dead Men Do Not Sell Timber*, National Genealogical Society Quarterly 101, pp175-188,
Peterson, A R

38. *Dictionary of Canadian Biography*, Vol. 6, Ingersoll, L K

39. *www.historyofparliamentonline.org*

40. *Dictionary of Canadian Biography*, Vol. VIII, Cornell, P G

41. *The History of The City of Chester*, p415, Hemingway, J

42. *www.wrexham-history.com*

43. *www.georgianera.wordpress.com*

44. National Library of Wales, *Glansevern Estate Records*, Refs. 7994-7997

45. ibid., Refs. 8001-8006

46. ibid., Refs. 7031-7033

47. *www.parliament.uk*

48. National Library of Wales, *Glansevern Estate Records*, Ref. 7987

49. ibid., Refs. 7055-7037

50. ibid., Refs. 6840-6841

51. ibid., Refs. 7452-7495

52. National Museums Liverpool: memorial to William Earle

53. *Liverpool Albion,* 25th March 1839

54. National Library of Wales, *Glansevern Estate Records*, Ref. 8772

55. *The Spectator*, 4th January 1913

56. National Library of Wales, *Glansevern Estate Records*, Ref. 6904

57. National Library of Wales, *Glansevern Estate Records*, Ref. 6864

58. *Caernarvon and Denbigh Herald,* 10th August 1861

59. *www.welshpoollanding.com*

60. *Chester Courant*, 20th August 1856

61. *www.genuki.org.uk/big/wal/Archives/NLWjournals/GreatLandowners,* James, B

Chapter Two

1. *History of the City of Chester from its Foundation to the Present Time*, Vol. 2, p283, Hemingway, J

2. *1815: Regency Britain in the Year of Waterloo*, p209, Bates, S

3. *The Time Travellers Guide to Regency Britain*, pp18-19, Mortimer, I

4. *The Regency Revolution*, pp78-79, Morrison R

5. *Chester Courant,* 13th January 1824

6. *The Time Travellers Guide to Regency Britain*, pp150-151, Mortimer, I

7. *1815: Regency Britain in the Year of Waterloo*, p250-251, Bates, S

Chapter Three

1. *A Walk Around the Walls and City of Chester*, p24, Broster, J

2. By Thomas Ravencroft of Pickhill, *The Dictionary of Welsh Biography* online, Jenkins, R T

3. *Old Chester*, p123, Crickmore, H H

4. *The Cheshire Sheaf*, Series 1, Vol. 2, p92

5. ibid., pp110-111

6. *The Dictionary of National Biography*, Vol. 8, pp16-17

7. *The Cheshire Sheaf*, Series 3, Vol. 35, p42

8. ibid., Series 1, Vol. 1, p141

9. www.*historyofparliamentonline.org*

10. *Old Chester*, p118, Crickmore, H H

11. *The Cheshire Sheaf*, Series 3, Vol. 22, p21

12. *www.historypoints.org*

13. *The Cheshire Sheaf*, Series 1, Vol. 1, p248

14. ibid., Series 3, Vol. 22, p21

15. ibid., Series 3, Vol. 32, p103

16. *The Time Travellers Guide to Regency Britain*, pp30-31, Mortimer, I

17. *Catherine Gladstone*, pp1-7, Drew, M

18. *Mrs Catherine Gladstone*, p5, Hilderley, J

19. *History of the City of Chester from its Foundation to the Present Time*, Vol. 2, p260, Hemingway, J

20. *The Cheshire Sheaf*, Series 3, Vol. 10, p93

21. *Catherine Gladstone*, p8, Drew, M

22. ibid., p12

Chapter Four

1. *Chester Courant,* 3rd February 1824

2. www.*chesterwalls.info*

3. *The Continuing Story of 'Mad Jack' Mytton – Number One London*

4. *Roberts' Chester Guide*, p137

5. *Chester Courant,* 3rd February 1824

Chapter Five

1. Cheshire Bishops' Transcripts, 1576-1933

2. *www.ucl.ac.uk*

3. *History of the County Palatine and City of Chester*, Vol. 3, p905, Ormerod, G

4. *Chester Chronicle*, 29th November 1799

5. *Holy Trinity Parish Registers,* 1532-1837

6. *History of the City of Chester from its Foundation to the Present Time*, Vol. 2, p256, Hemingway, J

7. *History of the Ancient City of Chester*, p242, Fenwick, G L

8. He was satirised as such by William Makepeace Thackeray in the character of Sir George Tufto in *The Book of Snobs*, published in 1848

9. *The Poole Family of Poole Hall on the Wirral*, pp194-195, Poole, M E

A painting of Poole Hall, accompanied by some brief history, hangs in the Grosvenor Museum, Chester.

10. *Chester Courant,* 21st January 1817

11. *Chester Courant,* 31st October 1809

12. *The Cheshire Sheaf*, Series 3, Vol. 10, p23

13. *The Time Travellers Guide to Regency Britain*, pp317-319, Mortimer, I

14. *www.naomiclifford.com/horace-cotton-ordinary-newgate*

15. *www.peterberthoud.co.uk/post/the-newgate-prison*

16. *www.historyofparliamentonline.org/ History of the City of Chester from its Foundation to the Present Time*, Vol. 2, p417, Hemingway, J

17. *History of the City of Chester from its Foundation to the Present Time*, Vol. 2, p268, Hemingway, J

18. *Australian Dictionary of Biography* online

19. *The Complete Letters of Henry James* 1876-1878, Vol.1, p94

20. *Chester Courant,* 15ᵗʰ January 1828

21. *The Interest*, pp207-217, Taylor, M

22. *blogs.bl.uk/music/2012/08/wandering-minstrels.html* – The British Library: The Wandering Minstrels – The Story of a Forgotten Victorian Orchestra

23. *Chester Chronicle*, 24ᵗʰ July 1829

24. For a detailed account of the Humberstons' time at Newton Hall, please refer to the author's previous work, *A Short History of Newton Hall, Chester*

25. *The Cheshire Sheaf*, Series 3, Vol. 20, p345

26. *Dictionary of National Biography*, Vol.4, p1227

27. *Tom Brown's Schooldays*, pp211-212, Hughes, T (OUP, 2008). The author is not to be confused with Thomas Hughes, FSA of Chester (1826-1890)

28. *Dictionary of National Biography*, Vol.4, pp1228-1229

29. *The Windows of the Cloister,* Chester Cathedral, p249

30. *History of the Ancient City of Chester*, p244, Fenwick, G

Chapter Six

1. *Chester Courant,* 16ᵗʰ March 1824

2. ibid., 30ᵗʰ March 1824

3. *www.historyofparliamentonline.org*

4. *Chester Courant,* 16ᵗʰ March 1824

5. *www.timetravel-britain.com*

6. *A Regency Visitor*, pp282-283, Pückler-Muskau, H

7. *Chester Courant,* 2ⁿᵈ March 1824

8. ibid., 23ʳᵈ March 1824

9. ibid., 30ᵗʰ March 1824

Chapter Seven

1. *History of the Ancient City of Chester*, p422, Fenwick, G

2. *The Cheshire Sheaf*, Series 3, Vol. 49, pp123-125

3. *The Cheshire Sheaf*, Series 3, Vol. 11, p4

4. *History of the City of Chester from its Foundation to the Present Time*, Vol. 2, p299, Hemingway, J

5. *Chester Courant*, 12ᵗʰ January 1796

6. *Manchester, Mercury*, 9ᵗʰ August 1808

7. *Two Paintings of Liverpool in 1680: A Reassessment*, p1, Tibbles, A

8. *An Account of the Oil Painting 'Liverpool in 1680'*, pp45-64, Stewart-Brown, R

9. *The History of the Island of Antigua*, p392 and 396, Oliver, V L

10. *An Account of the Oil Painting 'Liverpool in 1680'*, p61, Stewart-Brown, R

11. *www.ucl.ac.uk*

12. *England and Wales, Prerogative of Canterbury Wills 1384-1858*

13. *www.liverpoolhistorysociety.org.uk: Vanished Streets: Chorley Street*, 1725-1924, Jones, G

14. *An Account of the Oil Painting 'Liverpool in 1680'*, p31, Stewart-Brown, R

15. *Former British Colonial Dependencies, Slave Registers*, 1813-1834, pp617-625

16. *www.ucl.ac.uk*

17. ibid.

18. *Sunderland Daily Echo*, 6ᵗʰ August 1919

19. *Derby Daily Telegraph*, 12ᵗʰ August 1919

20. *University Archives and Records Center* online

21. *History of the County Palatine and City of Chester*, Vol. 1, p115, Ormerod, G

22. *The Cheshire Sheaf*, Series 3, Vol. 35, pp77-78

23. *History of the County Palatine and City of Chester*, Vol. 2, p510, Ormerod, G

24. *Chester Courant*, 15ᵗʰ March 1803

25. *Chester Chronicle*, 3ʳᵈ September 1824

26. *History of the City of Chester from its Foundation to the Present Time*, Vol. 2, P351, Hemingway, J

27. *Chester Chronicle*, 9ᵗʰ April 1830

28. *England and Wales, Prerogative of Canterbury Wills 1384-1858*

29. ibid.

30. *www.whoownsengland.org*

31. *Chester Courant*, 26ᵗʰ November 1845

32. ibid., 28ᵗʰ February 1845

33. ibid., 30ᵗʰ June 1852

34. UK and Ireland Incoming Passenger Lists, London 1936

35. *Horsham Express*, 23rd July 1889

36. *Chester Observer*, 3rd February 1894

Chapter Eight

1. *Chester Courant*, 27th April 1824

2. ibid.

3. ibid., 13th April 1824

4. *Hansard*, Vol. 11, 12th April 1824

5. *Chester Courant*, 6th April 1824

Chapter Nine

1. *The Cheshire Sheaf*, Series 3, Vol. 5, p330

2. Ibid., Series 3, Vol. 2, p84

3. *Dictionary of Canadian Biography* online, Vol. 1, Hunt, E

4. *History of the County Palatine and City of Chester*, Vol. 1, p484, Ormerod, G

5. *Chester, A History*, p73, Ward, S

6. *The Law Society Gazette* online, Morton, J

7. *www.findagrave.com*

8. *A Genealogical and Heraldic History of the Commoners of Great Britain and Ireland*, Vol. 4, p359, Burke, J

9. *England and Wales, Prerogative of Canterbury Wills 1384-1858*

10. *Chester Chronicle*, 14th April 1814

11. *Watergate St - The Rows Research Project*, p33, Brown, A N, Grenville, J C

12. Sedan chairs were a feature of the city at this time and could be hired at Chester Cross. 'Sedan House' on City Walls Road was specifically designed with this form of transport in mind.

13. *Chester Chronicle*, 17th January 1823 and *Chester Courant,* 21st January 1823

14. *The Time Travellers Guide to Regency Britain*, p59, Mortimer, I

15. *Chester Chronicle*, 23rd January 1824

16. *www.oteley.com* and www.parksandgardens.org/places/oteley

17. *www.gwrychcastle.co.uk/history*

18. *Chester Chronicle*, 2nd January 1829

19. ibid., 9th January 1829

20. *England and Wales, Prerogative of Canterbury Wills 1384-1858*

21. *www.glamorgancricketarchives.com*

22. *Herapath's Railway Journal*, 17th May 1845

23. *Birmingham Gazette*, 23rd April 1845

24. *North Wales Chronicle*, 8th August 1857

25. *Wrexham Advertiser*, 27th November 1883

26. *www.sl.nsw.gov.au/stories/hunter-valley*

27. *www.scribd.com*

28. *Regency Cheshire*, p103, Wilkes, S

29. *The Cheshire Sheaf*, Series 3, Vol. 45, p37

30. *History of the City of Chester from its Foundation to the Present Time*, Vol. 2, p268, Hemingway, J

31. *Chester Chronicle*, 24th April 1831

32. UK Foreign and Overseas Register of British Subjects 1628-1969

33. *The Daily Post*, 19th January 1860

Chapter Ten

1. *Chester Courant*, 4th May 1824

2. *The Cheshire Sheaf*, Series 3, Vol. 1, p73

3. *Chester Courant*, 11th May 1824

4. ibid., 4th May 1824

5. ibid., 18th May 1824

6. ibid., 11th May 1824

7. ibid., 18th May 1824

8. *www.regencyhistory.net*

9. *Chester Courant*, 25th May 1824

10. ibid., 1st June 1824

11. *Cheshire History*, No. 62, pp42-66

Chapter Eleven

1. *The Cheshire Sheaf*, Series 3, Vol. 10, p116

2. *Chester Chronicle*, 11th January 1822

3. *The Cheshire Sheaf*, Series 3, Vol. 39, p54

4. *www.roydenhistory.co.uk*

5. *History of the County Palatine and City of Chester*, Vol. 2, p731, Ormerod, G

6. *www.roydenhistory.co.uk*

7. *Chester Characters*, p33, Wall, B

8. *The Cheshire Sheaf*, Series 2, Vol.1, p171

9. *The Cheshire Sheaf*, Series 3, Vol. 39, p54

10. *Squire and Tenant: Life in Rural Cheshire, 1760-1900*, pp 6-7, Scard, G

11. *www.fitzwalter.com*

12. *The Cheshire Sheaf,* Series 2, Vol. 5, p317

13. *England and Wales, Prerogative of Canterbury Wills 1384-1858*

14. *Chester Chronicle*, 12th January 1827

15. *www.hymnologyarchive.com*

16. *www.fitzwalter.com*

17. *The Cheshire Sheaf,* Series 3, Vol. 43, p32

18. *Edinburgh Evening News,* 20th July 1898

19. *www.fitzwalter.com*

20. *Chester Chronicle*, 12th January 1856

21. *www.fitzwalter.com*

22. *East India Register and Directory*, Bengal, p6

23. *www.ucl.ac.uk*

24. *www.findagrave.com*

25. *Sydney Evening News,* 14th September 1883

26. *Chester Chronicle*, 22nd October 1938

27. *Truth*, 26th April 1933

28. *Chester Chronicle*, 28th February 1845

29. *England and Wales National Probate Calendar, 1858-1995*

30. *Beneath the Surface*, Vol. 2, p44, Backford, Mollington and District Local History Society

31. *Old Chester*, pp93 and 99, Crickmore, HH

32. *Reynolds's Newspaper,* 7th June 1914

33. *Coventry Evening Telegraph,* 6th June 1914

34. In March 1915 the *Votes for Women* publication reported on 'Our Wounded in Paris – Men and Women Working Together'. The Hotel Majestic had been transformed into a hospital for critically wounded servicemen. Singled out for special mention amongst the volunteer workforce were Miss Mary Blomfield – who had led the appeal to the king – her mother and her sister, their comfortable Cotswold home a world away. The Rear Admiral was their first cousin, once removed.

Chapter Twelve

1. *Chester Courant*, 29th June 1824

2. ibid., 15th June 1824

3. *John Bull*, 14th June 1824

4. *Chester Courant*, 15th June 1824

5. This institution was first mentioned in the Chester press in 1816

6. From the *Chester Courant,* 8th June 1824, and the *Chester Chronicle,* 11th June 1824

7. From the *Chester Courant,* 15th June 1824, and the *Chester Chronicle,* 18th June 1824

Chapter Thirteen

1. *The Cheshire Sheaf,* Series 3, Vol. 33, p96

2. Ibid., p106

3. *Dublin Weekly Nation,* 10th April 1858

4. *Chester Courant,* 7th October 1800

5. *Bishop's Transcripts, 1576-1933*

6. *History of the County Palatine and City of Chester,* Vol. 2, p367, Ormerod, G

7. *The Cheshire Sheaf,* Series 3, Vol. 7, p18

8. ibid., Series 3, Vol. 57, p32

9. *Chorlton Hall,* p5, Hess J P

10. *Chester Courant,* 26th October 1806

11. As reported by Hemingway, *History of the City of Chester from its Foundation to the Present Time,* Vol. 2, p352

12. *History of the County Palatine and City of Chester,* Vol. 2, p367, Ormerod, G

13. John Rylands Library Manchester, Refs. R.81524:916 to R.81524:925

14. *History of the County Palatine and City of Chester,* Vol. 2, p367, Ormerod, G

15. *Magna Britannia,* Vol. 2, Part 2, Cheshire, p355, Lysons

16. *George Ormerod, Historian of Chester,* p39, Hess J P

17. *Chester Chronicle,* 14th April 1814

18. *History of the City of Chester from its Foundation to the Present Time,* Vol. 2, p271, Hemingway, J

19. *The Cheshire Sheaf,* Series 3, Vol. 33, p96

20. *www.genealogy.com*

Chapter Fourteen

1. *Chester Chronicle,* 6th July 1824 and *Chester Courant,* 23rd July 1824

2. *Chester Chronicle,* 30th July 1824

3. ibid., 6th July 1824

4. These and many other sketches are wonderfully captured in *George Cuitt (1779-1845) – 'England's Piranesi'* by Peter Boughton and Ian Dunn

5. *Chester Chronicle,* 23rd July 1824

6. Drawn from the *Chester Chronicle,* 6th to 30th July 1824

Notes

Chapter Fifteen

1. *Chester Courant,* 8th February 1827

2. *www.boolehistoryheritagesociety.org.uk*

3. *Politics and County Government in Wales - Anglesey 1780-1914*, p36, Griffith, W P

4. *The Dictionary of Welsh Biography online*

5. Barbados Marriages 1643-1800, Vol. 1, p273 and 374

6. *England and Wales, Prerogative of Canterbury Wills 1384-1858*

7. ibid.

8. *Bury and Norwich Post,* 24th September 1824

9. *www.boolehistoryheritagesociety.org.uk*

10. *www.grandtour.amdigital.co.uk*

11. *www.bbc.co.uk/shropshire/content/articles/2007/03/01/slavery_plymley_diaries_feature*

12. *England and Wales, Prerogative of Canterbury Wills 1384-1858*

13. *www.oldbaileyonline.org*

14. *www.boolehistoryheritagesociety.org.uk*

Chapter Sixteen

1. *Chester Chronicle,* 6th August 1824

2. ibid., 20th August 1824

3. ibid., 6th August 1824

4. ibid., 13th August 1824

5. ibid., 20th August 1824

6. ibid.

7. *Chester Chronicle,* 13th August 1824

8. ibid.

9. *Chester Chronicle,* 27th August 1824

10. ibid., 6th August 1824

Chapter Seventeen

1. *The Family Shakespeare* by Thomas Bowdler was released in several editions, the first two of which appeared in 1807 and 1818.

2. *Dr Johnson's Ancestors and Connexions, p423*, Reade, A L

3. *Chester Courant,* 30th March 1824

4. ibid., 13th August 1824

5. *Chester Chronicle,* 17th September 1824

6. ibid., 8ᵗʰ October 1824

7. *The Life of Samuel Johnson*, p1217, Boswell, J

8. *Pearson v Bank of England*, cited as a precedent in the *Law Chronicle*, 28ᵗʰ August 1824

9. *The Life of Samuel Johnson*, p627, p1037 and p1098, Boswell, J

10. *Dr Johnson's Lichfield, p215*, Hopkins, M A

11. *Dr Johnson's Ancestors and Connexions,* p423, Reade, A L

12. *Shakespeare: the 'lost years'*, p102, Honigmann, E J

13. *A Diary of a Journey into North Wales in 1774*, p32, Johnson S

14. *The Cheshire Sheaf*, Series 1, Vol. 1, p10

15. *The Life of Samuel Johnson*, p917, Boswell, J

16. Information board at St Chad's Church, Lichfield

17. *Old Chester*, p55, p59 and p167, Crickmore, H H

18. *Bolton Chronicle* 2ⁿᵈ September 1854 and *Eddowes Shrewsbury Journal* 6ᵗʰ September 1854

19. *The Ipswich Journal*, 26ᵗʰ May, 1860

20. *Dr Johnson's Ancestors and Connexions,* p423, Reade, A L

21. *www.grandnationalultimatehistory.com*

22. *Dictionary of National Biography*, Vol. 2, p952

23. *Hereford Journal*, 4ᵗʰ March 1818

Chapter Eighteen

1. *Chester Chronicle*, 3ʳᵈ September 1824

2. *A Regency Visitor*, pp136-137, Pückler-Muskau, H

3. *Chester Chronicle*, 3ʳᵈ September 1824

4. ibid., 17ᵗʰ September 1824

5. ibid., 24ᵗʰ September 1824

6. *The Time Travellers Guide to Regency Britain*, p18, Mortimer, I

7. *Chester Chronicle*, 17ᵗʰ September 1824

8. ibid., 24ᵗʰ September 1824

Chapter Nineteen

1. *Pallot's Marriage Index*, 1780-1837

2. *The Leeds Intelligencer*, 16ᵗʰ August 1791

3. *History of the County Palatine and City of Chester*, Vol. 3, p775, Ormerod, G

4. *Magna Britannia*, Vol. 2, Part II, p400, Lysons

5. *History of the County Palatine of and Duchy of Lancaster,* Vol. 2, p109, Baines, E

Notes

6. *London Courier and Evening Gazette*, 19th September 1835

7. *www.boltongenealogica.blogspot.com*

8. *The Cheshire Sheaf*, Series 3, Vol. 12, p67

9. *England and Wales, Prerogative of Canterbury Wills 1384-1858*

10. *Chester Courant*, 28th February 1792

11. *Chester, A History*, pp80 and 81, Ward, S

12. ibid., pp88-89

13. *Chester Chronicle*, 9th October 1795

14. *The Cheshire Sheaf*, Series 3, Vol. 36, p32 and p41

15. A notice in the *Chester Courant*, 6th March 1798 being one example

16. *Chester Chronicle*, 16th March 1798

17. *The Cheshire Sheaf*, Series 3, Vol. 6, p81

18. *Landlord Control and Motivation in the Parliamentary Enclosure of St. Mary's-on-the-Hill Parish, Chester*, p96, Higson, P J W

19. *Old and Odd Memories*, p209, Tollemache, L

20. *The Cheshire Observer*, 20th March 1937, under the headline 'Hero of First Grand National', following centenary celebrations at Aintree

21. *Grace's Guide to British Industrial History* online

22. *www.natwestgroup.com*

23. *www.britishlistedbuildings.co.uk*

24. *England and Wales, Prerogative of Canterbury Wills 1384-1858*

25. *The Life of Samuel Johnson*, p915, Boswell, J

26. *Chester Courant*, 15th June 1898

27. *The Cheshire Sheaf*, Series 3, Vol. 9, p63

28. *www.christleton.org.uk*

29. *England and Wales National Probate Calendar, 1858-1995*

30. *The Cheshire Sheaf*, Series 3, Vol. 9, p111

31. *The History of the County Palatine of Chester*, p212, J H Hanshall and *The Cheshire Sheaf*, Series 3, Vol. 44, p59

32. *Chester Chronicle*, 16th July 1824

33. ibid., 20th August 1824

34. ibid., 3rd September 1824

35. ibid., 17th December 1824

36. National Archives, Ref. HO 7/2

37. *Chester Courant*, 3rd May 1831

38. *Chester Chronicle*, 13th September 1832

39. *Liverpool Mail*, 22nd November 1845

40. *England and Wales National Probate Calendar, 1858-1995* and *Cheshire Sheaf*, Series 2, Vol. 1, p85

41. *Chester Chronicle*, 23rd October 1846

42. *Magna Britannia*, Vol. 2, Part II, p431, Lysons

43. *Chester Courant*, 5th March 1839

Chapter Twenty

1. *Chester Chronicle*, 29th October 1824

2. ibid.

3. ibid., 22nd October 1824

4. ibid., 8th October 1824

5. ibid., 29th October 1824

6. *The Time Travellers Guide to Regency Britain*, p353, Mortimer, I

7. *Chester Chronicle*, 15th and 22nd October 1824

8. ibid., 29th October 1824

9. ibid.

Chapter Twenty-One

1. *www.findagrave.com*

2. *History of the City of Chester from its Foundation to the Present Time*, Vol. 2, P13, Hemingway, J

3. *Old Chester*, p17, Crickmore, H H

4. *England and Wales National Probate Calendar, 1858-1995*

5. National Archives Ref. E18/740/7/14C

6. *www.thoughtco.com*

7. Extracted from the Abstract of *Poland's Last King and English Culture*, Butterwick, R

8. *Curiouser and Curiouser*, blog post from Cheshire Archives and Local Studies

9. *Chester Courant*, 19th May 1818

10. *The Cheshire Sheaf*, Series 3, Vol. 25, p35

11. *History of the City of Chester from its Foundation to the Present Time*, Vol. 2, p245, Hemingway, J

12. *www.historyofparliamentonline.org*

13. *Chester Courant*, 17th May 1831

14. *England and Wales National Probate Calendar, 1858-1995*

15. *Chester Courant*, 1st September 1831 and 2nd April 1832

16. *The Cheshire Sheaf*, Series 1, Vol. 1, p203

17. *Chester Courant,* 29th November 1831

Chapter Twenty-Two

1. *Chester Courant,* 26th November 1824

2. ibid., 5th November 1824

3. ibid., 26th November 1824

4. ibid.

5. *Chester Chronicle,* 19th November 1824

6. *www.bristolandavonarchaeology.org.uk*

7. *Forgery, Fiscal Trauma, and the Fauntleroy Case*, pp401-415, Malton, S

8. *Chester Chronicle,* 12th November 1824

Chapter Twenty-Three

1. *The Cheshire Sheaf*, Series 3, Vol. 2, p84

2. *Some Account of General Robert Venables of Antrobus and Wincham, Cheshire*, p7, Townshend, L P and Venables, E A L

3. *History of the City of Chester from its Foundation to the Present Time*, Vol. 2, p216, Hemingway, J

4. *Oswestry Advertiser,* 22nd August 1877

5. *www.62ndregiment.org*

6. *www.oswestrygenealogy.org.uk*

7. *England and Wales National Probate Calendar, 1858-1995*

8. *Chester Courant,* 21st January 1823

9. *Oswestry, Advertiser,* 5th October 1870

10. *Dictionary of National Biography* online

11. *www.stsepulchres.org.uk*

12. *Grace's Guide to British Industrial History* online

13. *Lancashire Evening Post,* 6th November 1912

14. *Morning Herald,* 6th February 1846

15. *Manchester Courier,* 10th October 1846

Chapter Twenty-Four

1. *London Courier and Evening Gazette,* 5th September 1825

2. *Chester Chronicle,* 3rd December 1824

3. ibid., 10th December 1824

4. ibid.

5. ibid., 17th December 1824

6. ibid., 24th December 1824

7. ibid., 3rd December 1824

8. *Cheshire Magazine* online

9. *Chester Chronicle*, 3rd December 1824

10. ibid., 31st December 1824

11. ibid., 7th January 1825. There were 25,758 births recorded in 1824, compared with 20,237 deaths, only two of which related to people over a hundred years old.

12. *Chester Chronicle*, 10th December 1824

13. ibid.

14. ibid., 31st December 1824

15. ibid.

Chapter Twenty-Five

1. *The Cheshire Sheaf*, Series 3, Vol. 45, p26 and Vol. 15, p46

2. *Gore's Directory of* Liverpool, 1820 gives his address as 29 Duncan Street, St James. His profession and location are also confirmed in his marriage certificate of the same year.

3. *Holy Trinity Parish Registers*, 1532-1837

4. *Chester Chronicle*, 14th October 1824

5. ibid., 3rd November 1824

6. *Hull Packet*, 6th October 1832

7. *Holy Trinity Parish Registers*, 1532-1837

8. *Gloucester Citizen*, 30th December 1891

9. *The Nottingham Journal*, 29th September 1937 and *The Scotsman*, 30th September 1937

10. *www.rafweb.org*

Epilogue

1. *Chester Chronicle*, 5th June 1829

2. *Trades' Free Press*, 5th September 1829

3. *Chester Chronicle*, 1st December 1826

4. *www.findagrave.com*

5. *Chester Courant*, 18th July 1826

6. *Roberts' Chester Guide*, p136

7. *History of the Ancient City of Chester*, p247, Fenwick, G L

8. *Victoria History of the County of Chester*, Volume 5, Part I, p155, ed. Lewis, C and Thacker A

9. *Cambridge Chronicle*, 13th November 1829

10. *Perthshire Courier*, 23rd June 1825

11. *Liverpool Mail*, 8th February 1845

12. *Cheshire Observer*, 26th December 1885

13. *The Cheshire Sheaf*, Series 3, Vol. 32, p98. The entry reads, "'H" (i.38 etc) was Miss Humberston, sister of Col. Humberston.'

Family Trees

1. Mrs Coupland

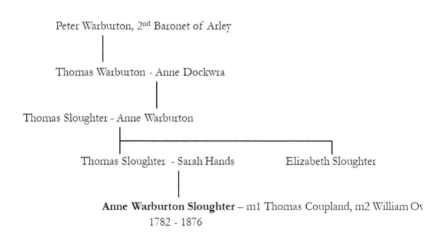

Peter Warburton, 2nd Baronet of Arley

Thomas Warburton - Anne Dockwra

Thomas Sloughter - Anne Warburton

Thomas Sloughter - Sarah Hands   Elizabeth Sloughter

Anne Warburton Sloughter – m1 Thomas Coupland, m2 William Ow
1782 - 1876

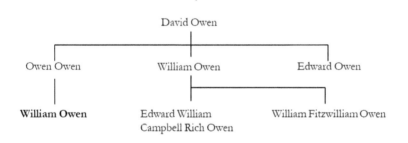

David Owen

Owen Owen   William Owen   Edward Owen

William Owen   Edward William   William Fitzwilliam Owen
Campbell Rich Owen

2. Mrs Glynne

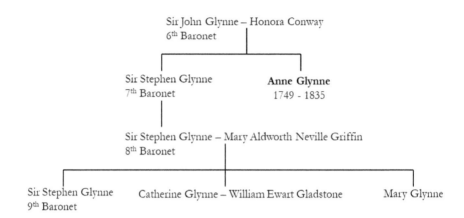

Sir John Glynne – Honora Conway
6th Baronet

Sir Stephen Glynne   **Anne Glynne**
7th Baronet   1749 - 1835

Sir Stephen Glynne – Mary Aldworth Neville Griffin
8th Baronet

Sir Stephen Glynne   Catherine Glynne – William Ewart Gladstone   Mary Glynne
9th Baronet

3. Mrs Humberston

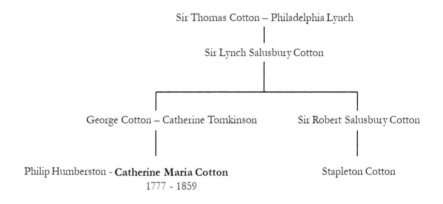

Sir Thomas Cotton – Philadelphia Lynch

Sir Lynch Salusbury Cotton

George Cotton – Catherine Tomkinson   Sir Robert Salusbury Cotton

Philip Humberston - **Catherine Maria Cotton**   Stapleton Cotton
1777 - 1859

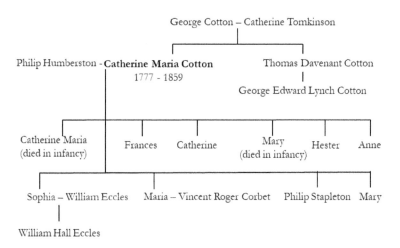

George Cotton – Catherine Tomkinson

Philip Humberston - **Catherine Maria Cotton**
1777 - 1859

Thomas Davenant Cotton

George Edward Lynch Cotton

Catherine Maria (died in infancy)　Frances　Catherine　Mary (died in infancy)　Hester　Anne

Sophia – William Eccles　Maria – Vincent Roger Corbet　Philip Stapleton　Mary

William Hall Eccles

4. George Johnson

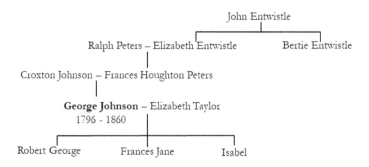

John Entwistle

Ralph Peters – Elizabeth Entwistle　Bertie Entwistle

Croxton Johnson – Frances Houghton Peters

George Johnson – Elizabeth Taylor
1796 - 1860

Robert George　Frances Jane　Isabel

5. Mrs Mainwaring

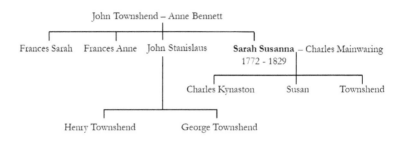

6. Mrs Massie

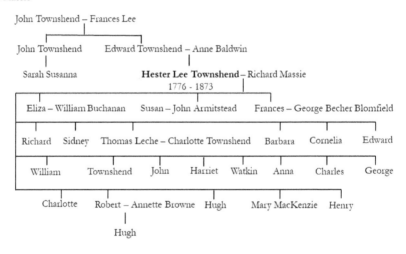

Family Trees

7. Mrs Nicholls

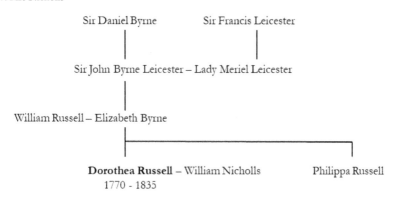

Sir Daniel Byrne   Sir Francis Leicester

Sir John Byrne Leicester – Lady Meriel Leicester

William Russell – Elizabeth Byrne

Dorothea Russell – William Nicholls   Philippa Russell
1770 - 1835

8. Mrs Panton

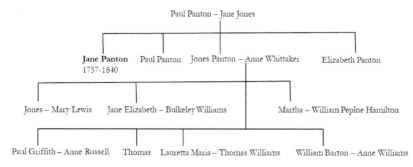

Paul Panton – Jane Jones

Jane Panton   Paul Panton   Jones Panton – Anne Whittaker   Elizabeth Panton
1757-1840

Jones – Mary Lewis   Jane Elizabeth – Bulkeley Williams   Martha – William Peploe Hamilton

Paul Griffith – Anne Russell   Thomas   Lauretta Maria – Thomas Williams   William Barton – Anne Williams

9. George Pearson

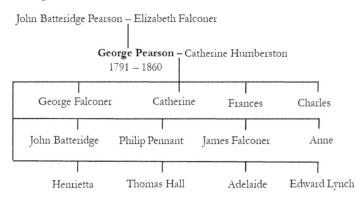

John Batteridge Pearson – Elizabeth Falconer

George Pearson – Catherine Humberston
1791 – 1860

George Falconer	Catherine	Frances	Charles
John Batteridge	Philip Pennant	James Falconer	Anne
Henrietta	Thomas Hall	Adelaide	Edward Lynch

10. Mrs Potts

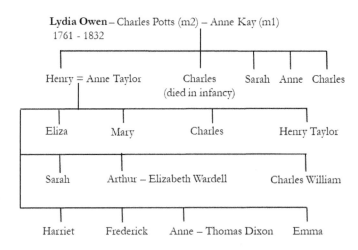

Lydia Owen – Charles Potts (m2) – Anne Kay (m1)
1761 - 1832

Henry = Anne Taylor	Charles (died in infancy)	Sarah	Anne	Charles
Eliza	Mary	Charles	Henry Taylor
Sarah	Arthur – Elizabeth Wardell	Charles William
Harriet	Frederick	Anne – Thomas Dixon	Emma

Family Trees

11. The Misses Townshend

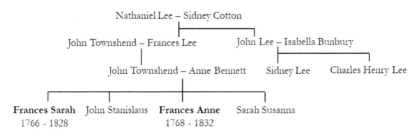

Nathaniel Lee – Sidney Cotton

John Townshend – Frances Lee John Lee – Isabella Bunbury

John Townshend – Anne Bennett Sidney Lee Charles Henry Lee

Frances Sarah John Stanislaus **Frances Anne** Sarah Susanna
1766 - 1828 1768 - 1832

12. Miss Venables

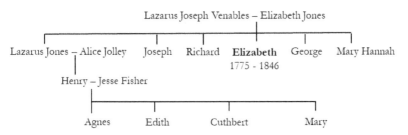

Lazarus Joseph Venables – Elizabeth Jones

Lazarus Jones – Alice Jolley Joseph Richard **Elizabeth** George Mary Hannah
1775 - 1846

Henry – Jesse Fisher

Agnes Edith Cuthbert Mary

13. Dr Norris

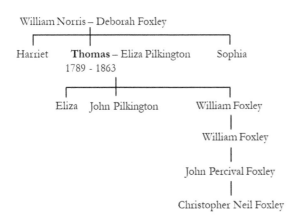

William Norris – Deborah Foxley

Harriet **Thomas** – Eliza Pilkington Sophia
1789 - 1863

Eliza John Pilkington William Foxley

William Foxley

John Percival Foxley

Christopher Neil Foxley

Acknowledgements

I am fortunate to live not far from the centre of Chester, so I have ready access to institutions upon which much of the research in this book is dependent. These include the reference library in Storyhouse, Cheshire Archives and Local Studies, the Grosvenor Museum, and Chester Cathedral. Gladstone's Library in nearby Hawarden was invaluable as a source of information on the Glynne family, as was John Rylands Library in Manchester in respect of Mr and Mrs Nicholls. Further afield, the National Library of Wales in Aberystwyth rendered a treasure trove of data on the Owen family, and documents at the National Archives at Kew shed important light on the official duties of Henry Potts. I would like to thank the staff at each of these locations, not just for making me feel welcome and providing the material requested, but also for promoting an atmosphere conducive to research and often taking an active interest in my work. The importance of their role as custodians of our history and heritage cannot be overstated.

Many generations have passed since 1824. Whilst we know that some book club members had no direct descendants, others will have a multitude. It was never in my scope to track these people down and my enquiries rarely touched the present day. If, by chance, you are reading this and you are descended from a figure in the book, I hope you will understand and not take exception to anything I have written about your ancestor.

By happy accident, I did come into contact with direct descendants of two book club members. Brother and sister Julian and Claire Armitstead are three times great-grandchildren of Richard and Hester Lee Massie. I had the great pleasure of meeting Julian at his home in Oxford, enjoying his hospitality and savouring the family records he so generously shared. Amongst them were the Massie portraits that feature in the illustrations in this book. I also met Robert Mainwaring – three times great-grandson of Charles and Susanna Mainwaring – and his wife, Dawn, who still live at Oteley. They too took a kind interest in my work and supplemented my research with family stories and memorabilia. It is encounters such as these that really bring history to life.

In preparing the book for publication, there are several people to whom I am much indebted. Lisa Dowdeswell of the Society of Authors was happy to assess my publication options and passed on guidance that eased the decision-making process. Sue Speed provided sage advice from a copy-editing perspective and Robin Green was assiduous in his proofreading duties. Any aberrations that remain are entirely my own. Andrew Chapman at preparetopublish.com supported me expertly through the final stages of publication. The cover image – an extract from David Hodgson's 1831 work, *The Exchange* – is reproduced with the kind permission of the Grosvenor Museum, Chester. Jessie Petheram's role in supplying it is particularly acknowledged. Lesia at German Creative ably assisted with the cover design. Illustrations that feature in the body of the book are accompanied by credits where copyright is known to exist and specific permission has been granted. Contemporary pictures were taken by me.

Family and friends have shown great patience in awaiting the output from this project and have been by my side every step of the way. I am extremely grateful to everyone involved and only hope the end-product lives up to expectations.

Chris Fozzard

Chester

November 2024

Index

Abashy, Duke, 27
Act of Union, 6
Adelaide, Queen, 46
America, 26, 36, 38, 48, 54, 55, 92, 137, 142, 155, 233, 235, 256, 317, 333, 346, 348, 362
  War of Independence, 16, 102, 239
American Revolution, 36, 317, 333
Anne Warburton. *See* Owen, Anne
Anne, Queen, 16
Arley Hall, 11, 12, 13, 14, 44, 140
Armitstead, Lawrence, 195
Armitstead, Reverend John, 189, 194, 195, 197
Art of Social Life, 3, 157, 166
Australia, 12, 37, 57, 81, 104, 171, 196, 198, 199, 233, 274, 361
  Sydney, 57, 104, 160, 198, 199
Balance of Comfort, 4, 331
Baldwin, Thomas, 181, 184, 286
Banks, Joseph, 215
Barnston family, 160, 218, 289
Benin, 27
Berriew, Montgomeryshire, 32, 49, 50, 51, 54
Birkenhead, 62, 211, 296, 307, 360
Bleak House, 53
Blomfield, Charles, 46
Blomfield, Eleanor, 202
Blomfield, George Becher, 82, 143, 176, 189, 201, 202, 322
Blomfield, Mary, 202
Blomfield, Sir Arthur, 202
Bonaparte, Napoleon, 6, 61, 78, 99, 154, 219, 239, 245, 282, 317, 347
Bonnie Prince Charlie, 69, 122, 186, 193
Boswell, James, 6, 262, 289, 364
Bowdler, Ann, 269
Bowdler, Harriet, 316
Bowdler, Thomas, 3, 259, 269, 316
Boxing, 63
Boydell, Charles, 171
Boydell, John junior, 72
Boydell, John senior, 72
Boydell, Josiah, 73, 75
Boydell, Samuel, 75
Boydell, Thomas, 72, 76, 159
Brassey, Thomas, 345

Brighton, 62, 69, 80, 90, 178, 347, 349
British Geological Society, 301
Brougham, Henry, MP, 206
Broughton, Flintshire, 17, 40, 41, 70, 76
Brown, Henry, 149
Brown, William, 149
Browne, Major Sylvester, 198
Buchanan, John Phillips, 188
Bunbury, Henry, Colonel, 317
Bunbury, Sir Henry, 316
Burgess, George, 176, 231, 232, 255, 272, 273, 275, 293, 304, 326, 342, 359
Byrne, Elizabeth, 216
Byrne, Sir John, 3rd Baronet of Timogue, 216
Byron, Lord, 42, 64, 92, 122, 148, 181, 182, 190, 191, 207, 234, 238, 275, 341, 362
Calcutta, 80, 82, 92, 112, 113, 121, 305, 336, 363
California Gold Rush, 54
Cambridge, University of, 19, 260, 336, 355
Campobello, 34, 35, 36, 37, 38, 39, 45, 50, 52, 54, 55, 56
Canada, 36, 37, 45, 56, 317, 328
Canning, George, 29, 91, 336
Castle Camps, 267
Catalani, Madame, 61, 89
Charles II, King, 68, 129, 158, 160
Cheshire Hounds, 172, 173, 284
Cheshire Sheaf, 1, 2, 4, 21, 141, 215, 227, 282, 291, 365
Chester
  Abbey Court, 217, 283, 336
  Albion Hotel, 31, 104, 172, 175, 209, 319
  Archaeological Society, 193, 194, 202
  Assizes, 189, 217, 359
  Bolland's Entry, 5
  Bridge Gate, 69, 252
  Bridge Street, 5, 62, 87, 150, 151, 168, 273, 304, 309, 342, 351
  Bridge Street Row, 5, 304
  Cathedral, 5, 11, 95, 98, 110, 126, 138, 146, 151, 158, 161, 176, 188, 190, 202, 216, 217, 223, 225, 227, 231, 243, 253, 254, 259, 261, 265, 274, 284, 286, 288, 292, 296, 297, 300, 307, 319, 323, 325, 336, 338, 363
  City Library, 5
  civic election, 307

Commercial Buildings, 5
Cuppin Street, 181, 341
Dixons and Wardell's Bank, 56
Eastgate Street, 31, 52, 56, 65, 168, 254, 286, 327, 342, 359
Exchange, 15, 60, 99, 119, 126, 226, 237, 260, 288, 290, 294, 303, 307, 315, 327, 339
Feathers Hotel, 52, 61, 83, 87, 212, 273, 304, 360
Female Penitentiary, 237
Fletcher's Buildings, 5
Foregate Street, 61, 125, 151, 177, 272, 306, 316, 319, 326
General Public Library, 5
Grey Friars, 43, 44, 46, 47, 85, 86
Grosvenor Bridge, 44, 85, 193
Holy Trinity, 79, 98, 109, 140, 159, 161, 167, 176, 187, 188, 195, 202, 216, 227, 259, 291, 294, 319, 351, 352
House of Industry, 253, 305, 326, 342
Infirmary, 22, 47, 62, 114, 118, 146, 169, 175, 191, 216, 219, 244, 246, 295, 332, 353
King Street, 106, 137, 168, 177, 218, 220, 224, 225, 226, 242, 254, 255, 271, 277, 291, 292, 295, 354, 364
King's Buildings, 106, 168, 225, 277, 278, 287, 292, 295, 296, 299
King's School, 89, 111, 126, 239, 265, 344
Lower Bridge Street, 31, 87, 104, 110, 175, 176, 252, 303
Midsummer Fair, 229
Nicholas Street, 69, 85, 86, 144, 141, 220, 228, 271, 290, 291, 296, 354, 363
Northgate Street, 5, 60, 87, 113, 120, 125, 127, 140, 177, 218, 242, 243, 244, 273, 274, 281, 288, 292, 295, 297, 306, 307, 314
Overleigh Cemetery, 146, 176, 286, 290, 300, 332, 360
Pied Bull Inn, 48, 85, 176, 226
Priory, 11, 20, 21, 22, 23, 26, 30, 31, 52, 56, 57, 196, 290
Queen's School, 291
Racecourse, 121, 138, 149, 172
River Dee, 15, 61, 64, 72, 75, 88, 105, 118, 197, 229, 230, 241, 251, 252, 254, 261, 281, 288, 293, 320, 327, 342, 343, 360
Roodee, 89, 138, 174, 319
Rows, 5, 123, 175, 304, 326
Royal Hotel, 31, 61, 79, 83, 89, 101, 104, 114, 143, 167, 168, 175, 180, 189, 220, 242, 251, 295, 306, 320, 321, 326, 327, 340, 360, 363
Self-Denial Union, 218, 224
St Bridget's, 87, 106, 108, 109, 114, 149, 151, 155, 187, 191, 192, 193, 200, 253, 254, 306, 338
St John's, 11, 14, 15, 17, 18, 20, 21, 22, 30, 31, 39, 40, 57, 60, 87, 89, 98, 131, 143, 145, 175, 208, 210, 216, 241, 253, 254, 266, 305, 341, 343

St Mary's-on-the Hill, 113
St Mary's-on-the-Hill, 16, 103, 114
St Olave's, 110, 259, 322, 323
St Oswald's, 95, 151, 218, 219, 278, 292, 335, 336, 339
St Peter's, 110, 126, 160, 161, 229, 259, 271, 282
Stanley Place, 46, 146, 187, 190, 191, 193, 198, 200, 213, 271, 274, 277, 291, 313, 319, 321, 322, 333, 334, 338, 346, 354, 364
Stanley Street, 142, 322
Theatre Royal, 60, 62, 167, 315, 319
Water Gate, 43, 69, 88, 118, 277
Watergate House, 280, 277, 290, 291, 297, 298, 300
Watergate Street, 62, 147, 158, 161, 162, 163, 167, 168, 176, 186, 274, 284, 290, 297, 299, 313, 315, 322, 326, 327, 341, 360, 364
White Lion, 61, 87, 138, 149, 223
Whitefriars, 5, 87, 98, 102, 109, 254, 363
Chester Chronicle, 5, 17, 31, 41, 59, 70, 85, 86, 106, 142, 162, 164, 173, 194, 199, 200, 226, 232, 254, 352
Chester Courant, 1, 59, 209, 325
Chipping Camden, 17
Chorlton, nr Chester, 218
Clarkson, Thomas, 246
Clayton, Thomas, 24
cockfighting, 88, 89, 121, 175, 205
Coddington, 184, 185, 186, 187, 189, 199
Coelebs in Search of a Wife, 3, 259
Cole, William, 241, 254
Combermere Abbey, 97, 159, 174, 264
Comforts of Human Life, 3, 277, 354
Cook, Captain James, 207, 362
Cook, Thomas, 193
Copeland, Ann, 28, 29
Copeland, John, 26, 27, 28, 35
Corbet, Sir Andrew, 108, 141, 175
Corbet, Vincent Roger, 108, 140
Corn Laws, 6, 92
Cotton
    Catherine Maria. *See* Humberston, Catherine Maria
    George Edward Lynch, 102, 110, 113, 145
    Reverend George, Dean of Chester, 95
    Reverend James Henry, 235
    Sir Thomas, 96, 264
    Sir Willoughby, 107, 111
    Stapleton, 99, 104, 159
Coupland
    Reverend Peter, 28
    Richard, 19
    Thomas, 11, 18, 19, 22, 23, 24, 25, 26, 28, 220
    Valentine, 19, 29, 333
cricket, 170, 199
Crimea, 108, 190, 193
Cromwell, Oliver, 68, 96, 332

Cuitt, George, 231
Dale, Joseph, 152
Davies, Mary, 13, 185
de Quincey, Mrs, 20–23
de Quincy, Thomas, 20–23
Delamere, 89, 222
Demerara, 65, 120, 177, 206, 235, 256, 260, 295
Denney, Plato, 34
Dickens, Charles, 103, 144
Don Juan, 181, 238
Doré, Louis, 62, 89
Dunham-on-the-Hill, 232, 255, 341, 359
Earle
   John, 24, 25
   Sir Hardman, 285
   T & W & Company, 25, 28
   Thomas, of Leghorn, 25
   Thomas, of Spekelands, 24, 25, 285
   William, of Everton, 24, 25, 26, 27, 28, 29, 51, 197
   William, of West Derby, 25, 27
Eaton Hall, 12, 60, 143, 144, 176, 187, 200, 211, 229, 266
Eccles, William Hall, 108
Eccleston, 31, 142, 143, 144, 187, 192, 198, 199, 200, 201, 279, 344, 360
Edward I, King, 67
Ellesmere Port, 101, 255, 281, 284
Emma, Lady Hamilton, 73
Entwistle, Bertie, 129, 133, 134, 139, 142, 177, 197
Entwistle, Edmund, 138, 145, 158
Entwistle, John, 129, 130, 131, 135, 138
Fauntleroy, Henry, 282, 329, 345, 346, 361
Fletcher, John, 5
Flinders, Matthew, 37
Flora Britannica, 3, 215, 228
Forshaw, James, 237, 294, 339, 359
Foxley, Thomas, 351
France, 23, 26, 45, 74, 78, 79, 99, 107, 122, 152, 154, 173, 178, 191, 235, 251, 275, 282, 283, 301, 306, 317, 346, 348
Franklin, Benjamin, 137
Freemasonry, 71, 279, 319
George II, King, 165
George III, King, 46, 101, 172, 231, 239, 287, 315, 317
George IV, King, 62, 84, 231, 347
George Johnson, 125–40
George V, King, 203
George VI, King, 356
Gladstone, John, 29, 65, 101, 134, 268, 308
Gladstone, Quamina, 65
Gladstone, William Ewart, 77, 86, 268, 361
Glansevern, 32, 33, 39, 40, 42, 43, 44, 47, 49, 51, 54, 55, 57, 142, 212, 278
Glan-y-Afon, 286, 287, 290, 297, 299, 345
Glynne

Anne, 8, 2, 67–86, 69, 70, 75, 78, 79, 80, 82, 83, 84, 85, 86, 143, 144, 141, 159, 164, 212, 228, 239, 268, 291, 313, 354
   John Conway, 70, 71
   Lady Augusta, 77
   Lady Mary, 78, 79, 80, 81, 82, 83, 84, 159
   Reverend Sir Stephen, 7th Baronet, 77, 79
   Sir John, 6th Baronet, 67–86
   Sir John, Lord Chief Justice, 68, 69
   Sir Stephen, 9th Baronet, 67–84, 170, 319
Goldsmith, Oliver, 76, 121
Grand National, 268, 284
Great Exhibition (1851), 55
Great Reform Act (1832), 33, 106
Greece, 5, 92, 122, 181, 182, 191, 207, 235, 237, 309, 329
Grosvenor
   Anne, 185
   Gilbert, 60
   Richard, 2nd Marquess of Westminster, 31, 32, 89, 143, 144, 154, 189, 194, 320
   Robert, 1st Marquess of Westminster, 142, 200
   Sir Richard, 12, 15
   Sir Thomas, 159
   Thomas, Earl of Wilton, 32, 47
   Thomas, General, 320
Gruithuisen, Professor, 257, 309
Guide to Domestic Happiness, 3, 183, 187
Guyana, 25
Hague, Entwistle, 134, 136
Hamilton, William Peploe, 249, 251, 253, 262, 298
Hampton Court, 40, 42, 44, 47, 52
Handel, George Frideric, 89, 344
Hardy, Sir Thomas, 36
Hardy, Thomas, 234
Harrison, George, 47, 48, 56, 105, 244, 304, 339
Harrison, Thomas, 44, 120, 172, 241, 252, 280, 286, 290, 300
Hawarden, 2, 67, 68, 69, 70, 71, 72, 73, 75, 76, 77, 78, 79, 80, 81, 82, 83, 84, 85, 86, 97, 144, 143, 160, 176, 189, 210, 230, 253
   Gladstone's Library, 78
Haygarth, Dr John, 63, 352
Heber, Reginald, Bishop of Calcutta, 41, 80, 92, 306
Hemingway, Joseph, 40, 59, 79, 127, 140, 162, 226, 290, 292, 295, 314, 320, 323, 332
Henry VII, King, 339
Henry VIII, King, 185, 207
HMS Victory, 36
Hogarth, William, 74, 205
Holyhead, 29, 62, 117, 150, 170, 329, 344
Hoole, 149, 180, 184, 208, 241, 246, 249, 286, 288, 297, 307, 327, 357
House of Commons, 33, 45, 68, 92, 106, 118, 119, 120, 153, 159, 173, 206, 320
Howson, Dean, 190, 201, 202, 363

Hughes, Hugh Robert, 109, 189, 298
Hughes, Thomas, 21, 365
Hughes, Thomas Catt, 365
Humberston
  Anne, 365
  Catherine, 262
  Catherine Maria, 3
  Frances, 110
  Philip, 31, 95, 98, 99, 101, 102, 103, 105, 117, 118, 127, 188, 205, 224, 262, 298, 303, 321, 325
  Philip Hugh, 113, 115
  Philip Stapleton, 100, 109, 113, 114, 115, 140, 174, 187, 190, 195, 285, 360
Hunt, Henry, 361
Hunter Valley, NSW, 171, 198, 322
Huskisson, William, 65
Illustrations of Country History, 4, 313
India, 33, 81, 104, 105, 112, 113, 146, 169, 194, 196, 198, 206, 207, 235, 267, 273, 275, 305, 306, 335, 348, 362
Irish Potato Famine, 361
Jacobite Rising, 69, 186
Jamaica, 26, 27, 29, 65, 91, 96, 97, 104, 107, 130, 224, 256, 275, 332
James II, King, 138
Jenner, Edward, 352
John Rylands Library, 221
Johnson
  Bertie Entwistle, 133, 134, 139, 142
  Croxton, 128, 132
  Frances, 135
  George, 3, 125–40, 165, 200, 228, 262, 294, 295, 296, 298, 299, 360
  Robert George, 140, 142, 144, 146, 198
Johnson, Dr Samuel, 6, 97, 121, 245, 262, 263, 264, 265, 266, 268, 289
Kean, Edmund, 251, 315
Keats, John, 51, 64
Kemble, Charles, 315
Kent, Duchess of, 43
Ladies of Llangollen, 80
Law, George Henry, Bishop, 29, 176, 231, 329
Lee, Charles Henry, General, 317
Lee, Sidney, 316
Leeke
  Stephen, 292
Leeke, Stephen, 281, 288, 289
Leicester, Meriel, 217
Lepanto, 3, 237
Leycester, Peter, 217
Lichfield, 259, 262, 263, 264, 265, 266, 269, 343, 378
Lindeman, Dr Henry, 171
Lisbon, 23, 30, 71, 251, 254
Little Belt Affair, 142
Liverpool, 19, 20, 24, 25, 26, 27, 28, 29, 30, 35, 51, 54, 57, 61, 62, 65, 87, 88, 92, 101, 117, 120, 128,

129, 130, 132, 133, 134, 135, 139, 153, 178, 179, 181, 197, 205, 211, 224, 226, 233, 234, 251, 252, 255, 257, 268, 274, 291, 294, 295, 299, 304, 307, 308, 310, 327, 328, 329, 334, 340, 343, 344, 351, 360
  Clayton Square, 24
  International Slavery Museum, 24
  Merseyside Maritime Museum, 29, 129
  Walker Art Gallery, 51
Llandudno, 64, 267
Llangollen, 80, 281, 347
London Missionary Society, 65, 177
Lord Combermere. See Cotton, Philip Stapleton
Lowe, George, 151, 176, 280
Lymm, 127, 128, 140, 141, 142, 167, 279
Lynch, Philadelphia, 96
Lynch, Thomas, 96, 97
Lysons brothers, 30, 221, 222, 223, 224, 226, 228, 264, 279, 301
Magna Britannia, 30, 221, 224, 228, 279, 301
Mainwaring
  Charles Kynaston, 147, 163, 165, 167, 274
  George, 158
  Mark Kynaston, 334
  Reverend Charles, 161
  Sir Harry, 159, 172, 175, 189
  Sir Thomas, 217
  Sir Watkin Randall Kynaston, 172
  Sir William, 158
  Susanna, 157–74
  Townshend, 169, 324
Manchester, 9, 19, 21, 23, 37, 63, 65, 87, 88, 93, 104, 119, 128, 136, 137, 139, 149, 152, 176, 178, 185, 195, 216, 221, 224, 230, 232, 255, 278, 279, 285, 344, 361
Markland, Robert, 224
Marriage Act, 2, 9, 10, 18, 32, 127
Marsh, George, 185
masquerading, 61, 164, 166, 183, 334, 354
Massie
  Charles, 197
  Edward, 192
  Eliza, 188
  Harriet Vyse, 187, 195
  Hester Maria, 183–203
  Hugh Hamon junior, 198
  Hugh Hamon senior, 198
  John Bevis, 195
  Maud Cleopatra, 191
  Reverend Richard, 148, 184, 185, 295, 313, 321
  Robert George, 198
  Thomas Leche, 190, 324, 362, 363
  Townshend, 195
  Watkin, 195, 202
Mauritius, 37
McCready, William Charles, 307

Moel Famau, 284, 287, 290, 299
Monasteries, Dissolution of, 11, 157, 266, 332
Mount Barker, WA, 12
Mrs Coupland. *See* Owen, Anne
Mytton, 'Mad' Jack, 89, 168, 175, 295, 347
Nash, John, 223
National Archives, 219, 295
National Library of Wales, 39
Nelson. Admiral Lord, 36, 73, 233
New Brunswick, 34, 35, 39, 56
New Lanark, 9
New South Wales, 104, 155, 171, 198, 199, 206, 235,
    274, 308, 314
Newton-by-Chester, 1, 4, 110, 113, 114, 144, 208,
    307, 327, 365
Nicholls
    Benjamin, 74, 137, 216, 235
    Dorothea, 3, 215–28
    William, 24, 215, 216, 218, 219, 221, 224, 225, 227,
        241, 282, 301
Nigeria, 26, 28
Norris
    Christopher Neil Foxley, 356
    Dr Thomas, 8, 2, 4, 10, 18, 32, 67, 74, 95, 96, 115,
        125, 157, 165, 183, 187, 189, 215, 228, 237, 238,
        253, 259, 262, 278, 313, 331, 332, 351, 355,
        351–57, 364, 365
    Eliza, 351
    Eliza Jane, 351
    John Pilkington, 351, 355
    Stephen Leslie, 355
    William, 351
    William Foxley (grandson of Dr Thomas), 356
    William Foxley (son of Dr Thomas), 352
Norris, Robert, 28
Nova Scotia, 34, 36, 56, 102
Old Bailey, 247, 329, 345
Ormerod, George, 97, 212, 218, 226, 279, 351, 359
Ormskirk, 19, 26, 29, 129
Oswestry, 54, 55, 109, 170, 333, 334, 335, 336, 338
Oteley Park, 147, 159, 161, 167, 169, 274
Owen
    Anne, 38, 42, 45, 48, 52, 53, 20, 82, 168, 169, 242
    Arthur, 34
    Cornelia, 50, 52, 54, 55, 188, 319
    David, 34, 35, 36, 50
    Edward William Campbell Rich, 37
    Owen, 33, 50
    Robert, 9, 10, 32
    Sir Edward, 45, 50, 54, 195
    William, 32, 33, 48, 54, 57, 70, 280
    William Fitzwilliam, 37, 38, 39, 45, 50, 52, 53, 54,
        55, 92
    William senior, 33, 34, 35
Paganini, Niccolo, 89
Paine, Thomas, 361

Panton
    Elizabeth Maria, 237–48
    Jane, 3, 237–48
    Jane Elizabeth, 241
    Jones, 240, 241, 242, 247
    Lauretta Maria, 242
    Martha, 240
    Paul Griffith, 243, 244, 245, 247
    Paul junior, 239
    Paul senior, 238
    William Barton, 242
Panton v Williams, 248
Parkgate, 109, 122, 140, 175, 184, 186, 188, 205, 229,
    257, 294, 315
Parkinson, William, 232, 255, 273, 341, 359
Pearson
    Adelaide Sophia, 268
    Anne, 267
    Charles, 267
    Edward Lynch, 267
    George, 259–69
    George Falconer, 267
    John Batteridge junior, 267
    John Batteridge senior, 259, 262
    Philip Pennant, 267
    Thomas Hall, 267
Penn, William, 96, 332
Pennant, Thomas, 75, 238, 260
Pennsylvania, 96, 137
Peters, Frances Houghton. *See* Johnson, Frances
Peters, Ralph I, 129, 130, 137
Peters, Ralph II, 129, 131
Peters, Ralph III, 129, 134, 135, 136
Peters, Richard, 137
Peters, William, 137
Pigot's Commercial Directory, 5
Pitt, William, the Elder, 70
Plan of the City of Chester, 1833, 15
Plessington, John, 185
Pontsycyllte Aqueduct, 281
Porter, Lucy, 262, 268
Potts
    Anne, 291
    Arthur, 285
    Charles junior, 282, 287, 288, 292, 294, 296, 297,
        298
    Charles senior, 278
    Charles William, 286
    Eliza, 283
    Emma Susan, 294
    Frederick, 289
    Henry, 127, 141, 143, 280, 277, 279, 289, 290, 300,
        301, 319, 334, 343, 345
    Henry Taylor, 284, 296, 297, 298
    Lydia, 3, 277–302
Prince Regent. *See* George IV, King

Princess Victoria. *See* Victoria, Queen
Pückler-Muskau, Prince Hermann, 120, 229, 272
Pulford Hall, 190, 199, 201
Queon, You Fung, 233
Raffles, Sir Stamford, 256, 275
Rasselas, 3, 121, 125
Richards, Philippa, 227
Richardson, Richard, 287, 297
Roman Catholic Relief Act, 361
Rome, 51, 138, 185, 186, 348
Roosevelt, Franklyn D, 56
Royal Humane Society, 261, 271
Rugby School, 107, 111, 257, 336, 354
Russell, Dorothea. *See* Nicholls, Dorothea
Russell, Reverend William, 216
Ruthin, 143, 144, 298
Sadler, Windham William, 179, 180, 181, 208, 209, 210, 211, 212, 230, 234, 255, 274, 277, 292, 293, 307, 309, 310
Saltney, 17, 75, 77, 194, 283, 286, 297
Sandwich Islands, King and Queen of, 182, 207, 233, 275, 362
Scott, Sir George Gilbert, 161, 192
Scott, Sir Giles Gilbert, 356
Scott, Sir Walter, 66, 245
Seven Years' War, 16, 34, 36, 317
Seward, Anne, 263
Shakespeare, William, 3, 74, 109, 259, 264, 269, 314, 316, 317
Sheridan, Richard Brindsley, 223
Short History of Newton Hall, Chester, A, 1
Shrewsbury, 34, 117, 118, 120, 126, 170, 283, 289, 339
Siddons, Sarah, 315
slavery, 6, 24, 25, 26, 28, 30, 35, 38, 63, 90, 96, 97, 107, 130, 131, 135, 136, 154, 181, 195, 220, 224, 235, 246, 261, 279, 291, 356, 363
Sloughter, Elizabeth, 17, 18, 31, 40, 41, 42, 43, 47, 51, 84, 85, 86, 98, 143, 141, 164, 169, 189, 262, 282, 291, 324, 354
Sloughter, Thomas junior, 11, 16, 17
Sloughter, Thomas senior, 11, 12, 13, 15, 17, 41, 42, 163, 176, 216
smallpox, 63, 231, 232, 274, 352, 362
Smirke, Robert, 223
Smith, John, missionary, 91, 120, 177, 348
Society for Promoting Christian Knowledge, 92, 105, 200, 262, 305
Society for Promoting Christianity amongst the Jews, 253, 271
Socrates, 5
Spain, 23, 26, 79, 96, 99, 207, 251, 329, 348
St Paul's Cathedral, 13
St Werburgh, 11, 194, 266, 286
Stanley, Sir John, 61, 166, 321
Stanley, Sir Thomas, 205

Stephenson, George, 255
Stephenson, Robert, 285
suffragette movement, 203, 361
Tales of the Castle, 2, 67
Tarleton, John, 130
Tarporley, 211, 319
Taylor, Reverend Mascie Domville, 128, 145
Telford, Thomas, 118, 150, 230, 251, 281, 360
Thackeray, Dr William Makepeace, 175, 299
Thames, River, 64, 328
Thomas, Dr Honoratus Leigh, 73
Thrale, Henry, 264
Thrale, Hester (Mrs), 97, 264, 265
Tomlinson, Mercy, 62, 87, 360
Tower of London, 68, 96, 222
Townshend
    Barbara Anne, 321
    Edward, 184, 313
    Edward Venables, 184, 188, 191, 319, 332
    Elizabeth, 331–38
    Frances Anne, 313–24
    Frances Sarah, 313–24
    George, 171, 198, 314, 322
    Henry, 322
    John Stanislaus, 162, 171, 188, 314, 315, 319, 321
    John, of Trevalyn, 184, 313
    Lee Porcher, 323
    Mary Charlotte, 323
    Sir Robert, 160, 314
Townshend, Hester Maria. *See* Massie, Hester Maria
Trafalgar, Battle of, 36, 219
transportation, 274, 294
Turner, Joseph, 69, 86, 354
Upton-by-Chester, 113, 114, 115, 194, 273, 286, 307, 327
Vanity Fair, 53
Venables
    Agnes, 336
    Cuthbert, 336
    Edith, 336
    Edward, 335
    Elizabeth, 8, 4, 331, 333, 334
    Jessie Maria, 338
    John, 335
    Joseph, 333
    Lazarus, 333
    Lazarus Jones, 334, 335
    Mary, 336
    Mary Hannah, 333, 338
    Reverend Henry, 336
    Richard, Archdeacon, 335
    Robert, 96, 332
    Rowland Jones, 335
Victoria, Queen, 44, 84, 112
Warburton
    Diana, 14

George Egerton, 12
Lady Christiana, 14
Margaret, 40, 41, 42
Sir George, 12, 14, 16, 42
Sir Peter, 13, 32
Walter, 14, 15
Wardell, Elizabeth, 286
Wardell, William, 286, 291
Washington, George, 137, 318
Waterloo, Battle of, 6, 61, 64, 100, 188, 282, 317, 323, 347

Wedge, Thomas, 287, 297, 298
Wellington, Duke of, 55, 61, 104, 172, 289, 347
Welshampton, 148, 161, 169
Welshpool, 32, 36, 55
Wilberforce, William, 65, 177, 260
William III, King, 138, 216, 329
William IV, King, 46, 84, 163
Willoughby, William, 180, 211, 327, 340, 360
Woolliscroft, John, 61
Yarker, Robert, 110, 259, 322

About the Author

Chris Fozzard is a teacher, social historian and writer. He has researched local history for many years and uses this as the basis for his writing, as well as for providing walks and talks in and around Chester, where he lives. He has had one book published previously – *A Short History of Newton Hall, Chester* – in 2022.

www.ingramcontent.com/pod-product-compliance
Ingram Content Group UK Ltd.
Pitfield, Milton Keynes, MK11 3LW, UK
UKHW032244110325
4954UKWH00002B/202